COLUMBIA:

THOSE WHO HONORABLY SERVED

MARK A. CLARKE

Cover photo by Lenny Hall

Published by CCE *Publishing*, Edgewater, Florida

Printed in the United States of America

ISBN 978-1-7373017-0-7

COLUMBIA:

THOSE WHO HONORABLY SERVED

MARK A. CLARKE

CCE PUBLISHING

EDGEWATER, FL

Mark A. Clarke

DEDICATION

To Susan Teaney Clarke
one of the remarkable people who goes unheralded
and remains unknown.

TABLE OF CONTENTS

Revolutionary War

Columbia County NY 7th Regiment

Albany County NY Militia 10th Regiment

Albany County NY Militia 8th Regiment

Albany County NY Militia 9th Regiment

Civil War

NY 128th Regiment

World War I

Columbia County Veterans

World War II

Columbia County Veterans

Korean War

Columbia County Veterans

Vietnam War

Columba County Veterans

Bibliography

Acknowledgements

INTRODUCTION

This book is a product of more than twenty years of inquiry.

I say inquiry because when peering into the lives of fellow veterans I am curious as to what compels them to do the things they do.

This book is made up of brief biographies of veterans and their faithful service to their country, family and communities. Whatever motivated them, their service remains an enduring gift to others.

Perhaps this is best illustrated in a story told to parishioners in a small church in Upstate New York by a visiting priest who spoke about his youth, his faith and what motivated him to become a priest.

"As a young boy my native country, Poland, was invaded and occupied by Nazi Germany in 1939. The Nazis ruled with a brutality that was difficult to comprehend. They had a strict policy that when a German soldier was killed, ten citizens from the nearest town would be selected and executed by firing squad. The entire town was to be assembled in the center of town to view this cruel event. It would serve to be a lesson to all the inhabitants of the region without exception. Men, women and children. Everyone.

"One day in late autumn a German soldier was killed near our town. A short while later several trucks entered our village and assembled all of its citizens to the center square. Separating the men from their families, a German major began to select ten men from the village, one by one. Randomly he pointed his finger to a man saying "you" and then two of his men would force him to line up against a stone wall in the village square. One of the unlucky men who were chosen stepped forward and addressed the German major.

"Respectfully he pleaded, 'Please Major, I ask that you spare my life. I ask it not for me but for my children. Winter is coming and who will care for them when I am gone?' For his effort he was beaten and forcefully placed in line with the other doomed men. While this man was being roughly treated, an older man from the village quietly stepped from the cowered masses and passively addressed the major.

"'Major, winter will be upon us shortly and in Poland it can be very

harsh and this man has several children that must be fed and kept warm. I have no children. Please allow me to take his place.' The German major, caring only that there be ten villagers shot for the one dead soldier, ordered the older man to take the place of the condemned man. When this had been done, the ten were lined up against a wall and then shot one by one in front of the entire village.

"I know this story to be true," the priest continued, "because the man who begged that his life be spared for his family was my father. And the man who was shot in his place was our village priest. It was then that I decided to become a priest. I vowed to take the place of the man who gave his life in place of my father."

Pausing he took a seat, leaving the dazed congregation in silence.

Evil comes to us in many forms. Across the span of time there have been countless men and women who have risen up in opposition. The following pages are filled with stories of men and women in service to their fellow man for the greater good.

Their service was a gift to others. They did it for many reasons. Some did it for love of country or family or community. Some did it because of their faith. That older, childless man in a black robe did it for all of these reasons on that cold Polish afternoon in 1939.

As I reflect on the past, a mere thank you seems hardly appropriate for the service of these men and women. But if you will, a thank you will do splendidly ... for a start.

Mark A. Clarke

SECTION 1

BIOGRAPHIES

This section is a collection of biographies of the men and women from Columbia County who served in the armed forces of the United States of America from the Revolutionary War, the Civil War, World War I, World War II, the Korean and Vietnam conflicts, Intervention of Lebanon, the invasions of Grenada and Panama, the Gulf War, Afghanistan War and Iraq War.

On the following pages, the biographies of these brave soldiers, who so honorably served, appear here in alphabetical order.

Gerald Edwin Alger, Jr.

Gerald Edwin Alger, Jr. was born October 29, 1954 to Gerald E. and Viola (Black) Alger in Troy, NY. After he graduated from Hudson High School he received an Associate's Degree in business administration from a college in Atwater, CA.

Gerald enlisted in the United States Air Force on August 20, 1973 at Hudson, NY. During the course of the next twenty years, Tech. Sgt. Gerald Alger, Jr. acquired the skill and knowledge which distinguished him as a K11270, aircrew instructor and in-flight refueling operator technician.

He attended the Noncommissioned Officer Academy, where he excelled in courses that prepared him for important leadership and supervisory assignments in a military career that included Vietnam, Lebanon, Grenada, Panama and the Persian Gulf.

T/Sgt. Gerald Alger, Jr. was assigned to the 4017th Combat Crew Squadron, a part of the Strategic Air Command, whose duties included KC 135 refueling operations. Aerial refueling is a difficult and dangerous operation, which requires utmost skill and precision. Aerial refueling is essential to ensure vital support for any successful airborne operation. Attesting to his dedication and achievements, his commander writes to his parents,

"... it is my recent privilege to present the distinctive Silver Wings of an aircrew member to your son. Those who do are very special, dedicated to their country's freedom."

For his selfless dedication to his country, T/Sgt. Gerald Alger, Jr. was awarded the following citations: Meritorious Service Medal, Air Medal, AF Commendation Medal, AF Outstanding Unit Award with four Oak Leaf Clusters, Combat Readiness Medal, AF Good Conduct Medal with four Oak Leaf Cluster, National Defense Service Medal with Bronze Star, Armed Forces Expeditionary Medal with two Oak Leaf Clusters, AF Overseas Long Tour Ribbon, AF Longevity Service Award Ribbon with four Oak Leaf Clusters, NCO Professional Military Education Graduate Ribbon and the AF Training Ribbon.

On August 31, 1993, after 20 years of service, Gerald was honorably discharged at Castle AFB, CA. In the years that followed he worked for the Register Star, Price Chopper and Tyson Chicken Company as Plant Manager. Gerald was a member of the Hudson American Legion Post 184 and a communicant of New Life Christian Church, Clarksville, AK. He was married on Okinawa, Japan (1/14/78) to Akemi and they raised two sons: Shawn and Stephen.

At the age of 51 Gerald passed away on March 27, 2006 in Clarksville, AK and was interred in the Saratoga National Cemetery. He exemplifies America's very finest, who dedicate themselves each day to protect our country and to ensure our freedom.

William Morris Armstrong

William Morris Armstrong was born April 5, 1926 to Homer B. and Gertrude G. (Morris) Armstrong in Hudson, NY. He attended public schools, and during the summer William worked as a life guard at Bash Bish Falls. William graduated from Hudson High School in June 1944 and then enrolled in Clarkson College at Potsdam, NY as a cadet corporal with a course of study in the Department of Military Science and Tactics.

William entered the United States Navy on September 5, 1945 in Hudson, NY. He received basic training at the United States Naval Training Station at Great Lakes, Illinois. William Armstrong was promoted to seaman 2nd class in October 1945. After marching in the rain during a parade, William subsequently became ill with rheumatic fever and was treated at a naval hospital. Rheumatic fever, an inflammatory disease, affects the heart, joints, skin and brain. Because of its disabling effects, E2 Seaman William Armstrong was honorably discharged on April 2, 1946 at the United States Naval Hospital, Dublin, Georgia.

William returned home and finished his degree in Civil Engineering at Clarkson College in 1950. He met his wife Joanne Cermola, and they were married on February 10, 1952 at Our Lady of Mount Carmel in Hudson, NY. In the ensuing years, William worked with the New York State Public Works as a Civil Engineer (retired 1975) and privately as a land surveyor. He and Joanne raised five children: Robert, Susanne, Jon, David, and James.

William was active in his community. He sang tenor with the Hendrick Hudson Male Choir and was a member of the American Legion Post 184, Past Commander of the Disabled American Veterans, Honor a Veteran Committee and Past President of the Junior Chamber of Commerce. William was a respected and dedicated leader with the Boy Scouts of America and was a member of the coveted "Order of the Arrow".

William died on February 17, 2012 and was buried in Cedar Park, Hudson, NY. He leaves behind his loving wife, Joanne, five children, seven grandchildren and three great grandchildren. He was 86 years old.

Kenneth J. Atkins

Kenneth J. Atkins was born July 27, 1921 in Andee, New York to Dean and Maude L. (Roe) Atkins. Ken was one of sixteen children who attended Andee Central School District and worked as a farmhand on a dairy farm in Salisbury Mills in Orange County, NY.

Kenneth entered the United States Army on April 12, 1946. After attending Engineer Basic Training, Private Kenneth J. Atkins graduated to the Army Service Forces Technical School at Fort Belvoir in Virginia. This ten week course trained him as a rigging specialist. His duties would require him to use derricks, cranes, gin poles, A-frames, cableways and chain blocking in the raising and moving of heavy equipment. Proficiency in the splicing of wire and manila rope and the tying of all kinds of knots were essential to his duties.

As a rigger Pvt. Kenneth J. Atkins was assigned to Camp Stoneman, California, which was a hub for all troops making their way to the Pacific battlefields. Three days before the surrender of Japan, just over a million men came through the Stoneman staging area, and it would be used as a separation center which ensured that returning soldiers could be promptly returned to their homes.

Upon deactivation of military personal after the end of WWII, on December 28, 1946 Pvt. Kenneth J. Atkins was honorably discharged at Camp Beale, CA. In addition to qualifying with the M1 Rifle, he was awarded the World War II Victory Medal.

Kenneth married Doris Doolittle on April 16, 1955 and moved to Columbia County where he raised three children: Doris M., Ruth A. and Kenneth E. He worked as a dairy farmer for many years and was affiliated with Hoards Dairyman Magazine. Three years prior to his passing, he worked for Peter J. Schweitzer Paper Mill in Ancram, NY. Kenneth was remembered by family members, as "Our hero. He taught us about hard work and respect. He loved America and all of us grew up knowing that the American flag was for freedom and honesty."

Kenneth passed away on December 24, 1975 and was buried in the Copake Cemetery, Copake, NY. He left behind three children, five grand- children and ten great-grandchildren. He was 54 years old.

George Lloyd Ball

George Lloyd Ball was born in Pine Plains, NY on January 6, 1924. Living in Copake, NY, he entered the United States Army in 1945. After basic training, he was trained as a truck vehicle mechanic. Staff Sgt. George Ball served overseas with Army Air Force (A.A.F) as an aircraft maintenance technician. The A.A.F., formally the Army Air Corps, was charged with the responsibility of all facets of aviation in the army. At its peak during WWII, 2.4 million men and women serviced approximately 80,000 aircraft. He remained part of an occupational force and decided to make the military his career.

Upon the outbreak of the Korean War, he was called again to serve his country. He was promoted to E-6 on May 12, 1966 and reenlisted on May 19, 1970. He served once more in conflict as hostilities escalated in Vietnam. SSgt. George Ball served three tours of duty in South East Asia where he was awarded a Personal Presidential Citation from then-President Richard M. Nixon and another from Gen. William Westmoreland Commanding General of Armed Forces in Vietnam.

Having served in the armed forces from 1945, he retired from the United States Army in 1972.

For his service to his country he received the following: WWII Victory Medal, A.A.F. Button, Army of Occupation Medal, Korean Service Medal, Bronze Star Medal, Vietnam Service Medal, Vietnam Campaign Medal and the Good Conduct Medal.

George and his wife Barbara (Beecher Ball) moved to West Copake after his retirement and remained active in his community. He was a member of the American Legion Post 1160 in Copake Falls, NY and a life member of the VFW Post 7955 in Copake, NY. George passed away in 1993.

Genesio Benvenuto

Genesio (Jerry) Benvenuto was born December 20, 1921 in Norwood, MA to Genessio and Domenica Benvenuto. Prior to his enlistment, Jerry attended high school at Niskayuna and worked for Oneglis and Gervesini, Inc. of Torrington, Conn. He graduated high school on May 25, 2001 under Operation Recognition.

On August 6, 1942, Tec 5 Jerry Benvenuto was inducted in the United States Army, attended basic training and subsequently trained as a heavy vehicle operator. On January 20, 1943 Jerry was assigned to the Quarter Master Corp, as a special vehicle operator in Burma and India.

After Japan took control of the Chinese coast and Indochina, the Burma Road became a vital supply link between India and China. The Allies needed to maintain an overland supply route to China, thus pinning down a large Japanese army. Tec 5 Benvenuto operated heavy tractor trailers and trucks along the Burma and Stillwell roads. In spite of debilitating diseases, malaria, leeches, jungle ulcers, monsoons, and often driving in blackout conditions to advanced positions, Jerry transported vital materials that were the lifeblood of the Allied war effort, thus, helping to bring about the capitulation of the Japanese forces in Southeast Asia.

On October 17, 1942 Tec 5 Jerry Benvenuto was honorably discharged at Camp Pickett, Va. He was awarded the following citations: Bronze Star, Distinguished Unit Badge, Asiatic Pacific Theater Medal and the Good Conduct Medal.

Jerry returned home on October 14, 1950 and married Rebecca Mesick. For the next five decades he worked in law enforcement as a Chatham police officer, Ghent town constable and retiring from the Columbia County Sheriff's Department in 1984 as deputy sheriff.

His commitment to community was distinguished. Jerry was past commander of the Italian American War Veterans, Post 192, and Chatham Legion

Post. He served on the County American Legion Committee and in 1991 was honored as Legionnaire of the Year for N.Y.S. 3rd District. In addition, he was Ghent highway superintendent, president/trustee and co-founder of Columbia Co. Sons and Daughters of Italy, past fire chief of Ghent Vol. Fire Co., American Community Center Director of the American Legion Boys State, Columbia Co. Veteran's Van Service Coordinator, a valued member of the Ghent Rod and Gun Club, Hudson Moose Club, and Kinderhook Elks. Jerry was a respected member of the Honor a Vet Committee and he worked tirelessly at the V.A. hospital and for veteran's organizations. His allegiance to his country is equaled only by his commitment to veterans and community. His legacy and motto should read, "Anything for a Vet."

Jerry left behind a son, Michael, a daughter-in-law, Marie and a lovely grand-daughter, Nina. His passing is sadly noted by friends, neighbors, family, and veterans alike.

Bernard Bernhoft

On April 12, 1922 at Silver Lake, WI, Bernard Bernhoft was born to Frederick and Catherine (Ihling) Bernhoft. Grade school consisted of a one room schoolhouse in Kinderhook, and later he attended Martin Van Buren High School.

Bernard entered the service on October 24, 1942 at Albany, NY. After his initial training, he was assigned to duty at Fort Benning, GA (10/30/42), Camp Barkley, TX (11/13/43), and Ft. Knox, KY (3/3/44). Cpl. Bernhoft completed a course on motor mechanic (3/44) gliderman (6/44) and was then assigned to the 12th Armored Division, 56th Regiment. This armored infantry unit sailed for overseas duty on July 17, 1945 on the SS Matsonia as a part of the invasion of Japan. Cpl. Bernhoft's unit remained in the Pacific Theater of Operation several months after V-J Day. On January 30, 1946 he returned to the United States on the aircraft carrier, the Steamer Bay. While assigned to the Western Pacific, he served as an auto mechanic, truck driver and reconnaissance car crewman. Cpl. Bernhoft was honorably discharged on February 8, 1942 at Fort Dix, NJ.

After the war Bernard returned home and married Agnes D. Shaw in 1955. They raised four children: Brenda, Nanci, William and Steven. He worked as an electrician while raising a family in Columbia County. He was a member of the IBEW Local 724 Union and retired in 1981, after 20 years. He was an active member of the VFW in Stuyvesant Falls, and the American Legion in Chatham and Valatie.

His wife recalls: "As with many WWII veterans, Bill didn't share much about his experiences during his service time. His children do know, however, their dad was very proud of having served his country. He instilled his love of flag and country to his family."

For his service to his country, Cpl. Bernhoft was awarded the following: the American Service Medal, the Asiatic-Pacific Service Medal, the Good Conduct Medal and the World War II Victory Medal.

Bernard died on August 11, 2002. He was 80 years old.

Donald G. Bertram

Donald G. Bertram was born March 4, 1925 to George and Mary (Lauster) Bertram in Stuyvesant, NY. As the eldest son of six children, Donald completed farm chores (feeding chickens and milking cows) before attending school in Claverack, East Chatham and then Greenport. He completed his education while serving in the Army.

Donald was drafted in the United States Army on July 5, 1943. He completed basic training at Ft. Dix and was assigned to the Pacific Theater of Operation as an ammunition handler with 103rd Infantry. He participated in combat operations in New Guinea and the Philippines, where he contracted malaria. Arriving back in the United States, PFC Bertram was discharged on January 27, 1946.

Three months later he reenlisted and served in Italy with Headquarter Company, 3rd Infantry Division as a rifleman. Cpl. Bertram met and married his wife Pasqualina Rosalia Aiello on August 27, 1948 in Trieste, Italy.

For the next two decades SSgt Donald Bertram served overseas and stateside. In the course of his military career, he was stationed in Cuba, Panama, New Caledonia, New Zealand, New Guinea, Philippines, Japan, Italy, Germany and numerous posts across the United States. Although he suffered bouts of malaria and significant hearing loss, several certificates of proficiency, rigorous training and appointment as temporary sergeant first class attests to his military abilities and acumen. After twenty years of service to his country, he was honorably discharged on January 1, 1964.

SSgt. Donald G. Bertram was awarded the following: Bronze Star, Combat Infantry Badge, Asiatic Pacific Service Medal w/Bronze Service Arrowhead, Philippines Liberation Ribbon, WWII Victory Medal, Good Conduct Medal, Army Occupation Medal, and the American Theater Ribbon.

As a civilian Donald worked for the railroad, Chatham Police, Paramount Fuel and Valley Oil as well as the Hudson School District. He was a member of Ghent VFW Post #5933 and enjoyed bowling, golf, country music, ballgames and Scrabble.

On January 12, 2010 Donald passed away and was buried in Memory Gardens Cemetery, Colonie, NY. He left behind a wife, Lee, three children, Doris, Linda and David, five grandchildren and three great-grandchildren as well as dear friend and companion Margaret Delong. He was 84 years old.

Wallace T. Blass

Wallace T. Blass was born in Ancram, NY on April 3, 1913 to Harry and Carrie Blass. Wallace attended school in Columbia County. He was recognized for his baseball ability in the eastern part of the county. In addition, Wallace was known for his political involvement, having served as a Democratic committeeman from the Ancram Election District. He was a past grand master of the Gallatin Lodge of Odd Fellows, and prior to his enlistment, he worked as a technician in the laboratory of the Ancram paper mills for several years.

In January 1943 Wallace enlisted in the United States Army and received basic training at Camp Maxey, TX. Upon completion of artillery mechanics' school at Fort Sill, OK, he was assigned to the 25th Infantry Division (a.k.a. the "Tropic Lighting Division" because of its impressive fighting record on Guadalcanal) in the Pacific Theater of Operation.

Sgt. Wallace T. Blass fought with the Field Artillery in the New Guinea Campaign and took part in the Philippines invasion. From late February to early May of 1945, the 25th Infantry Division was engaged in operations in the Caraballo Mountains. They drove up a corridor from San Jose to Balette Pass in what one historian described as:

> *". . . some of the fiercest fighting of the Pacific war . . . (the Division) fought its way through the Japanese defenses on one hill after another with the key Balette Pass . . . ."*

On April 20, 1945 while engaged with hostile forces across a steep ravine on two hills called the "Wolfhound" objectives, Sgt. Blass was killed near Balette Pass on the Island of Luzon, Philippines. He was buried in the 25th Division Cemetery, Luzon Philippines, but on August 17, 1945 his remains were reinterred in Cedar Park Cemetery in Hudson, NY.

Sgt. Wallace T. Blass was awarded the Purple Heart as well as campaign ribbons. Wallace left a wife, Helen, a son, Worth, two brothers and three sisters. Sgt. Wallace T. Blass died on his son's birthday. He was 32 years old.

John Wesley Blunt

John Wesley Blunt was born May 18, 1840 in Stuyvestant, NY to Henry and Eliza (Burbank) Blunt. His family moved to the Town of Austerlitz when he was a youth. Like most boys of his day, he received little schooling - going to work at an early age on his father's farm.

In October 1861, a train rolled into Chatham and John, with his brothers,

Rusten, Robert and Joseph, left for Hudson to enlist in the Union forces. John, tall and slim, grew a flowing moustache and later added a goatee like many gallant youth of that era. He joined Company M, 6th New York Cavalry and as an able leader, he was promoted to sergeant and then Company first sergeant within a year. He was mustered into officer ranks as a 2nd lieutenant in March 1863, won his silver bars in the same year and on December 14, 1864 was made captain with rank from October 21, 1864 - in recognition of his actions at the Battle of Cedar Creek.

The Battle of Cedar Creek began at dawn, October 19, 1864, when the Confederate Army surprised the Federal Army at Cedar Creek. Maj. Gen. Philip Sheridan arrived to rally his troops, and, in the afternoon, launched a crushing counter attack, which recovered the battlefield. This Union victory broke the back of the Confederate Army in the Shenandoah Valley, resulting in 8,575 casualties (US 5,665, CS 2,910). Abraham Lincoln rode the momentum of Sheridan's victories in the valley and Sherman's successes in Georgia to re-election.

As a first lieutenant in Company K, 6th New York Cavalry, John Wesley Blunt was recognized for actions taken on October 19, 1864 at Cedar Creek, VA. thus earning our nation's highest award, the Medal of Honor. His citation reads:

> *"The President of the United States of America, in the name of Congress, takes pleasure in presenting the Medal of Honor to First Lieutenant John W. Blunt, United States Army, for extraordinary heroism on 19 October 1864, while serving with Company K, 6th New York Cavalry, in action at Cedar Creek, Virginia. First Lieutenant Blunt voluntarily led a charge across a narrow bridge over the creek, against the lines of the enemy."*

Capt. Blunt was transferred to the 2nd Provisional Cavalry on June 17, 1865, where he made major (brevet) in the NY Volunteers. He was mustered out with his company, August 9, 1865, at Louisville, KY.

Returning to Chatham, he married Almina Lanphear on January 7, 1867. They had three children: Roy John, Amy, and Florence. Capt. Blunt became a legendary figure at the Chatham Fair, where he served as Grand Marshall in the parades held annually. With his Civil War Comrades, he helped organize Gen. John A. Logan Post GAR that met in the Masonic Hall on Park Row. His nephew, Arthur Blunt, remembered him as a great talker, particularly when reunited with his brothers, Joseph, Rusten and Robert.

John Wesley Blunt died on January 21, 1910 in Chatham, NY and was buried in the Chatham Rural Cemetery. He was 69 years old.

Gerard J. Boehme

Gerard Joseph Boehme was born April 14, 1945 to Thomas and Rita Boehme in Brooklyn, NY. He attended and was graduated from Chatham Central School.

Gerard enlisted in the United States Navy on February 2, 1965. After initial training, he was assigned to sea duty with the USS John W. Thomason (DD760). This destroyer was commissioned in October 1945 and received seven battle stars in the Korean War and three in the Vietnam War. For the next three years and nine months, Boatswain's Mate 3rd Class Gerard Boehme was assigned to sea duty in the Pacific. It was during this time that BM3 Boehme served in support of operations in which the USS Pueblo was taken captive by the North Koreans in international waters, thus creating a yearlong international incident. In addition, he served in support of United States Armed Forces off the coast of the Republic of Vietnam.

BM3 Boehme was discharged on October 14, 1969 from the United States Navy at the Brooklyn Naval Station where he was transferred to the Navy Reserves. For his service he was awarded the following citations: the National Defense Service Medal, the Armed Forces Expeditionary Medal (Korea), the Vietnam Service Medal and the Republic of Vietnam Campaign Medal.

Gerard married Regina Joeks on April 6, 1974 at St. Mary's, Rensselaer, NY, raising two girls: Kelly and Kristy. For the next 30 years, he worked for the New York State Thruway Authority (where he retired in 1999) and remained active in civic affairs. He was a member of the Ghent VFW Post 5933, serving on the Color Guard, a member of the Chatham and Ghent Fire Departments and a communicant of St. James Catholic Church in Chatham, NY.

Gerard died at the age of 62 on November 8, 2007 and was buried at St. James Cemetery in Chatham, NY. His wife, Regina, remembers:

> *"He was one of the most likeable people I've ever met. Two things that stand out when I think of him were his sense of humor and his pride of having served in the United States Navy."*

Gerard represents the countless many who serve this country selflessly, that we may enjoy our freedom, and who stand ready to protect our way of life.

Theodore S. Bombola

Theodore S. Bombola was born March 28, 1923 in Ipswich, MA. He attended school in Massachusetts, enlisted in Boston, MA on May 28, 1940 and entered active duty in the United States Army on January 16, 1941. Prior to his enlistment, he worked as a longshoreman for the Indian Wharf Co. in Boston, MA, where he operated a hoist, loading and unloading cargo from ships.

During basic training Theodore qualified marksman on both the rifle and the carbine. Later he received additional training as a truck driver and automotive mechanic. Shortly thereafter, the Japanese bombed Pearl Harbor which propelled Tech 5 Sgt. Theodore Bombola and the United States directly into the path of WWII.

T/5 Sgt. Bombola served 16 months in France and England with the quartermaster's gas supply company. He was then assigned to HQ Company, 101st Infantry Regiment and was charged with the responsibility of inspecting, maintaining and repairing trucks and other military vehicles. His duties included: relining brakes and brakes systems, repairing transmissions, transfer cases, rear end and overhauling motors. In a citation signed by President Harry Truman, it states:

"To you who answered the call of your country and served in its Armed Forces to bring about the total defeat of the enemy, I extend the heartfelt thanks of a grateful Nation."

T/5 Sgt. Theodore S. Bombola was awarded the following: Good Conduct Medal, American Defense Service Medal, Victory Medal, American Theater Campaign Ribbon, and the European-African-Middle Eastern Theater Campaign Medal.

T/5 Theodore Bombola was honorably discharged from Fort Devens, MA on December 3, 1945 and took up residence in East Chatham with his wife, Adeline, their son Teddy Jr. and daughter, Theresa. On July 4, 2000 Theodore passed away at the age of 77 and was interred in St. James Cemetery in Ghent, NY.

It is noteworthy that Theodore should leave this world on Independence Day, a day for which we celebrate our independence, an ideal that he helped to preserve.

Ernest Clifford Bower

Ernest Clifford Bower was born in Hudson, NY on February 27, 1929 to Leo and Vera (Baldwin) Bower. He attended Livingston Grammar School, Germantown Central School (graduated June 1946) and later attended Albany Business College, receiving a degree in Business Administration in 1956.

Ernest was working for the Mohawk Novelty Company in Hudson NY, when he was drafted into the United States Army on November 1, 1950. He received basic training at Ft. Eustis, VA, qualifying with the M-1 rifle and carbine. PFC. Ernest Bower was assigned to Company D, 120th Engineers Combat Battalion located in Inchon, Korea. Upon completing his term of enlistment, PFC. Ernest Bower returned to the United States and was honorably discharged on Nov. 1, 1952. He was awarded the following: Korean Service Medal with Bronze Service Star and the United Nations Service Medal.

Ernest reenlisted in the United States Army on February 25, 1957 in Albany,

NY. After basic training he received additional training at Fort Lee, VA at the Quartermaster School. Specialist 4 Ernest Bower was assigned to Headquarters and Headquarters Company at the Army Garrison at Fort Campbell, KY as a quartermaster supply specialist. In April of 1958, Sp/4 Ernest Bower was assigned to the Pacific on the Island of Eniwetok with a "secret clearance" dating Oct 16, 1958. From April through August 1958, twenty-two near-surface nuclear denotations were conducted on Eniwetok. On July 7 and Aug. 4, 1958, Sp/4 Ernest Bower's records indicate that he was exposed to (1.08 rad./.61rad) doses of radiation on the Island of Eniwetok. After October of that year, a nuclear test moratorium was enacted. Upon completion of his military obligation, Sp/4 Ernest Bower was honorably discharged for a second time (Feb. 24, 1960) and returned to his home in Columbia County.

In the years that followed Ernest worked at a funeral home and New York State Motor Vehicle Department in Albany, NY for more than twenty years.

Living in Linlithgo, NY, Ernest died on November 30, 1994 and is buried in Cedar Park Cemetery, Hudson, NY. He left behind two sisters: Ruth and Dorthy Bower. He was 65 years old.

Philip Richard Bower

Philip R. Bower was born May 9, 1925 to Leo and Vera (Baldwin) Bower in Hudson, NY. Growing up in Hudson, Philip was educated in the local school district.

Philip entered the United States Army on May 16, 1944. He completed basic training at Ft. Dix, NJ where he qualified with the M-1 Garand and then received additional training as a carpenter. On October 31, 1944, Philip was assigned to the infantry in the Panama Canal. The Panama Canal was invaluable for the defense and commerce between the Atlantic and Pacific oceans. Recognizing its importance, both Japan and Germany had plans to attack the canal. Submarines did venture near the canal but the Panama Canal was never in imminent danger. As a part of his assignment, Philip attended ordinance school as an armorer artificer, attaining the rank of Tech Sergeant (T-5). He was responsible for maintenance and care of weapons in his unit, therefore protecting this valuable asset which proved to be strategically important to the allied success during WWII. T/Sgt. Philip R. Bower returned to the states on February 14, 1946 and was honorably discharged on February 26, 1946 at Ft. Dix, NJ.

For his service he was awarded the following: American Service Medal and the WWII Victory Medal.

Philip met and married Thelma Snyder on September 24, 1948 at Livingston, NY, and they raised four children. Employed by Atlas Cement Co. of Hudson,

Philip worked as an electrician and carpenter while sidelining as a plumber for Jim Ryan for more than 20 years. He was a member of Hudson Washington Hose Fire Co, American Legion Post #184, Hudson Fish and Game Club and the Hudson Boat Club.

Philip passed away on November 14, 1984 and was buried in Cedar Park Cemetery in Hudson, NY. He left behind his wife, Thelma, four children: Philip (Jr.), Lawrence, Vera Ellen and Leo, 14 grandchildren and 13 great-grandchildren. He was 59 years old.

Thomas G. Bower, Sr.

Thomas George Bower, Sr. was born January 20, 1931 to Leo and Vera (Baldwin) Bower in Fishkill, New York. Growing up in Livingston and Germantown, he attended and graduated from Germantown Central School.

Thomas was drafted into the United States Army on February 11, 1952 in Albany, NY and received his basic training in Massachusetts. Thomas received additional training as a clerk typist and attended the Adjutant General School in May 1952. As a clerk typist, Cpl. Thomas G. Bower was assigned to Headquarters Unit Detachment 1 and worked with senior field grade command. His duties would take him to Korea for a brief time and then the Hawaiian Islands as a trainer of troops. In the course of his service, he was a part of the Reactionary Disaster Team that deployed in response to "Broken Arrow," a term referring to a military nuclear incident. Cpl. Thomas G. Bower, Sr. was credited with four months and five days overseas duty. On February 11, 1954, having completed his tour of duty, Cpl. Thomas G. Bower was honorably discharged and then transferred to the New York Army Reserves Military District, where he completed his military obligation.

For his service he was awarded the following: National Defense Medal and the Good Conduct Medal.

Returning home to Hudson, NY, Thomas met and married Margaret Steir on January 30, 1955. Together, he and Margaret raised three children. For the next thirty years, he work for IBM in the experimental department and ran a private business, Thomas Tree Service. He retired in 1985.

Thomas was active in Germantown Boy Scouts Troop 122 serving as Scout Master and Boy Scout Commissioner, Germantown American Legion #346 as Commander/County Commander, and Chairman of the Board of Appeals.

Thomas passed away on November 18, 2016 and is buried in Germantown Cemetery. Pre-deceased by his wife Margaret, at 85 years old Thomas left behind three children: Thomas, Jr., Pamela and David.

Leman William Bradley

Leman William Bradley was born March 6th, 1820 in Salisbury, Conn. to Leman and Nancy (Everts) Bradley. He worked for the Holley &Company, cutlery manufacturers of Lakeville, Conn. in the early 1850s. On May 10, 1854, he married Catherine Livingston Northrup, who was born in Austerlitz, NY but resided in Brooklyn, NY. At the time of his enlistment, Leman and his family lived in Hudson where he worked as a dealer in cutlery. Here they raised their three children: Minnie C. Bradley (9/28/55), Elizabeth M. Bradley (10/16/57), and Archer E. Bradley (2/13/60).

At 41 Leman enlisted in the 14th Infantry Regiment of the NYS Volunteers on April 30, 1861 and was commissioned first lieutenant into K Company on May 17, 1861. He was subsequently discharged at Washington, DC on September 24, 1861 due to disability.

Leman reenlisted as a first lieutenant into the 94th Infantry Regiment of the NYS Volunteers at Albany, NY. 1st Lt. Bradley later transferred to the 64th Regiment, NYS Volunteers. Promoted to the rank of captain on April 20, 1862, he was wounded in the arm at Fair Oaks, VA on June 1, 1862. Upon his recovery, he returned to his command where he was promoted to major on November 17, 1862.

The 64th Regiment, NYS Volunteers, 4th Brigade, 1st Division took part in the three-day battle at Gettysburg, PA. The regiment sustained casualties of 15 killed and 64 wounded and 19 missing, Maj. Bradley assumed command of the 64th while its commander Col. Bingham recovered from his wounds.

Promoted to lieutenant colonel (May 4, 1864) and in command of the 64th, he participated in the assault of the Muleshoe at the battle of Spotsylvania, VA. They secured the colors of the 44th Virginia, however, Lt. Col. Bradley was wounded in the arm and left for dead on the field but recovered. He mustered out of service on October 5, 1864 with the rank of colonel.

Leman returned to his family in Hudson, NY where he continued his trade as a cutlery dealer and where he retired in 1880. Upon his wife's death (Catherine) in 1890 he went to live with Dr. Howard Bradley and family. He died on August 13, 1912 and was interned in the Cedar Park Cemetery his wife. He was 92 years old.

Wesley Bradley

Wesley Bradley was born February 16, 1830 in Salisbury, CT, the son of Milton and Ester Everts Bradley. He moved to Hudson, NY where, on September 12, 1854, he married Mary Miller and where their three children: Minnie C. Bradley (9/28/55), Elizabeth M. Bradley (10/16/57), and Archer E. Bradley (2/13/60) were born and raised.

Wesley came from a military family. His maternal grandfather, Nathaniel Everts, Jr. was captain of a company of militia in the Revolutionary War and his great-grandfather was a captain of a company of volunteers in the French and Indian War. It seemed natural that on September 27, 1862 Wesley enlisted and was commissioned as a second lieutenant of Company A, 159th New York Volunteers.

It was in April 1862 during the American Civil War that Union forces began operations against New Orleans. The Union fleet had bombarded two old masonry forts which quickly surrendered and then destroyed the small Confederate fleet that gave them support. Without firing a shot, Confederate troops evacuated New Orleans, thus leaving Louisiana open to invasion and serving as a base for continued Union operations. The Confederates had been occupying Baton Rouge and completed river batteries and trenches at Port Hudson. Military activities subsided until the spring of 1863; then there was a series of engagements between Confederate and Union forces.

Assigned to the 3rd Brigade, 4th Division, 19th Corps, the 159th Regiment Infantry or the "2nd Duchess and Columbia Regiment," they occupied Baton Rouge, La., from December 17, 1862, and would remain there until March 1863. On January 14, 1863 Lt. Wesley Bradley was promoted to first lieutenant and transferred to Company E.

In April and May of that year, Lt. Bradley along with the 159th New York Volunteers were engaged in several engagements with Confederate forces in Louisiana. It was sometime during the Western Louisiana campaign that Lt. Wesley Bradley was severely wounded. He was subsequently transported to the St. James Hospital in New Orleans, LA and he died on May 10, 1863. He was later buried in the GAR Plot in Cedar Park Cemetery in Hudson, NY. His headstone records the cause of death as, "died of wounds received in battle." He left a wife and three children.

William Anthony Brown

William Anthony Brown was born in Hudson, NY on September 5, 1949. He started his education by attending Stottville Elementary and finished high school at St. Mary's Academy in Hudson, NY, earning a Regents Scholarship. He majored in civil technology at Hudson Valley Community College in Troy, NY.

As a young man, he excelled in sports. He played Little League and Youth League Baseball, making the all-star team several times. He enjoyed running, karate and boxing.

In January of 1969, William enlisted in the United States Marine Corps and completed his basic training at Parris Island. Subsequently, he trained at Camp LeJeune and Camp Pendleton. While in the Marine Corps, he continued with his boxing and remained undefeated in several bouts.

In June of 1969, William was assigned to the 26th Marines, but would later be assigned to the 1st Marines, in Vietnam. On March 29, 1970, Easter Sunday, while engaged with hostile forces, Cpl. William Anthony Brown was killed in action. He was 20 years old.

He was awarded the Purple Heart, the Combat Action Ribbon, the National Defense Medal, the Military Merit Medal, the Vietnamese Service Medal with Star, the Vietnamese Campaign Medal, Gallantry Cross w/Palm and the N.Y.S. Conspicuous Service Medal.

His selfless dedication to duty is in keeping with the finest tradition of the United States Armed Forces and is a credit to his family, community and the United States Marine Corps.

Robert Andrew Cadby, Jr.

Robert Andrew Cadby was born March 23, 1922 to Robert and Geneva Cadby in New York City. He grew up in Hillsdale and attended Roeliff Jansen Central School. After his graduation on December 26, 1941, he enlisted in the United States Navy and entered the service the following January 16th.

Robert received training at Newport, RI and was transferred to Martinique, where he awaited assignment to the recently built light cruiser the USS Juneau. Recently launched October 25, 1941, the USS Juneau was assigned blockade patrol off Martinique and Guadeloupe and then brief alterations on the east coast. Seaman Second Class Robert Cadby sailed with the USS Juneau on its next cruiser in the Pacific Ocean.

Rendezvousing with the carriers Wasp and Hornet, the USS Juneau joined Task Force 18 under the command of Admiral Noyes. For the next three months it would engage in some of the most fierce sea battles of WWII. On September 15, the Wasp was sunk and the USS Juneau helped rescue 1,910 survivors. It then joined the USS Hornet and assisted in three actions repulsing Japanese advances at Guadalcanal.

In early November, the USS Juneau left New Caledonia to help escort transport to Guadalcanal. It was attacked by 30 enemy aircraft, downing six planes. The USS Juneau was again attacked on November 13 by a large Japanese naval force and with the cruiser Atlanta they closed with the enemy. Receiving a torpedo to the port side, the USS Juneau was forced to withdraw. Listing badly and operating on one screw, she was again attacked by the Japanese submarine 1-26. Avoiding two torpedoes, the USS Juneau was struck by a third. After a large explosion she broke in two and sunk. S2c Cadby and five Sullivan brothers were among the 687 who lost their lives.

For his service to his country S2c Robert Cadby, Jr. was awarded the following: Purple Heart and a Presidential Citation. In a letter from the Secretary of the Navy, Secretary Frank Knox writes:

> *"The bravery of those who make possible the victories at Guadalcanal will long be remembered by a grateful people."*

A memorial service was given in his honor at the Hillsdale Methodist Church. VFW Post #7552 honored Robert Cadby, Jr. and Ralph Shutts, Jr. (another local fallen serviceman) by naming its post in his memory – "Cadby-Shutts Veterans of Foreign Wars Post #7552." His name also appears on the Town of Hillsdale Honor Roll of WWII. Robert was only 20 years old.

Gerald Bradford Card

Gerald Bradford Card was born June 5, 1923 in Philmont to Willis and Hazel (Barringer) Card. Growing up in Philmont, he attended Philmont Union Free elementary and high schools and then worked locally as a heavy truck driver.

Gerald entered the United States Army on January 20, 1943 in Albany, NY. After basic training he was trained as a light truck driver and on March 31, 1944 he departed for the European Theater of Operations.

Assigned to Patton's 3rd Army with the 731st Field Artillery Battalion, Tech 5 Sgt. Gerald Card saw action in Normandy, Northern France, the Ardennes, Central Europe, and the Rhineland. As a part of Patton's 3rd Army, T/5 Sgt. Gerald Card entered Europe in July of 1944 and fought across France, in the Battle of the Bulge, secured a bridgehead over the Rhine and liberated the Mauthausen-Gusen concentration camps. It was engaged for 281 days, liberated 82,000 square miles of territory, 1500 cities and towns, captured 956,000 enemies and killed or wounded 500,000 others.

After serving until the end of the war he arrived home and was honorably discharged at Ft. Dix, NJ on October 31, 1945. For his service T/5 Sgt. Gerald Bradford Card was awarded the following: Bronze Star, European-African-Middle Eastern Service Medal, WWII Victory Medal and the Good Conduct Medal.

Gerald returned home and married Betty Ann French. He worked as a milkman for Van's Dairy in Hudson, NY, Warp Knit Mill, in Mellenville, NY (25 yrs) and later he worked for Charter Supply in Philmont where he retired after 15 years.

He remained active in his community. He was a member of the Philmont American Legion Minkler-Secry Post 252, Philmont United Methodist Church (sang in the choir), Mellenville Vol. Fire Dept.(50 yr member), Hudson Chapter of the SPEBSQSA Barber Shop Singers, Highlanders Barbershop Quartet, Community choir and the Claverack Senior Citizens.

Gerry passed away on January 24, 2004 in Philmont and is buried in the Mellenville Union Cemetery. His wife having predeceased him, Gerry left behind two daughters: Linda and Geraldine, four grandchildren and twelve great grandchildren. He was 80 years old.

Cariseo Brothers
Sisto J. Cariseo
(Mar. 8, 1915 - Jan. 20, 1982)
Nicholas I. Cariseo
(June 1, 1918 - Feb. 2, 1987)
Patsy D. Cariseo
(Oct. 11, 1921 - June 20, 2000)

The Cariseo brothers, Sisto, Nicholas, Patsy, were born to Pasquale and Maria Luigi Cariseo and were raised and attended school in Hudson, NY.

Sisto J. Cariseo entered the United States Army on August 27, 1943. PFC Sisto Cariseo was trained as a rifleman and assigned to the Company C, 314 Infantry. Dispatched to the European Theater of Operation, he saw action in Central Europe, Normandy and the Rhineland. During the course of action he was wounded and was awarded the Purple Heart. In addition, he received the European-African-Middle Eastern Service Medal, and the Good Conduct Medal. On October 4, 1945, Sisto was honorably discharged at Fort Dix and he returned home to raise his family and begin his own successful construction business.

Nicholas was employed by the Mohawk Novelty Co. when he entered the United States Army on August 22, 1942. After training Tech/5 Nicholas Cariseo was assigned to the 43 Military Police Platoon and saw action in the Pacific specifically on the Island of Luzon in the Philippines. Nicholas was honorably discharged on February 9, 1946 and as awarded the following medals: American Service Medal, Asiatic-Pacific Service Medal, Philippines Liberation Ribbon, WWII Victory Medal and the Good Conduct Medal.

Nicholas returned to Columbia County where he and his wife, Elizabeth, owned and operated The Savoia Restaurant in Hudson and later relocated to West Palm Beach where they continued with the restaurant business for the next 20 years.

On October 17, 1942, Patsy was drafted into the United States Army at Albany, NY. Trained in the infantry, Sgt. Patsy Cariseo was a squad leader in Headquarters Company of the 389th Infantry. While on state side maneuvers, Sgt. Patsy Cariseo was injured by an accidental explosion from which he suffered a lung injury. As a result he was medically discharged in 1943 and returned to civilian life. For the next 40 years he worked for Empire Markets and Grand Union and retired as its manager. In addition, he was a long time member of the Disabled American Veterans and a 26 year member of the Catskill Elks.

PFC Sisto Cariseo, Tech/5 Nicholas Cariseo, and Sgt. Patsy Cariseo were three brothers born with a common heritage and instilled with common values. And they, like countless other siblings throughout our nation's history, came to the aid of their country when they were called upon.

One brother would see action in the Pacific, another wounded in Europe, while a third would suffer a disabling injury in a state-side training accident. Each did his part to preserve and protect the freedoms and liberties that we enjoy each day. When called, they came, when asked, they served and when needed, they measured up to the task. They are a credit to their family, their friends and their communities.

Ronald Andrew Carlucci

Ronald Andrew Carlucci was born January 2, 1935 in Hudson, NY to Augusto and Sara (Gasparri) Carlucci. He attended Hudson Central School and graduated in June 1952.

Ronald entered the United States Army on May 20, 1954. After basic training at Ft. Dix, NJ, he received eight weeks of training as a teletype operator at Fort Gordon, GA. Private First Class Ronald A. Carlucci was assigned to duty in Japan in the signal corps and after completing seventeen months of overseas duty returned to the States. On May 3, 1956 PFC Ronald A. Carlucci was honorably discharged from active duty at Fort Dix, NJ and transferred to the Army Reserves as a signal corpsman until his military obligation was completed.

For his service PFC Ronald A. Carlucci was awarded the following: National Defense Service Medal and the Good Conduct Medal.

Ronald returned to Hudson, NY and met and married Florence Schmitt on February 21, 1960 at Our Lady of Mount Carmel in Hudson, NY. Together they raised two children, their son James and daughter, Lynn. In the years that followed, Ronald worked as a computer technician and field engineer for IBM in Kingston, NY. He retired in August 1991 after 25 years of service.

He remained active in his community. He was a member of the Washington Hose Fire Co. of Hudson (life), a 25-year member of the IBM Club, a member of the Jennings Willet American Legion Post in Germantown, as well as a communicant of Holy Trinity/St. Mary's Catholic Church in Germantown.

He passed away on September 15, 2014 in Germantown, NY and is buried in Cedar Park Cemetery in Hudson, NY. He was survived by his loving wife of 54 years, two children, and two grandchildren. He was 79 years old.

Salvadore Castanza

Salvator J. Costanzo was born November 11, 1942 to James and Mary (Forte) Costanzo. Raised in Schenectady, he was graduated from Linton High School.

Sal joined the United States Navy and served on the aircraft carrier the USS Coral Sea during the Vietnam War. He was awarded the Vietnam Service Medal, National Defense Service Medal, and the Vietnam Campaign Medal.

He met and married Nina C. Keene, raising their son David. Sal worked as an assistant to the director of NYS Department of Veterans' Affairs in Albany,. He was a life member of the Stuyvesant Fire Company and the Stuyvesant Falls VFW Post #9593 as well as a member of St. John's Lutheran Church in Stuyvesant. In his later years he enjoyed spending time with his grandson, collecting coins and watching sports.

Sal passed away at The Spring in Troy, NY on November 13, 2017. He is survived by his wife, Nina, his son, David, and his grandson, Mark. He was buried in St. John's Lutheran Church, Stuyvesant. He was 75 years old.

Wendell Everett Chamberlin

Wendell Everett Chamberlin was born in Abington, MA on July 8, 1925 to Harlan and Ruth Chamberlin. He grew up in Columbia County where he attended Roeliff Jansen Central School in Hillsdale, NY.

After graduating high school, on August 9, 1943 Wendell entered the United States Army. He completed basic training at Fort Benning, GA. and received training in the Army Specialized Training Program at Cornell University.

PFC Wendell Everett Chamberlin was assigned to Headquarters Company, 289th Infantry, 75th Division, 9th Army in the European Theater of Operations. The 289th Infantry was constituted on 24 December 1942 and assigned to the 75th Infantry Division, which was then activated on April 15, 1943 at Fort Leonard Wood, MO. It embarked New York Port on November 14, 1944 with a brief stop in England; it then landed in France on December 13, 1944. The 289th Infantry was engaged in several major campaigns in the Rhineland, the Ardennes-Alsace and Central Europe, including the Ardennes, Salm River, Colmar Packet, Rhine River and the Ruhr.

In an excerpt written in the Stars and Stripes , the fighting was characterized:

"Christmas Eve, 1944: In the biting, stinging cold of the Ardennes, men who never before had seen a German soldier came to grips with the Nazis in a slashing bayonet duel. These were green troops — fresh from the States — these men . . . suffered many casualties. But their hold was tenacious."

Another writer characterized the conditions as, *"strong resistance, poor visibility, snow, and extreme cold."*

On April 25, 1945, while participating in combat operations in Germany, PFC Wendell Everett Chamberlin was killed in action. He was awarded posthumously the Purple Heart and Bronze Star. He was 19 years old.

Morgan H. Chrysler

Morgan H. Chrysler was born in Ghent, Columbia County, NY on September 30, 1822. Educated in Ghent, he lived for a time in Hudson, and while there married Amelia Groat of Ghent. He subsequently lived on the Groat Farm in Ghent.

Upon the outbreak of the Civil War, he enlisted as a private in the 30th New York Volunteer on April 7, 1861. Morgan was assigned to Company G, 30th Volunteer Infantry Regiment and was elected captain of Company G by its men on June 1, 1861. He became a major on March 11, 1862, lieutenant colonel on August 30, 1863; and colonel of a Regiment of Cavalry on December 13.

Chrysler fought in the battles of the Peninsula Campaign, Second Bull Run, Antietam and Chancellorsville. When enlistments expired for the 30th NY Volunteers, he was authorized to reorganize them into a cavalry unit called the 2nd New York Veteran Cavalry known as the Empire Light Cavalry. Briefly stationed at Washington, DC, they were assigned duty in Louisiana and participated in campaigns of the Red River (LA) and Mobile (AL).

Morgan Chrysler was brevetted major general on March 13, 1865, one of only four men who rose from private to major general during the Civil War. For a brief time he was military governor of the District of Northern Alabama before he was mustered out in 1866.

After the war, Chrysler led a private life serving at the New York State Custom House, New York Assembly as sergeant-at-arms and the Pension Department as special examiner until his death.

Gen. Chrysler lived in Valatie and founded the Major Thomas M. Burt Post #171(83 members) and the Grand Army of the Republic (GAR) in Valatie. The GAR, a national organization of Civil War veterans, boasted 400,000 members nationwide.

Morgan H. Chrysler died on August 24, 1890 in his home that he shared with

his wife on Broad St., Kinderhook, NY. He was interned in Prospect Hill Cemetery, Valatie, NY. He left behind his lovely wife, Amelia and a son, Clifford, a retired captain who also served in the Civil War. Morgan was 67 years old.

Harrison Clark

Harrison Clark was born April 10, 1942 in Chatham, NY. Little is known of his
boyhood years in Columbia County; however, he enlisted in the 125th New York
Infantry on August 27, 1862 as a corporal in Company E. This regiment was organized and mustered in for three years at Troy, NY on August 27-29, 1862.

The 125th New York Infantry Regiment under the command of Col. Willard
was attached to General Hays' Brigade, 3rd Division, 2nd Corps. On July 2, 1863
the Army of the Potomac marched to Gettysburg, PA. Confronting Gen. Robert
E. Lee's forces. On the second day of the Battle of Gettysburg, the 125th NY Infantry Regiment received heavy fire while crashing headlong into the Confederates of Gen. William Barksdale's Mississippi brigade.

In Cpl. Harrison Clark's own words,

" It was about seven o'clock in the evening of July 2,1863, as we moved
down into the fight, the sun was sinking low in the west and the heavens
were ablaze with its splendor, in marked contrast with the lurid fires of
death towards which we were marching. We were halted amid a heavy
cloud of smoke in front of a swale and a new growth of trees. Through
the smoke covering the field we could dimly see the outlines of men mov-
ing about. We commenced to fire, but the word was shouted: 'firing on
your own men,' and the command was given to 'cease firing.'
We soon learned our mistake. The color-bearer at my right fell, mortally
wounded, and before the old flag could touch the ground, I caught it, and
on we rushed with loud cries; on, with bullets whizzing by our ears,
shells screaming and cannon balls tearing the air, now bursting above
and around us, laying many of our comrades either low in death, or
bleeding with terrible wounds. Most of our color guard were killed or
wounded."

On the following day after the defeat of Pickett's Charge, Cpl. Clark jumped
over a stone wall and followed the rebels "down the board fence where the flag
received 15 bullet holes." This three-day battle resulted in 26 killed (including
the brigade commander, Col. Willard), 104 wounded and 9 missing of the 125th
NY Infantry. Cpl. Harrison Clark's actions resulted in his receiving a field promotion to color sergeant.

Later on May 6, 1864 at the Battle of the Wilderness, Harrison Clark advanced
the flag to within 10 feet of the enemy's line and held the position even though he

was severely wounded in the leg. This singular act resulted in a battlefield promotion to second lieutenant; however, his wound proved to be so severe that his leg was amputated.

Returning home, Harrison continued to be active in veteran's affairs. In 1889 he was elected Commander for the Department of New York of The Grand Army of the Republic. For his actions at Gettysburg, some 32 years after the battle, on June 11, 1895, Harrison Clark received our nation's highest award, the Medal of Honor.

Harrison Clark died on April 18, 1913 and was buried in section 112, plot 153 in the Albany Rural Cemetery in Menands, NY. He was 71 years old.

Joseph Paul Conte

Joseph Conte was born in Hudson on July 19th, 1923 to John and Anna Conte.

Joseph was a very strong swimmer, enjoyed ice hockey and hiking. He attended elementary school at St. Mary's Academy and was a member of the Hudson Boy's Club. He left high school to work as a roofer with Van Vorst Roofers of Schenectady.

With the devastating attack on the American fleet at Pearl Harbor, Joseph was compelled to enlist in the armed services. Although his first choice was the navy, he entered the United States Marine Corp at Albany on June 1, 1942. After completing basic training at Parris Island, he went to Camp Lejune and then volunteered for paratrooper training at Cherry Point, North Carolina.

Joseph embarked for the Solomon Islands from California to take part in some of the worst fighting to date on Vella Lavella, Choiseul and Bougainville. Sick with yellow fever, he was evacuated from Bougainville to a hospital ship to Guadalcanal. Joseph was ordered home and disembarked in California. He then flew to LaGuardia Field, New York City and took the train to Hudson for a well-deserved thirty-day leave.

Joseph returned to the west coast, Camp Pendleton, California and took part in forming the new 5th Marine Division. Turning down the opportunity of remaining state side as a drill instructor, Joseph went with the 5th Marine Division to Hawaii for further training. With a deep sense of duty and wanting to "go back and be with my buddies," Joseph was assigned to A Company, 1st Battalion, 28th Regiment, 5th United States Marines.

On February 19th, 1945 Joseph's outfit went ashore on the southeast coast of Iwo Jima. He was in the first wave to be received by this violent, volcanic island. Five days later the 28th Regiment helped secure Mount Suribachi and then headed west and north up the coast of the island. On the 3rd of March, Joseph was severely wounded by shrapnel and evacuated for a second time to a hospital ship where on March 6, 1945, he succumbed to his wounds and buried with full military honors at sea.

Joseph Conte received the Purple Heart, the Asiatic Pacific Campaign Medal, the World War II Medal, a Presidential Citation, and earned four Battle Stars. His sense of duty is in keeping with the highest tradition of the United States Marine Corp and his sacrifice is enshrined in the hearts of a grateful community and indebted nation.

Lyle Philip Coon

Lyle (Phil) Coon was born January 8, 1943 in Hudson, NY to Lyle F. and Inez (New) Coons. He attended Martin Van Buren Elementary School in Kinderhook and graduated from Ichabod Crane High School in Valatie. Growing up on his father's farm, Lyle, known by family and friends as Phil, loved to help with the pumpkins and field corn. He had a fascination with the Indian arrow heads that he would find in the plowed fields. One, a prized clovis point, was thought to date back thousands of years.

Shortly after graduation, Phil enlisted for four years in the United States Air Force in 1 July of 1960 and reenlisted on September 26, 1964. Little is known about his first four years; however, in his second tour of duty SSgt. Lyle (Phil) Coon was assigned to the Strategic Air Command (SAC) working as an administrative supervisor. In the ensuing four years, SSgt. Lyle (Phil) Coon was stationed in Germany, Crete, Taiwan and Kelly Air Force Base, TX. During this period of our history, the Cold War was in full swing and SAC was the answer to the real and present nuclear threat of the communist Soviet Bloc. By February 1968 the war in Vietnam was beginning to heat up. Several months after the Tet Offense, SSgt Lyle (Phil) Coon was honorably discharged at Kelly Air Force Base, TX. on September 25, 1968.

For his service to his country, SSGT Lyle (Phil) Coon was awarded the National Defense Medal and the Air Force Good Conduct Medal.

Phil returned to Columbia County and worked on the farm with his father. He met and married Lynn Cesternino in 1983 and went on to worked for Sonoco Crellin. Described as a "private person", yet, "well-liked and a good brother," February 23, 2002, Phil died and was buried in West Ghent Cemetery after a short illness. He was only 59 years old.

Herbert Oakley Coons

Herbert Oakley Coons was born May 25, 1918 at Red Hook, NY to Cecil and Margaret Coons. In his youth, he grew up in Germantown, where he attended school. Prior to his enlistment, Herbert worked for Tinkle Paugh as a mechanic and a general farmhand. On December 30, 1940, Herbert enlisted along with his friend Albert Lockwood in the US Army at Hudson, NY.

Herbert received basic training at Fort Dix, NJ and Advanced Infantry Training at Fort Benning, Ga. As an infantry rifleman Pvt. Coons was assigned to the Eastern Theater of Operation with the advent of World War II. He participated in the campaigns of North Africa, Sicily, and Anzio.

Anzio, a small town located on the western shores of Italy, was the scene of one of the longest and bloodiest battles of World War II. Struggling to break through heavy German resistance, the Allies faced a determined foe under the command of Field Marshall Albert Kesselring. However, victorious for five months (1/44 - 5/44) the Allies frequently fought a visible enemy hand-to-hand and often endured lengthy periods of deadly artillery as well as battling the invisible enemies of infection, disease and dysentery. The Allies incurred 60,000 casualties before Anzio would be secured.

While at Anzio, Pvt. Coons contracted acute yellow atrophy of the liver from contaminated food and water at the Anzio Beach Head. He was transferred to the West Point Military Academy Hospital for medical treatment. Having spent three weeks home on leave with his family in the spring of 1945, he succumbed to his illness on April 3, 1945 at the Military Academy Hospital at West Point. Pvt. Herbert Coons was buried at Union Cemetery in Mellenville, NY. At the age of 26, Herbert left behind his parents and his only sibling, Marion L. Noren. Marion remembers him fondly, stating Herbert was *"friendly . . . likable . . . with a very good disposition."*

For his dedication and service to his country Pvt. Herbert Oakley Coons was awarded the Good Conduct Medal, the Combat Infantryman's Badge with three Battle Stars, the Purple Heart, and a Presidential Citation at Anzio.

The price of our liberty is those sacred few who have shed their lives on the precious alter of freedom.

John C. Cordato

John C. Cordato was born to John and Molly (DeJoy) Cordato on October 12, 1932 in Hudson, NY. He grew up and attended the Hudson City School District. Upon his mother's death, he enlisted in the United States Army.

After basic training John served in Korea during the Korean War. He returned home and on July 1, 1956 he married Alice Platner. For the next 10 years he worked for Lone Star Cement Plant in Hudson, NY where he and Alice raised their son John, Jr.

In 1966, John enlisted in the Navy and was trained as an equipment operator with the Seabees. On January 9, 1970, EO2 John Cordato was Honorably Discharged from the Navy whereupon he enlisted a second time in the Army. For the next eleven years Staff. Sgt. John C. Cordato worked with the Army Corps of Engineer traveling to and from the States; twice to the Republic of Vietnam. Throughout his service to his country, he was awarded numerous citations and commendations for his proficiency and gallantry.

Staff Sgt. John Cordato was awarded the following: Army Service Ribbon, Overseas Service Ribbon, National Defense Medal with Oak Cluster, Republic of Vietnam Campaign Medal, Combat Infantryman Badge, United Nations Service Medal, Korean Service Medal with two Bronze Service Stars, Presidential Unit Citation (Army), Presidential Unit Citation (Navy), Army of Occupation Medal (Germany), Vietnam Service Medal with one Silver and one Bronze Service Star, Army Good Conduct Medal with Silver one Loop, Army Achievement Medal, Expert Rifle Badge, Rep. of Vietnam Engineer Badge, Army Commendation Medal and Vietnamese Cross of Gallantry with Palm.

John worked for Lone Star Cement Plant (Hudson, NY), Providence Hall and Columbia Greene Community College. He was a member of the VFW, American Legion, Hudson Elks #787, 50-year member/Past Treasurer of Washington Hose and communicant of Our Lady of Mt. Carmel Church, Hudson, NY.

John died on February 28, 2011 and is buried in Cedar Park Cemetery, Hudson, NY. He left behind his lovely wife Alice, his son John, two grandchildren and five great-grandchildren. He was 78 years old.

Leonard G. Cordato, Jr.

Leonard G. Cordato was born to Leonard and Enrichetta Cordato on March 15, 1919 in Hudson, NY. Growing up in Hudson, he attended grammar and high school in the Hudson School District.

Leonard entered the United States Army on July 21, 1937 as a private. After basic training, he was assigned to the 1st Cavalry Division at Fort Knox, KY where he attained the rank of Private First Class and served as a squad leader. On July 20, 1940, he was assigned to the 1st Armor Regiment and attended Topography School. Placed in the Army Reserves, PFC Leonard G. Cordato was discharged and then reenlisted in the Army on November 12, 1940 in New York City.

In January 1941 he was promoted to corporal and then to sergeant in April 1941. Sgt. Cordato was assigned to the 18th Infantry Regiment, 1st Cavalry Division where he served as a platoon leader with an Intelligence and Recon Platoon.

Assigned to the Eastern Theater of Operations, Staff Sgt. Leonard Cordato saw action in Algeria-French Morocco, Tunisia, Sicily, Normandy, Northern France, and the Rhineland. On April 23, 1943 he was wounded in the battle of El Guettar after a German shell exploded, fracturing his nose and taking shrapnel to the face. He earned the Bronze Star for ground combat in Algeria, FR. Morocco and again on D Day Omaha Beach in Normandy France. On September 16, 1944, he received the Belgian Fourragere at Liege, Belgium.

As platoon leader in an intelligence and recon platoon, Leonard Cordato spearheaded some of the most vicious fighting in the European conflict. He was in the assault landing in Africa (first wave) as well as Sicily and participated in a pre-invasion recon mission for the Normandy Invasion (D Day minus 60 min.).

Staff Sgt. Leonard Cordato was awarded the Bronze Star with Oak Leaf Cluster, the Purple Heart, Combat Infantryman's Badge, American Defense Service Medal, EAME Service Medal and the Belgian Fourragere. He was honorably discharged on June 23, 1945 at Ft. Dix, NJ.

On August 15, 1949, Leonard enlisted in the United States Army Reserve and remained until November 8, 1951. He was then assigned to the Company D, 31st Infantry Battalion New York National Guard attaining the rank of 1st Lieutenant.

Leonard married Harriett Parker, and they had four children: Harriett, Leonard, Mary and George. Remembered as an artist and family man, Leonard was self-employed as a neon and sign painter. He remained active in his community with the American Legion and VFW until his death.

On October 28, 1968, Leonard G. Cordato passed away of a cerebral hemorrhage and was buried at Cedar Park Cemetery, Hudson, NY. He left behind a wife and four children. He was 49 years old. The family has since grown to eight grandchildren and seven great-grandchildren.

Charles Cunningham

Charles Cunningham was born in Hudson, NY and entered the United States Army in New York City. He trained as a cavalryman and was assigned to Company B, 7th U. S. Cavalry under the command of Lt. Col. George Armstrong Custer.

With the discovery of gold, adventurous citizens rushed into the Black Hills of the Dakota Territory thus encroaching upon treaty rights and causing Indian unrest. Messengers were sent to the Indian leaders Crazy Horse and Sitting Bull, ordering them to return to the reservation by January 31, 1876.

On May 17, 1876, twelve Companies of the 7th Cavalry left Fort Abraham Lincoln with orders to return, if necessary by force, the Indians to the reservation. Cautiously, the 7th Calvary followed a trail which lead them into the Big Horn Valley, and on the morning of June 24th, Col. Custer was informed by scouts that there appeared to be a very large pony herd some 15 miles in the distance, thus indicating that the Indians they were tracking were camped along the Little Big Horn River and much larger than they had anticipated. Disregarding the intelligence gathered by his scouts, Col. Custer divided his 600 cavalrymen into four forces. Capt. Benteen would scout to the west, Major Reno would attack the Indian village from the south, Capt McDougall would guard the pack-train and he would attack from the east.

Maj. Reno's small force was violently repelled by what was later estimated to be in the thousands. He was joined on the bluffs in a defensive position overlooking the Little Big Horn River by Benteen's command as well as the pack train. Heavy rifle fire suggested Custer's command was engaged in heated action to the north.

Cpl. Charles Cunningham, who was initially assigned to guard the pack-train, was ordered to reinforce the defensive perimeter of the remnants of Maj. Reno's Command. Throughout the long hot day and into the night, the besieged 7th Calvary suffered numerous casualties with the constant and repeated close quartered attacks of the superior Sioux and Cheyenne forces. Despite injury, Cpl. Cunningham, "declined to leave the line when wounded in the neck during heavy fire and fought bravely all (the) next day." The following day General Terry rescued what remained of the 7th Calvary; however, Lt. Col. Custer and 261 of his men lost their lives.

On October 5, 1878 Cpl. Charles Cunningham was issued our nation's highest award, The Congressional Medal of Honor, for his heroic actions under extraordinary circumstances in spite of personal injury.

Albert Norman Dallas

Albert Norman Dallas was born in Hudson, NY on September 4, 1935 to Albert and Dorothy (Kline) Dallas. He attended Ockawamick Central School until his junior year when he enlisted in the United States Air Force. Albert would receive a GED from Troy, NY and in 1977 he received an AAS Degree for Human Services from Columbia Green Community College.

Living in Philmont, NY shortly after hostilities concluded in Korea, Albert enlisted in the United States Air Force on January 17, 1955 in Albany, NY. After basic training, he was trained at Keesler Air Force Base in Mississippi as a radio operator. Airman Second Class Albert Norman Dallas was assigned to overseas duty with the 21st Communication Squadron where he served in Germany and France. On January 17, 1957, Albert married Margarete Werner in the base chapel at Darstadt, Germany. On February 7, 1959 having completing his term of service, A/2C Albert Norman Dallas was honorably discharged at McGuire Air Force base, NJ. He received the Good Conduct Medal for his service and was then assigned to the Air Force Reserves.

Albert and Margarete returned home where they raised a family in the hamlet of Philmont. Throughout the ensuing years, Albert worked as a carpenter and a counselor for the mentally handicapped. Retiring in 1993 because of a disability, Albert continued to be active in his community. He was a communicant of Sacred Heart of Philmont as well as a Eucharist minister. In addition, he was a volunteer fireman (fire police) in the Philmont Volunteer Fire Company and assisted at the Nutrition Center in Philmont. He helped start the Special Friends Program in conjunction with Mental Health in Hudson. He also was honored for his work with the Catskill Boys Club for his work with adolescents.

His wife recalls, *"Albert was proud to have served his country. It is not easy as a young man to go to another country with no knowledge of the language. He was happy though for the experience. He loved his family which grew every year. All in all he liked others and was well-liked by all."*

Albert died on December 23, 2005 and was buried in the Sacred Heart Cemetery, Philmont. He left behind a lovely wife, Margarete, six children, fifteen grandchildren and ten great grandchildren. Albert, a Korean era veteran, was 70 years old.

Taylor S. Danar

Taylor S. Danar was born September 30, 1925 to Max and Tillie (Nesson) Danar in Fordham Hospital in the Bronx, NY. He attended school in Brooklyn, NY where he obtained a high school diploma.

Working for Wm. H. Weintraub Co. at Rockefeller Plaza (NYC) in Production Advertising, Taylor entered the United State Navy on January 21, 1944 in New York, NY. After four weeks of basic training at the Naval Training Center in Sampson, NY, he received additional 20 weeks training at Radio School at the same station. As a radioman, he was assigned to the Pacific Theater of Operation with the 7th Fleet. Radioman 3rd Class Taylor S. Danar was assigned to the Vice Admiral's Staff and served on various communications command ships throughout the South Pacific. While serving with the 7th Amphibious Force under Vice Admiral Daniel E. Barbey, he was involved with operations on Manus Island, Admiralty Islands and then Hollandia, New Guinea. After cessation of hostilities in the Pacific, RM3 Taylor S. Danar was honorably discharged on February 2, 1946 at Lido Beach Long Island, NY.

For his service RM3 Taylor S. Danar was awarded the following: Asiatic Pacific Medal with star, Philippine Liberation Medal with star, WWII Victory Ribbon and the American Campaign Medal.

Taylor returned to New York City and worked as an executive sales manager for W. A. Kreger (30 years) and then (top sales executive) with Quad Graphics where he retired on January 1, 2001 after 35 years. Having two children from his previous marriage, he married Elaine Georgiades on August 27, 1977 in New Jersey. Taylor was an avid golfer, dancer, world traveler and had a love for all kinds of music. He published a book entitled, Almost around the world traveler (2008).

Residing in Livingston, NY, Taylor passed away in Hudson, NY on March 30, 2017 and was cremated. He left behind his wife Elaine and two children: Robin and Richard. He was 91 years old.

Albert James Darling III

Albert James Darling III (Jimmy) was born in Webster, MA on May 7, 1946 to Albert J. and Marjorie (Kemp) Darling. In 1951 the family moved to Yorktown Heights, NY. Albert attended school and was a member of the Boy Scouts.

In 1961 his parents purchased a farm, and Albert along with his four brothers, Mark, David, Jeff and Mathew and sister, Nancy, moved to Craryville, NY. He attended Roe Jan School in Hillsdale.

On February 23, 1966, Albert enlisted in the United States Marine Corps. After basic training at Parris Island, PFC Darling received training as a wireman and was assigned to a communications platoon to Company B., Battalion Landing Team 1/3. The newly rehabilitated BLT 1/3 was a part of Special Landing Force Alpha.

On April 28, 1967 elements of the BLT 1/3 landed by helicopter in Que Son Valley. On the evening of May 2nd, Company C was attacked by hostile forces. With the support of USAF AC-47, "Puff the Dragon" gunships, "Spooky" flare planes, Marine artillery and the BLT's own supporting arms, the communists were driven from their positions. On May 10th, while resuming their sweep and destroy operation, PFC Darling's company became engaged in a day-long action with a sizable Viet Cong force.

Taken under intense and accurate sniper fire, they maneuvered to a defilade position behind some rice paddy dykes. Two of PFC Darling's fellow Marines were attempting to take a wounded man to safety but were unable to maneuver him up a steep slope. Albert and another Marine immediately responded to their call for assistance. As they approached the wounded man, they received several rounds of sniper fire. Locating the sniper, PFC Darling returned fire and killed him. As he was returning to a safer position, another sniper shot and instantly killed PFC Darling.

The first operation for Special Landing Force Alpha was costly, In the sixteen days of the operation, along with PFC Albert Darling III, the battalion had 54 marines killed and 151 wounded. The enemy suffered 181 killed and 66 captured.

For his service he was awarded the following: Purple Heart, Bronze Star with V (for valor), Vietnam Service Medal, Vietnam military Merit Medal, Vietnamese Cross of Gallantry, National Defense Service Medal and NYS Conspicuous Service Medal.

PFC Albert James Darling III was proud to be a marine and gallantly gave his life for his country. His remains were interned in Dudley, MA. He was only 21.

James A. Dawson

James A. Dawson was born March 6, 1920 to Robert and Anne (Armstrong) Dawson in Mt. Vernon, NY. Growing up in Hillsdale, NY, he attended and was graduated from Roeliff Jansen High School in June, 1938. He later attended SUNY at Cobleskill Ag/Tech. College, majoring in agriculture.

Working as a dairy tester, James was drafted to the United States Army on August 4, 1944. Having completed basic training and advanced infantry training; James was assigned to the European Theater of Operation to the 358 Infantry Battalion as a machine gunner. On February 10, 1945 while engaged with enemy forces in the "Battle of the Bulge", Tech Sgt. James A. Dawson was severely wounded by artillery fragmentation and evacuated to England for medical treatment. Upon recovery from his wounds, he was then assigned to 398th Military Police Battalion in France after which he was subsequently honorably discharged on July 26, 1946 at Fort Dix, NJ.

For his service, Tech Sgt. James A. Dawson was awarded the following: Bronze Star, Purple Heart, WWII Victory Medal, European African Middle Easter Campaign Medal, Good Conduct Medal and the Combat Infantry Badge.

Returning to Columbia County, James married Carolyn Lossow on September 19, 1948 in Hillsdale, NY and together they raised three children: James, John and Bonnie. During the next three decades, he worked as a farmer, milk tester and truck driver with highway maintenance for Columbia County Solid Waste, retiring after working 20 years with the county. He remained active in his community as a Mason, a member of the Hillsdale VFW and a communicant of the North Hillsdale Methodist Church.

On May 27, 2017, James A. Dawson passed away and was buried in the North Hillsdale Rural Cemetery. He left behind his wife Carolyn, three children, four grandchildren and five great-grandchildren. He was 97 years old.

James Vincent DeCaprio

James Vincent DeCaprio was born in Hudson, NY on December 15, 1923 to

Anthony and Philomena (Esposito) DeCaprio. Raised in Hudson, he attended the local elementary school and high school, receiving his high school diploma.

James entered the United States Navy on November 15, 1943 in Hudson, NY. He received basic naval training and radioman training at the Navy Training Station at Sampson , NY. He was then sent to Amphibious Training Base in Solomons, Md. For the next two years, Radioman Second Class James DeCaprio was assigned to the USS LST 267, USS LST 53 and USS LST 133 in the Asiatic-Pacific Theater of Operations.   An LST or Landing Craft Tank, is designed to support amphibious operation by directly carrying tanks, vehicles, cargo and troops from ship onto the shore. RM2 James DeCaprio participated in the landing in Northern France (Normandy), Southern France and the Philippines (Luzon). RM2 James V. DeCaprio fought in both the European and Pacific theater of operations and was involved is several major operations. He was honorably discharged on February 9, 1946 at Lido Beach, NY.

For his service he was awarded the following medals: Asiatic Pacific Medal with star, Philippine Liberation Medal, European Theater Medal with two stars, Victory Medal, American Theater Ribbon and the Good Conduct Medal.

James returned home but on January 19, 1958 married Louise Luponio in Alife, Italy. They raised four children: Anna, Joann, James, Jr. and Lisa. He worked as a produce manager at the Grand Union in Hudson, NY, retiring on disability. He was an active member of the Italian American War Veterans and Phoenix Hose Fire Co. #5.

James passed away on July 17, 1983 and is buried in Cedar Park Cemetery, Hudson, NY. He left behind his wife Louise, four children, seven grandchildren and two great-grandchildren. He was 59 years old.

David Franklin Decker

David Decker was born July 6, 1945 in Hudson, NY to Harry and Alice Decker. He grew up in Hudson and was graduated from Hudson High School in 1963.

David enlisted for three years in the United States Army on July 23, 1963. After his initial training, Specialist Fourth Class David Decker was trained as a medic and was stationed in Germany. Having served the previous three years in Germany, he reenlisted for a second term of four years in 1966 and volunteered for duty in Vietnam.

On July 31, 1968, Sp4 David Decker was assigned to the 568th Medical Company, 44th Medical Brigade, Helicopter Evacuation Unit near the Mekong Delta in the Republic of Vietnam. The 44th Medical Brigade was formed on December 30, 1965 and was activated on January 1, 1966 at Fort Sam Houston, TX. It was deployed to Vietnam, where it participated in 12 of the 17 campaigns, including Counteroffensive, Counteroffensive Phases II through VII, Tet Counteroffensive; Summer-Fall 1969; Winter-Spring 1970 and Sanctuary Counteroffensive.

While serving his first one-year tour of duty in Vietnam, Sp4 David Decker was killed on April 13, 1969 in a non-hostile motorized vehicle accident. His body was flown home and a funeral with full military honors was held at St. Matthew's Lutheran Church. Specialist Fourth Class David Decker's remains were interned in Cedar Park Cemetery, Hudson, NY by a military honor guard from Fort Dix, NJ.

Sp 4 David Decker received the following citations: Good Conduct Medal and the Expert Marksmanship Badge.

In a personal comment a friend writes:

"You were one of the brave that answered the call. You honor us by your service and sacrifice. We now honor you each time we stand and sing the words, 'the land of the free and the home of the brave'. Thank you for your bravery, courage and dedication to our country and freedom. Rest in peace and honor."

He is honored on Panel 27W – Line 72 on the Vietnam Veterans Memorial in Washington, D.C. *"Greater love than this hath no man that a man lay down his life for his friends."*

Paul Joseph Dooley

Paul Joseph Dooley was born June 16, 1925 to Anthony and Catherine Dooley in Rice County, Minnesota. He attended Faribault Elementary School and subsequently was graduated from Faribault High School in Minnesota.

Paul entered the Merchant Marines in Minnesota on December 7, 1941, the day the Japanese attacked Pearl Harbor. He served in the escort service for Allied war ships during World War II. While in the service to his country, two of the ships that he served on were sunk. He was discharged August 15, 1945 in New York City. From 1945 to 1950 Paul was employed as a civilian with the Merchant Marines.

On April 22, 1950, Sgt. Dooley returned to active duty in the United States Army and saw combat with the infantry in the 1st Army in Korea. Sgt. Paul Dooley was honorably discharged from the United States Army for a second time at Fort Devans, MA on September 14, 1952.

He was awarded the following: two Combat Infantry Badges for WWII and Korea, Merchant Marine Service Medal, Mediterranean Service Medal and Pacific War Zone Medal.

Paul was a member of the American Legion, a communicant of St. Luke's

Church in Chatham and a 4th Degree Honorary member of the Knights of Columbus.

On November 24, 2000, Paul Joseph Dooley died and was buried in Saratoga National Cemetery.

His wife recalled, *"Paul was a man who was so full of love for God, for his country, for the Flag and his family. He was proud to be an American and to have served his country in time of war. To receive the honor he had at the Saratoga Veteran's Cemetery and will receive from this program would have meant so much to him and means so much to his family and friends. A program such as this makes all of us proud to be Americans who honor their veterans!"*

Paul Dooley leaves behind a loving wife, Dorothy, three children: Carol Ann, Greg and Brian and five grandchildren. He was 75 years old.

Leonard William Dorren

Leonard William Dorren was born October 3, 1916 to Florence (Talbot) and Peter Dorren in Paterson, NJ. Although an "ace student," he was forced to quit school to assist his father with the dairy business. Getting up a 2 a.m., Leonard would "hitch the horses to the wagon, ride to the dairy, load the wagon with milk, cream and butter, and deliver the goods to homes through the area." He received a correspondence high school diploma.

In 1935 during the Depression, Leonard enlisted in the United States Navy lured by a poster that suggested, "Join the Navy and See the World". After basic and oil burning boiler school, Leonard was assigned to the USS New Orleans (CA32) where he met and married his best friend's (Charlie) sister Dorothy Van Wert in Honolulu, HI.

On December 7, 1941 Leonard heard low-flying planes outside his Naval Base apartment and "recognized the Japanese symbol, a red circle on the wings of a plane," and he "lock(ed) eyes with one of the pilots." Immediately returning to his ship, which was under engine repair, Len fired at the attacking planes from the deck of the ship with a pistol. In the coming years, Chief Warrant Officer Len Dooren would engage the enemy in seventeen Pacific Battles including: Coral Sea, Midway and the Solomon Islands.

On November 30, 1942 at the Battle of Tassafaronga, he received a commendation for actions he took when a Japanese torpedo blew the bow off his ship, killing 180 crew members. On same day, he received news that his brother, Bobby, was killed aboard the USS Hornet. CWO 3 Len Dorren would serve 23 years in the navy and retire in 1958.

He was awarded the: Good Conduct Medal with three stars, American Defense Service Medal w/ star, American Campaign Medal, Asiatic-Pacific Campaign

Medal w/12 stars, European-African Middle Eastern Campaign Medal, WWII Victory Medal, Navy Occupation Service Medal, Philippine Liberation Ribbon and the National Defense Service Medal.

For the next 25 years he would work for the insurance industry attaining the management position of Vice President of Coroon and Black of New York, Inc. In the interim, he and Dolly lived on Queechy Lake in Canaan, NY and raised four children: Douglas, Leonard, Dorothy and Noralen.

Len remained active in his community. He was a member of the Queechy Lake Club, the Canaan Historical Society, the Northern Columbia County Rotary and served four terms as Supervisor of the Town of Canaan.

Leonard died on December 25, 2012 and was buried at the Dutch Reform Church in Claverack, NY. He was 96 years old.

William Henry Doss, Jr.

William Henry Doss, Jr. was born in 1931 in Stottville to the parents of Mr. and Mrs. William H. Doss, Sr. He attended Stottville Union Free School and then Hudson Central School until he decided to pursue other aspirations. While still residing with his parents, he started a business where he would pick up milk from county farmers and deliver it to the Borden Plant located in Chatham.

In October of 1949, William enlisted in the United States Army, and he received basic training at Fort Knox, KY. After additional training, he reported on February 1, 1950 for active duty with the 31st Infantry Regiment, 7th Infantry Division, which was then located in Japan.

On December 6, 1950, while serving as an ammunitions driver for the service company in the 31st Infantry near Hagaru-ri, Cpl. Doss was separated from his unit. Telling a fellow soldier that he was "going back to his buddies," he was taken prisoner and subsequently died while a prisoner at Camp #5 at Pyongyang, North Korea. Official records list the remains of a: "Doss, William H. Cpl. RA12350120 Svc. Co 31st Inf." to U.S. custody in 1954 and buried in the Punch Bowl, Hawaii in 1956.

He was awarded the following: Purple Heart, Prisoner of War Medal, Korean Service Medal, United Nations Service Medal and the National Defense Service Medal.

Cpl. William H. Doss, Jr. was honored on May 24, 2002 with Clifford Johnson, Donald McNaughton, and Richard Powell – all served in the 7th Infantry Division and died within five days of each other during the same offensive.

Walter Doty, Jr.

Walter Doty was born March 13, 1930 in Hudson, NY to Walter and Sophia Piesta Doty. Walter grew up in Hudson and attended Hudson Central School.

Living on Allen Street, Walter enlisted in the United States Army on September 8, 1948 in Albany, NY. Walter took basic training at Ft. Dix, NJ and attended construction engineer school at Camp Stoneman, CA. Cpl. Walter Doty was assigned to a duty station in Mazsu, Japan as a part of the Allied Occupational Force.

In November 1950, when the Korean War broke out, Cpl. Walter Doty was assigned to the Marines at the Chosen Reservoir. While temperatures dropped to 40 below zero, he helped transport the dead south to Hungnam Harbor. With the evacuation of military and civilian personnel, he helped destroy the vast quantities of supplies and ammunition that remained behind. After two years and nine months of overseas duty, Cpl. Walter Doty was assigned to the 118th Transportation Company at Fort Eustis, Va., where he was honorably discharged on October 14, 1952.

He was awarded the following: Army of Occupation Medal with Japan Clasp, Korean Medal with silver star the United Nations Service Medal, the Good Conduct Medal and the National Defense Service Medal.

Returning home Walter married Caroline White and they raised seven children. Walter worked at Deno's Auto Body during the day and Chris' Auto Body at night. In his later years, he worked at DeBrino Caulking and retired after eight years in 1988. On October 7, 1989 he married Betty Roberts in Hudson, NY.

Walter remained active in his community. He was the Past Commander of VFW 1314 and the Korean War Veterans, as well as serving on the committee for the Korean War Monument that is located in front of the Hudson City Courthouse.

Walter passed away on April 27, 2016 in Berlin, NY. He left behind his wife, Betty, seven children: Rosemary, Betty Ann, Carolann, Walter (III), Robert, Michelle, and Kimberly, 20 grandchildren and 28 great-grandchildren. He was 86 years old.

Walter Doty, Sr.

Walter Doty was born June 5, 1891 to Ben Z. and Jennie (Webster) Doty in Amsterdam, NY. Growing up in New York, he attended high school in Hoboken, NJ. Walter worked on a tugboat until he entered the United States Army on March 28, 1918 at Hoboken, NY.

Finishing basic training in Fort Dix, NJ, Pvt. Walter Doty was given advanced training as a horseman in the cavalry. Cavalry units prior to World War I were considered an effective shock tactic in land warfare. The advent of the machine gun, barbed wire, trenches and artillery fire reduced their effectiveness, and they were replaced by the armored tank. Horses, however, were used effectively for transporting materials to the front until the end of the war. Pvt. Walter Doty remained stateside and thus completed his military service in New Jersey and was honorably discharged on March 8, 1920 at Hoboken, NJ.

Walter moved to and resided in Hudson, NY where he married Sophia Piasta on May 7, 1921. During the ensuing years, he worked at Lane Construction, Van Wyack Coal Company, while he and Sophia raised their five children: Fred, Helen, Anna, Joseph and Walter, Jr. Walter served with the Hudson fire police at No 8 Fire Company, and during World War II, he served as an air raid warden in Hudson, NY. After 30 years with the Hudson Department of Public Works, Walter retired in 1964.

Fondly remembered as one who was dedicated to family and friends, Walter passed away on February 4, 1974 in Hudson, NY, where he was buried in Union Cemetery. He was 85 years old. He left behind a wife, five children, sixteen grandchildren and twenty great-grandchildren.

Lawrence Earl Dunton

Lawrence Earl Dunton was born March 15, 1915 to Raymond and Edith Archer Dunton in Port Chester, New York. He grew up in Canaan and Chatham, NY where he attended school. He was active in the Boy Scouts and his favorite subject was chemistry.

Shortly after the attack on Pearl Harbor, Lawrence enlisted in the Marine Corps at Springfield, MA. He was assigned to active duty on January 22, 1942 and completed basic training at Paris Island. After additional training, he was then assigned to the Pacific Theater of Operations on the Island of Samoa.

Fearing the airfields on Guadalcanal were a threat to Australia (an ally), the 1st Marine Division landed on August 7, 1942, where they encountered heavy resistance. On Sept. 18, 1942, Cpl. Dunton joined hostilities on the "Canal" with Company A, 1st Battalion, 7th Regiment of the 1st Marine Division. The 1/7th's famous commander, Lt. Col. Lewis (Chesty) Puller, led his marines in several strategic battles along the Matanikau and the Lunga River.

On October 24, a listening post from the "understrenghted" 1/7, detected signs that the Japanese were planning to attack and overrun Henderson Air Field. Screaming "Banzi", the crack Sendai Division charged the 1/7 position and a fierce battle ensued, in what would come to be known as the Battle of Bloody Ridge. A historian notes,

"When A Company on the left fired all of its ammunition, Puller told

Capt. Regan Fuller to hold with the bayonet. The enemy regrouped and
came on again, a half dozen times."

At a critical moment, the Japanese penetrated the Marine lines but were repulsed with the help of 25-year-old Sgt. "Manila John" Basilone, who would receive the Medal of Honor for his heroics. The Japanese would lose some 23,000 men while the Americans would incur 1,598 killed and 4,709 wounded before hostilities would end on Guadalcanal.

The significance of this victory is that the United States and its allies would take the strategic initiative which they would not relinquish until cessation of hostilities.

Rabaul, a massive enemy base on the eastern end of New Britain Island, was the next important objective. To neutralize this threat, the 1st Marine Division landed the day after Christmas at Cape Gloucester, New Britain. From December 26, 1943 to April 30, 1944, Cpl. Lawrence Earl Dunton would battle a determined enemy, the jungle, monsoon rains and disease at Cape Gloucester. The victory cost the marines 310 killed and 1,083 wounded.

Cpl. Lawrence Earl Dunton returned to the United States and was discharged on October 12, 1945 at Camp Lejeune, NC. He was awarded the Honorable Service Lapel Pin and the Asiatic Pacific Campaign Medal.

Lawrence returned home, married Anne Mary Girdler in 1949 and raised a family: Susan, Timothy and Bill. He retired from General Electric after 33 years. On March 24, 1991 Lawrence died and was buried in Canaan, New York. He was 76 years old.

Howard David Dwy

Howard David Dwy was born August 20, 1930 in New Milford, CT to Howard L. and Hope (White) Dwy. Raised in Ancram, David graduated in 1947 from Roeliff Jansen High School in Hillsdale, NY. After graduation he worked as a bookkeeper for AC Bristol in Copake, NY.

Dave entered the United States Army on December 11, 1953 and received training at Fort Dix, NJ. Specialist Four David Dwy received additional training for 10 weeks at an Ordinance School qualifying as an ammo supply specialist. Stationed in Columbia, SC Spec/4 David Dwy was then assigned to Headquarters and Headquarters Company, 411th Engineers Brigade in France . On September 11, 1955, Spec/4 David Dwy was transferred to the Stand by Reserves and remained as such until he was honorably discharged at Camp Kilmer, NJ on November 30, 1961.

For his service Spec/4 Howard David Dwy was awarded the Good Conduct Medal and the National Defense Service Medal.

While in the reserves, David received an associate's degree from Westchester Community College and a bachelor's degree at Empire State College. Dave met Jane Pascoe, and they were married on February 4, 1961 in Scranton, Pa. He worked for Lane Construction Corp, and with his business degree, he then worked as a business manager for twenty-six years at Taconic Hills Central School, from where he retired in 1993. Together he and Jane raised four children: Kevin, Craig, Pamela (Reed) and Karen (Hathaway).

David was active in his community. He was a member of the Masonic Lodge #396, a 32 degree Scottish Rite Mason, a Shriner in the Kalurah Temple (Binghamton, NY), a communicant and a board member of St. John's Lutheran Church in Ancram, NY, and the Supervisor of the Town of Gallatin.

On February 11, 2000 David passed away and was buried in Union Cemetery Ancram, NY. He left behind his loving wife, Jane, four children: Kevin, Craig, Pamela and Karen and eight grandchildren. He was 69 years old.

Arthur A. Eppler

Arthur A. Eppler was born June 10, 1923 in Yonkers, NY to Arthur J. and Anna K. Eppler. Growing up in New York, Arthur was graduated from Saunders Trade School on June 24, 1941 and went to work as a machine operator for Jenkins Brothers, Bridgeport, CT. He met and married Elizabeth Emily Giovanna at St. Mary's on August 15, 1942.

On February 21, 1943, Arthur entered the Army Aviation Cadets in New York City, NY. During next few years, Arthur learned to fly twin engine airplanes. Successfully completing basic training, Arthur went on to finish Elementary Flying and Ground School (12/4/43). It was then three months Co-Pilot training (C-46) at Reno, NV, and then finally nine months training as a pilot for twin engines at Freeman Field, IN.

On May 23, 1944 1st Lt. Arthur A. Eppler was assigned to the 1344th Army Air Force based Unit in the Far East. With a brief stop in India, he flew on to China where he spent the next several months flying resupply missions in the twin engine C-46 cargo plane . 1st Lt. Arthur Eppler's unit was a part of the India-China Division/Air Transport Command located in Hsinching, China.

Their mission was the transportation of supplies, personnel, equipment and aircraft in India and China. Flying over the eastern end of the Himalayan or "The Hump" was characterized as "risky business . . . where turbulence and abominable weather was the norm." At war's end the Americans lost 468 aircraft as well as 1300 personnel. An additional 81 aircraft and 345 personnel went unaccounted; 1200 personnel were rescued.

For his service, 1st Lt. Arthur A. Eppler received the following: Asiatic-Pacific

Service Medal, Am. Campaign Medal and the World War II Victory Medal.

Art worked as a machine operator, a salesman at A&A Driving School, Sales and Cottage Bakery, a turn lathe operator and self-employed at JenArt Ceramics. He married his second wife, Jennie Louise DiGioia on April 13, 1956 in New Mexico.

Active in his community, Arthur was a Little League coach, Boy Scoutmaster for Troop 581, a life member of the VFW National Home, the American Legion, and Sunrise Bible Fellowship.

Art died on November 21, 2001 in Red Bluff, CA and is buried in Oak Hill Cemetery Red Bluff, CA. He left behind: three children: Anna F. Hall, John A. and Arthur J. Eppler, three grandchildren, and one great-grandchild. He was 78 years old.

Francis Fabiano

Francis Fabiano was born April 11, 1926 to Antonio and Margaret (Guido) Fabiano in Hudson, NY. He attended Hudson City School District, graduating high school in June of 1944.

Francis enlisted in the United States Navy on September 5, 1944 at Albany, NY. After basic training, he received training at the Fire Control School at Fort Lauderdale, FL. He was assigned to a heavy cruiser, the USS Los Angeles (CA – 135) as a fire controlman 3rd class.

The USS Los Angles held a compliment of 1000 men. After its initial shakedown out of Guantanamo Bay, Cuba, the USS Los Angeles sailed for the Far East on October 15, arriving at Shanghi, China, on January 3, 1946.

For the next seven months, FC3 Francis Fabiano was stationed in Hong Kong and Shanghai; while serving with the 7th Fleet along the coast of China and in western Pacific to the Marianas.

He was honorably discharged on June 22, 1946 at Lido Beach, Long Island, NY. He was awarded the: American Campaign Medal, Asiatic Pacific Campaign Medal, China Service U.S. Navy Medal and WWII Victory Medal.

Returning home he married Sarah Ann DuFour on October 1, 1949 and worked as a general carpenter; building and refurbishing homes. During the ensuing years, they raised three children: Francis, David and Teresa and established the contracting business of A. Fabiano and Sons. After 17 years, Francis retired in 1991 and worked as a Greenport Building Inspector for four years.

Francis was active in his community. He was a Boy Scout Master for Troop #105 and #107 (16 yrs), a member (27 yrs) and Commander of Greenport VFW Post #6142, VFW All State Commander (4 times), a member of Hudson Elks Lodge #787 serving on the Bingo Committee, a chairman of the Elks Veterans

Committee (14 yrs), AMTRAC Concession volunteer (4 yrs) and a lifelong member of St. Mary's Church, Hudson, NY.

At 83., Francis passed away on December 17, 2009 and was interned in Cedar Park Cemetery, Hudson, NY. Francis was "a people person, a devoted, dedicated, hard working husband and father; always encouraging his children to do their best."

His service to his country and community is sterling and he will be greatly missed.

Richard Willie Fennoff

Richard Willie Fennoff was born March 28, 1935 in Landoff, NY to Willie and Gladys (Steerey) Fenoff. Richard was an acolyte of the Episcopal Church, attended Glenco Mills Elementary in Glenco Mills, NY and graduated from Hudson High School, Hudson NY. Richard then worked in produce for the Great Atl. & Pac. Tea Company.

Living in Hudson, Richard enlisted in the United States Navy on May 19, 1954. Having attended basic training on August 7, 1954, he completed Radioman Class "A" school at the USN Training Center at Bainbridge, MD and was then assigned to the U.S. Naval Station at Newport, RI.

As hostilities on the Korean Peninsula terminated, America found itself embraced in a Cold War with the Soviets and its eastern European satellites. RM2 Richard Fennoff was assigned to the USS Taconic (AGC-17), a command ship in the Atlantic Fleet. As a radioman he was responsible for transmitting and receiving radio signals and processing all forms of telecommunications through various transmission media aboard ships, aircraft and at shore facilities along the eastern coast, Atlantic Ocean and Mediterranean Sea.

After having completed his tour of duty, on May 14, 1958, RM2 Richard Fennoff was honorably discharged from active duty and assigned to the Third Naval District, NY as a reservist. He remained a reservist until May 18, 1962.

For his service he was awarded the following: National Defense Service Medal and the Good Conduct Medal.

Richard met and married Eleanor Wheeler on July 7, 1957 in Christ Church, Hudson, NY. He worked as a draftsman while they raised their two children: Lori and Ron. After retirement he worked as a driver for a healthcare consortium until 2000.

Richard was active in the Boy Scouts, Ghent Little League, Ghent 4-H, the Hudson Whalers Pop Warner (coach), and was a communicant of West Ghent Reformed Church, Ghent, NY.

Richard passed away on September 20, 2007 while living in Ghent, NY and was buried in the West Ghent Cemetery. He left behind his loving wife Eleanor, their two children and four grandchildren. He was 72 years old.

John A. Fino

John Albert Fino was born in Hudson, NY on October 6, 1923 to Rocco and Josephine Fino. He grew up there and attended Hudson High School. Graduating in June of 1942, John wert to work for the Watervliet Arsenal. Because of his important war related job, John qualified for a military deferment. However, his friends recalled that he would frequently call his Draft Board asking when he could get into the Army. He was summoned to active duty on February 12, 1943 as a private in the United States Army.

Pvt. John Fino received training in the United States and was assigned to combat duty in the European Theater of Operations with Company A, 7th Engineers Battalion. He landed in occupied France with his unit in the second wave after D-Day. The 7th Engineers Battalion was attached to General George C. Patton's famous 3rd Army, and for the next several months, John was engaged in extensive action throughout Europe as the Allied Forces fought their way into Nazi Germany. Although quite young, his meritorious service would earn him a battlefield promotion to corporal.

On February 25, 1945 while engaged in hostilities with enemy forces, Cpl. John A. Fino was killed in action. A lone white cross bearing his name marks his final resting place at the military cemetery in Hamm, Luxembourg.

His sister reflected:

"We thought about bringing him home after the war, but we felt that he belonged with his friends."

Later John's commanding officer, Gen. George C. Patton would request that he also be laid to rest in the same military cemetery along with those men who had faithfully and gallantly died.

"In grateful memory of Corporal John A. Fino who died in the service of his country. ...He stands in the unbroken line of patriots who have dared to die that freedom might live, and grow and increase its blessing. Freedom lives and through it he lives – in a way that humbles the undertaking of most men."

– Franklin D. Roosevelt

Cpl. John A. Fino's family posthumously received the Purple Heart for injuries he incurred in that last engagement that cost him his life. He was 22 years old.

Theron C. Folmsbee

Theron C. Folmsbee was born May 14, 1912 in Stockport, NY to Stuart and Eva (Van Allen) Folmsbee. He grew up in Columbia County where he attended school in Stuyvesant Falls.

He entered in the army on March 1, 1944 in the Brizzie Building in Chatham, NY. He received basic training at Fort Dix, NJ and additional training at the Infantry Training Center at Camp Blanding, FL. Staff Sgt. Folmsbee was assigned on August 17, 1944 to the European Theater of Operation with Company G, 110th Infantry , 28th Division, 3rd Army.

Early that fall, Staff Sgt. Folmsbee was engaged in the bitter fighting in the Hurtgen Forest. Moved for rest and relaxation in a "quiet sector" near Wiltz, Luxembourg, the 28th Division was then quickly sent as replacements to the Battle of the Bulge. Staff Sgt. Folmsbee's position was overrun, which resulted in him being wounded and separated from his company for a time. After healing from his wounds, he continued with his unit until the war's end. He was shipped back to the States on August 2, 1945 and was honorably discharged at Fort Jay, NY on November 19, 1945.

Staff Sgt. Folmsbee received the Silver Star from Major General Norman D. Cota for heroism in Germany on March 9, 1945. The citation reads as follows:

". . . for gallantry in action against the enemy on 9 March 1945 in Germany. Sergeant Folmsbee and his squad spearheaded an attack of his company on the enemy located in the town of Anweiler, Germany. Adroitly covering an open stretch of 250 yards, he surprised the enemy at a road block at the entrance of the town and captured more than 120 prisoners, including 10 machine gunners and ammunition bearers. His aggressive and courageous action enabled his display of leadership and gallantry. Sergeant Folmsbee reflects credit upon himself and the Armed Forces of the United States."

For his service to his country, he was awarded the following citations: Silver Star, Purple Heart, WWII Victory Medal, European-African-Middle Eastern Medal with three Battle Stars, American Theater Medal, Good Conduct Medal and the Expert Rifleman Badge.

Theron returned to his wife and family in Stuyvesant Falls. During the next several decades he was employed as a carpenter with the Kingston Local. Along with raising a family, he was a member of Chatham American Legion Post 42, Stuyvesant Falls VFW 9593 (charter member), Emanuel Lutheran Church, and Fire Co. #2 (Fire Commissioner). Also, he served as Constable for the Town of Stuyvesant.

Theron passed away on February 28, 1985 at the age of 73 and was interned in Stuyvesant Falls Cemetery. He left behind a wife, Edith, two sons, Theron and

Todd, four grandchildren and four great-grandchildren. Theron was a devoted husband and loving father who served his country and community with honor and distinction.

Leo Forando

Leo Forando was born April 24, 1923 in Hudson, New York. He attended elementary school and high school in Hudson.

Leo enlisted in the United States Army on January 27, 1943 in Hudson, New York. Qualifying with the M1 Garand in basic training, PFC Leo Forando received additional training as a carpenter and was assigned to the European Theater of Operations to Company A, 306 Quartermaster Battalion.

PFC Leo Forando saw immediate action with the Quartermaster Battalion in Central Europe and the Ardennes. An army's effectiveness extends only as far as it supply lines. A standing army requires not only "beans, blankets and bullets," but those men who provide the skills and services for those in line companies. If objectives were to be met and victory was to be secured, cadres of soldiers were needed to ensure that the materials and manpower would be provided to support a successful war effort.

PFC Leo Forando was one of the countless unknown, who shared the hardships of combat in an auxiliary capacity, yet was vital to the war effort. His and untold others' contributions are evident, although their names may be lost in the pages of history. However, they proudly shared and rightfully earned the World War II Victory Medal.

After the secession of hostilities, PFC Forando remained in Europe as part of an occupational force until he returned to the States and was honorably discharged from military service on January 27, 1946 at Fort Dix, NJ. In addition to the WWII Victory Medal PFC Leo Forando was awarded the American Service Medal, the EAME Service Medal, and the Good Conduct Medal.

Leo returned home and worked for Julliard Company. On January 19, 1946, he married Dorothy Wraught and raised four children: Roger, Clifford, Kathleen and Sharon. He remained active in the community. He was a member of the Greenport VFW Post 6142, Hudson Fish and Game Club, Stottville Rod and Gun Club and Hudson Power Boat Association, Deacon of the First Presbyterian Church and Charter Member, former Captain, Assistant Captain and Chief of the Greenport Pumper #3 Fire Company. He continued working with Clifford Rivenburg Garage and Columbia Automatic Transmission until 1985 when he retired.

Leo Forando died April 27, 1999 in Hudson and was buried in the Stuyvesant Falls Cemetery. He left behind three children, 11 grandchildren and 13 great grandchildren. Leo was 76 years old.

Frank R. Fratellenico, Jr.

Frank R. Fratellenico was born on July 14, 1951 to Frank and Jennie Frantellenico in Sharon, CT. When he was eight, he moved with his family to Austerlitz, NY. With his three sisters, he was raised on the family farm along Route 203, outside of Spencertown. He honed his skills as an outdoorsman, and after graduating from Chatham High School, Frank enlisted in the United States Army in September 1969.

After basic and initial training, Frank volunteered, like his father and uncle, to become a paratrooper. After completing airborne training at Fort Benning, in May 1970 he was assigned to 502nd Infantry Regiment, 1st Brigade, 101st Airborne Division, Rep. of Vietnam.

Known as "Rocko", Cpl. Frank Fratellenico quickly established himself as a gallant soldier. In June 1970 he exposed himself to hostile fire, thus enabling his squad to capture a sniper and eliminate another. His actions earned him the Bronze Star.

Two months later, while serving as a rifleman with Company B in Quang Tri Province, Vietnam, Cpl. Frantellenico and his squad were pinned down by intense enemy fire from two well-fortified bunkers. At great personal risk to himself, he maneuvered forward and using hand grenades neutralized one bunker which was occupied by a number of enemy soldiers. While attacking the second bunker, Cpl. Frantellenico was struck by enemy fire, causing him to fall, dropping a live hand grenade that he was preparing to throw. Mindful of the imminent danger to his comrades, Cpl. Frank Frantellenico, Jr. retrieved the live grenade, falling on it an instant before it exploded, resulting in his death. His heroic actions prevented death or serious injury to four of his comrades and inspired his unit to subsequently overrun the enemy position. For his action he was awarded our nation's highest award, the Medal of Honor. It states in part,

"Cpl. Fratellenico's conspicuous gallantry, extraordinary heroism and intrepidity at the cost of his life, above and beyond the call of duty, are in keeping with the highest traditions of the military service and reflect great credit on him, his unit and the United States Army."

Cpl. Frank R. Fratellenico, Jr. was awarded the following: Medal of Honor, Purple Heart, and Bronze Star for Meritorious Service, Good Conduct Medal and the Army Commendation Medal.

Franks remains were interred on a hillside overlooking the family homestead. They were later disinterred, cremated by the family when they relocated from the area. He left behind his father, mother, and three sisters. Frank was only 19 years old.

Frank Froggatt

Frank Froggatt was born on June 13, 1910 to Franklin and Nora (Ahearn) Froggatt in Birmingham, England. The Froggatts immigrated to New York City when Frank was in grade school. Growing up in Woodside, Long Island, Frank graduated from high school and went to worked for an advertising agency.

Frank entered the United States Army on August 8, 1942 at Fort Jay, NY. After basic training Frank trained as an anti-aircraft machine gunner. On April 26, 1944 Private First Class Frank Froggatt arrived in the European Theater of Operations and was assigned to B Battery, 870th Field Artillery Battalion.

As a part of 12 Army Group, 66th Infantry Division, PFC Frank Froggatt's 105-mm howitzer was a lightweight towed weapon which fired a 33 pound projectile in support of the infantry. His unit took part in the D Day Invasion and later saw action in the St. Nazaire and Lorient pockets, where the enemy forces surrendered to his division upon the end of hostilities in Europe on May 8, 1945. His unit served as an occupational force in Koblenz, Germany.

Receiving shrapnel wounds to his back, PFC Frank Froggatt was awarded the Purple Heart. He returned to the States and was Honorably Discharged at Fort Dix, NJ on November 9, 1945.

PFC Frank Froggatt was awarded the following: Purple Heart, European African Middle Eastern Service Medal, American Service Medal and the Good Conduct Medal.

Returning to New York City, Frank married Edith H. Hunter on May 6, 1948 in Christ Church, Manhattan, and they went on to raise two daughters: Jane and Barbara. For the next 32 years, Frank worked as an elevator operator at an office building at 347 Madison Avenue, New York City. He retired on June 3, 1975 and he and Edith relocated to their summer home in Copake Falls, NY.

Frank served twice as the commander of the Patrick F. Kelly VFW in Manhattan. He was a communicant of St. Johns in the Wilderness in Copake Falls, NY.

Frank passed away in Copake Falls on February 20, 1982, and was buried at the church of St. Johns in the Wilderness, Copake Falls, NY. He left behind a wife, two daughters, four grandchildren and seven great grandchildren. He was 82 years old.

Frank Gamello

Frank Gamello was born on November 28, 1916 in Stuyvesant, NY to Guy and Rose Gamello. He attended school at Rossman. Frank was just short of 13 years old when the Depression came.

His daughter, JoAnn, recalls, "My father told me that, 'Life is hard,' and for him it was." His "teen years were about work and how to help support the family." He, like many of his generation, would not complete high school because of difficult times and familial obligations.

Frank was drafted on February 12, 1941 while working as a kiln burner. After basic training, he received additional training as an anti-aircraft gunner.

After December 7, it became clear that PFC Frank Gamello would remain in the Armed Forces for the duration of the war. He arrived in the Europe Theater of Operation on September 5, 1942 and was assigned as a crewman to Battery C, 108th Anti-Aircraft Battalion. In the course of the next three years, PFC Gamello would participate in the campaigns in Algeria French Morocco, Tunisia, Sicily, Rome, Arno, Southern France, Central Europe and the Rhineland.

For his service to his country PFC Frank Gamello was awarded: the American Defense Service Medal, the Good Conduct Medal, and the European African Middle Eastern Service Medal with seven battle stars.

Frank was discharged from the Army on September 11, 1945 at Fort Dix, NJ. He returned home, met and married Anna Merante on October 21, 1945. In the ensuing years he and Anna raised two children: Guy and JoAnn. Frank was a self-employed barber for more than 50 years and an active member of the Stuyvesant Rod and Gun Club.

His daughter recalled: *"(My father's) generation had faced the worst and had survived. Even more they triumphed, yet they never bragged about it. To me, they were the 'Quiet Generation'. Going on with their lives, understanding that life is hard and one has to face it head on. What was important to my dad, was that we had a roof over (our) heads, food on the table and his children got the education he did not. He was a survivor . . . he knew how to survive."*

At the age of 82, Frank Gamello passed away on December 28, 1998 and was buried in Stuyvesant Fall, NY. As the "Greatest Generation" passes on, their personal sacrifices for, and singular love of country, community and family are lessons worthy of admiration and their enduring legacy.

Charles P. Gamello, Sr.

Charles P. Gamello, Sr. was born on October 10, 1923 to Gaetano and Rose Gamello in Newton Hook, NY. He attended grade school at Rossman School in Columbiaville, NY and graduated from Martin Van Buren High School in Kinderhook, NY.

Employed at the Watervliet Arsenal, Charles entered the United States Army on June 1, 1943 in Albany, NY. After his basic training in Kentucky, he was assigned to the European Theater of Operations with the 29th Infantry Division, 115th Infantry Regiment. For the next two years Sgt. Gamello would see action throughout Europe as a squad leader of a machine gun crew.

On June 6, 1944 the 29th Infantry Division, 115th Infantry Regiment. assaulted "Fortress Europe" on the beaches of "Bloody Omaha" beach. They continued to press the enemy in places like St. Lo in Northern France, the "Battle of the Bulge" and then into Germany crossing the Roer, Rhine and Elbe rivers. On August 3, 1944, Sgt. Gamello was wounded by shrapnel in the hip at St. Germain. He was evacuated to England for treatment and opted to rejoin his unit where he remained until the end of the war. Sgt. Gamello was honorably discharged on January 21, 1946 at Ft. Dix, NJ.

For his service to his country, he was awarded following medals: Purple Heart, WW II Victory Medal, American Service Medal, EAME Service Medal, Combat Infantry Badge and the Good Conduct Medal.

During the next few decades Charles returned to civilian life, and worked for the Metropolitan Life Insurance Co., as a carpenter, a construction worker, and for the State of New York Dept. of Social Services from which he retired after 20 years as a medical claims examiner.

Charles was active in St. Mary's Catholic Church (Nassau), Village of Nassau Trustee and Water Commissioner, Town of Nassau Republican Committeeman, President of the Nassau Baseball Association where he was once a coach and manager of Little League, Babe Ruth and American Legion baseball. His wife recalls, "Baseball was his whole life."

Charles died at the age of 81 on November 7, 2004 and was buried at the Saratoga National Cemetery. He left behind a loving wife, Elizabeth, four children and five grandchildren.

On the 60th anniversary of the end of WWII, we pause in quiet recognition of Sgt. Charles P. Gamello, Sr., who faithfully and selflessly did his part to protect and defend our lives and our liberties that we enjoy today.

Edward Gibbons

Edward Gibbon was born June 14, 1929 to John and Eulalia Gibbons in Stuyvestant, NY. He grew up in Stuyvestant, where he attended elementary and high school.

On September 18, 1950, Edward enlisted for four years in the United States Air Force. After his basic training, Edward received Military Police training at Tyndall Air Force Base, FL and was then assigned for duty with the Air Police on Korean Peninsula. Airman 2nd Class Edward Gibbons served just shy of 15 months during hostilities during the Korean War.

Returning to the States, he was discharged on July 17, 1954 at Grandview Air Force Base, Grandview, MO.

For his service, A/2C Edward Gibbons was awarded the Good Conduct Medal, the Korean Service Medal (2 BSS), the United Nations Service Medal and the National Defense Service Medal.

Edward returned home and on September 25, 1955 and he married Shirley Jean Coon at the Church of Nativity in Stuyvesant, NY. In the ensuing years, Edward worked as a meat cutter, delivering heating oil for Agway, was a heavy equipment operator where he was a small business owner/operator of a bulldozer and backhoe. He retired after 20 years as Supervisor of Highways for the Town of Ghent.

He remained active in his community. He was a member of the Stuyvesant Fire Company, American Legion, VFW, the Korean War Vets, and the Hook Boat Club, where he served as treasurer.

Edward died on May 23, 2006 at the Barnwell Nursing Home and was buried at the West Ghent Cemetery. He was 77 years old.

Edward served alongside those who went in harm's way to promote democracy and defended freedom around the world. He represents our nation's finest; recognized and honored in the company of a select few.

John William Gillespie

John William Gillespie was born November 10, 1892 in Brooklyn, NY to William and Annie (Ryan) Gillespie. Raised in New York City, working as a clerk, he was inducted in the United States Army on March 28, 1917 in Brooklyn, NY.

After his basic training, John W. Gillespie was assigned to Battery B, 59th Artillery in France. He saw action in the St. Mihiel (9/12/18-9/15/18) and the Meuse Argonne offenses (9/26/18-11/11/18). His duties included the placing of communication panels to distinguish between contested forward positions. Private First Class John W. Gillespie was honorably discharged on Feb. 5, 1919 at Fort Upton, NY.

He enlisted in the National Guard and was assigned to 8th Company, 13th Coastal Defense Command. Cited for his "excellent, honest and faithful" character, he was again honorably discharged at the rank of 1st Sergeant on April 25, 1921. For his service, he was awarded the Victory Medal.

John and Katherine (Sweeney) were married on June 1, 1922 in Brooklyn, NY and raised two children: John William, Jr. and Dorothy Katherine. John worked as a banker for Hannover Trust Bank and the New York Federal Reserve. In mid-century the Gillespies moved to Copake, NY where John was a member of Copake Grange. He and his wife remained communicants of Saint Bridget's Catholic Church in Copake Falls, NY until their deaths.

John passed away on January 26, 1975 at the VA hospital in Albany, NY and was buried in Copake Falls, NY. He left behind his wife, Katherine, two children: John and Dorothy and seven grandchildren. He was 82 years old.

Katherine Gillespie

Katherine Sweeney was born February 25, 1897 in New York City to William J. and Annie (Gray) Sweeney. Working as an executive secretary, Katherine was inducted in the United States Navy on May 3, 1918.

After her basic training, Yeoman 1st Class Katherine Sweeney was assigned to the 3rd Naval District, USN Fleet Supply Base in South Brooklyn, NY. Yeo. 1c (F) Katherine Sweeney worked in the Provisions and Clothing Depot until she was honorably discharged on July 31, 1919 in Brooklyn, NY. For her service she was awarded the Victory Button.

Katherine and John were married on June 1, 1922 in Brooklyn, NY and raised two children: John William, Jr. and Dorothy Katherine. Katherine worked at the New York Cotton Exchange as executive secretary. In mid-century the Gillespies moved to Copake, NY. She and her husband remained communicants of Saint Bridget's Catholic Church in Copake Falls, NY until their deaths.

Katherine passed away at the VA hospital in Seattle, WA on October 31, 1986 and was buried beside her husband, John, in Copake Falls, NY. She left behind two children: John and Dorothy and seven grandchildren. She was 89 years old.

Lloyd Glasser

Lloyd Glasser was born on May 31, 1918 to in Philmont, New York. He attended school in Philmont, where he graduated with honors in June of 1935. He worked as a bookkeeper in Chatham, NY for the NY State Electric and Gas Company for six years.

Enlisting in the Army Air Corps on June 13, 1942, Lloyd received primary training at Pine Bluff, Arkansas, basic training at Winfield, Kansas and graduated a pilot from Pampus, Texas and was then commissioned a 2nd lieutenant. In December 1943, 2nd Lt. Lloyd Glasser was assigned to the 434 Troop Carrier Group, 9th Air Force in the European Theater of Operation. He flew C47, transporting troops, supplies and wounded servicemen to and from the battlefield where he accrued more than 700 hours of flying time.

Second Lt. Lloyd Glasser participated in paratroop and glider landings in Airborne Operations in France (Overlord) and Holland (Market Garden) and supply operations in Belgium (Battle of the Bulge). Operation Overlord was the largest seaborne invasion in history. It involved almost 3 million troops crossing the English Channel from England to Normandy in then-German-occupied Fortress Europe. Second Lt. Glasser's unit received a Presidential Citation for their part of the D Day Invasion.

Market Garden was the largest airborne operation in history, delivering more than 34,000 paratroopers in a failed attempt by the Allies to cross of the Rhine River, the last major natural barrier to an advance into Germany. The Rhine would remain as such until an Allied Offensive in March 1945.

The Battle of the Bulge was a result of the German's attempt to split the British and American forces, capture the port of Antwerp and encircle and destroy four Allied armies. In a stunning show of resistance by surrounded American forces at Bastone, the Germans were forced to withdraw with critical losses that ultimately led to their defeat a few months later.

Second Lt. Glasser was killed on January 13, 1945 in a mid-air collision while supporting troops in the Battle of the Bulge and was buried in Plot A, Row 6, Grave 33 of the Epinal American Cemetery at Epinal, France. He was awarded the Air Medal with Oak Leaf Cluster and a Presidential Citation. He was 26 years old.

Wilbur A. Gramlich

Wilber A. Gramlich was born March 13, 1913 in New York City, NY. In his youth he attended grade school in the Bronx, NY where he graduated from Stirasm High School.   While living in Copake, NY, Wilber attended Michigan Tech University in the ROTC program, where he graduated with a degree in Electrical Engineering in 1942.

Upon graduation, Wilbur entered the United States Army and was commissioned a 2nd lieutenant on June 16, 1942. He then attended Transportation Quartermaster School and Engineer Field Officer School. Serving in Algeria French Morocco and Tunisia as motor transportation officer during WWII, he returned to the United States and served in the engineers in NY, NJ, VA, and LA. until 1945; attaining the rank of captain.

Cpt. Wilber Gramlich remained in the Army Reserves until April 11, 1951 when he served as commanding officer of the Company D, 76 Armored Medical Battalion. in Korea. Throughout the 1950s Maj. Wilbur Garmlich was stationed with the ROTC Polytechnic Inst. in Brooklyn, NY, the 299th Engineer Battalion, and V Corps with the USAREUR, and the 593d Engineer in Granite City, IL. Elevated to the rank of lieutenant cornel, Wilber Gramlich was assigned for a year to the Military Assistance Advisory Group (MAAG) in Vientiane, Laos in November 1961.

Lt. Col. Gramlich returned to the states and served with the Army Engineers at Headquarters 5th Army in Chicago, IL until May of 1964 where he became a Plans Officer for USARPAC at Ft. Shafter, HI.

In the three decades of service, he served around the world in the United States, Europe, Japan, Korea and Laos and was honorably discharged with 60 percent disability.

For his service Lt. Col. Wilber Gramlich was awarded the following: Bronze Star, Legion of Merit w/ OLC, Army Commendation Med., EAME Campaign Med., American Theatre Campaign Med., WW II Vic. Med., Korean Svc Med., UN Svc Med., Nat'l Def Svc Med. with OLC, Rep. of Kor. Unit Citation with C/S Bars, as well as awards for meritorious service.

Wilber returned to Copake with his wife Ella (Hopkins) and daughter, Mary Alice and was the owner and operator of Copake Electric. He was a member of the Knights of Columbus, Copake Vol. Co. and Rescue and Columbia County Taxpayers Association.

Wilber died on January 2, 1994 in Chandler, AZ and was buried in Queen of Peace Cemetery, Mesa, AZ. He was 80 years old.

Gilbert John Gregory, Jr.

Gilbert J. Gregory Jr. was born December 18, 1935 in Providence, RI to Gilbert J. and Mabel (Norton) Gregory. He attended school in Providence, RI until the 11th grade and soon thereafter entered the service.

Gilbert entered the United States Navy June 22, 1954 and after basic training he received additional training as aviation boatswain mate. Having served briefly in the Naval Reserves, BM2nd Class Gilbert J. Gregory, Jr. reenlisted on September 10, 1958 at the US Naval Recruiting Station in NYC and was assigned to duty on the USS Saratoga (CVA-60). Having qualified as an aircraft flight orderly on the C-118B (12/16/63) he reenlisted again on August 14, 1964 at Pawtuxet River, MD and on December 27, 1964 was assigned to duty on the USS Lexington (CVS -16).

It was while serving on the U.S.S. Lexington (Lady Lex) during naval operations in the Mediterranean Sea that he was severely injured. The navy was conducting touch and go landings and takeoffs with naval aircraft when the incident occurred. While an aircraft was being raised to the main deck, a reserve fuel tank dislodged from the aircraft and severed the right leg of Aviation BM2nd Class Gilbert J. Gregory, Jr.

After extensive hospitalization at the naval hospitals at Pensacola, FL (7/20/67), Albans, NY (2/22/68) and Brooklyn, NY 5/27/68), he was placed on the temporary disability retirement list on June 17, 1968. After 13 years, 11 months 7 days Aviation BM2nd Class Gilbert J. Gregory was retired on March 1, 1971 at the U.S. Naval Station Brooklyn, NY with a disability pension. For his service to his country he was awarded the National Defense Ribbon.

Gilbert returned home and lived in Nassau Lake, NY, met his first wife and they had five children. He met and married his second wife Carolyn Marano on October 29, 1988 in East Greenbush, NY. Throughout the years, Gilbert enjoyed assembling wooden ship models. He was an active member of the Stephentown Veterans.

Gilbert passed away on March 27, 2017 while living in Chatham, NY. His remains were cremated and remain with the family. He left behind his wife Carolyn, seven children: Darleen, Donna, Debra, Kevin, Dawn, Edward (Bemis) and Michael (Bemis), twelve grandchildren and five great-grandchildren. He was 81 years old.

Ralph C. Ham, Sr.

Ralph C. Ham, Sr. was born May 22, 1923 to Edward and Lena (Potts) Ham at Athens, NY. Growing up in Hudson, NY Ralph was educated at Hudson Central School.

Working for two years as a delivery man for Donald F. Gohl of Union Turnpike, Hudson, NY, Ralph was inducted into the United States Army on January 13, 1943. After basic training, Ralph trained as a medic. After 15 months of service he was promoted to Section Leader with the rank of corporal and then after 19 months to medical NCO.

Sgt. Ralph C. Ham, Sr. was assigned to the Western Pacific Theater of Operation, where he was a medical NCO with 311th General Hospital. For the next eight months, Sgt. Ham supervised the personnel of a medical unit in the care and treatment of the sick, injured and wounded. He assisted in the supervision of operations of hospital units or dispensaries; the inspection of military facilities; as well as the preparation of medical records and reports. On January 26, 1946, Sgt. Ralph C. Ham, Sr. returned to the United States and was honorably discharged at Fort Dix, NJ on February 3, 1946.

He was awarded the following citations: American Service Medal, Asiatic Pacific Service Medal, Good Conduct Medal, and Philippines Liberation Ribbon. He also received one Bronze Star (Service) for his participation in the Luzon Campaign.

Ralph returned to Columbia County and went to work for Donald F. Gohl, where he met and married Emily Thomas on December 30, 1946. They raised three children: Ralph, Jr., Marilyn and Mark. Ralph then worked for the Hudson City School District (John L. Edwards) and retired after 20 years.

Ralph was a devoted and caring husband, father, grandfather and great-grandfather. He was active in the Stuyvestant fire company, where he served as chief and the Stuyvestant Reformed Church, serving as an elder. He was well known for his cooking abilities and putting on many dinners in the community.

Ralph died at the age of 70 on August 10, 1994 and was buried in the Stuyvesant Cemetery. He left behind three children, seven grandchildren and six great-grandchildren.

Richard P. Hatch

Richard P. Hatch was born June 4, 1924 in Canaan, NY to Abram and Maude (Sweeney) Hatch. After attending school, he went to work locally as a farmhand.

On November 22, 1943 Richard entered the United States Armed Forces at Albany, NY. He received basic training at Fort Dix, NJ where he qualified as sharpshooter with the M1 rifle and advanced infantry training at Jacksonville, FL.

On July 1, 1944 PFC Richard Hatch departed the United States and upon his arrival on July 15, 1944, he was assigned to the 48th Maintenance and Repair Squadron in the European Theater of Operation. Although PFC Hatch was trained for the infantry, he was reassigned as a truck driver. His duty required him to transport supplies and ammunitions for the United States Army Air Force which was vital in the war effort in Europe.

PFC Hatch participated in the campaigns in Italy (Rome-Arno), Southern France and Central Europe where he received an injury to his foot. At one of his duty assignments, Richard served with Little Jimmy Dickens, the famed "Grand Ole Opry" country music star to be. After VE Day, Richard remained in Germany as an occupying force until the 22nd of December 1945 when he returned to the United States and was discharged from Fort Dix, NJ on December 30, 1945.

On July 28, 1946 Richard married Cora Blace and they would raise six children: Sandra, Shirley, Terry, Mark, Pennie and Ken. In the passing years, Richard worked as a heavy equipment operator for the Valente Gravel and as a welder for George Van Sant, where he retired on June 4, 1986. He was an active member of the VFW and Honor Guard for Disabled American Veterans.

For his service to his country PFC Richard P. Hatch was awarded the EAME Service Medal, WWII Victory Medal, the Good Conduct Medal, the Purple Heart and a Certificate of Appreciation from the Army Air Force.

On September 6, 2002, Richard passed away and was interned in the Flatbrook Cemetery in Canaan, NY. He leaves behind a lovely wife, six children, eleven grandchildren and ten great-grandchildren. His wife, Cora, fondly remembers Richard as "a very good father and is much missed by his children."

We owe a debt of gratitude to Richard Hatch and all those who protect and defend our country – those who share in the common risk and a common fate in the name of freedom and for the cause of liberty.

Edward J. Hawks

Edward J. Hawks was born to John and Dorothy Hawks on July 10, 1929 in Hudson, NY. He attended Greenport Elementary and Hudson High School, graduating in June 1948. For the next four years he worked as a cooler tender for Lone Star Cement Company of Hudson, NY.

With the onset of the Korean War, Edward was drafted and entered the United States Army on January 10, 1952 at Albany, NY. After his basic training he received additional training as a Combat Construction Specialist. Cpl. Edward Hawks was assigned to the Far East Command with Company D, 578th Combat Engineers, 40th Division in Korea. He participated in three major military offensives while assigned to the Combat Engineers on the Korean peninsula.

The 40th Division saw heavy action in Korea most notably in an area around the Punch Bowl, so named because of the shape of the terrain. In October of 1952 communist forces launched a series of major operations in an effort to dislodge the American forces from this key terrain.

The weeks that followed resulted in heavy fighting by the 40th Division, charged with the responsibility for defending key positions like Heartbreak Ridge and the Punch Bowl.

In the early morning hours of October 22-25 and November 3-4 enemy bugles signaled an attack along this front. Its main focus was Hill 851 or Heartbreak Ridge. Repelling the enemy time and time again, the 40th Division held fast. The 578th Combat Engineers played a part in this heroic effort.

For his service, Cpl. Edward Hawks was awarded: the National Defense Service Medal, Korean Service Medal with three service stars and the United Nations Service Medal. He was discharged from active duty at Camp Kilmer, NJ on November 13, 1953.

In September 1957 Edward married Blanche (Hendrickson) in Hudson, NY. Edward worked for Universal Atlas, Lorbrooks and L&B Products. In the ensuing years they raised three children.

Edward remained active in community affairs, recalls Jack and Betty Hallenbeck, lifetime friends. He was a proud member of Hudson VFW Post 1314 and the Hudson Korean War Veteran's Chapter 283.

Edward died on April 20, 2012, while living in Stottville, NY and is buried in Union Cemetery in Mellenville, NY. He left behind his wife, Blanche, three children: Bruce (Cornwallville), Edward J., Jr. (Ghent), and Joanne Hawks-Stevens (Stottville), four grandchildren and two brothers John and Richard from Greenport and Texas, respectively. Edward J. Hawks was 82 years old.

Martin J. Healy

Martin J. Healy was born April 22, 1917 in Hudson, New York to Thomas and Elizabeth Healy. As a boy he attended Saint Mary's Academy for elementary and high school, graduating in 1934.

Prior to his enlistment in the United States Army Air Corps in September 1942, Martin worked as a salesman for Kristman Maskin men's clothing store on Warren Street in Hudson, NY.

Martin was assigned to train in Nevada and was trained as a navigator on a B-17 commonly known as the "Flying Fortress." It was thus named because of its heavy armament and its ability to endure great punishment and still fulfill its mission. He continued his training with his crew until they were assigned to combat duty in the European Theater of Operations in the early spring of 1943.

First Lt. Healy flew numerous missions over hostile territory in occupied Europe. On May 15, 1943 while on a dangerous mission over Germany, 1st Lt. Healy's B-17 was shot down by enemy anti-aircraft fire.

The War Department notified his family and listed him as "missing in action." The hopes of his safe return by his family and friends were soon dashed when a few months later he was listed as "killed in action" by the War Department. He was buried in Cuxhaven-Brahwald, Germany.

After the war, his family requested that Martin J. Healy's body be exhumed and buried at home. Today his remains are interred in the old part of Cedar Park Cemetery in Hudson, NY along with his family. First Lt. Martin J. Healy was awarded the Purple Heart.

Prior to his enlistment, Martin was active in his church. He became the president of the Saint Mary's Alumni Association and rose to be a grand knight in the Knights of Columbus. His friends remember him as *"a highly intelligent young man who succeeded in whatever he attempted to do."* After the war, he planned on attending college and studying law.

First Lt. Martin J. Healy, like many other young men of his time, gave up his dreams and ultimately his life on what Abraham Lincoln called "the altar of freedom" that we might enjoy the freedoms that we possess today. As a boyhood friend said of him, *"In our eyes he died a hero and he will never be forgotten by anyone that he touched."*

William Laing Heermance

William Laing Heermance was born in Kinderhook, Columbia County on February 23, 1837 and was educated at Kinderhook Academy.

Prior to the Civil War, he departed for New York City in pursuit of a career in business. Upon opening hostilities at Fort Sumter, his sense of duty prompted him to raise a company of two hundred men.

Securing arms and hiring a hall to drill at his own expense, he was elected captain of this company. However, feeling unqualified to lead it in active service, he enlisted in Company F, 83rd New York Volunteers as a private. Serving that summer in Maryland and the Shenandoah Valley; on October 23, 1861, he was then commissioned first lieutenant. in Company M of the 6th N.Y. Cavalry and later in the fall of following year, he was commissioned captain of Company C of the same outfit.

On the night of April 1863, his regiment was near Chancellorsville, VA, where his command was surrounded by Gen. Fitzhugh Lee's Cavalry (CSA) and order to surrender. He was ordered to break by fours to the right and cut his way through with sabers.

Capt. Heermance's squadron being on the right was the first to strike. In a hand-to-hand engagement, he sabered his way through the Confederate Cavalry. In the process, he was shot in the arm and the ball entered his stomach. Wounded, he subsequently was captured and taken to Libby Prison.

For his "most distinguished gallantry in action near Chancellorsville," he would receive our nation's highest award, The Congressional Medal of Honor.

In November of 1864, he mustered out of the service because of a severe wound he sustained to the head.

Cpt. Heermance participated in more than sixty engagements, including two raids around Richmond and was in all of the principal battles in which the Army of the Potomac was engaged. He was wounded three times (twice left on the battlefield for dead), a prisoner of war and became Columbia County's first Medal of Honor recipient.

On February 25, 1903 he died at the age of 66 in Yonkers, NY.

Michael Hess

Michael Hess was born October 14, 1752 in the Manor of Livingston (Germantown) in the County of Columbia to Johannes and Anna Margaretha (Scherp) Hess. Michael was baptized on November 12, 1752 at the Reformed Church of Germantown and grew up in that community.

Residing in Claverack, NY, Michael served as a private in the militia from January 15, 1776 until the fall of 1780; a total active service of at least ten months.

Pvt. Hess served in the defense of the Hudson and Mohawk valley regions under command of the notable leadership of Gens. Schuyler and Robert Van-Rensselaer.

In 1777, Pvt. Hess was a part of Col. VanRensselaer's Regiment that guarded

Albany, Half Moon Point, Still Water, Saratoga, and forts Miller, Edward and George. For the next few years his militia was frequently order into service to seek out and pursue "robbers and tories" in the Town of Claverack and the outlying regions.

On October 19, 1780, Pvt. Michael Hess' militia under the command of Gen. VanRensselaer and with Col. Lewis Dubois, Col. John Brown and Oneida warriors, (numbering about 1,500), engaged the 1,000-man raiding force of Sir John Johnson and the Mohawk leader Joseph Brant in the Mohawk Valley. Resulting in an American victory, the Battle of Klock's Field cost the Americans 39 killed (including Col. Brown); the loyalist casualties were not reported, however, 40 were captured.

Michael married Margaret Schauer on February 10, 1784 at the Reformed Dutch Church in Claverack, NY. Together they raised twelve children: Margaret (10/18/1786), Johannes (a.k.a. John, b. 12/18/1786), Elizabeth (a.k.a. Betsy), Catherine, (7/29/1791), Maria (a.k.a. Polly, b. 3/19/1794), George Willem (b. 8/20/1796), Jacob (b. 11/9/1798), Cornelia (b. 2/17/1801), Cathlina (b. 2/17/1801), Laurance Landt (b. 11/13/1802), Jeremias (b. 1/6/1804) and Rachel (b. 12/8/1808).

On August 25, 1832, Michael Hess applied for and received a soldier's pension for his service to what would become the United States of America.

Michael died on December 5, 1838 in Claverack, NY and is buried in the Teal Plot, Ogden Farm, Roxbury Road, Claverack, NY. He was 80 years old and 11 months. Next to him lies his wife Margaret (b.11/14 1765), who died January 16, 1839.

Rodney W. Hingle

Rodney was born January 26, 1919 to Chester and Ella Hingle at Baldwin, NY. Growing up in Baldwin, he attended Plaza Elementary and Baldwin High School.

Graduating in 1938, Rodney received 400 hours of training in fabricate aircraft at Freeport Aviation, Freeport, NY. He went to work for Gruman Aircraft Corp in Long Island, NY. Using blueprints, Rodney used hand tools, automatic drills and riveting machines to assemble aircraft wings.

Rodney entered the United States Army on September 20, 1943 at 10 Pacific St, Baldwin, NY as a private. After basic training he was trained as a carpenter where he was assigned on September 15, 1944 to the 1657 Engineer Utility Detachment in the Eastern Theater of Operation.

Tech 5 Sgt. Rodney Hingle was a supervisor of a crew of twelve men who built bridges, barracks and infrastructure that would be necessary in aiding the allied thrust across Europe onto final victory. Tech 5 Sgt. Rodney Hingle was honorably discharged on April 19, 1946 at Fort Dix, NJ.

For his service, he was awarded the Good Conduct Medal, the American Campaign Medal, the European-African-Middle Eastern Campaign Medal and the World War II Victory Medal.

Rodney returned home to Copake, NY and married Alice on April 7, 1956 at the Freeport United Methodist Church in Freeport, NY. In the subsequent years Rodney worked for Gruman Aerospace, Sherman Roofing Co., and Long Island Lighting Co; while he and Alice raised four children: Nora, Linda, Kevin and Keith. He was head usher in his church: United Methodist Church and was a member of the International Brotherhood of Electrical Workers.

Rodney passed away on May 6, 2007 in Greenville, NY and was buried at the National Cemetery at Schuylerville, NY. He was 88 years old.

Edward J. Hofem, Jr

Edward J. Hofem, Jr. was born October 11, 1919 to Edward and Elizabeth (Anderson) Hofem in Hudson, NY. Growing up in Hudson where he attended school, Edward later worked as an auto washer.

Edward was inducted in the United States Army on July 10, 1942, where he attended Basic Training on July 24, 1942. Trained as a rifleman and qualifying with the M1, Edward was assigned to the European Theater of Operation with the 820th Signal Service Company on December 6, 1943.

For the next two years, Edward attained the rank of corporal and served as a squad leader in Europe. Cpl. Edward J. Hofem, Jr. was involved in the Rome, Arno, and North Apennines campaigns. During this period his unit distinguished itself and Edward earned the Bronze Star Medal. Later, Edward worked in food service where he helped prepare meals, attended mess hall stoves, and served food in the capacity of kitchen helper.

Edward was honorably discharged November 30, 1945 at Fort Dix, NJ. For his service to his country, he was awarded the following: Bronze Star, Combat Infantry Badge, American Service Medal, Distinguished Unit Badge, European African Middle Eastern Service Medal and the Good Conduct Medal.

Edward returned to Columbia County where he married Hazel Kohn in a ceremony in Hudson, NY in 1948. For the next 40 years Edward worked in the printing department of the Universal Match Factory, from which he retired.

Edward remained active in his community. He was a member of the Christ Episcopal Church, the Hudson American Legion and a fifty-year member of the J.W. Edmonds Hose Fire Company and the Hudson Elks Lodge #787.

Edward resided at the Fireman's Home in Hudson at the time of his death, August 8, 2007. He left behind his wife, Hazel, a sister, Gertrude, four nieces:

Karen, Marilyn, Elaine, and Joanne, and a nephew, Geoffrey. He was buried in Cedar Park Cemetery, Hudson, NY. Edward was 87 years old.

Wilfred J. Holmes

Wilfred Jay "Jasper" Holmes was born April 9, 1900 in Stockport, NY to John Eric and Ester F (Moett) Holmes. He grew up in Stottville where he attended grade school.

Upon graduating from Hudson High School, he attended the United States Naval Academy, where he graduated in 1922 with a degree in Engineering.

During the next decades "Jasper" Holmes was a line officer in the Navy serving aboard the Battleship Nevada. He attained the rank of lieutenant, commanding the submarine S-30 stationed in the Pacific in the Hawaiian Islands.

It was at this time that as a skilled writer, he began writing and publishing essays and short stories under the pen name Alec Hudson; some of which was published by the Saturday Evening Post. Several of these articles were about the theoretical way of a foreign power to attack the United States through Pearl Harbor. Holmes literally charted the war that was to come six years later. An arthritic back would prevent him from sea duty and in 1936 he retired.

With a degree in engineering, Jasper Holmes secured a position as an instructor at the University of Hawaii. He was called back into active service in mid-1941 and although lacking cryptographic experience, he was assigned to Ultra Intelligence.

Rated above top secret, he helped compile intelligence which determined the strength, composition and movements of various Japanese units which led to breaking the JN-25 naval and diplomatic codes.

This resulted in major victories in the Pacific like the Battle of Midway, the shoot-down of Admiral Isoroku Yamamoto and the destruction of the Kido Butai or Japanese flotilla that participated in the attack on Pearl Harbor. To each submarine skipper who sunk a ship of the Kido Butai, Cpt. Jasper Holmes awarded a bottle of Scotch.

After the war Cpt. Jasper Holmes returned to the University of Hawaii, where he taught physics, electrical and civil engineering and math. He became the Dean of Engineering and later published a memoir of his wartime experiences in a book, *Double Edged Secrets: U.S. Naval Intelligence Operations During World War II*. He retired in 1965 and Holmes Hall, an engineering building on campus, was named in his honor.

At 86, Cpt. Wilfred "Jasper" Holmes died on January 10, 1986 at Honolulu, Hawaii and was buried at the National Memorial Cemetery of the Pacific. He left behind a wife, Isabell (West), and a son, John Eric.

Bruce Holtaling, Sr.

Bruce Holtaling was born October 29, 1949 in Hudson, NY to William and Mary Holtaling. He attended grade school in Stottville and graduated from Hudson High School in 1967. In his youth Bruce enjoyed hunting and fishing.

Bruce was working for Stan Martin Ford when he was drafted on June 5, 1969 into the United States Army in Hudson, NY. After finishing basic training at Fort Dix, NJ he completed additional training as a light infantryman in Washington State, qualifying expert with the M16.

Specialist 4 Bruce Hotaling was assigned overseas duty with Company D, 3rd Battalion, 1st Infantry, 11th Infantry Brigade, Republic of Vietnam. After ten months of active combat, Spec. 4 Bruce Holtaling became ill and was transferred to hospitals in Japan, Alaska and Long Island, NY. Recovering from having weighed less than 100 lbs., he was honorably discharged on January 14, 1971 and transferred to the United States Reserves until June 4, 1975.

For his service he was awarded the following: Army Commendation Medal, Combat Infantry Badge, Vietnam Service Medal, Vietnam Campaign Medal, and the National Defense Service Medal.

Bruce met and married Rosemary Doty on March 21, 1976 in Hudson, NY. During the ensuing years, they lived in Hudson, NY and raised their son, Bruce, Jr. and four children from a previous marriage: Frank, Anna, Chuck and Wally. Bruce worked as an assembler for L&B Products and a molder for KAZ in Hudson, NY.

Bruce passed away on October 13, 2015 and is buried in St. Patrick Cemetery in Catskill, NY. He left behind his lovely wife, Rosemary, a son, Bruce, eleven grandchildren and six great-grandchildren. He was 66 years old.

Edward W. James

Edward W. James was born December 11, 1920 in New York City. After high school Edward went to work as a millwright for the Miller Colt Firearms Company.

He entered the Armed Services on May 2, 1943 at Fort Devens, MA and subsequently received training at Tyndall Field and Sheppard Field, TX as a gunner on a B 17. On April 30, 1944, Tech/Sgt. Edward W. James was assigned to combat duty in the European Theater of Operations with the United States Army Air Corp.

As a left waist gunner on a B 17, Tech/Sgt. James saw action over Normandy, France and on July 21, 1944 while on his seventeenth mission over Regensburg, Germany; his B 17 received heavy flak damage. In a letter dated October 24, 1944 to his family, the pilot of the B 17, Lt. Henry Laird, states:

"We had 3 engines shot out by flak and we could not make it home on one engine. We were hit at 26,000 feet and I ordered my boys to jump after we got down to 5,000 feet. . We bailed out over the small country of Luxembourg. Six of us made it back o.k.; four of my boys got the bad breaks and were taken prisoner."

Tech/Sgt. James' "bad break" came when he landed and was taken prisoner by the Gestapo. He was later assigned to Stalag Luft 4 and remained there until he was liberated at the end of the war by the British Army under Gen. Montgomery.

While a P.O.W., James' family received a letter from the War Department awarding him the Air Medal with Oak-Leaf Cluster. The citation reads:

"For meritorious achievement while participating in heavy bombardment missions over enemy occupied Continental Europe. The courage, coolness, and skill displayed upon these occasions reflect great credit upon himself and the Armed Forces of the United States."

Tech/Sgt. Edward W. James was awarded the American Theater and the European-African-Middle Eastern Ribbon, the Good Conduct Medal, the Air Medal w/ two Oak Leaf Clusters, the Victory Medal, the NYS Conspicuous Service Award, a Personal Presidential Citation from President Clinton and was a Life Member of the V.F.W. Post 7955 of Copake, NY.

Tech/Sgt. Edward W. James' dedication and sacrifice is representative of all those brave man and women who selflessly served their country for the cause of freedom. He passed away on September 15, 1997.

Merwin Harlan Jennings

Merwin Harlan Jennings was born July 14, 1895 to Harold and Grace Jennings of Germantown, NY. He attended Germantown Central School and worked as a farmer from 1910 until his induction into the Army.

On September 21, 1917 Merwin was inducted into the United States Army and for the next two months received training at Camp Devens, MA. Transferring to Camp Gordon, GA, for the next five months Pvt. Jennings received additional infantry training and was then assigned to Company K, 328th Infantry, 82nd Division.

In May 1918, Jennings' unit left the States (Boston) for Foreign Service with the American Expeditionary Force, (AEF). The 82nd Division first landed in England (Liverpool) and then France (Le Havre), where preparations were made for the 328th to advance to the front.

Pvt. Jennings first saw action in the Toul and Marbache sectors in the St. Mihiel offensive. The St. Mihiel was a dress rehearsal for the Argonne Offensive. The Argonne Offensive was marked by vicious fighting and gave rise to two notable incidents: the Lost Battalion and Sgt. Alvin York.

On October 7th the 82nd Division advanced into the Argonne Forest area to assist the 77th Infantry Battalion (aka The Lost Battalion) which was under the command of Maj. Charles Whittlesey. The 77th Infantry Battalion became surrounded by hostile German forces and for several days was becoming systematically decimated. Company G (Sgt. Alvin York) and Company K (Pvt. Merwin) of the 328th Infantry, 82nd Division crossed the Meuse River north of the Lost Battalion. As Sgt. Alvin York described it in his diary he states;

> "...*God would never be cruel enough to create a cyclone as terrible as that Argonne battle. ... all through the long night those big guns flashed and growled just like the lightning and the thunder when it storms in the mountains at home... and the Lost Battalion was in there somewhere, needing help most awful bad! ... Our loses were very heavy. ... They just stopped us dead in our tracks.*"

Sgt. Alvin York would receive the Medal of Honor for *"fearlessly leading seven men, he charged with great daring a machine gun nest ... taken together with four officers and 128 men and several guns."*

Out of 670 men of the Lost Battalion, 191 were able to walk out of the fire storm. On October 20, 1918, Pvt. Merwin Jennings was killed in continued action in the Argonne region. His body was returned to the United States and interned in the Reformed Cemetery in Germantown. He was 23. In the memoirs of his commanding general, Maj. Gen. Duncan paid tribute to the fallen American soldier saying, *"Our country is richer because of his life."*

The Jennings-Willets American Legion Post #346 was so named to honor the memory of Pvt. Merwin Jennings. Our lives are richer because of him. We owe a debt of gratitude for his sacrifice and pay tribute to him, that we may enjoy the gift of life and freedom.

Robert F. Jette

Robert F. Jette was born November 3, 1943 to Felix and Lucille (Marcil) Jette in Adams, MA. Growing up in Adams, MA he attended Notre Dame Elementary and Adams High School, graduating June, 1963. He received an Associate's Degree from Berkshire Community College in 1963.

Robert entered the United States Air Force on September 11, 1963 in Albany, NY. After basic training he received additional training as a weapons control systems mechanic.

Senior Airman (SrA) Robert Jette was assigned to the 62 Fighter Interceptor Squadron at K.I. Sawyer Air Force Base in Michigan.   This squadron was a part of the 410th Bombardment Wing (SAC) which was made up of the McDonnell

F-101 (Voodoo) supersonic jet fighter. Its mission was to maintain an alert against a Soviet bomber threat.

The remainder of SrA Robert Jette's enlistment would be servicing the weapons control systems of the F-101 Squadron as it maintained the air defense in North America. He was recognized as Avionics Man of the Month (8/67). On September 10, 1969 he was honorably discharged at K.I. Sawyer Air Force Base, MI.

SrA Robert Jette was award the following: Small Arms Expert Marksmanship, Good Conduct Medal, National Defense Medal and Airman of the Month (8/67).

Bob returned home and received a bachelor's degree in finance from North Adams State College (1977). He married Linda LeBlonde and they raised two children: Lisa and David. On August 10, 2002 he married his second wife, Jacqueline Dupuis, in Adams, MA. Working as financial hospital comptroller for Columbia Memorial Hospital in Hudson, NY, he retired in 2013.

Bob was active in his community as president of the Lions Club (1983-84), a volunteer for the Valatie Food Pantry and communicant of St. John the Baptist Church in Valatie, NY. Bob was an avid skier, hiker and mount climber. He enjoyed golf, travel, following college basketball and attending his grandchildren's sporting events.

Robert passed away on February 5, 2016 in Kinderhook, NY and was buried in Bellevue Cemetery in Adams, MA. He left behind his lovely wife Jacqueline, two children: Lisa and Ryan, and two grandchildren. He was 72 years old.

Clifford Stanley Johnson

Clifford Stanley Johnson was born in Valatie, New York in 1930 where he grew up and attended Martin Glynn High School. At 17 while living with his father, Clifford obtained employment with the Village of Valatie where his father was also employed.

On October 3, 1949 Clifford enlisted in the United States Army. He received training in the United States and then was assigned to Headquarters Company, 57th Field Artillery Battalion, and 7th Infantry Division in Korea.

On December 6, 1950 while engaged in hostilities in the vicinity of Hagaru-ri, North Korea, the 20-year-old corporal was reported missing in action. With the end of hostilities three years later, on December 31, 1953 he was presumed dead.

Cpl. Clifford Johnson was awarded the Purple Heart. His remains were never recovered. Clifford joined his brother, Nathan (who also died in combat while serving in WWII) in the supreme sacrifice to his country for the noble cause of freedom.

Cpl. Clifford Stanley Johnson was honored on May 24, 2002 with William H.

Doss, Jr., Donald McNaughton, and Richard Powell; all serving in the 7th Infantry Division and died within five days of each other during the same offensive.

Donald Milton Johnston

Donald M. Johnston was born April 22, 1918 to Barson and Grace Powell Johnston in Mellenville, NY. He attended Philmont Elementary and High schools, graduating in June of 1935. Prior to his enlistment he worked as a mechanic.

Donald entered the United States Army on August 8, 1942 in Albany, NY as a 2nd lieutenant and was promoted to 1st lieutenant in May of 1944.

Lt. Donald M. Johnston was assigned to the 8th Air Force, 303 Bomber Group (Hells Angels), 360 Squadron as a B-17G pilot in the ETO. Stationed at Molesworth, England, he flew 36 missions over France and Germany. After flying the B-17 named "Iza Vailable Too" on a bombing mission of a railway station in Berlin, he received flak damage causing a fire on his #2 engine. In the after action report he stated:

> *"Flak had damaged the fuel line and the engine caught fire when the fuel booster pump was turned on. At about 300 feet over the runway, the #4 engine became a ball of fire. As I cleared the runway, onto the grass side, my main concern was injuring any of our crew as they cleared our burning aircraft. Alone I departed through the cockpit side widow to the left wing."*

What was left of his B-17 was used as spare parts. Lt. Don M. Johnston returned to the states and was assigned to the 563rd AAF Base Unit. He was honorably discharged on November 14, 1945 at Drew Field, FL.

For his service 1st Lt. Donald M. Johnston was awarded the following: Distinguished Flying Cross, Air Medal w/3 Bronze Oak Leaf Clusters, Good Conduct Medal, American Campaign Medal and the EAME Campaign Medal.

Don returned home and was employed at B.W. Johnston Construction Co. and later was the maintenance supervisor at Taconic Hills Ockawamick Central School; where he retired in 1984. Active in his community, he as a member of Philmont Rod and Gun Club (life), American Legion Post #252, Commissioner of Mellenville Fire District, and Claverack Republican Club (charter member) and the Philmont Santa Claus Club.

Don passed away on February 2, 2009 and was interned in the Sacred Heart Cemetery, Philmont, NY. He left behind three children: Marcia, Mary and Michael, eight grandchildren and several great-grandchildren. He was 91 years old.

Eldridge Charles Jones

Eldridge Jones was born in Hudson, NY on December 30, 1930 to Milton and Ethel Jones. He grew up in Hudson where he attended elementary and high school. Upon graduation he went to work (3 yrs) for the Vans Dairy in Hudson as a pasteurizer.

Eldridge enlisted in the United States Army on February 11, 1952 in Albany, NY as a private. After basic training at Fort Dix, NJ he received training in the infantry and was assigned to Korea.

Known as the "Forgotten War," the Korean War would cost the United States 33,741 lives: 23,615 KIA, 92,134 WIA, 4,820 MIA or declared dead and 7,245 POWs. 2847 of these died while prisoners of war.

From August 9, 1952 until June 12, 1953 Sgt. Eldridge Jones saw combat with Company M, 47th Infantry. On November 10, 1953 he was honorably discharged at Fort Dix, NJ and transferred to the Army Reserves.

Sgt. Eldridge Jones was awarded the following: Korean Service Medal with three Bronze Service Stars, United Nations Service Medal, Commendation Ribbon with Medal Pendant and the Combat Infantry Badge.

Eldridge returned home to Hudson where he met and married Lorraine Dallas on April 23, 1954 in the Philmont Methodist Church. In the years that followed, they raised four children: Janet, Karen, Mary Ann and Glenn. Eldridge worked for 33 years as an electrician for Witham Electric in Hudson, NY until his death. He was an active member of the Stockport Fire Company and the Philmont Methodist Church.

He died on June 11, 1994 and is buried at Mellenville Union Cemetery. His daughter recalled that her dad was a *"family man"* and his wife fondly adds, *"Eldridge went to work, came home and spent time with the family. He was a wonderful friend, everyone liked him."* In addition to his wife and four children, he is survived by eight grandchildren and one great-grandchild. He was 63 years old.

Edward J. Keeler

Edward J. Keeler was born October 29, 1918 to Frank and Rose (Brennan) Keeler in Hudson, NY. He attended St Mary's Academy and was graduated from Hudson High School. Prior to entering the armed forces he served as an undertaker's apprentice.

Edward enlisted in the United States Army on March 4, 1941. After basic training, he attended military intelligence school. Edward was assigned to the Headquarter Company 2nd Battalion 18th Infantry, of 1st Infantry Division when it was reactivated in Texas. Assigned to the European Theater of Operations, he departed for England from Ft. Devens. Tech Sgt. Edward J. Keeler saw action in

North Africa, Sicily, France, Belgium and Germany. Receiving the Bronze Star, the citation reads in part:

"... heroic achievement in connection with military operations against the enemy in the vicinity of St. Lauren-sur-Mer, Normandy, France 6, June 1944. Despite heavy enemy fire Sgt. Keeler moved fearlessly about open beach assembled and reorganized a command group. Sgt Keeler's initiative and heroic devotion to duty contributed materially to the success of the invasion. "

Tech Sgt. Edward J. Keeler was awarded the Combat Infantry Badge, eight battle stars, Bronze Star with cluster, Pre-Pearl Harbor Ribbon, the American Defense Service Medal, ETO Ribbon and Arrowhead, Distinguished Unit Badge with two Oak Clusters, European-African-Middle Eastern Service Medal, and the Good Conduct.

Edward was discharged at Fort Dix on June 23, 1945 and returned to his father's farm in Columbia County. He met and then married Mary O'Brien on May 7, 1949. They built a home on the family farm and raised eight children: Margaret, Joe, Kevin, Timmy, George, Mary Dowd, Patrick and Terry. Licensed as an undertaker, he started a business "Wilbert Burial Vaults" with his brother-in-law, George O'Brien in 1949. His son's Joe, Timmy and Kevin took over the vault business when he retired in 1983.

Edward remained active in the community. He was a charter member of the Claverack Lions Club, serving as president and district governor, and active in the Eyes for the Blind Program. He was a member of the Hudson VFW, American Legion, and the Elks Club.

On January 4, 2006 Edward passed away and was buried next to his wife in Cedar Park Cemetery in Hudson, NY. He left behind eight children, eighteen grandchildren and one great-grandson.

Richard Harold Keil

Richard Harold Keil was born in Stuyvesant Falls, NY on March 18, 1922 to George and Elizabeth Keil. He grew up and attended school in Stuyvesant Falls. Richard worked on a farm and then worked for the Fort Orange Paper Company.

On November 17, 1942 Richard entered the United States Army in Albany, NY. He received basic and advanced training at Cam San Luis in Obisdo, CA.

On August 27, 1944 he was assigned to the 104th Timer Wolfs Division in the European Theater of Operation. He saw action in Belgium, Holland, Central Germany from the Siefried Line to the Rhine River.

Tech Sgt. Keil was wounded on October 26, 1944 and was evacuated to England to recover. He returned to the front lines and resumed his duties. While on leave and waiting for assignment to the invasion of Japan, the war ended.

T/Sgt. Richard Keil returned to the United States on July 2, 1945 and was honorably discharge on November 2, 1945 at Camp San Luis in Obisdo, CA.

He was awarded the following: Purple Heart, Bronze Star, European Campaign Medal, American Campaign Medal, WWII Victory Medal and the Good Conduct Medal.

Richard married Elizabeth Phillips on June 30, 1946 at St. Mary's Parish in Stuyvesant Falls, NY. He worked as a paper stripper with the Fort Orange Paper Company for more than 44 years, retiring in 1985.

Richard was a life member of the Stuyvesant Falls VFW Post #9593 and served as commander, life member of Stuyvesant Falls Fire Co., life member of Glencadia Rod and Gun Club. He served as the tax collector for the Town of Stuyvesant Falls for 14 years and was a volunteer in the Fireman's Silver Medal Club. He was awarded the prestigious Abraham Lincoln Award.

Richard Harold Keil passed away on April 27, 2003 and was interned at St. Mary's Cemetery in Stuyvesant Falls, NY with full military honors. He left behind a loving wife, Elizabeth, two sons: Paul, Gary and three grandchildren.

John H. Kelley

John H. Kelley was born August 6, 1925 to Charles and Emma (Heideman) Kelley at Enfield, CT. Growing up, he attended school in Hudson, NY.

Prior to entering the military, John was a taxi driver. He enlisted in the United States Army on February 2, 1943 at Albany, NY. Upon completing basic training at Camp Blanding, where he qualified with the M1 rifle and the 30 caliber machine gun, Pvt. John Kelley was assigned to the 77th Division as an automatic rifleman.

The 77th Infantry Division, the Statue of Liberty Division, was activated on March 25, 1942 and was assigned to the Pacific Theater of Operation (PTO). Having received amphibious and jungle warfare training in Hawaii, the 77th Infantry Division was assigned to operations in the Western Pacific and the Philippine Islands. As an automatic rifleman, Pvt. John Kelley saw action in Eastern Mandates, New Guinea and Southern Philippines. It was here where Pvt. John Kelley was severely wounded.

After almost one year to the day that he entered the conflict, Pvt. John Kelly returned to the States on March 26, 1945. He was honorably discharged on November 1, 1945 at Fort Dix, NJ.

Prior to his honorable discharge on November 1, 1945, John married Josephine Squillace on July 29, 1945. He returned to Columbia County where he went to work as a taxi driver, L and B and for Harder's Express. In the years that followed, he and Josephine raised three children: Donna, John J. and Beverly.

John remained active in community affairs. He was chairman of the Hudson Zoning Board of Appeals, governor and life member of the Loyal Order of Moose #1184, past president and life member of Washington Hose Co. #3, life member of the Federation of Polish Sportsmen, member of Nativity/St. Mary's Church Stuyvensant Falls, Hudson Elks Lodge #787, V.F.W. Post 1314, American Legion Post #184, Disabled American Veterans, and the former Our Lady of Mt. Carmel Church and Holy Name Society.

For his service Pvt. John Kelley earned the American Service Medal , the Asiatic Pacific Service Medal , Philippines Liberation Ribbon with Bronze Star, and the Purple Heart.

John died Wednesday, June 3, 2009 at the Albany Medical Center. He was buried at Cedar Park Cemetery, Hudson, NY. He left behind a wife, three children, six grandchildren and four great- grandchildren. He was 83 years old.

Robert Francis Kelly

Robert Francis Kelly was born June 6, 1925 to Edward Kelly and Ethel Harder Kelly in Valatie, NY. He grew up on Mechanic Street in Valatie, graduating from Martin H. Glynn High School in 1943.

Robert tried to enlist in the armed forces but was initially rejected because of hearing loss, however, on July 9, 1945 while working as a plumber's helper, he was drafted in the United States Army. After his induction in Albany, NY, Robert received basic training at Fort Dix, NJ. He received additional training as a medic and was then assigned to the 996th TSU SGO Medical Detachment at Mason General Hospital at Brentwood, NY.

Staff Sgt. Robert Kelly was Ward Sergeant in the Psychiatric Department at Mason General Hospital. As a part of his duty, SSGT Kelly escorted patients to and from the facility as well as tended to the needs of those who were suffering from various mental conditions associated with the harsh realities of combat. They suffered from what was then called "battle fatigue" but is now termed PTSD or Post-traumatic Stress Disorder.

Robert, the youngest of four brothers who served in WWII (Edward – Navy, Truscott – Marines, and John – Air Force), was honorably discharged on December 9, 1946. He was awarded the World War II Victory Medal and the American Theater Service Medal.

He returned to Valatie working as a plumber, window caulker, office worker and retired from the State of NY Dept of Taxation and Finance in 1992. He married Nancy Keller on July 12, 1952 at the St. John the Baptist Church in Valatie and they raised a son, Robert Edward.

Robert remained active in his community. He was a member of John W. McConnell American Legion Post #47 of Valatie (which he helped build), he was a founder of the Valatie Santa Claus Club, served on the Boy Scout Troop Committee, was a volunteer in his church (St. John the Baptist), and was the recipient of the Winchester-Western Inc. Commemorative Award for his military service and outstanding service to the American Legion. He also received the "Spirit of Valatie Award" for his 60 years of community service.

Robert was remembered as "quiet and unassuming, doing things without fanfare. If someone needed help, he was there."

He died on February 23, 2010 and is buried at St. John the Baptist of Valatie. He left behind his loving wife, Nancy, his son, Robert and three grandchildren.

Donald J. Kirker

Donald J. Kirker was born April 9, 1928 to Mr. and Mrs. Henry and Frances Kirker. He attended St. Mary's Elementary School and graduated from St. Mary's Academy in Hudson, NY.

As a strapping 5-foot-11, blond-haired, blue-eyed young man, Donald enlisted in the Marine Corps in Albany, NY on July 15, 1946 and was trained as a radio operator. He was then stationed at Cherry Point, North Carolina, serving for an unspecified period of time as a radioman on the Marine Corps Commandant's airplane. Donald was temporarily assigned to duty in Puerto Rico from February to March of 1947 and was then discharged at Cherry Point, NC on January 30, 1948.

Completing his first tour of duty, Donald enlisted in the Third Marine Corps Reserve District in Albany, NY on October 21, 1948; obtaining the rank of corporal. He went to work as the lumberyard manager for Speer-Kirker Co. Inc. in Hudson, NY.

In June of 1950, the communists of North Korea crossed the 38th parallel into South Korea. Cpl. Kirker entered active duty on August 19, 1950 in Albany, NY and attended the U.S. Army Security Agency School at Carlisle Barracks in Pennsylvania for training as a high speed radio operator.

Donald was assigned to 1st Radio Company, FMF, Camp Pendleton, Oceanside, California. He attained the rank of sergeant and was honorably discharged on July 9, 1951. Sgt. Donald J. Kirker was awarded the World War II Victory Ribbon and the Good Conduct Medal.

Donald was a communicant of Holy Family Church of Stottville, NY, and a member of the Holy Name Society. He was an active member of the Rogers Hose Fire Company and the Federation of Polish Sportsman of Hudson, NY. He retired as a quality control supervisor for Marshall Erdman Assoc. of Madison, WI in

1987.

On June 8, 1989 Donald J. Kirker passed away at the age of 61 and was buried in Stuyvesant Falls, New York. He leaves behind his lovely wife, Norma, eight children, (Debra Kirker, Richard Kirker, Mary Kirker-Fay, Kathleen Kirker, Paul Kirker, Teresa Stockley, Peter Kirker and Michael Kirker), twelve grandchildren and two great grandchildren.

Sgt. Donald J. Kirker's dedication and service to his country during two wars is in the finest tradition of the United States Marine Corps and has earned the deepest respect and admiration from his friends, family and a grateful nation.

Robert C. Knabbe

Robert C. Knabbe was born May 27, 1926 in Queens, NY to Roger and Hellen Swartz Knabbe. In 1935 his family moved to Ghent where Robert attended Chatham School.

Robert entered the United States Army on September 1, 1944 in Albany, NY. After basic and infantry training, he qualified as a sharpshooter in and was assigned to Company C, 255 Infantry Regiment, 63rd Infantry Division in Europe.

The 63rd Infantry Division, a.k.a. the "Blood and Fire" Division, saw intense action from Sarreguemines (France) through the Siegfried Line to Worms, Mannheim, Heidelberg, Gunzburg and then liberated several Nazi concentration subcamps at Landsberg by the end of April 1945. The 63rd Division spent 119 days in combat and suffered 8,019 total battle casualties while capturing more than 21,000 of the enemy.

While leading a squad in April 1945, Sgt. Knabbe stepped on a land mine, which resulted in the amputation of his left leg, wounds to his left hand, right thigh and hearing loss. For more than a year he received medical care at Walter Reed Medical Hospital in Washington, DC. where he was honorably discharged on May 2, 1946.

Sgt. Robert C. Knabbe was awarded the following citations: Purple Heart, European African Middle Eastern Service Medal, Good Conduct Medal, WWII Victory Medal, American Campaign Medal, Combat Infantryman Badge, and the Rifle Sharpshooters Medal.

Robert returned home where he worked as a heavy equipment operator for Mark Kearney Sand and Gravel of Greenport and later for the Columbia County Highway Department, where he retired in 1988.

Robert was a charter, life member and past commander of Ghent VFW Post 5933. He was a 62-year member and past chief of the Ghent Fire Company. In addition, he was a board member emeritus of the Ghent Union Cemetery Association.

His lovely wife, Nancy recalled:
"Bob had a great love for his family and his country. As much as he could he would help to promote veterans and their causes. His biggest delight was his 10 grandchildren and before he died he knew he would soon have twin great-granddaughters."

Robert Knabbe died on October 14, 2005 and was interred in the Ghent Union Cemetery.

He forfeited a leg that his fellow man could stand tall, free.

George A. Koren

George A. Koren was born September 22, 1912 in Livingston, Illinois to Anton and Anna (Kuher) Koren. His family moved to Columbia County where he attended and graduated from Hudson High School. As a young man he went to work in construction for James J. McKinney Co.

With his construction background, George enlisted in the Navy February 28, 1942 in Albany, NY and served with the United States Navy Reserve, 7th Naval Coast Battalion in the Pacific with the Navy Seabees as Ship Fitter 1st Class.

During WWII, the Seabees were vital to the victory in the Atlantic and Pacific Theaters of Operation. They served on four continents and on more than 300 islands. After $11 billion and numerous casualties, they constructed 400 advanced bases.

In the Pacific where George served, the Seabees built 111 major airstrips, 441 piers, 2,558 ammunition magazines, 700 square blocks of warehouses, hospitals to serve 70,000 patients, tanks for the storage of 100,000,000 gallons of gasoline, and housing for 1,500,000 men. They suffered numerous combat deaths and earned 2,000 purple hearts. Literally, success can be attributed to the efforts of George Koren and his fellow Seabees in paving the road to the allied victory in WWII.

George Koren was discharged on November 11, 1945 at Lido Beach, Long Island. For his service to his county, he was awarded the following citations: Navy Good Conduct Medal, WWII Victory Medal, American Campaign Medal, Asiatic Pacific Campaign Medal, European-African-Middle Eastern Campaign Medal, Honorable Service Lapel Pin (Ruptured Duck) and the Discharge Button.

Upon his discharge, George returned to work for James J. McKinney Co. He worked on the construction of the Rip Van Winkel Bridge, where he survived an accidental fall during it construction. He was a foreman with that firm until his death. His wife, Viola (Witko) Koren was the owner of Vi Cel Beauty Salon in Hudson.

George was an avid New York Yankee fan. He was a member of the Sacred

Heart Church, Polish Sportsman Club, Knights of Columbus and Hudson Elks.

George died May 23, 1957 at the age of 42 and is buried at Cedar Park Cemetery in Hudson, NY.

Harold Wayne Krambeck

Harold Wayne Krambeck was born September 25, 1929 to Harry and Dorothy (Tietz) Krambeck in Moline, IL. Raised in East Moline, he graduated from United Township High School in 1947. While attending school he worked at John Deere Harvester.

Harold entered the United States Army on August 4, 1948 in Rock Island Il. After basic training he was trained as a light weapons infantryman where he qualified expert with the M-1 rifle. Harold Krambeck was assigned to Company A, 3rd Infantry at Fort Myers, VA.

The 3rd Infantry was known as the "Old Guard" and is the Army's official ceremonial unit, escort to the president and provides security for Washington, D.C. It is the oldest active-duty infantry unit in the Army having served our nation since 1784.

While serving in this famed unit, Harold was promoted to private first class (7/15/49) and then corporal (10/3/50).

Cpl. Harold Krambeck served as a sentinel, Tomb of the Unknown Soldier with Company E, 3d Infantry Regiment and was authorized to wear the Guard, Tomb of the Unknown Soldier Identification Badge as a permanent part of his uniform. Cpl. Harold Krambeck was honorably discharged at Fort Myer, VA on June 17, 1952.

Harold married Elizabeth Altermer while in the armed services. They raised two children: Wayne and Ronnie. In the summer of 1977 he was married again to Viola Alger in a private ceremony in Hudson, NY. He worked as a mechanic with the Universal Match Factory, Hudson, NY and after 32 years he retired. He was a member of the American Legion Post #184 (34 years), where he served as its commander several years.

On November 13, 2018, Harold passed away and was interned in Cedar Park Cemetery, Hudson, NY presided by an honor guard from his former unit. He left behind his wife Viola, sons: Wayne and Ronnie, step-children: Sharon, Mike, David, Dennis and Cindy as well as several nieces, nephews, grandchildren and great-grandchildren. He was 88 years old.

Francis O. LaCasse

Francis Oliver LaCasse was born March 16, 1919 in Shelburne, VT to Oliver and Nora (Blain) LaCasse. Growing up in Vermont, he attended Essex Junction Public school.

Francis entered the United States Army on September 6, 1941 in Rutland, VT. His basic training was at Ft. Devens and then he received Armor training at Ft. Knox, KY, where he trained as a driver and gunner in a medium tank.

Assigned to the 751st Tank Battalion, they were shipped to the European Theater of Operation. First stop was Liverpool, England and then saw action as a part of operations in North Africa.

Tech Fifth Class (T/5) Francis LaCasse was a part of a medium tank crew of the Sherman M-4 tank, landed in Algeria and fought through Tunisia.

The 751st then landed in Salerno. On September 1943 T/5 "displayed conspicuous bravery in administering first aid to a wounded soldier while under heavy enemy shell fire." Although two fellow soldiers had been killed and another wounded, T/5 LaCasse remained with the casualty until he was evacuated one hour later and was subsequently awarded the Silver Star.

Having participated in the assault on Anzio and offensive to Rome, T/5 LaCasse returned to Ft. Knox where he helped train armored units for the Pacific Theater of Operation until the end of the war.

For his service he was awarded the following: Silver Star, European African Middle Eastern Service Medal with two Bronze Arrowheads and the American Defense Service Medal and Expert Tank Gunner Badge.

Francis returned home, met and married Anne Flannery on October 13, 1951and they raised two children: James and Stephen. He owned and operated a dairy business from 1955 to 1988 and continued to "rent out fields and buildings" until his death. He was a member of the American Legion Post 1160 in Copake Fall, NY.

Francis died on September 11, 2016 and was buried in the Saratoga National Cemetery, Schuylerville, NY. He was 97 years old.

Eric R. Lagerwall

Eric R. Lagerwall was born July 10, 1938 in Nyack, NY to Harry and Adelaide (Nelson) Lagerwall. He attended elementary and high school in Brooklyn; graduating from Midwood High School in 1956. He attended Hudson Valley Community College in Troy, NY and graduated in 1958.

Eric enlisted in the United States Coast Guard on March 12, 1958 in Brooklyn, NY. After his initial training, Seaman Eric Lagerwall was trained as a boatswain mate. Among the duties of a boatswain mate is to operate small boats; store cargo; handle ropes and lines; and direct work of deck force. In addition, they navigate the ship's steering; lookout supervision, ship control, bridge watch duties, visual communication and maintenance of navigational aids.

Seaman Lagerwall was assigned to the Third Coast Guard District on board the USCG Cutter, Sauk, based at Battery Park, New York City.

Sauk, was named after the Native American tribe from the mid-west. The 110-foot cutter was built in Brooklyn and commissioned on May 25, 1944. With a complement of 16 sailors, she was based in New York Harbor. Its mission included search and rescue, fire fighting, towing assistance, light ice-breaking, and law enforcement, including customs' boarding of merchant vessels entering New York Harbor.

Seaman Eric Lagerwall was discharged on February 15, 1962 at Battery Park, NY.

On August 20, 1960, while still in the Coast Guard, Eric married Martha Heltzle. They moved to East Chatham in 1962 and for the next 45 years he worked for Clifford Nelson Contracting, Ben Franklin Press, Ceramaseal and the Columbia County Highway Department as the motor equipment operator, retiring after 27 years.

Eric served as Town of Canaan Highway Superintend (3 yrs), animal control officer (25 yrs) and Deputy Town Clerk. He was a 50-year member, past president and chief of East Chatham Fire Company, member of the Chatham Rescue Squad (30 yrs), the Republican Association and Canaan Conservation Club.

Eric, a former Eagle Scout, was a Boy Scout leader and served on the District Council. He was a communicant of the Canaan Congregational Church where he taught Sunday School, served as deacon and trustee for many years.

Eric passed away on February 6, 2007 and was buried at Canaan Cemetery in Canaan, NY. He left a lovely wife, Martha, three children: Glen, Karen, Robert and seven grandchildren. He was 68 years old.

Joseph LaPorta

Joseph Nicholas LaPorta was born in Bronxville, NY on October 19, 1945 to Anthony and Vincenza (Vigilante) LaPorta, Jr. He attended and graduated Roeliff Jansen School in Hillsdale, NY in June 1963.

Joseph was drafted in the United States Army on November 4, 1965. After basic training he was trained as a food service specialist. Spec. 5 Joseph LaPorta was assigned to the Service Battery, 1st Battalion 92nd Artillery.

The 1/92nd Artillery was a three-firing battery, each with six 155 millimeter (M114A1) Howitzers. In February 1967 the 1/92nd departed for the Central

Highlands, Vietnam, its primary area of operations. As a mobile unit it served as direct fire or in support of military operations with the 4th Infantry and the 173 Airborne Divisions. The 1/92nd moved 111 times in their first four months in country.

After eight and a half months of Foreign Service, Spec. 5 Joseph LaPorta returned to USA and on October 28, 1967 was honorably discharged.

For his service Spec. 5 Joseph LaPorta was awarded the following: Vietnam Service Medal, Vietnam Commendation Medal, Overseas Service Bar, National Defense Service Medal, Good Conduct Medal and Expert Rifle Badge.

Joseph returned home, received a degree from Detroit Diesel from Western Electric in 1970. He was married to Karen Luango; they had two children: Douglass and Nicholas and then on April 21, 2010 Joseph married Charlene (Ryan) in Copake, NY. He worked as an engineer for Bell Systems and was a self-employed electrician.

Joseph was a member of the Hillsdale VFW (Commander), Copake VFW (Founding Member), Copake Comm. Rescue Squad (Captain/Director), Copake Fire Co. (life member), Farm Building Inspector, volunteer umpire, Commissioner of TH Storm Football, Town of Copake board member and Deputy Supervision.

Joseph died on April 18, 2016 and was interned in the Dutch Reform Church cemetery in West Copake. He left behind his loving wife, Charlene, two children: Douglass and Nicholas, three step children: Linda, Scott and Kristen, and 10 grandchildren. He was 70 years old.

Dallas Philip Laurange

Dallas Philip Laurange was born August 8, 1932 to Philip and Ruth (Stupplebean) Laurange in Chatham, NY. He grew up and attended school in Chatham.

Dallas was employed as a laborer with Keegans Trucking Company of Kinderhook from 1948 to 1952 when he was drafted in the United States Army on October 20, 1952. After basic training at Fort Dix, NJ , Dallas received advanced infantry training, specializing in light weapons.

PFC Dallas Laurange was assigned to Company A of the 14th Infantry in Korea. The 14th Infantry Regiment, known as the "Golden Dragons," engaged in almost constant combat duty along the 38th Parallel.

It was assigned defensive positions on "Heartbreak Ridge," "Punchbowl" and "Pork Chop Hill" as well as conducted aggressive combat patrols. The 14th Infantry earned five campaign streamers, a Republic of Korea Presidential Unit Citation for gallantry as well as three Medal of Honor recipients (two posthumously).

After one year, three months and twenty-two days overseas, PFC Dallas Laurange returned to the United States. He was released from active military service on October 2, 1954 at Camp Kilmer, NJ and was then transferred to the Army Reserves, where he was honorably discharged on September 30, 1960.

For his military service PFC Dallas Laurange received the following: the Korean Service Medal, the United Nations Service Medal and the National Defense Service Medal.

Dallas returned home to Chatham and worked for M.L. Gold of Hudson, NY, where he retired 30 years later. He was a proud member of the VFW and the American Legion. His long time friend and companion, Faith Boyce, remembers him as, "kind and very outgoing. He could not sit still – always working."

Dallas Philip Laurange died on April 20, 2007 in Columbiaville and was buried in the Union Cemetery in Mellonville NY. He left behind five children: Dallas Philip (Jr.), Mark, Tina, Timmy, and Holly; 17 grandchildren, 12 great grandchildren. He was 74 years old.

John N. Loos

John N. Loos was born March 27, 1920 in Hudson, NY to Kenneth and Mary (Hermance) Loos. He grew up in Hudson and attended elementary and high school. As a boy he played baseball and enjoyed watching boxing. He worked odd jobs for Bates and Anderson and the Columbia Dinner. Prior to his enlistment, he worked as a counterman for the Park Dinner located near the 7th Street Park.

On June 10, 1942, John was inducted into the United States Army in Albany, NY. He underwent basic training and was trained as a rifleman for the infantry at Fort Meade.

Upon completing his training, PFC John Loos was assigned to the 3rd Infantry Division, 7th Infantry where he saw action in North Africa (Algeria-French Morocco-Tunisia), Sicily, Italy (Naples-Foggia, Rome-Arno, Southern France and Germany (Rhineland).

While engaged with hostile forces in France, on September 25, 1944, PFC Loos was wounded by small arms fire. A bullet which had just killed a friend, severely wounded him in the hand. He was taken to the 32nd General Hospital where he recuperated and returned to his unit where he remained until the cessation of hostilities.

After the war John returned home, married Edith L. Smith (1946) and raised four children: John, Kenneth, Richard and Joann.

He worked for the Lone Star Cement Company and for a time was a security agent for the Pinkerton Security Service. John was active in the VFW Post 1314,

American Legion Post 184 and was a life member of the Phoenix Hose No 5 (Hudson Fire Dept.) where he once held the office of captain.

For his service to his country, PFC John Loos was awarded the EAME Service Medal, the Purple Heart and the Combat Infantry Badge. On June 4, 1971, John Loos died at the age of 51 and was buried in Cedar Park Cemetery in Hudson, NY.

Wilfred D. MacGiffert

Wilfred Dinwitty MacGiffert, Jr. was born in Hudson, NY on May 17, 1925 to Wilfred D. and Aleta (Scott) MacGiffert. He attended Stottville and Greenport elementary and then Hudson High School.

Wilfred (Bud) MacGiffert, Jr. entered the United States Navy on August 16, 1945 at the end of his third year of high school. After basic training at Camp Peary, VA, he was trained at Gulfport, MS as a motor machinist's mate.

MM3 Wilfred MacGiffert was assigned to the 133rd Navy Seabees, Company D, 5th Platoon in the Pacific Theater of Operations. With a stopover in Hawaii for jungle training and amphibious landing, he was attached to the 4th Marine Division.

The 133rd Seabees landed with the 4th Marine on the first day of the battle for Iwo Jima. Encountering all the hazards of frontline combat, they unloaded supplies, lay steel mats from the LSTs on the soft black sand and repaired and constructed the airstrips that would be vital to the continued offensive on Japan. Exhibiting the "CB Can Do" spirit, the 133rd Navy Seabees incurred 246 casualties alongside the marines in the battle for Iwo Jima.

MM3 Wilfred MacGiffert received the following awards: Asiatic Pacific Campaign Medal with star and arrowhead, WWII Victory Medal, Am. Campaign Medal.

Returning home he opened MacGiffert Brothers Garage with his brother Jack. He met and married Anne Buckley on May 16, 1948 and raised two children. Anne died in June of 1968 and he married Constance Grabowski on July 14, 1973 in Hudson, NY.

Upon retirement in 1990, he worked for Thorpe's GMC in Tannersville. Bud owned and raced a stock car in the 1950s.

He remained active in his community and was a life member of Greenport Fire Co. #1, Hudson Elks #787, and former director of Hudson Powerboat Society and Navy Seabee Veterans of America in Davie, FL.

Bud passed away on August 3, 2017 in the Fireman's Home in Hudson, NY and is buried in Cedar Park, Hudson, NY. He left behind two sons: Robert and Paul MacGiffert, three stepchildren: Joseph Barca, Maryann Bopp and John Barca; four grandchildren and three great-grandchildren. He was 92 years old.

John Mackowski

John Mackowski was born January 27, 1916 in Brooklyn, NY. A product of the tough streets of New York City, the Depression and a loving Polish family, he graduated from Grover Cleveland High School in Queens, NY.

On March 25, 1941 at the age of 25 and recently engaged to be married, John was drafted into the United States Army. He received training at Fort Belvoir and then was assigned to the 36th Combat Engineers at Westover Field, MA.

Increased hostilities in the Pacific resulted in his unit being assigned to the Philippines. On December 8, 1941 the Japanese bombed Clark Air Field and on the 22nd they landed at Lingayen Gulf in the Philippines. After several weeks of intense fighting his company was ordered to the small island of Corregidor, strategically located at the mouth of Manila Bay.

For the next ten weeks the isolated American forces fought courageously against overwhelming odds. Inevitably, Corregidor fell on May 5th and John became a Prisoner of War. He spent the next two and a half years as a P.O. W. at five different prison camps in the Philippines.

Life was harsh and often brutal. For the first three days of captivity there was no food or water and refusing to salute and bow to a Japanese soldier resulted in a savage beating.

For the thousands of American POW's there was little to no medical attention for the sick and wounded, inadequate food and water, open latrines which bred swarms of flies and other disease-bearing insects, dysentery, heat prostration, beri-beri, malaria, malnutrition and other debilitating diseases. Guards routinely beat and kicked the prisoners without cause or provocation and escape attempts resulted in summary executions. Forced labor was compulsory.

Because John refused to inform on a fellow American, he endured 22 days of "beating with bamboo," "kicking," "slapping" and "starvation," denied "water" or "sleep or rest," "uninterrupted interrogations," "hours standing in the hot sun . . .naked," and bound "in unnatural and painful positions."

Emaciated and weak from malnutrition and maltreatment, John returned weakened but unbroken from his brutal ordeal. He escaped death once more when the Japanese ship he was transported in was inadvertently sunk by an American submarine. Of the 750 Americans aboard, 83 survived. Rescued by submarine, John Mackowski escaped to the United States and on February 4, 1945 married his fiancé, Opaline.

Cpl. John Mackowski showed extraordinary courage in a hostile environment at great peril to himself. By his heroic action, he earned the everlasting admiration of his fellow prisoners and his countrymen. He is an inspiration to all who knew and loved him.

John is buried beside his wife in St. James Cemetery, Ghent, NY.

Michael Mahokin

Michael Mahokin was born to Paul and Mary Mahokin on April 18, 1924 in Hudson, NY. He attended 6th Street Elementary School and then Hudson High School. Due to Michael's academic excellence, he made the honor roll for all four years of high school and was inducted as a member of the Honor Society.

In addition, he played on the football team, was elected Vice President of this Class of 1940 and became associate editor for the high school yearbook, "The Blue and Gold." When Michael graduated, he was voted the "most pleasant boy" for the class of 1942.

Upon graduation, Michael went to work for General Electric Corporation in Pittsfield, MA. where he took mechanical courses. Michael briefly attended Andover College in Massachusetts and on February 12, 1943 he entered the United States Army in Hudson, NY.

Michael received training as an Army medic in the United States and then was shipped to the European Theater of Operation. He was initially assigned to the 177 Medical Corps where he attained the rank of tech. 5th class and saw action in France and Germany.

Tech/5 Sgt. Michael Mahokin was transferred to the 224th Medical Corps and with only two weeks with his new unit he went on his final mission.

While evacuating some wounded, his clearly marked medical evacuation plane landed and came quickly under intense enemy fire. With less than six weeks before V-E Day, Michael Mahokin was killed near the Rhine River on March 24, 1945. He would have been 21 on his next birthday.

Tech/5 Sgt. Michael Mahokin was buried in Margraten Military Cemetery in Holland. Later he was reinterred in the veteran's section of Cedar Park Cemetery in Hudson, NY.

Michael was credited with two campaign ribbons for the European Theater of Operations and posthumously awarded the Purple Heart.

John Wesley Marriott

John Wesley Marriott was December 2, 1933 to Resco and Mettie Sopher Marriotte at Pandora, OH, where he grew up and attended school.

On August 29, 1956 John was inducted in the United States Army at Finnlay, Ohio. After basic training he was trained as an artilleryman and assigned to Battery D, 2nd Battalion, 1st Field Artillery Regiment, Ft. Chaffee, AK.

Having attained the rank of private first class, in the course of his duties PFC

John Wesley Marriott was injured and received medical attention at Walter Reed Army Medical Center, Washington, DC. On March 31, 1958 he was "permanently retired by reason of physical disability" and received an honorable discharged.

John met and married Judith Samascott on March 31, 1974 at Niverville, NY. He worked as a self-employed welder and carpenter and retired in 1980.

Known as "Ginkey" to family and loved ones, he was a "quiet, gentle man who worked in the yard, taking rides in the country or sitting by the river. He enjoyed "drawing, fishing or flying kites" with his grandchildren; telling them "many times how blessed we all were to live in America and to never forget our great military – the best in the world."

John passed away on March 9, 2015 at Stratton VA Medical Center, Albany, NY. He left behind is loving wife, Judith, four children: Rhonda, Lori, Nora-Jean and Juliana, twelve grandchildren and seven great-grandchildren. He was 81 years old.

John Peter Massarella

John Peter Massarella was born on July 1, 1922 in New York City to Emanuel and Maria (Vitale) Massarella. He grew up in New York City, attending P.S. 84 Elementary School and Power Memorial High School.

John enlisted on September 24, 1942 in the United States Coast Guard at the 3rd Naval Station. SEA1 John Peter Massarella served honorably during World War II protecting the mainland and coastal waters of the United States.

He was honorably discharged on March 27, 1946 at the Personal Separation Center No. 3 in Brooklyn, NY and was awarded the Good Conduct Medal (8/24/42 - 8/23/45).

John married Catherine (Kay) Hunter on September 5, 1946 in Elkton, MD. Although living in Manhattan where they raised two children, John and Kay rented a summer home in Copake Falls. Kay, John, and the children, along with family members would spend summers in Copake Falls.

Working in the maintenance department for the 20th Century Fox Corporation, John spent weekends and vacations in Columbia County. After retiring from the City College of New York, he permanently resided in Copake Falls.

John became involved in the local community. He was active in the Roe Jan Young at Hearts and Closson Raught American Legion Post 1160. He especially enjoyed attending Taconic Hills sporting events and was a big fan of the local softball team. While residing in Manhattan, John served as post commander of the Kelly VFW Post 6140, where he proudly marched in the Memorial Day parades.

His daughter, Susan, recalled that he loved his family, friends and country. He was extremely patriotic and would fly the American flag on his 30-foot flag pole on his property in Copake Falls. Deeply moved by 9/11 when his daughter escaped from the 72nd floor of building one of the World Trade Center, he displayed the American Flag on his car window as a sign of patriotism and fidelity for his fellow countrymen.

John passed away on August 28, 2005 at the age of 83 and was interned in St. John in the Wilderness Cemetery located in Copake Falls, NY.

His daughter, Susan recalled, "My father was a kind, gentle man. He was always willing to lend a hand, drive neighbors to doctor's appointments, social events and shopping. (He had) friends of all ages – teenagers and seniors would come to his house to visit every day. He was there to listen, give advice, never criticizing. I am extremely proud to be Johnny Massarella's daughter."

John J. Mazur

John Joseph Mazur was born to John J. and Alice (Borosky) Mazur on February 22, 1928 in Hudson, NY. John attended grammar and high school until 1944, receiving a GED in 1953.

John entered foreign service with the Merchant Marines on May 27, 1944 during WWII aboard a merchant liberty steamer, the Alice H. Rice, from October 12, 1944 to January 20, 1945 and a diesel merchant ship, the Cape Igvak (C1-A), from February 5, 1945 to August 17, 1945.

Merchant ships faced danger from submarines, mines, armed raiders and destroyers, aircraft, "kamikaze," and the elements. About 8,300 marines were killed at sea, 12,000 wounded of whom at least 1 in 100 died from their wounds, and 663 were taken prisoner – a total killed estimated 9,300. One in 26 marines serving aboard merchant ships in WW II died in the line of duty, suffering a greater percentage of war-related deaths that all other U. S. services. In 1988 the Merchant Marines were granted veteran status.

John was inducted into the United States Army in February 8, 1952, receiving training at Fort Dix, NJ, where he completed Infantry NCO Academy.

In the next two years, Sgt. Mazur served as a platoon sergeant in Company I, 47th Infantry Regiment, and then a line Company with the rank of master sergeant.

On February 7, 1954, MSgt. John Mazur transferred to the Army Reserves where he served with Company B, 152d Engineer Battalion and Company C, 1st Battalion, 105th Infantry in Hudson, NY. On April 18, 1980, WO2 John Mazur was honorably discharged.

For his service, he was awarded the following: National Defense Ribbon, NYS Service Decoration, NYS Recruiting Medal, MYS Commendation Medal, Sharpshooters badge.

John was an administrative and supply technician for CG NYARNG Public Security Building on the State Campus, Albany, NY. He was active in the Citizen Band Radio Club where he served as president from 1963-64.

John was remembered by his daughter, Ellen, as having, "a great sense of humor and was very quick-witted and generous. He loved to build things and tinker. He would help anyone without expecting anything in return."

He passed away on December 24, 2011 and is buried in Cedar Park Cemetery, Hudson, NY. He was 83.

John B. McEvoy

John B. McEvoy, one of seven children, was born July 26, 1925 to Arthur and Katherine Broderick McEvoy of Hudson, NY. He attended school at St. Mary's Academy in Hudson where he graduated 1943 and later attended St Michael's College of Winoski, VT.

On July 24, 1943 he entered the United States Navy Reserves in New York and reported to the Navy Recruiting Training Station for basic training and then Storekeeper School at Newport, RI for advanced training.

He was assigned to a duty station in Brooklyn, NY and then to the 3rd Naval District where he was assigned to the USS Eurora (AP177).

SK2 McEvoy was honorably discharged from Lido Beach, Long Island, NY. For his service during WWII, he received the following awards: Victory Medal, American Medal and the European Theater Medal.

John McEvoy returned to Hudson where he worked for J. C. Rogerson & Co. of Hudson, NY, which was operated by his father and uncle. John married Jacqueline Hunter of Stuyvesant Falls on March 1, 1949 and they raised a son, Dennis. Upon the retirement of his father and uncle, John become part owner of J.C. Rogerson & Co and remained president until his death in 1994.

His wife, Jackie, a registered nurse, worked for Columbia Memorial Hospital, the Fireman's Home and the Columbia County Department of Social Services where she retired in 1982.

John remained active in community affairs. He was a former commander of the Hudson American Legion Post 184, president of the J.W. Edmonds Hose Co. #1, a life member of the Columbia County VFW Post 1314 and the Ancient Order of the Hibernians. In addition, he served on the Board of Assessment Review of the City of Hudson, Memorial Day chairman, co-chairman of the City of Hudson Bicentennial as well as the 200th anniversary of the Edmonds Hose and H.W. Rogers Hose Co. No. 2. fire companies.

John passed away on June 10, 1994 and is buried in Cedar Park Cemetery,

Hudson, NY. He leaves behind his lovely wife, Jackie, a son, Dennis, and two grandsons, Ryan and Timothy.

When his country needed him, he heeded the call. His service to his country and his community attests to his compelling character and we, his family and friends, are testimony of his enduring legacy.

Albert E. McGee

Albert E. McGee was born to Albert and Mary (Hood) McGee on July27, 1929 in Woonsocket, RI. He grew up in Hudson while attending school at Hudson Central School District.

Employed as a sales clerk, Albert enlisted in the United States Army on October 5, 1946 in Albany, NY. Qualifying with the M1 in basic, he received additional training as a military policeman. Pvt. Albert E. McGee was assigned to occupied Japan on December 30, 1946, where he served with the 720 Military Police Battalion for the next two years.

In August 1945, the 720 Military Police Battalion was positioned in the city of Tokyo for the primary purpose of conducting Law and Order missions in the occupied city. Due to a shortage of personnel in 1948 the 720th MP Battalion was attached to the 410th MP Co. whose primary mission was command and control.

Returning to the United States in 1948, Pvt. Albert E. McGee was honorably discharged at Stoneman, CA on April 1, 1948 and assigned to the active reserves.

Albert was called back to active duty during the Korean War and he was assigned to Fort Campbell before being shipped to the Korean theater of operations as an MP in the spring of 1951. He was again released from military duty December of 1953.

Returning home from WWII Albert worked as a pressman at the V&O Press. In July of 1950 he married Mildred Pulver and they resided in Mellenville, NY, where they raised their daughter, Rindy. In 1955 he married his second wife, Beverly Bluto, in Orlando, FL. Continuing to work as a printer in Orlando, FL, he and his new wife raised two boys: Edward and John.

Pvt. Albert E. McGee was awarded the WWII Victory Medal and the Army of Occupation Medal.

Albert died on March 31, 1965 of an aneurism and was buried in Greenwood Cemetery, Orlando, FL. He was 35 years old.

Donald McNaughton

Donald McNaughton was born October 30, 1931 to Mr. and Mrs. John McNaughton in North Bellmore, Long Island and moved to Philmont in 1946 where he attended high school.

On December 12, 1949, Donald enlisted in the United States Army in Hudson, New York. He received training with mortars in the United States and was assigned to Company M, 31st Infantry Regiment, 7th Infantry Division, which was then stationed in Japan.

At the outbreak of the Korean War, PFC Donald McNaughton's unit was ordered to combat where they became engaged with hostile forces on the eastern shore of the Chosin Reservoir, North Korea. On December 2, 1950 PFC Donald McNaughton was killed in action from a machine gun bullet.

A letter dated December 22, from a friend, Cpl. Gerald DellaValle of Marsteller, Pennsylvania to Donald's parents, stated Donald died in the corporal's arms. Cpl. DellaValle wrote:

"Just before he died his last works were 'Please write to my mom' and I told him that I would and I held his hand until he died. Donald was a very good soldier and he knew his job and he did it well. He was hit by a machine gun bullet . . . . He did a wonderful job in protecting a lot of wounded and that's when he got hit. It sure hurts me to write this letter."

Nineteen year old PFC Donald McNaughton's remains were never recovered. A memorial was dedicated in his honor at the Philmont baseball field. He was posthumously awarded the Purple Heart.

PFC Donald McNaughton was honored on May 24, 2002 with William Henry Doss, Jr., Clifford Johnson, and Richard Powell; all serving in the 7th Infantry Division and died within five days of each other during the same offensive.

Allen Lee McWhirt, Sr.

Allen Lee McWhirt, Sr. was born October 27, 1932 in Hudson, NY to Rubin and Martha McWhirt. Growing up in Craryville, Allen attended primary and secondary school at the Roeliff Jansen Central School.

In his youth, he worked part time on the Elmer Nelson Farm, drove dump truck for Leroy Michael and during the summer caddied at the Copake Country Club.

On November 12, 1952, Allen was drafted in the United States Army at Albany, NY and attended 16 weeks of basic training at Indiantown Gap, PA,.

In April 1953, Sgt. Allen McWhirt, Sr. was assigned to combat duty in the Republic of Korea to the 3rd Battalion, L Company, 179th Infantry Regiment, 45th Infantry Division.

The 45th Inf. Div., known as the "Thunderbirds," was organized in 1920 as a part of the Oklahoma National Guard. Mobilized in WWII where it saw extensive action, then it was once again activated for the Korean War.

Replacing the 1st Cavalry Division in 1951, the 45th Infantry Division participated in four campaigns, fighting in the Chongjamal area, Heartbreak Ridge and
the Punchbowl. It suffered 4,038 casualties; 834 KIA, 3170 WIA, 1 missing, 33
POWs before the armistice in July 1953.

Having spent one year and 29 days as a leader of a machine gun squad, Sgt.
McWhirt, Sr. returned to the States. On May 21, 1954, Sgt. Allen McWhirt, Sr.
married PFC June (Joan) Schmeichel at the Army Chapel at Fort Lee, VA.

Sgt. Allen McWhirt, Sr. was awarded the following citations: the Combat
Infantry Badge, the Korean Service Medal with two bronze stars, the United Nations Medal, and the National Defense Medal with one overseas bar.

Discharged on November 11, 1954 at Fort Devens, MA, Allen and his
new wife returned home where Allen worked as a equipment operator and mechanic for the Town of Hillsdale Highway Dept. under superintendents John Pollock, Sr. and Ed Rodman.

For the next few decades, Allen and June lived in Hillsdale, NY and raise their
three children.

Allen enjoyed hunting, fishing, trapping, swimming and playing horse shoes
with family and friends. In 1956 he joined the Cadby Shutts Post #7552 VFW in
Hillsdale, NY.

On October 30, 1964 Allen Lee McWhirt, Sr. passed away in the Veteran's
Hospital in Albany, NY. He was buried at the United Methodist Church Cemetery
in North Hillsdale, NY. He was 32 years old.

Military service is a legacy that Allen instilled in his family. Several members
of his family have served in the armed forces or are now presently serving. We
are grateful for his and their service to our country.

Ralph Melino, Sr.

Ralph Melino was born July 20, 1933 to Joseph and Lucinda (Garafalo) Melino in Hudson, NY. Raised in Hudson, he attended St. Mary's Catholic School
before enlisting in the Armed Services.

Ralph entered the United States Army on April 16, 1953. After his basic training, he was assigned to post war Germany with the American occupational forces
as a stalwart member of NATO.

NATO was initiated as a deterrent to the growing threat of communism
throughout the world, specifically Soviet Russia and satellite countries in Western Europe.

It was while driving a jeep in Munich, Germany with Company A., 2nd Infantry Regiment, 5th Infantry Division that PFC Ralph Melino, Sr. was injured in an
accident. This resulted in a plate being placed in his left eye socket and the per-

manent and partial lose of sight in that eye.

On March 12, 1955, PFC Ralph Melino, Sr. returned to the States. He was honorably discharged on March 31, 1961.

Ralph married Denise Crowley and they raised two children: Ralph, Jr. and Judy. He worked as a construction equipment operator with Faxon Excavating of Ghent at the time of his death.

Ralph remained active in his community. He was a member and past state vice commander of the Phillmont Minkler /Seery American Legion Post 252, a member of Ghent VFW, member and Americanism Chairman of Hudson Elks #787 as well as a VA volunteer. The numerous offices that he faithfully served with these organizations are lasting testaments to his commitment to country and community.

Ralph Melino passed away on September 1, 1989 and was buried at Sacred Heart Cemetery in Philmont, NY. He leaves behind his wife, Denise, son and daughter-in-law, Ralph and Mary Melino, Jr., daughter and son-in-law, Judy and Kevin Skype, and two grandchildren, Kody and Jenna Skype. Ralph was 56 years old.

Thomas C. Merante

Thomas C. Merante was born July 10, 1931 in Niagara Fall, NY to Agnes (Scott) and Dominic Merante.

Thomas enlisted and entered the United States Army on Dec. 31, 1948. After receiving military training in the States, Thomas was assigned to Battery D, 507th Antiaircraft Artillery, Automatic Weapons Battalion at Camp McGill, Japan.

On Sunday, June 25, 1950 communist forces from North Korea crossed the 38th Parallel into the Republic of Korea. Having first been place on alert, a detachment (mostly volunteers) from the 507th , was assigned to an air-transported mission of an unknown destination. Known as Detachment X, it was comprised of three officers and 32 men who operated four M-55, quadruple-mounted .50 caliber machine guns. One of those men was PFC Thomas Merante.

On Thursday, June 29, PFC Thomas Merante along with Detachment X boarded C-54 airplanes and flew to South Korea. Still smoldering from a previous attack, they unloaded the M-55's at Suwon Airfield and prepared for an imminent attack. Shortly before dusk, four planes approached the airfield, bombing and strafing as they approached. PFC. Merante's position was hit and he was wounded in the left leg by shell fragments.

PFC Merante was evacuated from Korean by Gen. Douglas MacArthur's two seated plane. Credited with being the first soldier wounded in the Korean Conflict, his photograph appeared in Life Magazine and in numerous newspapers at the time. U.S. Sen. Irving Ives (R-NY) visited him at Walter Reed Hospital, and his wife wrote a letter of reassurance to his parents in Hudson.

Thomas was honorably discharged on June 9, 1950 and returned to Hudson where he married Ann D'Angelo in 1958 and raised a son, Peter.

Thomas remained active in community affairs. He was a respected member of Mt. Carmel Church and VFW Post 1314. Known for his generosity, Thomas gave freely and often to the needy.

In 1969 he was credited with the rescue of a 9-year-old girl from drowning in the Hudson River. Letters of recognition were sent from then Congressman Hamilton Fish, Jr., Gov. Nelson Rockefeller, and President Ronald Reagan.

Having worked at Kadin Brothers where he retired, Thomas Merante died on March 5, 1989 and is buried at Cedar Park Cemetery, Hudson, NY.

PFC Thomas Merante was awarded the Purple Heart, Bronze Star with "V", Army of Occupation Medal (Japan), Korean Service Medals with Star and the State of NY Conspicuous Service Medal.

As he was in life, Thomas Merante will be remembered for his dedicated service to his country, his community, and his fellow man.

Rondell John Mercer

Rondell John Mercer was born August 15, 1918 in Pleasant Valley, NY. He graduated from Millerton High School and attended SUNY at Delhi.

Rondell enlisted in the United States Marine Corp on November 26, 1942 at Pittsfield, MA. He went to Parris Island where he took basic training and then to New River, NC where he was trained as a radio operator. Cpl. Mercer was assigned to the 4th Signal Company, Headquarters Battalion, 4th Marine Division at Camp Pendleton, CA, which subsequently was assigned to the Pacific Theater of Operation.

For the next two years Cpl. Mercer would become engaged in some of the toughest fighting in the Pacific. He saw action in the Battle of Roi and Namur (Feb. 1-12, 1944), Saipan (June15-July9, 1944), Tinian (July 24 - Aug. 2, 1944) and Iwo Jima (Feb 19-March 16, 1945).

For his service to his country, Cpl. Mercer received the following: Asiatic Pacific Service Ribbon (three stars), American Campaign Robbon, WWII Victory Medal, USMC Achievement Award, Presidential Unit Citation (one star), and two letters of commendation from the Commanding General of the 4th Marine Division for: "excellent service in the line of duty as radio maintenance man during the invasion and capture of Saipan, Marianas Island 15 June to 9 July, 1944" and "for excellent service during operations against the enemy on Iwo Jima, Volcano Islands".

Rondell married Julie (Christenson) on July 6, 1946 and they raised three children: Ellen, Peter and Joan. He was the head of transportation for, and retired from, the Chatham Central School District.

He was an avid sportsman and was a member of the Kinderhook Sportsmen's Club. Although he rarely spoke of his military experiences, he was proud to have been a marine and remained active in veteran's affairs. He was a charter member of Ghent VFW Post 5933 where he served as commander and was granted a life membership.

John Arthur Mesick

John A. Mesick was born October 4, 1924 to Ernest and Juanita (Raught) Mesick in Valatie, NY. He grew up in Ghent and attended school in Columbia County.

John entered the United States Army on March 8, 1943. He qualified as a sharpshooter with the M1 carbine in basic training and received additional training as an artillery crewman on a 155 Howitzer. John was assigned to the European Theater of Operation with Battery C, 21st Field Artillery Battalion, 5th Infantry Division, 3rd Army. His unit was active in Northern France, Rhineland, Ardennes-Alsace and Central Europe.

Cpl. John A. Mesick made an amphibious landing in the first wave on D Day Omaha Beach, Normandy Coast. Confronted by a fortified seawall comprised of artillery, machine guns and land mines, it resulted in 2,400 American casualties.

Making his way across Europe, Cpl. John Mesick saw heavy action throughout Europe at places like the Battle of the Bulge and aided in liberating Buchenwald, a concentration camp. During his service he was temporarily listed as missing in action.

In defending a French town in fierce combat, Cpl. John Mesick was awarded the Croix de Guerre (Cross of War), a high French military honor, by Gen. Charles DeGaulle. In addition, he was awarded the EAME Theater Ribbon with five Bronze Stars and the Good Conduct Medal.

Returning home July 5, 1945, he was honorably discharged on October 4, 1945 at Camp Atterbury, IN.

John returned to Columbia County, met and married Frances Gustafson on August 6, 1949 and they raised four children: Jack, Chris, Jim and Pati.

Working for the Columbia Rensselaer Telephone Company for the next 45 years, he served his community as mayor, police chief and fire chief of Chatham.

He was a life member of Ghent VFW #5933, the Chatham American Legion Post #42 and the Ground Observer Corps during the" Cold War." He had a passion for fishing, hunting and golfing with his primary love for his family.

John passed away on December 31, 2019 at the Albany VA Hospital. He left behind his loving wife of 70 years, Frances, three children: Chris, Jim, and Pati, seven grandchildren, and several nieces and nephews. He was buried with military honors at St. James Cemetery in Ghent, NY. John was 95 years old.

Richard Irving Mesick

Richard Irving Mesick was born May 20, 1930 to John and Beatrice (Warfield) Mesick in Spencertown, NY. He attended Spencertown Academy and was graduated from Chatham High School in 1948 in three and a half years.

Richard enlisted in the United States Navy on October 14, 1948 in Albany, NY. After his basic training at Great Lakes, he trained as a gunner's mate, which consisted of the operation, maintenance and troubleshooting of Naval guns, basic explosives, small arms, Naval ammunition classification and safety. It was then at a dance that he met his future wife, Edna Vosburgh.

GM3 Richard Mesick was assigned to the USS Soley (DD 707), which hailed out of Guantanamo Bay, Cuba and conducted anti-submarine and hunter-killer exercises with Task Force 81 along the eastern seaboard. Assigned to Hunter-Killer Task Force 24 in October 1949, the USS Soley participated in the Second Fleet exercise in the North Atlantic.

The USS Soley was in the Panama Canal when hostilities broke out on the Korean Peninsula. The USS Soley, assigned to the 6th Fleet, cruised the Mediterranean and the Northern European coast. It had the honor to represent the United States at the funeral of King Gustavus V of Sweden.

Richard married Edna on December 16, 1951 just before being assigned to the USS Ault (DD 698). As part of the 6th Fleet, the USS Ault cruised the Atlantic visiting England, France, Guantanamo Bay and Norfolk, Va.

GM3 Richard Mesick was honorably discharged at Norfolk, Va. on October 3, 1952.

In the ensuing years, Richard worked as an insurance salesman, a real estate agent, paint store owner and a self-employed painter/contractor.

He and Edna raised four children: Pamela, Patricia, Richard W., and Randall.

At the age of 40, Richard was stricken with a severe heart condition, which rendered him disabled. However, remaining active in his community, he was a member of the Ghent VFW, the Ghent Fire Company and the Masons.

Richard, 45, died on August 25, 1975 and was laid to rest in the Ghent Union Cemetery. In addition to his wife and children, he is survived by eight grandchildren.

John J. Mettler, Jr.

John J. Mettler, Jr. was born on February 7, 1923 in Hillsdale, NY to John and Lillian Mettler. He attended school in Hillsdale, graduating from Roeliff Jansen High School and studied veterinary medicine at Cornell University. Graduating in 1944 with a Doctorate of Veterinary Medicine, Dr. Mettler enlisted in the United States Army on July 10, 1944.

As a veterinarian, Dr. Mettler was commissioned in the quartermaster corps as a captain and was assigned to the Pacific Theater of Operation. Cpt. Mettler's responsibilities as a meat and dairy inspector consisted in part to ensure the safety of food products for the armed services in places like Guam, Saipan, Oahu and Chichi Jima.

His service extended beyond V-J Day until February 14, 1947, where he was discharged at Camp Beale, CA and returned to civilian life. For his service he was awarded the Asiatic Pacific Service Medal and the WWII Victory Medal.

For the next 38 years, Dr. Mettler served the community of Hillsdale as a veterinarian. He married Elinor Fox on July 19, 1947 at St. Bridget's in Copake Falls and in the ensuing years, he and his wife raised six children: Partrick, Jo Ann, Jeanne, Margaret, Sally, and Suzanne.

Dr. Mettler remained active in community affairs. He was a member of the Roeliff Jansen PTA, Lions Club, and Historical Society, Copake Fire Co. #2, Cadby Shutts VFW Quartermaster, NYS Veterinary Medical Society, Hudson Valley Medical Society president, chairman of Copake Planning Board and Zoning Board, assessor and contributed articles for magazines and authored three books.

Dr. Mettler died on March 27, 2001 and was remembered by his friends and associates as *"one of the most caring, honest persons"* with a *"strong sense of community"* and *"social conscience."* He was *"respected for his wisdom, his sense of humor, his character and respect for others. He touched a lot of people's lives in such a positive way,"* and was *"sorely missed by the community he served so well."*

Dr. Mettler was buried at St. Bridget's of Copake Falls. He was 78 years old.

Armour Conway Miller

Armour Conway Miller was born in Hudson, NY on April 18, 1921 to Azro Harmon and Martha (Conway) Miller. He attended the Claverack Elementary School and graduated from Romford Academy, CT. After one year at Cornell University, Armour enlisted in the United States Army Air Corps.

Upon completing his initial training, Cpt. Armour Miller was trained as a fighter pilot. He was subsequently assigned as a P38 pilot to the 1st Fighter

Group, 27th Squadron in the 15th Air Force in the European Theater of Operation.

As a fighter pilot Armour distinguished himself by shooting down six enemy aircraft and damaging two, thus, making him a fighter ace. Among his daring exploits, while serving as formation leader, he participated in a raid on the Ploesti Oil Fields.

It was believed that the Romano-Americano refinery at Ploesti was supplying one-third of the fuel oil for Nazi Germany. This highly controversial day light operation planned to have American bombers fly exceptionally low over the tightly defended refineries at Ploesti, Romania.

On Sunday, August 1, 1943 the mission was undertaken and deemed a success, thus greatly restricting the flow of oil or life blood to the Nazi war machine.

Of the 177 bombers taking part in the raid, 54 were lost and 53 additional were heavily damaged. Five Medals of Honor were awarded to the participants of this raid, the single most in any American military action. The 1st Fighter Group suffered its highest casualties of any mission in WWII.

Armour Miller would attain the rank of captain before being honorably discharged from military service.

For his service to his country during WWII, Cpt. Armour Miller was awarded the following: a Presidential Citation, the Distinguished Flying Cross and the Silver Star.

Returning home, Armour went into business with his brother, David. They owned and operated J.T. Lampman and Co., which manufactured feed and flour and various agricultural supplies in Claverack, NY. It would become Red Mills Inc. where he would serve as owner/president.

Armour married his first wife, Nita Newbold in May 1945 and they had three children: Martha, Thomas and Jeane. In June of 1964 he married his second wife, Betty Jane Ellenberger of Hudson, NY, and Nicholas, his fourth child, was born.

Active in his community, Armour was a member of the Phi Gamma Delta Fraternity, the University Club of Albany, and past president (12 yrs) of the Columbia Golf and Country Club.

Armour Conway Miller passed away on July 26, 1996 at the age of 75. He is buried at Cedar Park Cemetery, Hudson, NY. He left behind a loving wife, Betty, four children and several grandchildren.

Emmett Elliot Miller

Emmett Elliot Miller was born September 20, 1916 to Emmett and Emma Miller in West Taghkanic, NY. Growing up on the family farm with two brothers and two sisters, he attended Hudson High School.

Working as a diesel mechanic, Emmett enlisted on June 22, 1943 in New York City. After basic training at the Naval Training Station at Sampson, NY (West Seneca Lake), he attended additional training for diesel engines and then advanced diesel engines at Richmond, VA and Schoemaker, CA.

Motor Machinist Mate First Class (MM1) Emmett Miller was assigned to the Pacific Theater of Operations during WWII as a diesel mechanic and carpenter. First assigned to US Naval base at Guiuan, Philippines, he was then assigned to Manicani Island in Leyte Gulf, Philippines.

During the World War II, Manicani was a major naval repair facility, which maintained and repaired ships of the Pacific fleet. At its peak, Manicani Naval Facilities housed and accommodated up to 10,000 personnel. This facility was instrumental in maintaining a naval fleet that would ultimately culminate in the unconditional surrender of the Imperial Japanese forces and the closure of hostility of World War II.

MM1 Emmett Miller was honorably discharged on December 16, 1945 at Lido Beach, Long Island, NY.

For his service to his country MM1 Emmett Miller was awarded the following: Asiatic & Pacific Ribbon, American Theater Ribbon, Philippine Liberation Medal and the Victory Medal.

Emmet returned home and worked for the Columbia County Highway Department as a mechanic.

He married Melissa Windsor on Long Island and they raised two daughters: Deborah and Terry.

His granddaughter Kim recalls that; Emmett was a *"quiet and modest man who was very spiritual."* He was *"very active in his church congregation and was instrumental in planning and building the Trinity United Methodist Church in Hudson and was a member of its men's church club."* Emmet was an avid gardener and *"took pride in the vegetable and flower garden he cared for in his backyard."*

Emmet passed away on January 6, 1993 at his residence in Greenport. He was buried in the West Taghkanic Cemetery. He left behind a loving wife, two daughters, six grandchildren and five great-grandchildren. Emmet was 79 years old.

Francis William Miller

Francis William Miller was born October 29, 1948 in Hudson, NY to Ann (Breler) and William G. Miller. He attended Germantown Elementary and High schools.

On April 13, 1966 Francis enlisted for three years in the United States Marine Corps at the age of seventeen. After his basic training at Paris Island, SC, Francis trained as a repair shop machinist at Quantico, VA. In November of 1967, he received his GED, thus completing his high school education.

Sgt. Francis William Miller was assigned to a duty station in the Republic of South Vietnam where he worked on helicopters near the DMZ. After his tour of combat duty he was assigned to the 1st Marine Air Wing at the Marine Corps Air Station at El Toro (Santa Ana), CA.

Sgt. Miller was honorably discharged from active duty on April 2, 1969 and was transferred to the United States Marine Corps Reserves.

Sgt Francis William Miller was awarded the following citations: Rifle Marksman Badge, Good Conduct Medal (1st Award), National Defense Service Medal, Vietnam Service Medal and the Vietnam Campaign Medal.

Francis returned to Elizaville, NY where he joined VFW Post #7765 of Red Hook, NY.

Tragically, on June 2, 1969 Francis was killed by a drunk driver who had crossed into his lane on Rte 66. Home for only two months, he was buried in Cedar Park Cemetery in Hudson, NY. He was only 20 years old.

Clayton A. Mink

Clayton A. Mink was born October 8, 1920 to Charles and Lottie (Dewitt) Mink in Hudson, NY.

He enlisted in the United States Army on January 24, 1941 in Albany, NY. After basic training, he was given advanced training as an Army Air Corp aerial gunner.

Staff Sgt. Clayton A. Mink was assigned to the European Theater of Occupation with the 8th Air Force, 34th Bomb Group, 7th Bomb Squadron. Flying from Mendlesham Air Base, England, SSG Mink logged 21 combat missions on a B-24 called "The Nearsighted Robin." Completing additional training in a B-17, he was temporally assigned as a ball turret gunner on "The Wrangler," a B-17 on a mission to Kassel, Germany.

Several hours into the flight "The Wrangler" developed a hydraulic oil leak in the ball turret, causing the turret to malfunction and loss of visibility. The pilot then ordered SSG Mink to vacate the turret. While flying over Paderborn, Germany another B-17 collided with the tail section of "The Wrangler."

Amid sub zero temperatures and having exhausted the oxygen at 25,000 feet, SSG Clayton Mink and five of his ten flight crew managed to successfully exit the crippled airplane.

He was captured by German guards, incarcerated (Paderborn), interrogated (Frankfurt) and then transported by train (40x8 box car) to Stalag-Luft IV, near Grossstchow, Germany.

In the seven months of captivity, SSG Clayton A. Mink endured harshest treatment as a POW, which included interrogation, inhuman transportation in cramped cattle cars, prodded by bayonet, snarling police dogs, cramped living conditions, slept on straw-strewn barracks, meager rations, the monotonous and dreary life in captivity, physical abuse by insensitive guards, pangs of hunger, lacking basic medical treatment, an 80-day winter march along a highway "covered with vomit, slime and human excrement."

He describes the "death march" as "unbelievable, grueling, excruciating, horrible, inhumane, depressing and degrading. Where men (were) falling by the roadside physically unable to continue. Others who fell by the roadside no longer needed medical attention . . . (it was a mass of men with) gaunt facial features, long dirty hair, thin, unshaven, unbathed bodies covered with lice and body odors permeating the air."

SSG Clayton A. Mink was liberated on April 26, 1945 at Bitterfeld, Germany by a unit from the 104th Division and returned to the United States, and was discharged at Ft. Dix, NJ. He was awarded the Air Medal w/ two Oak Leaf Clusters, AMS Medal, EMES Medal and the Good conduct Medal.

He met and married Helen (Ward) on Oct. 26, 1945 and they had two children: Sharon and Pamela. He worked for the Columbia Co. Highway Dept. and retired after 25 years in 1983.

He was the past president of the Columbia Co. Civil Service Assoc., past commander of the Am. Legion Post the past president of the Admin. Board and Men's Club of the Germantown United Methodist Church. He was chairman of the Pastor's Relations Committee and recording church secretary.

Clayton died on May 12, 2010 and was buried at the Valley View Cemetery, German Town, NY. He left behind two daughters and two grandchildren. He was 89 years old.

Guy Minkler

Guy Minkler was born to Calvin and Sara Minkler in Stockbridge, MA on August 22, 1891. Growing up in Philmont, NY he attended the elementary course in the district school in Philmont. He met and married Florence Coyn and they raised a son, George.

In March of 1914 Guy enlisted in the United States Army. After basic training Sgt. Guy Minkler was assigned to the Infantry.

In the following years, he served in the Philippines, Texas, Mexico and at Fort William McKinley. In 1916 he was transferred to Camp Syracuse, NY and for the next eighteen months he served as a supply sergeant with Company A, 9th Infantry, 2nd Division .

In September 1917 the 2nd Division or the "Indianhead" Division, commanded by Maj. Gen. James G. Harford, landed in France and was assigned to the American Expeditionary Force (AEF) under the command of Gen. John J. (Blackjack) Pershing.

Sgt. Guy Minkler saw action at Bouresches, Belleau Wood, the Marne and Chateau Thierry. At 4:35 a.m. on July 18, 1918, while a "violent thunderstorm pelted the allies as they hurried into formation" the 2nd Division advanced "behind an artillery barrage," Sgt. Guy Minkler was killed in action at Chateau Thierry and was buried with the 9th Infantry Division at Oise-Aisne. He left behind a wife, Florence, and a son, George. He was 26 years old.

Howard P. Montague

Howard P. Montague was born March 27, 1926 to William and Loletia (Huddleston) Montague in Hudson, NY. Growing up in Philmont, he attended elementary and high school.

Howard entered the United States Navy on February 8, 1944 in Albany, NY. After finishing recruit training at Sampson, NY, Howard received additional training at Electricians Mate School at Sampson, NY, Degaussing School at Norfolk, VA and Firefighters School at Brooklyn, NY.

EM3 Howard Montague was assigned to the Pacific Theater of Operations on the USS Jesse Ruthford (D.E.347). Commissioned on May 31, 1944 this destroyer escort was named after mortally wounded Pvt. Jesse Ruthford who received the Navy Cross on the USS Lexington at the battle of the Coral Sea.

From the staging base on Manus Island, the USS Jesse Ruthford was assigned convoy escort to Leyte Gulf in support of recapturing the Philippines. During the ensuing months, the USS Jesse Ruthford escorted numerous convoys in the Pacific including escort duty to Okinawa, patrolling San Bernardino Strait, participating in the landing of allied forces at Borneo.

EM3 Howard Montague was honorably discharged on March 5, 1946 at Lido Beach, LI. For his service he was awarded the American Theater Medal, Asiatic Pacific Medal, Philippine Liberation Medal, and the Victory Medal.

Marrying Verna Boyles on September 25, 1945, Howard returned home and became co-owner and president of Montague Coal and Oil Co. and a school bus company, the Howard Montague Inc. He and Verna raised seven children: Carol, Bill, Linda, Paula, Phyllis, Richard and Howard.

He remained active in his community. He was past president of the Philmont Rotary Club, served on the Ockawamick School Board, commissioner of the Mellenville Fire Company, Post Commander of Minkler-Seery American Legion Post 252, and assessor for the Town of Claverack.

Howard passed away on June 25, 2010 and was buried in the Sacred Heart Cemetery, Philmont, NY. He left behind his wife of 66 years, Verna, seven children, 17 grandchildren and 13 great grandchildren. He was 84 years old.

Ronald Montague

Ronald Montague was born June 12, 1924 to Mr. and Mrs. William Montague of Philmont. He graduated from Philmont High School and enlisted in the United States Marine Corps on November 2, 1942.

After receiving training at Parris Island, SC, Camp Lejune, NC, and Camp Pendleton, CA, Ronald was assigned to the 4th Marine Division as a machine gunner.

Cpl. Ronald Montague participated in four major engagements in the South Pacific; Roi-Namur in the Marshall Islands, Saipan and Tinian in the Mariana Islands and Iwo Jima. On Tinian, his heroic actions earned him the Purple Heart and Bronze Star for:

> *"...heroic achievement in action against the enemy while serving as a gunner in a machine gun squad of an assault rifle company . . . after being wounded by the enemy who had made two direct assaults with hand grenades and grenade launchers on this position..."*

During the attack, the gun crew ran low on ammo and Ronald went for supplies. Although painfully wounded, he continued fighting, leaving three dead enemy at the edge of the foxhole. He refused evacuation until further danger from enemy attacks ended.

On February 19, 1945 elements of the 3rd, 4th, and 5th Marine Divisions landed on Iwo Jima against an opposing force of 20,000 Japanese. It took several weeks of fierce fighting to secure the island by late March. One soldier wrote:

> *"It takes courage to stay at the front on Iwo Jima. It takes something we can't tag or classify to push out ahead of these lines, against an unseen enemy ... an enemy capable of suddenly appearing on your flanks or even at your rear, and of disappearing back into his hole ... It takes courage to crawl ahead, 100 yards a day, and get up the next morning, count your losses, and do it again. But that's the way it can be done."*

The price for Iwo Jima would be 5,453 dead and a total of 23,573 casualties. Adm. Nimitz would say of Iwo Jima, "Uncommon valor was a common virtue."

Cpl. Ronald Montague was killed on Iwo Jima on March 4, 1945 and was awarded the following citations: Bronze Star, Purple Heart with star, Presidential Unit Citation and Asiatic Pacific Medal with four stars. His body was exhumed from Iwo Jima at the family's request in 1948 and re-interred in Philmont's Union Cemetery.

Just 21, Cpl. Ronald Montague had that "uncommon valor."

Mary First Moon

Mary First was born October 11, 1921 to Frank and Eva (Ziemba) First in Hudson, NY. Growing up in Hudson, Mary attended Hudson Central School, graduating in 1940. She graduated in 1944 from Hudson City School of Nursing.

As a registered nurse, Mary worked at Columbia Presbyterian Hospital in New York City until she entered the service.

Mary entered the Army Nursing Corp as a registered nurse on May 1, 1945 with the rank of 2nd lieutenant. Assigned to the Station Hospital 1976th Service Command Unit, she performed general nursing duties.

2nd Lt. Mary First was one of more than 59,000 American nurses who served in the Army Nurse Corps during World War II. Their skill and dedication contributed to the extremely low post-injury mortality rate among American military. Thus, fewer than four percent of those who received medical care for wounds or disease died during WWII.

This is a credit to the skill and care provided by the nurses like 2nd Lt. Mary First. Because of demobilization, she was honorably discharged on June 16, 1946 at Camp Beale, CA.

For her service, 2nd Lt. Mary First was awarded the following: American Campaign Medal, WWII Victory Medal and the Meritorious Service Unit Plaque.

Mary returned home and went to work at Hudson City Hospital as a registered nurse.

She met and married Roland F. Moon on June 8, 1947. Becoming a full time homemaker, they raised three children: Robert, Marcia and Brian. Mary developed a reputation as a professional wedding cake baker. She belonged to the Nurses Bowling League and was a life-long member of the Sacred Heart Catholic Church in Hudson, NY.

Mary passed away on April 15, 1965 and is buried at Cedar Park Cemetery in Hudson, NY. She is survived by her three children, five grandchildren and one great-grandchild. Mary was 43 years old.

Roland F. Moon, Sr.

Roland F. Moon was born September 14, 1923 in Hudson, NY to Floyd and Viola (Curran) Moon. After graduating from Hudson High School, he enrolled in Syracuse University as a business major, where he was drafted into the Army on February 12, 1943.

After basic training he received additional training at Radio Mechanic School and Gunnery School in North and South Dakota. As a radio operator mechanic/ gunner, Staff Sgt. Roland F. Moon was assigned on January 16, 1945 to 601st Squadron, 398th Bomb Group, 8th Air Force in Nuthamstead, England.

As a radio operator on a B 17 S/Sgt. Roland Moon was responsible for receiving and sending directions, orders, keeping contact with airplanes in flight, radio mechanics as well as manning one of the 50 caliber machine guns located in the ceiling of his compartment.

He completed 6 combat missions over Europe as radio operator and while on his seventh he was wounded by enemy flack. Initially his squadron's mission was Egar, Czechoslovakia, however, the target was clouded over and they flew to the secondary target of Schweinfurt.

At 12,000 feet his B-17 jettisoned it payload and while coming off target an 88 mm shell penetrated the midsection of the B-17, severed Sgt. Moon's right leg and seriously injured the other. Given immediate medical attention by his crew, the pilot opted to land at an airbase in Nancy, France; where he was given life saving care. After extensive rehabilitation S/Sgt. Roland Moon was honorably discharged in Atlantic City, NJ on April 2, 1946.

For his service S/Sgt. Moon was awarded the following: Purple Heart, American Theater Medal, WW II Victory Medal, ETO Ribbon with Battle Star, and the Good Conduct Medal.

Roland married Mary First and they raised three children: Robert, Marcia and Brian. After Mary's death, Roland married Rosemarie Grandinetti on February 14, 1966 and they raised two children: Maria and Roland, Jr.

Roland was employed as the executive officer and investigator for the ABC Board until 1976 and then as an investigator for the NYS Worker's Comp. Board until 1986. He was owner/operator of "Leader Printing" in Hudson, NY.

Active in his community, Roland was a member of CH. Evans Hook and Ladder #3, Past Trustee of Hudson Elks 787, Commander of VFW Post 1314, life member of American Legion Post 184, board member of the Hudson Boys Club, and secretary of Mutual Racing Assoc.

Roland passed away on November 26, 2004 and was buried in Cedar Park Cemetery, Hudson, NY. He was 81 years old.

Raymond R. Moore Sr.

Raymond R. Moore, Sr. was born to Roland and Laura (Ogden) Moore on April 18, 1919 in Germantown, NY. He attended school in Red Hook and Germantown, graduating from Germantown High School in 1937.

Raymond was inducted in the United States Army on November 24, 1942 in Hudson, NY. He training included Communications Course and Amphibious

Staff and Command School.

As a communications officer he was assigned to the Pacific Theater of Operation with the 132nd Infantry. Capt. Moore saw action in the Northern Solomon Islands, Southern Philippines and Luzon and was wounded on March 29, 1944.

He was honorably discharged April 27, 1946 at Fort Dix, NJ.

Capt. Raymond R. Moore Sr. was awarded the: Bronze Star, Purple Heart, Combat Infantry Badge, Am. Defense Service Medal, Am. Campaign Medal, Asiatic-Pacific Campaign Medal with Bronze Arrowhead, Philippines Liberation Medal and the WWII Victory Medal.

Raymond married Kathrin (Wegfarth) Moore on November 14, 1942 in Columbus, Georgia.

His enduring love was captured in the war letters home, opening with: "Town of Heaven," "Date of Love," "19 Kisses," "Hugs" punctuated by the year it was mailed. In the ensuing years, he and Kathrin would raise six children: Carol, Maureen, Barbara, Pamela, Raymond and Ronald.

Raymond worked in several capacities after returning home: tractor, truck and chauffer driver, owner and operator with his mother) the 7th Street Hudson Paint Store, an agent for Prudential Insurance, and custodian for the Germantown Central School.

He remained active in community affairs. Showing movies at the American Legion Hall and coaching Little League expressed his love of children. He was a member of the Masons, Germantown American Legion, VFW and Volunteer Fire Company.

Raymond R. Moore Sr. died on August 22, 1980 and was buried in the Germantown Reformed Church Cemetery. He left behind his wife, mother, six children, and twelve grandchildren.   He was 61 years old.

Walter C. Morris

Walter Chester Morris was born August 21, 1937 to John S. and Evelyn (Quinon) Morris in Ghent, NY. Growing up in Columbia County, he attended Philmont Public School.

Living in Stottville and working as a construction machine operator, Walter entered the United States Army on August 4, 1956 in Albany, NY. Upon successfully completing basic training at Fort Dix, NJ, Walter was trained as a Bridge Specialist. In addition, he received military courses in: Chemical, Biological and Radiological Training, Survival/Escape and Evasion, Military Justice and Code of Conduct.

SP4 Walter C. Morris was assigned to Schwetzingen, Germany, where he met and married Doris Frank in a civil ceremony in Mannheim on September 26,

1957.

After this tour of duty, he was assigned to Headquarters and Service Company, 91st Combat Engineers Battalion, Ft. Belvoir, VA, as a bridge specialist with the United States Army Corps of Engineers.

Upon the end of his enlistment he was transferred to the United States Army Reserves with II US Army Corps of Engineers and was honorably discharged on August 31, 1962.

Walter worked for Sherman's Cement Plant, then as a tractor trailer driver for Harder's Express in Philmont, NY and finally as a Columbia County Veteran's Van driver until his retirement in 2012. He was a shop steward for the Teamsters Union Local #294, a member of the American Legion, Korean War Veterans and a volunteer at the VA hospital.

His daughter recalls that Walter's military service was the "best time of his life" and he was "always ready to serve and assist a veteran." Always smiling, he was a "grand example of service to our country. We miss that smile."

Walter passed away on April 29, 2014 and was buried in the Ghent Union Cemetery in Ghent, NY. He was survived by his daughter Susan, a sister Dorothy, a brother Alfred and two grandchildren; Andrew, Olivia. He was 76 years old.

Clifford William Mossman

Clifford William Mossman was born in Taghkanic, NY on February 12, 1913 to George and Florence Mossman. He grew up in Philmont, worshipped at the Philmont United Methodist Church and graduated from Philmont High School. He was known to his friends as "Grit" because of his outstanding athletic ability. His friends recall,

Clifford *"excelled at basketball . . . (however) . . . baseball was his game and batting left-handed he was considered a heavy hitter. He played in the outfield because of his strong throwing arm."*

On September 30, 1933 Clifford was married to Mattie Rasmussen and was employed as a spinner at High Rock Mills.

On November 6, 1942 he joined the United States Navy and he was trained as a signalman. SM1 Clifford Mossman was one of the original members assigned to LCI (G)- 365 (Landing Craft Infantry).

Built at Lawley Shipyards just south of Boston in 1943, this 158-foot landing craft was used to escort larger ships and to transport troops.

On July 21,1944 during the landing of Guam, USS LCI (G)-365 took 10 direct hits from shore guns, killing seven men and wounding fifteen. Clifford was one of those killed. A

As one sailor stated, *(it) "was designed for one purpose . . . One run to the beach, and you're gone, you're history. We lost seven kids, killed outright in the battle of Guam. The ship looked like a piece of cheese and ended up going back to Pearl Harbor to be rehabilitated."*

Fifty-seven years later, Lt. Hector would tell Wes Mossman, SM1 Clifford Mossman's son, "He was a really fine shipmate, a very popular person, and truly was an example to the other kids . . . a war hero, indeed he was."

SM1 Clifford Mossman was awarded the following: Bronze Star, the Purple Heart, and Asiatic Pacific Campaign Ribbon among others.

He left behind a widow and two small children: Bruce Wayne (6) and Wesley Clifford (4). At the time of his death, he was 31 years old.

Clinton J. Mossman, Sr.

Clint J. Mossman, Sr. was born on December 30, 1923 in Philmont, NY to Phillip and Lillian (Rockefeller) Mossman where he grew up and attended school.

Employed as a shipping clerk, he was drafted into the United States Army on January 4, 1943 in Albany, NY and was trained as a driver of a medium tank.

Assigned to the 264th Armored Replacement Battalion (5th Division) in the European Theater of Operations during WWII, Tec/5 Sgt. Clint Mossman fought in Naples, Foggia, Rome and Arno Campaigns in Italy.

While serving in combat, Clint was wounded by shrapnel in the knee. On February 28, 1946, Clint was honorably discharged at Fort Dix, NJ.

For his service he was awarded the following: Purple Heart, American Service Medal, EAME Service Medal, Good Conduct Medal and the World War II Victory Medal.

He told his mother, "God willing, if I'm lucky to return, I'll never leave Philmont."

True to his word, Clint returned to Columbia County and raised a family. During the next several decades, he worked for High Rock Mills, Fosters Refrigeration and Charter Supply and retired after 28 years. For the next 12 years, he worked for Michael Johnston Bus Company.

Clint was 1st vice commander/commander of Minkler-Seery American Legion Post 252, life member of Ghent VFW Post 5933, past commander of Columbia County American Legion, member of Claverack Lions Club, secretary and treasurer for Columbia Republican Committee, Columbia-Green Selective Service Committee, Boy Scout master, charter member and past president of the Philmont Rescue Squad, life member and president of the Rotary Club and life member of the Philmont Fire Co..

In addition, he served as trustee and chairman of the Philmont Planning Board, mayor of Philmont for more than 25 years, chairman of the WWII Cannon Committee, member of Monument Committee, and Columbia County Republican Executive Committee.

In 2001, Clint, along with other WWII veterans received their high school diplomas from Taconic Hills Central School.

Clint died on January 10, 2005 and laid to rest in the Mellenville Union Cemetery. He left behind his lovely wife Carol, a son Clint, Jr., a step-daughter Haidee and three grandchildren. He was 81years old.

Lewis Henry Mueller

Lewis Henry Mueller was born on August 23, 1924 to William and Mae (Helsey) Mueller in Germantown, NY. He attended Hudson elementary and high schools.

Lewis worked for Stottville Mills as a garnet machine operator before he enlisted in the United States Navy on January 12, 1943. After basic training at Sampson, NY, Lewis received training as a gunners mate at Newport RI.

On December 1, 1943, 1st Class Petty Officer Gunners Mate (GM1) Lewis reported aboard the USS LST 273 and on April 11, 1944 he was assigned to the USS LC (L) 1069 and attended AA Gunnery School. GM1 actively served during the assault and occupation of Okinawa and Japan.

He was honorably discharged at Lido Beach, L.I., NY on November 26, 1946.

GM1 Lewis Mueller was awarded the following: American Theater of War and the Asiatic Pacific Campaign Ribbon with two bronze stars.

Lewis married Hilda Ogden on March 29, 1947 in Hudson, NY. They raised four children: Alan, Carol, Gail and Colleen.

Lewis was owner and operator of Mueller's Grocery and the MGM Market. He worked for NY State Assembly for 30 years, retiring as foreman of the printing department in 1979.

Lewis served as 4th Ward alderman(4yrs), supervisor (16yrs), assist. chairman of the Board of Supervisors, chairman of Columbia County Civil Service and ABC Board. He received the Hudson Boys Club Man of the Year, and the Hudson Republican Party Abraham Lincoln Award.

He was a communicant of the St. Mark's Lutheran Church, Federation of Polish Sportsman, American Legion Post #184, VFW Post #1314, and H.W. Rogers Hose Company #2. He was remembered as "a very kind and devoted husband, father, grandfather, and great-grandfather . . . committed to helping people and his community."

Lewis passed away July 21, 2017 and is buried at Cedar Park Cemetery. He left behind his lovely wife, Hilda, and four children Gail, Carol, Alan and Colleen, seven grandchildren and sixteen great-grandchildren. He was 92.

James P. Mullins

James P. Mullins was born March 11, 1923 in New York City to Jeremiah and Catherine Ann Mullins where he attended St Veronica's Elementary and Chelsea Vocational School.

He entered the U.S. Army on February 11, 1943 in New York City. After receiving Basic and Advance Infantry Training, PFC Mullins was assigned to the 180th Infantry, 45th Division and sailed to North Africa in May of 1943.

From Casablanca, PFC Mullins and his unit convoyed by truck to Oran and then to Bizzerte by boxcar. On July 10, 1943, he made his first amphibious landing (LCT) in the invasion of Sicily.

With the end of hostilities, he and the 180th Infantry made their second amphibious landing at Salerno, where they were engaged in heavy mountain fighting all the way to Naples.

As scout and squad leader, PFC Mullins was charged with the difficult and often hazardous task of detecting the enemy and then reporting its size and location. On January 22, 1944 James made his third landing at Anzio.

On February 17, 1944 while engaged in fierce fighting, PFC Mullins was severely wounded in his right upper femur by grenade and rifle fire. For the next 18 months James required hospitalization for medical treatment and rehabilitation.

On August 14, 1945, James was discharged with a medical disability from the U.S. Army at Rhoads General Hospital, Utica, NY.

PFC James P. Mullins received the Purple Heart, Bronze Star, Combat Infantry Badge, Europe-Africa-Middle East Medal with four battle stars, Good Conduct Medal, Am. Campaign Medal, WWII Victory Medal and a Unit Citation.

James returned home and in the ensuing years, he dedicated himself to raising a family and community service.

He was vice commander of Ghent VFW, commander of Chatham American Legion, treasurer of Ghent Fire Co., a member of Ghent Rod and Gun, 45th Division Association, Anzio Beachhead Veterans and Little League coach.

In 1978 he retired from the N.Y.S. Thruway and he served for almost two decades as a councilman for Ghent.

James died January 10, 2002 leaving a lovely wife, Sara, three children, five grandchildren and two great grandchildren. His wife fondly recalled:

"Jim regretted never reaching Rome. However, when he arrived back in the United States, he was delighted when he awoke June 6th to the sound of ship whistles and church bells celebrating the D-Day invasion."

Benjamin A. Murell

Ben's parents, Benjamin and Madeline (Villa) Murell, emigrated from Italy in the late 1800s, met in Torrington, CT, married and gave birth to Benjamin A. Murell on January 7, 1981.

They moved to Columbia Street, Hudson, NY where Benjamin Sr. ran a small house-to-house vegetable route and small store. Later, his father worked in Gifford Woods Sheet Metal Shop as a molder.

Ben, the eldest son, attended St. Mary's Catholic School until his father developed a severe lung ailment, which resulted in Ben having to help raise his four siblings.

Ben's skill and passion for boxing was renowned. This 5-foot-4 son of an Italian immigrant, "Ben the Bomber Murell" became a Golden Gloves contender and a champion of the Adirondack Region.

On January 15, 1941 Ben enlisted in the United States Army. His civilian occupation was listed as pugilist, a professional boxer.

He was trained as a surgical technician or medic. After the advent of WWII, PFC Ben Murell was assigned to the 9th Division, 39th Infantry and saw intense action in Africa and Europe (Algeria-French Morocco, Tunisia, Sicily, Southern France, Normandy, and the Rhineland).

Although an unarmed medic, PFC Murell participated in some of the fiercest battles in Europe and awarded numerous awards, (including Division Boxing Champion).

PFC Ben Murell was discharged from the Army on July 10, 1945 at Fort Dix, NJ. For his heroism and service to his country he was awarded the following: Silver Star, Bronze Star, Purple Heart, Am. Defense Service Medal, Good Conduct Medal, European-African-Middle Eastern Service Medal w/ Silver and Bronze stars, WWII Victory Medal, Conspicuous Service Cross, Normandy Invasion Medal, Germany Occupation Medal, Am Campaign Medal and the WWII Medal; making him the most decorated WWII veteran in Columbia County.

When Ben returned home, he married Gladys and raised their son, Matt (named in honor of Matt Urban, a close friend and Medal of Honor recipient). Numerous organizations will attest to Ben's dedication to his community and his country.

He was a member of the American Legion, VFW, and director of the Columbia County Veteran Services. In addition, he was active in Hudson Elks, Eagles, Moose, Lions clubs (Lion of the Year) and Fire Co. #8, Knights of Columbus, Columbia County Sons and Daughters of Italy, past president (45 yrs) and board member (50 yrs) of Benjamin "the Bomber" Murell Little League, past president (12 yrs) Hudson Boy's Club, Hudson Lions Club, and Fed. of Polish Sportsmen.

Ben held elective office for 42 consecutive years. Among his charges were: Hudson 4th Ward supervisor (30 yrs), alderman City of Hudson (12 yrs) both as majority and minority leader.

Ben, a member of St Mary's, died June 16, 2003, and is buried with his wife in Hudson, NY. In addition to his son, he had one grandson, Andrew. He was 85 years old.

Charles R. Nichols

Charles R. Nichols was born December 22, 1930 to Dr. Charles L. Nichols and Elizabeth R. Nichols in Philmont, NY. Graduating from Philmont High in 1947, Charles attended Albany Academy and then Champlain College (Plattsburgh, NY), majoring in psychology.

Known as Doc, he enlisted in the United States Army on February 7, 1951. After basic training at Ft. Devins, Charles was assigned to Company B, 155th Infantry Regiment, 31 Infantry Division at Fort Jackson, SC. With additional training in leadership and chemical warfare, he was assigned to Company A, 14th Infantry Regiment, 25th Division in Korea.

Known as the Golden Dragons, the 14th Regiment was in almost continual combat in Korea along the 38th parallel in defensive positions or offensive patrols in the areas surrounding Heartbreak Ridge, the Punchbowl and Pork Chop Hill. These efforts earned the Regiment five campaign streamers and a Rep. of Korea Presidential Unit Citation for gallantry at Munsan-Ni; while SFC Charles R. Nichols was awarded the Combat Infantry Badge.

He returned home and honorably discharged on June 12, 1954.

For his service SFC Charles R. Nichols was awarded the following: Combat Infantry Badge, Expert Infantry Badge, and Korean Service Medal with two Bronze Stars, National Defense Service Medal, United Nations Service Medal, New York State Conspicuous Service Cross and the Republic of Korea War Service Medal.

Charles married Phyllis Young on July 29, 1951 and they raised two boys, Charles and Jonathan. He worked for Foster Refrigeration, Hudson, NY and Hudson City Saving Institute, where he retired after 30 years in 1992.

Charles remained active in his community. He was a member of the Philmont Second Reformed Church, Rescue Squad, Health Director, Rod and Gun, and American Legion Post 252; Hudson Masonic Lodge; Claverack Senior Citizens; Columbia County Historical Society, Chapter of the Korean War Veterans Assoc. and Car Club, NYS Sons of the American Revolution, and Military Heritage Institute; as well as Combat Infantrymen's Assoc., Amateur Trap Shooting Assoc., Comp. of Military Historians and Ye Olde Connecticut Gun Guild. In addition he was on the Town of Claverack and Philmont planning boards, and the Columbia County Industrial Development Agency.

Charles passed away on September 4, 2013 at the age of 82. After donating his body to science, his cremated remains were interred in Mellenville Union Cemetery.

Edward Bernard Novak

Edward Bernard Novak was born in Valatie, NY on September 2, 1921 to Frank and Sarah Novak. Moving to Stuyvesant Falls, Edward attended school and was a communicant of St. Mary's Roman Catholic Church.

Prior to enlisting in the United States Marine Corp on July 22, 1942 in Albany, Edward was employed at the Fort Orange Paper Company in Castleton, NY.

PFC Edward Bernard Novak received training at Paris Island, NC and was then assigned to Company C, 1st Battalion, 22nd Marines. His unit would soon be engaged in hostile activities in the Pacific Theater of Operation.

On February 22, 1944 Edward's unit was directed to land and secure Parry Island on the Pacific atoll of Eniwetok in the Marshall Islands.

Ordered to advance and secure their first objective (a line of enemy trenches and dugouts), PFC Edward Bernard Novak's platoon landed in the first wave on this ring-shaped coral island. While advancing amid a fierce fusillade of Japanese mortar and machinegun fire, PFC Edward Bernard Novak was struck and killed. He was 22 years old.

PFC Novak's company commander wrote to Edward's parents the following:

> *"Edward was a fine Marine and an excellent example of American manhood which is carrying on the present struggle in which our nation is engaged. He was well liked by his fellow Marines, and his passing has been a loss, none of us will forget. All the member of this company join me in expressing to you my deepest regret and heartfelt sympathy in your bereavement and render a final salute to a splendid Marine."*
> *- Captain C. F. Widdecke (USMC)*

In their first campaign, the 22d Marines stormed two Islands manned by veteran enemy troops and played an important role in the capture of a third on the Eniwetok Atoll. PFC Novak was one of 254 dead and 555 wounded Marines. His sacrifice is a constant reminder of the heavy price that one must pay for the cause of freedom.

After the war, Edward's remains were returned to the United States and was buried in St. Mary's Cemetery in Stuyvesant Falls with full military honors given by VFW Post 9593 from Stuyvesant Falls.

PFC Edward Bernard Novak was awarded the Asian Pacific and the Good Conduct Medals as well as the Purple Heart (posthumously). The American Legion "Clapp-Novak" Post of Kinderhook, NY was named in his honor.

Fred Oleynek

Fred Oleynek was born May 12, 1926 to Joseph and Emmy (Steinert) Oleynek in Essen, Germany. He grew up in New York City where he attended school.

Fred entered the United States Army on August 28, 1944 in The Bronx, NY. Earning the riflemen's sharpshooter's badge in basic training, he was then trained as a heavy weapons specialist.

PFC Fred Oleynek was assigned to the 2nd Battalion, Headquarters Company, 15th Infantry in the European Theater of Operations.

The 15th Division reached the Rhine River (11/26/44), fought in the Colmar Pocket, broke through the Siegfried Line, captured Nuremburg and remained on garrison duty in Germany until September 1946.

Engaged in heavy action in Central Europe and the Rhineland as a heavy weapons crewmember, PFC Oleynek earned the Combat Infantry Badge (CIB). Fred was injured in a jeep accident which required him to wear a body cast for a year. On June 5, 1947 he was honorably discharged.

In addition to the Rifle Sharpshooter's Badge and the CIB, PFC Fred Oleynek was awarded: Good Conduct Medal, American Theater Ribbon, Victory Ribbon, Two Bronze Battle Stars, and the European-African-Middle Eastern Theater Ribbon.

Fred returned home and attended Chicago University of Aeronautical Engineering. Graduating in 1950 with a BS in Aeronautical Engineering, he married Gloria Florio on February 17, 1952. Together, they raised eight children: Joseph, Jean, Paula, Fred, Marguerite, Stephen, Gloria and Susan.

Fred was employed as a private business owner, Air Compressor Plus and as a code enforcement officer for the Town of Austerlitz.

He remained active in the community; he was a member of the Ghent VFW and the Spencertown Fire Co.

Fred died on September 29, 2009 in Austerlitz, NY. He was 83 years old.

There is no greater duty than devotion and service to others. He honorably served his country and today we recognize and honor him for that service.

Franklin Thomas O'Neil, Sr.

Franklin Thomas O'Neil, Sr. was born March 28, 1926 in Hudson, NY to Daniel and Alice O'Neil. He attended high school and on September 23, 1943 enlisted in the U.S. Navy at the Recruiting Station in Albany, NY as an apprentice seaman. He was only 17.

Franklin received basic training at the Naval Training Station at Sampson, NY and then additional training at the Amphibious Training Base in Solomon, MD.

He was assigned to duty at Fort Pierce, FL and Norfolk, VA, before being stationed for the next year and a half on the USS Tennessee in the Pacific Theater of Operation.

The USS Tennessee was a massive battleship commissioned on June 3, 1920. It had a main battery of twelve 14-inch guns and sixteen 5-inch guns; was 642 feet long and 114 feet wide and displacing more than 40,000 tons. Before being decommission on February 14, 1947, it earned 10 Battle Stars while providing support for several major engagements in the Pacific. It received damaged on December 7 when the Japanese attached Pearl Harbor and saw action at Tarawa, Kwajalein, Eniwetok, Saipan, Guam, Tinian, Leyte, Iwo Jima, Okinawa.

Aboard the USS Tennessee, Franklin would see action in two of the bloodiest battles of WWII – Iwo Jima and Okinawa.

Franklin was honorably discharged on April 6, 1946 at Lido Beach, NY. Returning to Hudson, he married Claire Seaman on April 31, 1955 at St. Mary's Catholic Church and worked as an assembler/foreman at the V&O Press Company in Hudson.

He died on May 4, 1989 leaving his wife, Claire, and two sons, Tim and Frank, Jr. He was interred in Cedar Park Cemetery.

In keeping with the highest tradition of the United States Navy, S1 Franklin O'Neil, Sr. was awarded: The American Theater Medal, the Victory Medal, the Asiatic-Pacific Medal with three stars, the Philippine Liberation Ribbon with two stars and a Letter of Commendation for his service to his country and merits the sincere gratitude of a grateful nation.

Mario J. Palleschi

Mario J. Palleschi was born to Alvino and Angelina (Ferrera) Palleschi on June 23, 1931 in Schenectady, NY. He attended school at Nott Terrace High School and graduate in 1950.

Mario was drafted into the United States Army on March 25, 1952 in Albany, NY. After his initial training he was assigned to Company I, 22nd Infantry as part of the occupational force in Germany.

After VE day in Europe, the Allies helped the war-torn nations of Europe rebuild their economies and ease the plight of refugees and displaced persons. As tensions increased between Western democracies and the Soviet Union, an "Iron Curtain" descended on Europe, thus dividing Eastern and Western Europe between the former allies. A "Cold War" ensued.

The 22nd Infantry arrived in Germany in 1951as a part of the 4th Infantry Division. Under the newly formed North Atlantic Treaty Organization or NATO, it would serve as a deterrent to the expanding totalitarian communism regimes and in defense of the nascent European democracies.

Serving in the 22nd Infantry overseas for a year and a half, Cpl. Mario Palleschi was discharged at Camp Kilmer, NJ on March 2, 1954, where he was transferred to the Army Reserves in the New York Military District.

Cpl. Mario J. Palleschi was awarded the Occupational Medal (Germany) and the National Defense Service Medal.

Mario returned home and on February 13, 1955 married Jane Cunningham. Living at Kinderhook, NY, they raised four children: Paola, Mario Jr., Elizabeth and Peter.

He went into the hardware business in Columbia County, calling it "Valatie Paint and Hardware." For thirty years he was the owner and operator of Mario's Home Center in Valatie. Building and expanding his hardware business consumed a great deal of his time; however, he remained an active member of the Valatie VFW.

Mario died suddenly on May 26, 1991 and was buried at the St. John the Baptist cemetery in Valatie, NY. He left behind a wife, three children, and ten grandchildren. He was 59 years old.

Michael F. Paquin

Michael F. Paquin was born on September 28, 1939 to Leo and Theresa Paquin in the Bronx, NY. Growing up in Tannerville in the Catskill Mountains, he attended St. Ann's Academy in Albany, NY where he graduated in 1958.

Michael enlisted in the United States Army on April 9, 1959 in Albany, NY. After basic training at Fort Dix, NJ he was trained as a medical corpsman. Attaining the rank of private first class, Michael was assigned as a medic at Ireland Army Hospital at Fort Knox, KY.

Ireland Army Hospital was named in honor of Maj. Gen. Merritte W. Ireland, a surgeon and U.S. Army surgeon general and serves as a general medical and surgical care unit.

PFC Paquin broke his ankle while in the service which required several weeks of recovery in the hospital. Serving during the Cold War, he was stationed stateside (NJ, KY,TX), discharged on March 31, 1961 and transferred to the United States Army Reserves where he was honorably discharge on April 8, 1965. PFC Michael Paquin was awarded the Army's Good Conduct Medal.

Michael worked as a letter carrier for the United States Postal Service. He married Lucy Bradt in 1963 at St. Anne in Albany, NY. Together they raised six children: Mark, Scott, Christine, Denise, Ivonne and Nicole. Retiring from the USPS after 30 years, Michael worked the next five years on the campus of SUNY Albany.

Michael remained active in his community. He was a member of the Kinderhook Knights of Columbus and a past grand knight of the John J. Currant Council #7606, faithful navigator of the Donald E. LaValley Assembly of the Fourth Degree of the Knights of Columbus, and district deputy of District 68 of the Knights of Columbus. He was also the commander of the Disabled American Veteran Council #194 in Chatham.

Michael passed away on August 30, 2008 and was buried in Holy Sepulchre Cemetery in East Greenbush. He left behind five children, eight grandchildren and two step grandchildren. He was predeceased by a son, Scott. He was 68.

Michael W. Perdue

Michael's father, Franklin D. Perdue, came from Roanoke, VA and met his mother, Marlene Shappy, while his father was stationed at Ethan Allen Air Force Base in Essex Junction, VT. They were married in July of 1955, moved to Burlington, VT, where Michael was born June 7, 1960. The forth of eight children, he began his schooling at Donald P. Sutherland School in Nassau, NY and later attended elementary (1965-1974) and high school (1974-1978) at Chatham, NY, where he graduated in 1978.

Michael enlisted in the United States Navy on October 25, 1982. After basic training he was assigned to the USS Belleau Wood, which was stationed in the Pacific. This duty station took him to places like Hawaii, Korea, Hong Kong and the Philippines.

E4 Michael Purdue's duties on board the USS Belleau Wood included educational services, correspondence control, customer services, proctoring the Navy advancement examinations and duty yeoman.

In addition, as an enlisted surface warfare specialist, he was the junior member serving on the planning board for training and management, enlisted surface warfare qualifications board and the command professional development board.

Michael was released from active duty on October 23, 1988 at the Naval Reserve Personnel Center, New Orleans, LA and was transferred to the Naval Reserves where, for the next two years, he fulfilled his military obligation. During his service to his country, of which three years and seven months was sea service, Michael held the rank of E4, was an enlisted surface warfare specialist, rated Battle Efficiency "E" and was awarded the Sea Service Deployment Ribbon.

Michael went to work as an office manager for Pacific Church in San Diego, CA. Several years later he moved to Minneapolis, MN where he became a financial analyst for X-Cel Power Company. He is remembered as, "a proud and caring person. He worked hard and took pride in all his accomplishments".

Michael died on December 21, 2004 in Minneapolis, MN and is buried in St. James Cemetery in Ghent, NY. He was 44 years old. He left behind a mother, father and seven siblings: Frank, Jr., David, Kevin, Gary, Kathy (Sitzer), Joanne (Rowe) and Julie (Sitzer).

John Clifford Pfeiffer

John Clifford Pfeiffer was born April 21, 1947 in Hudson, NY to Wilfred and Eleanor Pfeiffer. He grew up in Hillsdale and attended Roeliff Jansen Central School where he was a member of the Conservation Club, and participated in volleyball, football, track and intramural sports.

His principal, Mr. Robert Robinson, remembered John as a *"willing worker ... quiet in his way (and) ... interested in all school activities."*

Prior to his enlistment in the United States Marine Corps, John *"endeavored to build himself up for the time when he planned to enlist." He felt that "... young men should not run from their duty. Their duty is to serve their nation to the best of their ability."*

On June 30, 1966, one week after graduating from Roeliff Jansen Central School, Private First Class (PFC) John Pfeiffer was inducted in the USMC and received basic training at Paris Island, SC. He received additional training as a gunner on the 106mm recoilless rifle at Camp Lejune, NC.

After a brief stay at Camp Pendleton, CA, he was assigned to Headquarters Company, 2d Battalion, 26th Marines, 3d Marine Division in Quang Tri Province, South Vietnam.

On May 16, 1967 while PFC Pfeiffer's battalion was conducting military operations from Cam Lo to the Demilitarized Zone in Quang Tri Province, his platoon was hit by heavy mortars and small arms fire. During this operation John died as a result of a gunshot wound sustained while engaged with enemy forces. In a letter from his Company Commander, Capt. Mulligan states,

> *"(John) was one of the finest Marines I had ever known. His exemplary conduct, leadership, and singular determination to do every job well were qualities that all of us respected. We will miss him and hope you will find some comfort in knowing this."*

John's remains were sent home and funeral services were held at the Hillsdale Methodist Church with full military honors. He was buried in North Hillsdale Cemetery; he was just 20 years old.

PFC Pfeiffer was awarded the: Purple Heart, National Defense Service Medal, Vietnam Service Medal, Republic of Vietnam Campaign Ribbon, Military Merit Medal, Gallantry Cross with Palm and the New York State Conspicuous Cross.

Robert V. Pinto, Sr.

Robert V. Pinto was born April 6, 1932 in Spencertown, NY to James V. and Caroline S. Pinto. He attended Spencertown and Chatham High School.

Growing up on the family farm with five brothers, Robert worked as a chauffeur for his father's taxi service. It was then that he met and married Mary Vinchiarello on April 5, 1952.

Robert enlisted in the United States Army on August 21, 1953. After receiving basic training at Fort Devens, MA he was assigned to overseas duty with Tank Company, 38th Infantry Regiment, 2nd Infantry Division in Korea.

Graduating the third highest in United States Armed Forces Ordinance School, Sgt. Robert V. Pinto served as a tank commander with the regimental tank company. Additional training included Track Vehicle Mechanic Course at the Tokyo Ordinance Depot, where he was awarded a Certificate of Proficiency.

In March of 1954 Sgt. Pinto and his tank platoon attained distinction when they received a rating of excellent; achieving a score of 1849 out of a possible 2000.

In July of 1960, Sgt. Robert V. Pinto, Sr. was honorably discharged from the United States Army.

Sgt. Robert V. Pinto was awarded the Combat Infantry Badge, the Korean Service Medal, UN Korea Service Medal, the Republic of Korea War Service Medal, and the National Defense Service Medal.

Returning home to his wife and two sons in Spencertown, Robert went to work in construction for Barris Johnson. He subsequently worked as a district lineman for the New York Central Railway and after retiring after twenty years with the railroad, Robert continued to work for Chatham Motors until 1980. Robert was an avid hunter and fisherman. He was a member of the Spencertown Rod and Gun, a 30-year member of the Spencertown Fire Co. and served as an umpire for the Little League.

Robert passed away on November 3, 1990, ten years after his wife, Mary's passing. He was buried at St. James Cemetery in Ghent, NY, leaving behind two sons: Robert and Steven, seven grandchildren and three great-grandchildren. Robert was 58 years old.

Frederick Richard Potts, Jr.

Frederick Richard Potts, Jr. was born November 20, 1924 in Hudson, NY to Frederick and Elsie May (Miller) Potts. He attended elementary and high school at Germantown Central School, graduating June 1, 1942.

Fred entered the Marine Corps on July 14, 1942 in Albany, NY at the age of 17. After basic training at Parris Island, he was trained as an automatic rifleman.

He was assigned to a machine gun crew with the 1st Batallion, 2nd Regiment, 2nd Marine Division just prior to the Battle of Tarawa. On this small island (3½ miles wide) the 2nd Marines suffered 1,000 dead, while killing almost 5,000 Japanese and came to be known as "Bloody Tarawa."

Engaged in some of the fiercest fighting of the Pacific, Cpl. Fred Potts, Jr. saw action on Saipan, Tinian, Okinawa and was part of the occupational forces at Nagasaki.

On Saipan, Cpl. Potts and three marines were assigned to protect the company's flank when 80 Japanese tried to out-flank them. With two wounded and a third sent back for help, Cpl. Potts was credited with 32 Japanese killed and was awarded the Bronze Star.

He was later wounded in the leg by shrapnel and received the Purple Heart. His unit lost two transports to Kamikazes on the first day of the invasion of Okinawa.

"It was enough to make a grown man cry with rage," he said.

He was honorably discharged on January 10, 1946 at Bainbridge, MD.

For his service Cpl. Fred Potts, Jr. was awarded the following: Bronze Star, Purple Heart, WWII Victory Medal WWII Am. Campaign Medal, Asiatic Pacific Campaign Medal, WWII Occupation Service Medal, Marine Corps Reserve Medal, Good Conduct Medal, National Defense Service Medal, and the Rifleman's Sharpshooters Badge.

Returning to Columbia County, Fred married Virginia Mae Spanburgh on June 16, 1947. They raised five children: Nancy, Fred, Cindy, Terry and Mary Ellen.

Fred worked for the New York State Police with the BCI for 33 years and retired on January 3, 1979.

He remained active in social affairs. He was the former commander of the Minkler-Seery American Legion Post in Philmont, NY, the Hudson Elks Club, the Hudson V.F.W. and the Philmont Rod and Gun Club.

Fred passed away on October 27, 1981at Port St. Lucie, FL and is buried in Reform Church Cemetery, Germantown, NY. He left behind his lovely wife, Virginia, five children, seven grandchildren and 12 great-grandchildren. He was 56 years old.

Richard M. Powell

Richard M. Powell was born in Philmont, New York to Milton and Anna Powell the year of the Stock Market Crash (1929). He grew up in Philmont where he attended school.

He entered the United States Army, receiving training in the United States and then was assigned to Company M, 31st Infantry Regiment, 7th Infantry Division.

On December 3, 1950 he was a part of an element of Task Force McLean. While heavily engaged with overwhelming numbers of Communist Red Chinese forces on the eastern shore of the Chosin Reservoir, North Korea, PFC Powell was killed in action. His remains were never recovered.

Along with his neighbor and childhood friend, Donald McNaughton, a memorial was dedicated in his honor at the Philmont baseball field.

PFC Richard M. Powell was awarded the Purple Heart, the Combat Infantryman's Badge, the Korean Service Medal and the United Nations Service Medal.

He was honored on May 24, 2002 with William Henry Doss, Jr., Clifford Johnson, and Donald McNaughton; all serving in the 7th Infantry Division and died within five days of each other during the same offensive.

Paul J. Proper, Sr.

Paul J. Proper, Sr. was born October 21, 1930 to Myron and Olia (Pectal) Proper in North Egremont, MA. Growing up in Craryville, NY, Paul attended Roe Jan Central School. After graduating in June, 1949 he worked as an auto mechanic.

Paul enlisted as a private in the United States Air Force on January 3, 1951 in Albany, NY. After basic training in San Antonio, TX, he was trained at Lackland AFB as an aircraft mechanic on bombers and then Aberdeen, MD.

Tech Sgt. Paul J. Proper, Sr. was assigned to duty in Pusan, Korea in August 1952 with the 5th Air Force, 78th Maintenance Squadron. He few on night missions on the Douglas B-26 bomber as flight mechanic.

The B-26s were credited with the destruction of 38,000 vehicles, 406 locomotives, 3,700 railway trucks and 7 enemy aircraft on the ground.

T/Sgt. Paul J. Proper, Sr. was honorably discharged on December 19, 1954 at Vance Air Force Base in Enid, OK.

For his service he was awarded the following: Bronze Star, National Defense Service Medal, United Nations Service Medal, Korean Service Medal and the Good Conduct Medal.

Paul met and married Marjorie E. Decker of Ancramdale, NY on April 13, 1952. They raised four children: Paul, Jr., Rosemarie, David and Jeffrey.

He worked as a deputy for the Columbia County Sheriff's Dept., becoming it first investigator and then undersheriff (1972). Elected sheriff in 1977, he would serve for the next 12 years in that capacity, retiring in (1989); serving briefly as sheriff in 2001.

Paul was president of the NYS Sheriff's Assoc.(life member), instrumental in the building the Columbia County Public Safety Facility in Hudson, NY (named in his honor), a member of: Clausson Raught Comm. Rescue Squad, Copake Fire

Co, (assist. chief, fire commissioner, life member), Hillsdale 612 Free Masons, Cadby Shutts VFW Post 7552, Columbia. Co. Korean War Assoc., director of Columbia Co. Fair Board (30+ yrs), communicant of West Copake Reformed Church.

Paul passed away on December 20, 2018 and is buried in Evergreen Cemetery in Pine Plains, NY. He left behind his loving wife, four children, eight grandchildren, and nine great-grandchildren. He was 88 years old.

Sigmund S. Przymylski

Sigmund S. Przymylski was born on July 3, 1925 on Long Island, NY to Adam and Mary Przymylski. Sigmund grew up and attended an elementary school in Brooklyn and graduated from a high school in Queens.

Sigmund joined the United States Army on October 8, 1943 in New York City. After completing basic and advanced training, he was assigned to the 3rd Infantry Division, serving in Central Europe and the Rhineland.

During the Battle of Anzio, PFC Sigmund Przymylski's fox hole took a direct hit by mortar fire and all were killed except Sigmund. He was hit by shrapnel to his hip and spine, unable to walk. Waiting for help, Sigmund's squad was reported missing in action.

Sigmund later recalled as he lay with his dead buddies, he wondered who would find him first. He knew if the Germans found him, he would be killed. He remembered the joy and relief he felt when he saw a platoon of American soldiers approaching him.

He was honorably discharged on December 30, 1945 from Fort Dix, NJ.

PFC Sigmund S. Przymylski was awarded the following: Silver Star, Bronze Star Purple Heart, WWII Victory Medal, Distinguished Unit Badge, European-African-Middle Eastern Service Medal and the Good Conduct Medal.

Sigmund returned home and married Leona Hess on February 13, 1949 in Brooklyn, NY. Together they raised five children: Stanley, Richard, Donna, Sandy and a foster son Andy.

They moved to Hastings, NY where Sigmund operated his own Deli business for more than 30 years. His customers nicknamed him "Whitey." Whitey sold the business and moved to Copake as a full time resident in 1986.

Whitey was a 50-year member of the VFW and American Legion, active in the Copake VFW and Copake Falls American Legion. He was also a member of the West Copake Fire Department.

His wife Leona remembers Whitey as a hard working man who was loved by everyone. She recalls how much Whitey loved his country more than anything else, except his family. At the age of 77 he often said, *"If I could, I would join the service and fight for my country all over again."*

Sigmund "Whitey" Przymylski passed away on September 25, 2004 at the age of 79. He is survived by his wife, Leona, five children, eleven grandchildren and nine great-grandchildren.

Joseph Henry Ptaszek

Joseph Henry Ptaszek was born to Michael and Nellie Ptaszik on August 11, 1915 in Upper Red Hook, NY. Residing at Atlas Lane, Hudson, NY in 1934 he enrolled in the CCC at Camp 52 out of Boston Corners, NY and prior to his service worked as a millwright.

Joseph volunteered for the United States Army on January 4, 1943 in Albany, NY. Qualifying as sharpshooter with the M1 in basic training, he received additional training on the 90mm gun.

Gunnery Technician Fourth Class (Gunnery TEC4) Joseph Ptaszek was assigned to Headquarters Battery, Harbor Defense of Boston, Ft. Banks, MA.

Serving in the military police, he was the gun commander on a 90mm gun crew. Consisting of thirteen men, TEC4 Ptaszek was charged with the responsibility of: loading, firing, supervising maintenance, control of operations, tactical employment of the gun and crew.

His 90mm fixed/mobile gun was used in defense of Boston Harbor against enemy aircraft, mechanized forces or small naval vessels. Collaborating with scientist from MIT, he trained the first gunnery crew to use radar-assisted artillery for the United States.

On March 25, 1946 he was honorably discharged at Ft. Devens, MA and served the next 10 years in the Naval Reserves of the Third Naval District.

He was awarded the American Theater Campaign Ribbon, Victory Medal, Good Conduct Medal and sharpshooter medal.

Joseph met Nellie Jenowich of Taghkanic, NY and they married on June 1, 1952. Together they raised their daughter Paula. Joseph and Nellie opened the Joe-Nel Trailer Park in Greenport, NY and later purchased Red Mill where they opened an antique shop.

He remained active in his community. He played baseball on the Columbia County Ukrainian team, a life member of the Greenport Fire Co. #1, Hudson Carpenters Local (40 yrs/pres.), Polish Sportsman's Club (67 yrs), Old Time Power Assoc. Engine Club (36 yrs)

On March 29, 2013 Joseph passed away and was buried in Hudson, NY. He left behind his daughter, Paula, and two grandchildren. He was 97 years old.

Leo J. Pulcher

Leo John Pulcher was born September 2, 1914 to John and Crescenthia (Paul) Pulcher in Hudson, NY. Growing up in Greenport, he attended Hudson School District and worked as an auto mechanic prior to his entering the service.

Leo was inducted in the United States Army on February 18, 1941 in Albany. After basic and infantry training at Camp Upton, Long Island, NY, Leo was assigned to Dodd Field, TX. In the ensuing years, Leo Pulcher attained the rank of first sergeant and conducted training in TX, LA, and CA.

On July 31, 1944 the 174th Combat Engineers departed from the Seattle, WA on the USS Flasher to the Hawaiian Islands, where they were trained in amphibious landings.

The 174th Combat Engineers were then assigned to duty in the Pacific Theater of Operations as a part of the liberation of the Philippines on October 15, 1944.

On April 1, 1945 at 1700 hrs, 1st Sgt. Leo Pulcher led his Company of Combat Engineers ashore on White Beach during the invasion of Okinawa. Under his direction they provided vital supplies to the infantry despite heavy enemy fire.

On May 16, 1945, 1st Sgt. Leo Pulcher was severely wounded by bomb fragments and was evacuated from Okinawa to undergo medical treatment. He was subsequently honorably discharged at Fort Dix, NJ on November 29, 1945.

For his service 1st Sgt Leo Pulcher was awarded the following: Bronze Star, Purple Heart, American Defense Service Medal, American Service Medal, Asiatic Pacific Service Medal, Good Conduct Medal, and Philippines Liberation Medal.

Returning home Leo married Viola Kuhner on November 17, 1946 and they raised four children: Elizabeth, Thomas, Leo and Viola.

He remained active in his community. He was a charter member of the Greenport Ambulance Squad, a life member and trustee of the Greenport Fire Dept., a life member of Hudson VFW Post #1314, honorary life member of the K of C Council #316 (3rd Degree), and a life-long member of the Holy Family Church in Stottville. Leo was the owner and operator of Pulcher's Motors until his death.

On January 19, 2010 Leo passed away and was buried in St. Mary's Cemetery, Stuyvesant Falls. Predeceasing his wife, he left behind four children, eight grandchildren and ten great-grandchildren. He was 95 years old.

Murray Winn Rathbun

Murray Winn Rathbun was born November 28, 1947 to Howard and Marion (Winn) Rathbun in Troy, New York. He attended Berlin Central School District and after graduating in June 1965, Murray worked for Seagrott Florest, Berlin, NY.

Murray was drafted in the United States Marine Corps and was inducted into the service at Garden City, NJ on December 5, 1968. He received basic training at Parris Island, where he qualified expert with the M-16.

He then received training in supply services, attaining the rank of E-5 or sergeant. Murray Winn was assigned to Headquarters and Supply Company, Supply Brigade, 1st Marine Division. in Vietnam as warehouse supply clerk.

Although every marine is a rifleman, Sgt. Murray Rathbun duties included just about all the inventory and supply in warehouses, including: receiving, inspecting, locating, storing, rotating, safekeeping, issuing, preparing, shipping, material return and disposal of supplies and equipment.

As a part of his duty Sgt. Rathbun was charged with the inventory of personal belongings of serious wounded or KIA marines. Having served a year in Vietnam and his term of service ended, Sgt. Murray Rathbun was honorably discharged on July 31, 1970 at San Diego, CA.

For his service he was awarded the following: Republic Vietnam Cross of Gallantry with palm and frame, Vietnam Service Medal with cluster, Vietnam Campaign Medal with device, National Defense Service Medal, Good Conduct Medal and Rifle Expert Badge.

Murray returned home and continued working for Seagroat Flowers Berlin, NY and then Fairpoint Communications where he retired after 30 years in 2001.

He met and married Anne Eaton on January 23, 2004 in Chatham, NY. They have three children; Scott Rathbun , Robert Borovich and Laura Leone (previous marriages). Murray was a member of the Berlin Vol. Fire Co. and the Stephentown Veterans Group.

Murray passed away in Chatham on July 17, 2012 and was buried in St. James Cemetery, Ghent, NY. He left behind his wife, Anne, a son Scott, two stepchildren: Robert and Laura Leone, six grandchildren and eight great-grandchildren. He was 64 years old.

Helmuth H. Renken

Helmuth H. Renken was born September 12, 1921 in Wulstoff, Germany to Heinrich and Ella (Rother) Renken. Raised in The Bronx, NY, he attended PS 46 elementary school and was graduated from Haarem High School.

Helmuth enlisted in the United States Army on Sept 17, 1942 in NYC. After basic training he received additional training at Weatherford, OK as an airplane maintenance technician for the Army Air Force and qualified for the AAF Air Crew Member Badge and the AAF Tech Badge.

On June 10, 1943 Sgt. Helmuth H. Renken was assigned to duty in China-Burma-India Theater with the Tenth Air Force. He was a flight engineer on C-46s that flew from India to China over the Himalayan Mountains (AKA "The

Hump"), transporting supplies to allied troops.

He was in charge of a crew of mechanics who performed line maintenance on airplanes, supervised their work accordance with technical orders and inspected planes to see that all repairs are properly made for flight.

The Tenth Air Force transported more than 500,000 tons of cargo with the loss of 594 aircraft and approximately 1,300 personnel killed and 345 missing. Their efforts were instrumental in the capitulation of the Japanese during WWII.

Sgt. Helmuth H. Renken was honorably discharged October 29, 1945 at Mitchel Field, NY and for his service was awarded the following: American Service Medal, Asiatic-Pacific Service Medal and the Good Conduct Medal.

Helmuth returned home, met and married Mary Mariak on October 17, 1953. Together they raised two daughters.

He worked as a mechanical engineer for the V&O Press in Hudson, NY for 30 plus years. He also worked for Comair Rotron (Saugerties, NY) and Servotec (Hudson, NY).

He remained active in his community as a founding member of the Greenport Pumper #3 Volunteer Fire Co and served as an officer for the American Legion.

Helmuth died on January 31, 2016 and is buried in Cedar Park Cemetery, Hudson, NY. He left behind two daughters: Linda and Susan, and two grandchildren: William Mintzer and Ellen E. Mintzner. He was 94 years old.

Harvey L. Ringer, Jr.

Harvey L. Ringer, Jr. was born to Harvey and Elizabeth Ringer, Sr. on January 1, 1917 in North Coplay, Pennsylvania. His family moved to Philmont, a thriving mill town in upstate New York, where he attended high school. Later, he was employed as a mechanic for Harders Trailer Corporation.

The surprise attack at Pearl Harbor on December 7th, 1941 prompted Harvey to enlist in the Armed Services. On January 16, 1942 he enlisted in the United States Army Air Corp and received training at Miami, FL and Chicago, IL.

Harvey's skill and sense of duty aided him in rising in the ranks quickly. Sgt. Ringer was assigned to combat duty with the 8th Air Force, 363 Squadron, 388 Bombardment Group stationed at Knellis Hall, England. As the oldest member on his B-17 named "The Expectant Father," this 27-year-old waist gunner was fondly referred to as "Pappy" by the rest of the crew.

On April 11, 1944 while on a bombing mission over Warnemunde, Germany bad weather forced his group to divert to a secondary target, an enemy airfield near Rostock, Germany. "Feathering" an engine damaged from a previous attack, "The Expectant Father" completed its bombing run and was heading back to England. While over the Baltic Sea, they were again attacked by German (ME-

190) fighters, thus setting the radio room on fire.

Crippled, "The Expectant Father" dropped out of formation, losing altitude quickly. While over the Baltic Sea, "Pappy" and three other crew members in the rear of the plane were forced to parachute from the burning aircraft. He and two comrades subsequently drowned in the icy sea. The remaining crew crashed landed on German soil and were taken prisoner.

Sgt Harvey's body was recovered on June 16, 1949. His remains were returned to the United States and he was buried in Union Cemetery, Philmont, NY.

Sgt. Harvey L. Ringer, Jr. received the N.Y.S. Conspicuous Service Cross, the Village of Philmont Medal of Honor; and on September 16, 1946 his father, Harvey L. Ringer, Sr., respectfully accepted the Purple Heart for his son who gave his life so that others might be free.

Joseph E. Robsky

Joseph E. Robsky was born April 17, 1972 in Hudson, NY to Joseph and Bonita Robsky. He was raised in Claverack where he attended Claverack Elementary, Hudson Middle School, and graduated from Hudson High School in 1990.

Upon graduation of high school Joseph enlisted in the United States Marine Corps in June of 1990. After Basic at San Diego, CA, he was trained as a combat metal worker and assigned to the 3rd Engineer Maintenance Company, 3rd Force Service Support Group in Okinawa and Japan (1991-1993).

After completion of two years of overseas duty, Joseph was assigned to the 3rd Light Armored Reconnaissance Battalion, 1st Marine Division at 29 Palms, CA.

He was honorably discharged as a corporal on October 15, 1994 to continue his education and pursue other interest.

While employed as a civilian welder, Joseph enlisted in the California National Guard as an infantryman in April 1996 and the following year he enlisted in the United States Army.

Specialist 4 (SP4) Robsky was assigned to the 1st Cavalry Division in Fort Hood, TX. He worked for a time as the assistant operations sergeant in S-2 and soon attained the rank of sergeant.

He was deployed to Bosnia for "Operation Joint Forge" in the summer of 1999. That same year he re-enlisted, he changed jobs.

He attended Explosive Ordinance Disposal School at Eglin, AFB, FL. Sgt. Robsky was then assigned to the 759th Ordnance Company, Fort Irwin, CA. where he was promoted to the rank of staff sergeant and team leader.

As a team leader, SSG Robsky deployed again this time with the 759th EOD in December 2002 in support of "Operation Enduring Freedom."

He crossed into Iraq with the 3rd Infantry Division where he and his unit provided valuable service neutralizing and disposing explosive devices. On September 10, 2003, while performing his duties, SSG Robsky was killed as a result of an explosion during hostile action.

SSG Joseph E. Robsky was awarded the following medals: Purple Heart, Bronze Star, US Army Commendation Medal, Kosovo Campaign Medial, US Navy Service Ribbon, National Defense Service Medal, US Army and Marine Good Conduct Medal.

SSG Joseph E. Robsky was interred in the Claverack Dutch Reform Church. He was 31 years old.

Claude L. Rogers

Claude L. Rogers was born October 9, 1949 in Great Barrington, MA to Edwin and Evelyn Rogers. As a young boy he grew up in Columbia County and attended both elementary and high school at Roeliff Jansen where he graduated in 1968.

Claude was inducted in the United States Army on April 2, 1969 at Hudson, NY. He received basic training at Fort Dix, NJ and after additional training as an infantrymen, he was assigned to the 199th Infantry in the Republic of Vietnam.

The 199th Infantry was formed on March 23, 1966 at Fort Benning, GA and was assigned to Vung Tau, South Vietnam in November 1966. It served for four years in Vietnam and then returned to Ft. Benning where it remained inactive. Completing his tour of duty, Specialist 4 (SP4) Claude Rogers returned to the United States and was honorably discharged.

On July 16, 1972 he married June Hornung at the Craryville Methodist Church. In the ensuing years, Claude was employed at Pete's Esso Station in Craryville and Morandi Packing Company. Claude was active in the Craryville Fire Company No. 1, Craryville Rod and Gun Club and a member of the Craryville Methodist Church.

For his service to his country, SP4 Claude Rogers was awarded the following medals: Combat Infantry Badge, Vietnam Service Medal with two Bronze Stars, the Vietnam Campaign Medal, National Defense Service Medal with two o/s Bars, Army Commendation Medal with oak cluster, the Good Conduct Medal, and the Sharpshooter and Marksman Badge.

The Vietnam Conflict was one of the longest war in our history. Approximately 2.7 million Americans served in the war zone. Of those who served, 300,000 were wounded, 58,000 died and 2,100 remain missing and unaccounted for. It was said of those who served, "All gave some, some gave all."

Claude L. Rogers died on November 30, 1975 and is buried in the West Copake Cemetery. He was 26 years old.

Morton Wheeler Schermerhorn

Morton Wheeler Schermerhorn was born December 24, 1921 in Dover Plains, NY to Frederick and Minnie (Wheeler) Schermerhorn. He attended Columbia and Dutchess County Schools and completed his education while in the Armed Services.

Morton enlisted in the United States Marine Corps on July 10, 1942. After basic training where he qualified as marksman on with the M1 rifle, he received additional training for a light anti-aircraft gun crew.

Private First Class (PFC) Morton W. Schermerhorn was assigned to the Pacific Theater of Operation on December 3, 1942 until June 17, 1943 where he was then assigned as a guard at Camp Lejeune, NC.

PFC Morton Schermerhorn was honorably discharged on November 14, 1945 from the Redistribution Battalion.

While in the Marine Corps, Morton met and married Gladys Marie Matthews on August 19, 1944. Living in Ghent, they raised eight children: George, Joan, Kenneth, Gloria, Marcia, Rita, Peggy and Morton and was employed as a mason in Albany and Columbia County for 40 years.

Morton remained active in his community. He was a member of the Ghent V.F.W Post 5933 (post commander and color guard) , Ghent Fire Company, Ghent Sportsmen Association, Chatham American Legion Post 42, Masons Union #6 and communicant of Christ Evangelical Lutheran Church in Ghent.

In his leisure, Morton loved to paint signs, portraits, murals and sculpting where he earned an apprenticeship at Jonas Studios in Claverack, NY.

In addition, he enjoyed gardening, playing the piano, making and flying model airplanes. He built his own single hydroplane boat. He is remembered as a "wonderful example of love, faith and appreciation of those who served in the Armed Forces."

Morton passed away on October 27, 2005 and is buried in the Ghent Union Cemetery. He left behind his lovely wife, eight children, 18 grandchildren and 29 great-grandchildren. He was 83 years old.

Herman Fredrick Schmidt

Herman Fredrick Schmidt was born on May 29, 1890 to Louise and John Schmidt of Hudson, NY. He lived at 329 State Street where he grew up and attended public school. Prior to his enlistment in the NYS National Guard on November 6, 1907, he worked as a mill hand in a local firm.

Assigned to the NYS National Guard, Herman served as a cook for the next six years with Company F, 10th Infantry, where he attained the rank of sergeant.

Honorably discharged on September 18, 1913, for the next few years Herman was employed as a "bottler," and on October 24, 1916 he married Miss Louise Braker of Hudson, NY.

As the conflict in Europe drew America closer to war, Herman re-enlisted in Company F of the NYS National Guard. Then, for the second time, he was honorably discharged from the NYS National Guard where he answered the call to "federal service" which was preparing for armed conflict in Europe.

For the next several months, Herman was stationed at Camp Whitman, Fort Niagara and Camp Wadsworth as sergeant of Company F, 51st Pioneer Infantry, 4th Army Corps.

On July 26th, 1918 Sgt. Schmidt sailed for Brest, France where he and the 51st Pioneers saw action at St. Mihiel, the Meuse and Moselle River Sectors as well as operations in the Woerve.

The Battle of St. Mihiel was notable in that it was the first time that American Expeditionary Forces (AEF) organized, planned and fought independently under the command of its own leadership, Gen. "Black Jack" Pershing.

Sgt. Schmidt's unit was then assigned as a part of the 600,000 man AEF Meuse-Argonne Offensive of September 1918. Lasting six bloody weeks, at a cost of 26,277 killed and 95,786 wounded, an Armistice was finally signed on November 11, 1918, thus ending "the war that would end all wars."

Sgt. Schmidt served as a part of the Army of Occupation until July 3, 1919, where he returned to the States and was discharged. Herman remained in the National Guard and in 1935 he was recognized for twenty years of "Long and Faithful Service".

After the war Herman worked as a chef at the General Worth Hotel and started a drum and bugle corps where his daughter, Jeannette, served as majorette. Reflecting on her grandfather Nora Van Brunt stated,

"The flag from his grave side service was cherished by my parents and displayed at all important holidays. I was taught flag etiquette because of this and (I) have passed it along to my children and grandchildren."

Norman William Schneidt

Norman William Schneidt was born November 1, 1922 in Hoboken, NJ to William and Maude Schneidt. He attended Hudson High School and although Norman had not yet graduated from high school, he enrolled in preliminary flight courses at Massachusetts State College for glider Service in Westfield, MA.

Norman entered the service on August 17, 1942 as a private. He would attain the rank of captain.

In March 1943, Norman applied for admission to the Air Cadet Corps. In a letter of recommendation, his former high school superintendent wrote, "He is a young man of good personality, intelligence and character. ..."

Norman was assigned to combat duty in the Pacific Theater of Operation where he served as an aerial photographer with the Army Air Corps in the Philippines.

On August 27, 1944 he married Johanna Schoenmakers. At the conclusion of WWII Cpt. Schneidt was discharged from active duty on May 2, 1947 at Fort Dix, NJ.

Cpt. Norman Schneidt remained in the Air Force Reserves while raising a family and working at McCall Refrigeration of Hudson NY.

He was called to active duty with the advent of the Korean War and was assigned to the 370th Bombardment Squadron, 307th Bombardment Wing on Okinawa.

On November 8, 1952 while piloting a B-29 over North Korea (fifth mission) on a night bombing mission, Cpt. Schneidt's plane was hit midsection by a Russian MIG. Three crew members parachuted to safety, the remaining crew were listed as MIAs. Cpt. Schneidt's remains were never recovered. However, a plaque was placed in the Punch Bowl Cemetery in Hawaii in his honor.

Cpt. Schneidt was 30 years old at the time of his death and he left behind a wife, Johanna, and three children: Joanne, Norman and Carl.

For his distinguished service to his country during WWII and Korea, Cpt. Norman Schneidt was awarded the Air Medal, Purple Heart, American Campaign Medal, WWII Victory Medal, Korean Service Medal, Bronze Service Medal, United Nations Service Medal, National Defense Service Medal, Philippines Independence Ribbon, Pilot Badge and Gold Star Lapel Button Pin.

His sacrifice is a painful reminder of the personal price that is paid for the high cause of freedom. Our enduring gratitude is immeasurable.

Edward Joseph Schuster, Sr.

Edward Joseph Schuster Sr. was born to Mr. and Mrs. Ludwig Robert Schuster in New York City on July 30, 1921. Moving to Columbia County, Ed attended school at Ancram and graduated from Roliff Jansen High School in 1939.

On January 3, 1941, after Edward enlisted in the United States Marines for four years, he finished basic training where he received the rating as sharpshooter with the 45 cal. pistol.

While assigned to the 1st Marine Division as a member of a machine gun crew, Cpl. Edward Schuster participated in three major campaigns against the Japanese in the Pacific .Fearing the airfields on Guadalcanal was a threat to our ally, Australia, the 1st Marine Division landed on August 7th 1942 and for the next several months engaged a determined enemy. At the end of hostilities America would incur 1,598 killed and 4,709 wounded, at the cost of 23,000 Japanese.

In December of 1942, the 1st Marine Division made another landing on Cape Gloucester, New Britain. From January 1st 1944 to March 1, 1944 Cpl. Edward Schuster not only fought a determined enemy but the jungle, the monsoon rains, and a multitude of tropical diseases as well. Victory would come at the price of 310 marine dead and 1,083 wounded.

On September 15, 1944 Cpl. Schuster made his last amphibious landing on the Island of Peleliu. For the next four weeks in temperatures which reached 115 degrees, the 1st Marine Division engaged a tenacious enemy who were entrenched in hundreds of bunkers and caves. With 6,526 casualties (1,252 killed), the United States ended hostilities on Peleliu and the destruction of the Japanese garrison of some 10,500 men.

Cpl. Edward J. Schuster Sr. was honorably discharged from the United States Marine Corps on February 26, 1946 at the United States Naval Shipyard at Brooklyn, NY. He was awarded the Honorable Service Medal, the Honorable Discharge Button and the Good Conduct Medal.

Edward returned home and went to work for Kimberly Clark as a paper machine operator where he retired in 1984. His daughter, Patricia, fondly recalls of her father: *"He was an amazing man raising five children on his own, working a second and sometimes third job. He was known by many and liked by all."*

On March 28, 1998, Edward died at the age of 76. He left behind five children; Edward, James, Patricia, Kevin and Becky, twelve grandchildren and eleven great-grandchildren. Lest we forget. Semper Fidelis.

John William Seery

John Seery was born November 26, 1890 to John and Bridget Seery in Catskill, NY. John grew up and attended school in Catskill.

While living on Maple Avenue in Philmont, NY, John enlisted in Company F, 10th Infantry of the New York National Guard on July 20, 1917.

Federalized by presidential proclamation, Company F, 10th Infantry went to Fort Niagara for additional military training and was then sent to Camp Wadsworth, SC.

With Company F, PFC John Seery was assigned to the 197th Inf., 27th Division. His division sailed for Brest and arrived in the French port on May 11, 1918 as a part of the American Expeditionary Force (AEF).

PFC John Seery saw action in Belgium at Mount Kimmel, Vierstadt Cross Road, and the Hindenburg Line.

On September 29, 1918 at the Hindenburg Line, PFC John W. Seery was killed in action, his final resting place unknown. He was 27 years old.

Ralph H. Shadic

Ralph H. Shadic was born on August 17, 1931 to Homer C. and Hilda E. (Shattuck) Shadic in Hudson, NY. He attended Roe Jan Central School in Hillsdale, NY and graduated June 1950. He went to work for AC Bristol Corporation in Copake, NY as a truck driver until he entered the service.

Ralph was inducted in the United States Army on February 19, 1953 as a private (E-1) and after his basic training he was assigned to Clark Air Force Base in the Philippines.

Cpl. Ralph Shadic's duties required him to monitor seismic activities for underground testing of munitions around the world. He was released from active military service on January 31, 1955 at Camp Kilmer, NJ and was transferred to the Army Reserves where he was honorably discharged. For his service he received the National Defense Service Medal.

Ralph returned to Columbia County and went to work for AC Bristol CO. He began a business "Shadic Builders" and worked as a carpenter and mason for 45 years until he retired. He was also a building inspector for the Town of Copake.

In the interim, he met and married Joan M. Salvo in Brooklyn, NY on September 8, 1956. Together they raised three children: Pal, Christine and Brenda.

Ralph was active in his community. He was a member of the Cadby Shutts VFW, Copake Fire Co. #1, past president and life member of Community Rescue Squad, past president of the Roe Jan Young at Heart and a communicant of Our Lady of Hope Catholic Church. In addition he was a building inspector, council member and on the Zoning Board of Appeals from Copake, NY.

Ralph died on June 16, 2014 and was buried in St. Bridget's Cemetery, Copake Falls, NY. He left behind a wife and three children. He was 82 years old.

John Shaw

John T. Shaw was born January 8, 1932 to Robert and Frances (Doyle) Shaw in Poughkeepsie, NY. He attended Martin Van Buren School in Kinderhook.

Working as a farmer, John enlisted in the United States Marine Corps on August 7, 1950 in Albany, NY. After basic training Cpl. John T. Shaw was trained as a small arms technician and during the Korean War was assigned to Headquarter Company, 2nd Battalion, 8th Marines, and 2nd Marine Division in Korea. Cpl. John Shaw was discharged on March 13, 1952 and was awarded the following: U.N. Ribbon and the Korean Service Medal.

John returned home and worked for the NY State Police in 1956, where he attained the rank of sergeant. On September 19, 1959, in Hoosic Falls, NY, he married Kathleen McGuire. They raised five children: Sharon, John, Thomas, Robert and Kathleen.

After 20 years with the NY State Police, John retired in December 1976. During his 20 years, he had served as station commander of Claverack and New Lebanon.

Following his state retirement, he went to work for Amtrak Police Dept. in Rensselaer and then worked for Peduzzi Roofing Co. John ran for sheriff of Columbia County, was a member of the VFW Post 9593, Stuyvesant Falls, and Valatie Am. Legion, NY State Police Benevolent Assoc., Valatie Tri Valley Rod and Gun Club, and a communicant of St. John the Baptist Church Valatie, NY.

John passed away on August 18, 1981 and was buried at St John the Baptist Cemetery, Valatie, NY. He leaves behind his wife, Kathleen, five children, eleven grandchildren and seven great-grandchildren.

Robert Shaw

Robert William Shaw was born August 12, 1920 to Robert and Frances (Doyle) Shaw in Poughkeepsie, NY. He attended Pawling Public School District.

Living in Bedford Hills, NY and working as a fireman, Robert enlisted in the United States Army on August 19, 1942 in Upton, NY and entered the service on September 2, 1942. After training at Ft. Knox, KY and then Ft. Campbell, KY, he was trained as a gunner of a medium tank. He qualified with the Colt 1911 45 cal. pistol and the 30 cal. machinegun.

Assigned to Company A, 10th Tank Battalion, Tech. Sgt. Grade 5 Robert Shaw saw action in the Eastern Theater of Operation in Italy (Sicily), Northern France (Normandy) and Central Europe (Ardennes, Rhineland).

While serving with Patton's 3rd Army, on August 26, 1944 he was seriously wounded with shrapnel in action when his tank was hit and set ablaze. After receiving medical treatment in France and England he was honorably discharged on October 13, 1945 at Ft. Dix, NY.

For his service Tec/5 Robert Shaw was awarded the following: Purple Heart, Good Conduct Medal, EAME Service Medal with Bronze Arrow.

As a disabled veteran Robert returned home and worked as a mechanic. He was a member of the Valatie American Legion.

He died on August 6, 1968 in Kinderhook, NY and is buried at St. John the Baptist, Valatie, NY. He left behind a daughter Bonnie. He was 48 years old.

Wilson Shea

Wilson George (Harpy) Shea was born to James and Bertha (Baxter) Shea on April 6, 1919 in Hudson, NY. He attended St. Mary's Catholic School and upon graduation (1937) went to work as a machinist in the tool trade with V&O Press of Hudson, NY.

Harpy entered the United States Navy on November 23, 1942 in Albany, NY. After basic training the apprentice seamen completed sixteen weeks of naval training as a machinist at Sampson, NY and then on to Wentworth Institute in Boston, MA.

Machinist Mate 2 Class (MM2) Wilson Shea was assigned to the USS White Plains and took part of the following Pacific campaigns: Gilbert Islands, Marshall Island, Kwajalein, Roi, Marianas, Saipan, Tinian, Ulithi, Palau, Okinawa, the Philippine and Leyte Invasions.

He was awarded the following: Admiral's Commendation Ribbon, a Presidential Citation with Bronze Star, WWII Victory Medal and the WWII Asiatic Pacific Service Medal.

MM2 Wilson Shea was honorably discharged on October 21, 1945 at Lido Beach Long Island, NY.

Harpy married Mary Ann Fallarino on December 31, 1944 and after his discharge, returned to Columbia County and continued working for V&O Press until he retired after 47 years in the position of superintendent.

Harpy was very active in his community. He was a member of the J.W. Hoysradt Fire Company #8 (74 yrs.), communicant and usher for St. Mary's Catholic Church (60+ yrs), Past Exalted Ruler and District Vice President from Hudson Elks Lodge #787, Grand Knight in the Knights of Columbus, basketball referee (72 yrs.), and a member of: American Legion, VFW, Honor a Vets Committee, Hudson Fish and Game Club, Polish Sportsman Club, and Federation of Columbia County Sportsman. He received citizen of the year from the Albany Times Union Newspaper and the Hudson Rotary Club (2008).

Harpy passed away on September 24, 2014 at the Fireman's Home. He was buried at Cedar Park Cemetery in Hudson, NY. Predeceased by his wife Mary Ann,

Harpy left behind a nephew, Patrick Shea and a niece, Mary Pitcher Shea. Harpy was 95 years old.

Kenneth Elmer Sheffer

Kenneth Elmer Sheffer was born December 2, 1931 to Elmer and Gladys (Quick) Sheffer in Hudson, NY. Growing up in Hudson and graduating from Hudson High School in 1949, he attended Ithaca College for one year. Prior to enlistment, Ken was a painter and apprentice electrician for Stanley Walker in Hudson, NY.

Kenneth enlisted in the United States Air Force on December 27, 1950. After basic training, he attended Medical Field Service School and was trained as a medical technician.

Attaining the rank of corporal, Kenneth served as a senior clerk and medical technician at Luke Air Force Base, Phoenix, AZ during the Korean War.

Cpl. Kenneth Elmer Sheffer was honorably discharged on March 27, 1952 at Luke Air Force Base, Phoenix, AZ.

Ken returned home, met and then married Rachel Borrelle on May 26, 1956 at Mount Carmel Catholic Church in Hudson, NY. They raised four children: Valerie, Paula, Gary and Kenneth.

He worked for thirty-three years for IBM as a manager in Kingston and retired in 1989.

Ken remained active in his community. He was a member of the Hudson Elks Lodge #787, where he served as House Committee chairman and was a member of Edmund's Hose Fire Company in Hudson, NY.

His daughter recalls that he meant "the world to his wife, children and grandchildren" and that he was "ready to serve his country at whatever level needed."

Kenneth died on October 12, 2007 while residing in Wynantskill, NY. He was buried in Cedar Park, Hudson, NY. He was 75 years old.

Ralph Shutts Jr.

Ralph Shutts Jr. was born January 17, 1921 to Ralph and Ethel (Pagan) Shutts of Hillsdale, NY. He grew up on the family farm located near Rte 23 off Old Town Road. He helped his father (a painter and wallpaper hanger) raise chickens, pigs and Holstein dairy cows, which helped provide for the family through the hard times of the 1920s and 1930s.

Ralph attended Roeliff Jansen Central School and graduated in June 1939. His love of farming was cultivated in his youth. Often during the summer he would show dairy cows at the Chatham Fair. This prompted him to try his hand at farming on the family farm after graduation. Having lost his mother as a teenager and then his father a few years later, he decided to enlist in the United States Army.

Upon completion of his training, Ralph was assigned in 1940 to the motorized division of the 1st Battalion at Fort Benning, GA where he attained the rank of corporal.

On April 1, 1942 he was promoted to staff sergeant in the 1st Infantry Division of Artillery at Camp Blanding, FL. Ralph was subsequently assigned to Headquarters Company, 76th Infantry Division at Fort Mead, MD. He was promoted to master sergeant on September 22, 1942.

As the war went into full swing, Ralph was commissioned a second lieutenant on April 22, 1943 and was assigned to Company C, 114th Field Artillery Battalion at Camp Shelby, MI.

It was at Camp Shelby on June 7, 1943 that 2nd Lt. Ralph Shutts, Jr. lost his life. During a training exercise he was run over by a two and a half ton vehicle while he was sleeping on the ground. He was rushed to Camp Shelby hospital where he died of severe abdominal and head injuries. Second Lt. Shutts, Jr. was 22 years old.

Second Lt. Ralph Shutts, Jr. was buried in the family plot on Rte. 22 in Hillsdale, NY next to his mother and father.

VFW Post #7552 honored Ralph Shutts, Jr. and Robert Cadby, Jr. (another local fallen serviceman) by naming their post in their memory – "Cadby-Shutts Veterans of Foreign Wars Post #7552." His name also appears on the Town of Hillsdale Honor Roll of World War II, which is located alongside of the Civil War Monument in the center of town.

Irving Philip Siegel

Irving Philip Siegel was born on December 3, 1921 to Sam and Cecelia (Sasnowitz) Siegel in New York City. He attended school in the Hudson City School District, graduating in 1939. He attended UCLA at Berkley and New York University.

Known as Phil, he enlisted in the United States Marine Corps on May 12, 1942 in Albany, NY. After basic training at Parris Island, SC, he then trained as an aircraft mechanic.

PFC Irving Philip Siegel was assigned to the Pacific Theater of Operations with the Marine Fighting Squadron 422 (VMF 422). The VMF 422 was a Vought F4U Corsair squadron, known as the "Flying Buccaneers" and was a part of the campaigns of Kwajalein and Eniwetok.

PFC Phil Siegel was deployed on the island of Engebi, a triangular shaped island at the northern end of Eniwetok Atoll in the Marshall Island Group. While his unit was being attacked by enemy aircraft, a Japanese bomb exploded near his position. It resulted in a serious injury to PFC Phil Siegel's lower right leg that required immediate amputation (3/8/44). It would be two days before he could be flown from the island and receive the necessary medical attention on the Hawaiian Islands.

After extensive rehabilitation he was honorably discharged on December 13, 1944 at Mare Island Navy Yard, CA.

PFC Irving Philip Siegel was awarded the following: Purple Heart and Presidential Unit Citation.

Phil returned to Hudson, NY. He married Eileen Velda Bellock on June 30, 1946 in Detroit, MI and they raised two children: Alan and Jonathan.

Phil was a self-employed businessman for 39 years and retired while with Sam Siegel and Sons, Inc. He liked to travel, read, bowl and play golf. Aside from driving his 1967 Buick Skylark convertible, he liked to mostly spend time with his grandson, Sam.

Phil was active in his community. He was a member of Congregation Anshe Emeth, VFW, American Legion, Disabled American Veterans, Hudson Elks Lodge #787, Washington Hose Fire Co., B'nai B'rith, AARP and Winding Brook Country Club.

Phil passed away on November 23, 2006 in Hudson, NY and was interned with full military honors in Cedar Park Cemetery, Hudson, NY by a Marine Corps Color Guard. He was 84 years old.

Lowell Dale Sigler

Lowell Dale Sigler was born on March 27, 1933 to Leon and Margaret Kathryn Macy Sigler in Hudson, NY. He attended Ockawamick Central School and later obtaining a GED.

Lowell entered the US Army on April 9, 1951 in Albany, NY and completed basic training at the Hawaiian Infantry Center. SFC Lowell Sigler's military service extends two decades; serving in the U.S., Korea, Germany, Vietnam and the Dominican Republic.

Initially trained in light weapons infantry, his duties included platoon sergeant, section leader, motor sergeant, truck master, infantry operations and intelligence sergeant. His training included Light Weapons Inf., Track Vehicle Mechanic, Airborne Jump School, NCO Leadership Course, Emergency Med. Care, Div. Air Drop, Inf. Operations and Intellegence as well as Corp of Engineers Dive School, Harbor Master, Demolitions and Signal Corps.

SFC Lowell was assigned in 1951 to the Korean Peninsula for 14 months. He saw action in the CCF Spring Offensive1951, UN Summer/Fall Offensive 1951 and 1952 where he was wounded and awarded the Purple Heart. He served a second tour of duty in Korea (1960), Vietnam (1963) and the Dominican Republic (1965) with distinguished units that included the 1st Cavalry Division, the 82nd Airborne Division and the United States Special Forces.

After twenty years of service, SFC Lowell Dale Sigler was honorably discharged on June 30, 1971 and was awarded the following : Purple Heart, Combat Infantry Badge (second award), United Nations, National Defense (with Bronze Service Star) and Korean Service Medals (with four Bronze Service stars), Vietnam Campaign Ribbon (with Device), Rep. Vietnam Gallantry Cross with Palm Unit Citation Badge, Republic of Korea Presidential Unit Citation Badge, Armed Forces Expeditionary Medal, Parachutist Badge, Good Conduct Medal (fifth award), Expert Rifle Medal, Automatic Rifle, Carbine, Grenade Launcher and Pistol Bar.

Lowell married Janet Cole on June 21, 1953 in Hudson, NY and they raised four children: Deborah, Timothy, Steven and Mark.

Lowell worked at V&O Press and Johnny's Ideal Printing in Hudson, NY. and was a member of the Philmont Rod and Gun Club, Vice Commander of the Columbia County Chapter of 195 DAV and local veterans organizations.

Lowell died on February 3, 2009 and donated his body to Albany Medical College after which his remains were cremated. He left behind four children, nine grandchildren and six great-grandchildren. He was 75 years old.

William Henry Silliman

William Henry Sillman was born in Old Chatham, NY on December 11, 1911 to Lawrence and Julia (Thorne) Sillman. He attended Riders Mills Elementary and Old Chatham High School.

Although he never finished school, he was known as a hard working man who had "street smarts" and a love for family, community and country.

William entered the United States Army on September 23, 1943 in Albany, NY. He qualified with the Springfield 03 rifle in basic training and then received additional training in the area of transportation.

On May 12, 1944, Sgt. William H. Silliman was assigned to the European Theater of Operations with the 741 Railway Operations Battalion.

Railroads were strategically important to the war effort in Europe. Victory required reliable transportation for troops as well as supplies (beans, bullets and blankets). To ensure the men and supplies reached their necessary destinations, required a great deal of planning and skilled manpower.

Sgt. William Silliman provided that skilled manpower as engineer of Locomotive 110. He was one of countless many who performed a quiet, yet important assignment which culminated in victory over fascism in Europe.

Sgt. William Henry Silliman was awarded the European Middle Eastern Campaign Medal, the WWII Victory Medal and the Good Conduct Medal.

William returned to the States and was honorably discharge on April 2, 1946 at the Separation Center at Fort Dix, NJ.

For the next thirty-two years William put his skills to good use with the New York Central and Penn Central Railroads, and retired in 1974.

In the intervening years he married Katherine Traver in a ceremony in Chatham, NY on Easter Sunday 1947 and helped raised their son, David.

William remained active in his community. He was a member of the Ghent VFW, Rider Mills Historical Society, Old Chatham's Gentlemen's Club, Brotherhood of Railroad Trainman Union, Past Commander of Chatham American Legion Post 42, and the past superintendent of the Chatham Rural Cemetery. He was a communicant of the United Methodist Church of Chatham.

With great fondness his granddaughter recalls being taught how to drive, feeding ducks, or learning *"a little something about almost every gravesite in the cemetery."* Living next to the railroad, William liked to explain each type of car on the passing train to his grandchildren. For years he would *"scale the stairs to wind the clock that towers over Main Street in Chatham."* Life's lessons were simple to William, his granddaughter recalled: *"work hard, live life just and right, love your country and be thankful for those who lived before you, that we may live a safer life for generations to come."*

William passed away on March 17, 2000 and was buried in Chatham Rural Cemetery. He is missed by his family, friends and community. He was 88 years old.

George W. Sitser

George W. Sitser was born on April 4, 1925 to John and Josephine Sitser in Catskill, NY. He attended elementary school in Catskill and graduated from Ockawamick Central School in Philmont, NY.

George entered the United States Army on September 27, 1943. In basic training he qualified with the M1 Rifle, Carbine and the Colt 45 semi-automatic pistol. He then received additional training as an ammunition handler for a heavy machinegun squad.

PFC George W. Sitser was assigned to the 349 Infantry, 88th Division in the European Theater of Operation. Landing in Sicily on April 4, 1944, he participated in three major campaigns in Italy: the Rome-Arno, North Apennines and Po Valley; for which he received three campaign ribbons.

PFC George W. Sitser was honorably discharged on November 15, 1945 at Camp Breckinridge, KY.

PFC George W. Sitser was awarded the following: Combat Infantry Badge, WWII Victory Medal, European, African, Middle Eastern Theater Ribbon with three Bronze Stars and the Good Conduct Medal.

George returned home and married Adeline E. Coon of Red Hook, NY on November 5, 1947at the Methodist Church in Philmont, NY and went to work for the Atlas Cement Company for the next thirty-three years. Together he and Adeline raised two children: Linda and Robert.

George died on June 14, 2011 and is buried in Cedar Park Cemetery, Hudson, NY. He was survived by his two children, six grandchildren and five great-grandchildren. He was 86 years old.

James G. Smith, Jr.

James G. Smith, Jr. was born February 15, 1924 to James and Fabiola (Girard) Smith in Hudson, NY. Graduating from Hudson High School in 1942, he worked assembling refrigerators for McCalls Refrigeration in Hudson.

James enlisted the United States Marine Corp on December 14, 1942. After Basic Training at Parris Island, he received additional training for water distillation at Camp LeJeune, NC. PFC James G. Smith, Jr. was then assigned to H&S Company, 4th Engineering Battalion, 4th Marines in the Pacific.

For the next two years James participated in several major operations: Kwajalein Atoll, Saipan, Tinian and Iwo Jima. The 4th Marines received a Presidential Unit Citation for its part on Saipan and Tinian, stating (in part):

"Unflinching despite heavy casualty ... (and) unchecked by either natural obstacles or hostile fire, these ... indomitable men spearheaded a merciless attack which swept Japanese forces before it and ravaged all opposition ... in these vital islands."

On Iwo Jima, PFC James Smith saw the raising of the American Flag on Mt. Suribachi. The fighting there was described as "a nightmare in hell" with death resulting in "the greatest possible violence."

Adm. Nimitz stated, "Among the men who fought on Iwo Jima, uncommon valor was a common virtue".

After three years, PFC James G. Smith was honorably discharged on November 14, 1945 at Bainbridge, MD.

Jim returned home and attended college on the GI Bill. He met and married Ann Chaikowski and they raised two children: David and Patti. For the next thirty years, Jim worked as an industrial arts teacher at Ockawamick Central School, where he later retired.

Jim remained active in his community. He was a member of the Color Guard for the Ghent VFW, delivered Meals on Wheels, and was a communicant of

Christ Episcopal Church in Hudson.

James G. Smith, Jr. died on October 23, 2009 and was buried at Cedar Park, Hudson, NY next to his wife. He was 84 years old. Semper Fidelis.

Chester Pershing Smith

Chester Pershing Smith and his twin, Roland Foch Smith, were born in Hudson, NY on November 16, 1918 to Chester and Elsie Smith. Born just days after the armistice in WWI, they grew up and attended school in Hudson.

Chester went to work with his father, installing electrical appliances and equipment while Roland was employed as a maintenance man.

In October 1940 both enlisted in the Armed Services at the State Armory in Hudson, NY.

Chester received basic training at Ft. McClellan, AL and later additional training for chemical warfare at Edgewood Arsenal, MD. He attained the rank of staff sergeant where his duties included, telephone switchboard operator, topographic draftsman, message center chief and duty NCO.

During the next few years, SSgt. Chester Smith was assigned to duty stations at Camp Hawn, and Ft. Ord CA. He was then stationed at Pearl Harbor, and Hickham Field in the Hawaii Islands (3/42- 3/43), where he was assigned to protect and defend American assets and interests.

The remainder of the war was spent in the States (3/43-9/45) at Camp Hale and Camp Carson, CO. For his service to his country SSgt. Chester Smith was awarded the American Defense Service Medal, the Asiatic-Pacific Service Medal, the WWII Victory Medal and the Good Conduct Medal.

Chet married Mary E. Nimmons on June 4, 1944. When he returned home to his family, he became active in the American Legion Post 184 (former commander), the C.H. Evans Hose and Ladder Fire Co. #3 of Hudson and a charter member of the Honor a Vet Committee of Columbia County.

Chester died on February 27, 2005 at the age of 86 and is buried at Cedar Park Cemetery in Hudson, NY.

Roland Foch and his twin brother, Chester Pershing, are given the middle name honoring two generals who distinguished themselves during the WWI, as well as his father. It is fitting that these brothers – who were born, raised and enlisted together – be recognized and honored for their distinguished service to their country during WWII.

Harold J. Smith

Harold James Smith was born on November 23, 1925 to Edgar and Elizabeth (Storm) Smith in Hudson, NY. He grew up in Hudson where he attended elementary and high school.

Harold entered the United States Army on March 8, 1944 and after basic training, where he qualified with the M1 Garand, became an infantryman. Harold was assigned to the 386th Infantry Regiment in the European Theater of Operation on May 2, 1945.

Pvt. Harold Smith participated in combat operations in the Rhineland (Germany) until the end of hostilities and then returned to the United States on April 23, where he was honorably discharged on May 2, 1946.

For his service Pvt. Harold J. Smith received the following awards: Combat Infantry Badge, American Campaign Medal, Asiatic Pacific Campaign Medal, EAME Campaign Medal, and the World War II Victory Medal.

Harold returned home to complete high school where he met his future wife Anna Concra. Together they raised four children: James, David, Harold Jr., and Robert.

Harold was the owner and operator of the A-Z Cleaning Company in Hudson, NY for more than twenty-five years.

Active in his community, Harold was a member of the Hudson American Legion (and treasurer 20 yrs), Hudson VFW, and the Hudson Elks #787. He was also an alderman for the 2nd Ward in Hudson, NY from 1974-1980 and member of the Board of Director for the Hudson Development Corp.

Harold died on December 12, 2012 and was buried in Cedar Park Cemetery, Hudson, NY. He left behind four sons, five grandchildren and four great grandchildren. He was 88 years old.

Roland F. Smith

Roland Foch Smith and his twin, Chester Pershing Smith, were born in Hudson, NY on November 16, 1918 to Chester and Elise Smith. Born just days after the armistice in WWI, they grew up and attended school in Hudson.

Chester went to work with his father installing electrical appliances and equipment, while Roland was employed as a maintenance man. In October 1940 both enlisted in the armed services at the State Armory in Hudson, NY.

In the ensuing years, Roland saw action with the infantry in the Pacific Theater of Operation in Marshal, Marianas and Ryukyus island groups.

Attaining the rank of staff sergeant, he earned the following awards: Combat Infantry Badge, American Defense Medal, Asiatic-Pacific Medal and the Good conduct medal.

He was honorably discharge at Fort Dix, NJ on September 19, 1945.

Roland returned to Hudson and worked as a toolmaker of which he would retire later in life. He met and married Wilma Stupplebeen on March 9, 1946. Together they raised three sons: Peter, Richard and Ronald.

He remained active in the Hudson American Legion Post #184 serving as commander. He was a member of the C.H. Evans Hose and Ladder Company #3 of Hudson, NY and Hudson Elks Lodge #787.

Roland died on August 10, 2003 at the age of 85. He left behind his loving wife, Wilma, and his three sons.

Roland Foch and his twin brother, Chester Pershing, are given the middle name honoring two generals who distinguished themselves during the WWI, as well as their father. It is fitting that these brothers – who were born, raised and enlisted together – be recognized and honored for their distinguished service to their country during WWII.

Walter E. Smythe

Walter E. Smythe was born June 27, 1916 in Montreal, Canada to Walter and Kathleen (Gibbs) Smythe. He grew up in New York City where he attended All Hollows Catholic School.

Walter enlisted in the United State Army in the early spring of 1942 and received infantry training at Camp Croft, SC. After receiving training for infantry, demolitions and anti-tank, he was assigned to an anti-tank crew with the 9th Infantry Division in the European Theater of Operations.

On Dec. 11, 1942 the 9th Infantry Division was deployed overseas to invade North Africa. It pushed through Tunisia into Bizerte, which fell in May 1943. Tec. 5 Smythe then landed at Palermo, Sicily that August.

After being sent to England for the impending cross-channel invasion of France, he landed in Normandy on June 10, 1944, thus cutting off the Cotentin Peninsula and assisting in the capture of fortified Cherbourg Peninsula.

In July he participated in the breakthrough at St.-Lo and with the 9th Infantry Division swept across northern France. It held defensive positions near the Roer River from December 1944 through January 1945, then crossed the Rhine at Remagen Bridge on March 7, 1945, pushing into the German Harz Mountains.

After the Battle of the Bulge, the 9th Infantry Division was nicknamed "Old Reliable."

After seeing action at Algeria-French Morocco, Tunisia, Sicily, Normandy, Northern France, Rhineland, Ardennes-Alsace, and Central Europe during WWII, on August 10, 1945 Tec. 5 Walter Smythe was honorably discharged from the United State Army at Fort Dix, NJ. He was awarded the: Bonze Star, Purple

Heart, eight Battle Stars, three Invasion Arrowheads and the Combat Infantry Badge.

Walter returned home, married Emma Hoffmeister and raised their son, Walter G. Smythe. As a chemical engineer, he lived in Austerlitz, NY and worked for Dek Tillett Ltd. in Sheffield, MA, where he retired in 1978.

All the while, Walter was active in the 9th Infantry Division Association.

On August 24, 1989, Walter passed away at the Berkshire Medical Center and was buried with military honors at St. Peter's Cemetery in Great Barrington, MA. He left a wife, a son and three grandchildren.

We owe a debt of gratitude to Walter Smythe and all those who protect and defend our country, and share in the common risk and a common fate in the name of freedom and for the cause of liberty.

Robert E. Spoor

Robert E. Spoor was born to Burton A. and Geannette Spoor on February 8, 1923 in Schenectady, NY. Growing up in Schenectady he attended and graduated from Mt. Pleasant High School.

As a civilian meter reader, Robert enlisted in the United States Army on October 2, 1942 and entered active duty on July 20, 1943. In the interim period between enlistment and entering the service, Robert completed a 144-hour course, "Fundamental of Radio I, and "Fundamentals of Radio II" at Rensselaer Polytechnic Institute. After signal corps basic training, Robert received additional training at Central Signal School where he became a communications installer and repairman.

PFC Robert E. Spoor was assigned to the Eastern Theater of Operation, arriving in England on March 21, 1944. Assigned to the 3110th Signal Service Battalion, his responsibilities were installing and repairing telegraph and telephones as well as maintaining essential switchboards.

Having entered "Fortress Europe" at Normandy, he fought in Northern France and Central Europe, experiencing intense action in battles like The Battle of the Bulge in Belgium.

His unit received a Presidential Unit Meritorious Award for its vital role in communication preparations for the D-Day Invasion. Remaining in Europe as a part of the occupational forces, Robert set sail for the States in February 1946 and was then honorably discharged at Fort Dix, NJ on March 3, 1946.

PFC Robert E. Spoor was awarded the following: World War II Victory Medal, European-African-Middle Eastern Service Medal with two Battle Stars, Presidential Unit Meritorious Service Award, Good Conduct Medal and the Marksman's Rifle Badge.

Returning to civilian life, Robert went to work for Niagara Mohawk Power Corporation as a site planner.

He met and married Mildred Sweet on June 19, 1949 and in the ensuing years they raised two children: Robert and Barbara.

Robert remained active in his community. He was a member of the: VFW of Scotia, NY Fire Police, Treasurer for Hudson A.B. Shaw Fire Co., Elder for the Claverack Dutch Reformed Church, and Den Dad for Claverack Cub Scout Pack 121.

Robert passed away on February 2, 2008 and is buried in the cemetery at the Dutch Reformed Church in Claverack, NY. He left behind a lovely wife, Mildred, two children: Robert and Barbara. He was 84 years old.

Frederick J. Stark, Jr.

Frederick J. Stark was born April 25, 1925 to Frederick J. Stark, Sr. and Beulah Augusta Stark. After graduating from high school, Fred attended Iowa State University of Science and Technology and Syracuse University.

He entered the United States Navy on November 4, 1943 and after basic training he attained the rank of Apprentice Seaman. He was subsequently promoted to electricians mate 2nd class. He was assigned to the Pacific Theater of Operations and served in the Philippines and Okinawa campaigns.

He was honorably discharged on June 3, 1946 at Lido Beach, Long Island, NY. For his service EM2C Fred Stark was awarded the following: Asiatic-Pacific Medal w/2 stars, Philippines Liberation Medal, Occupation Medal and the WWII Victory Medal.

Fred passed away on Sunday, April 2, 2017. He left behind his wife, Joan; children Frederick, Phillip, William, Jean, Cathy Riegl of Taghkanic, three grandchildren Marc Riegel, Marie Stark, and Erick Stark, and three great grandchildren.

Benjamin Allen Stevenson

Benjamin Allen Stevenson was born on February 7, 1975 to John and Laura Stevenson in Albany, NY. He attended Ichabod Crane Central School (Valatie, NY), Doane Stuart (Rensselaer, NY), and Stimson Valley High School (San Antonio, TX).

Growing up, Ben was active in the Cub Scouts, Civil Air Patrol and a member of the St. Paul's Church in Kinderhook. His mother recalls that from elementary school, Ben wanted to be in the Army.

Although he recognized that being a soldier was a "dangerous occupation" Ben joined the United States Army on June 10, 1993 in San Antonio, TX. After basic, advanced and airborne training, Ben was assigned to Company D, 325 Infantry Battalion at Fort Bragg, NC.

Serving as a TOW gunner and squad leader, he was then assigned in 1996 to Company D, 82nd Aviation Battalion, where he served as an aircraft power plant repairer and supervisor for the next year and a half. He was then assigned to Katterbach, Germany to Company A, 601 Aviation Support Battalion.

MSgt. Benjamin A. Stevenson graduated from the JFK Special Warfare Center and Training as a Special Forces weapons sergeant in January 2000 and then assigned to Company B, 3rd Batallion, 5th Special Forces Group, Fort Campbell, KY. There he served as junior/senior weapons sergeant, Special Forces intelligence sergeant and assistant operations sergeant. In 2006 he was assigned to United States Special Operations Command, Fort Bragg, NC.

Having previously served in Kosovo, MSgt. Benjamin Stevenson's served ten tours of duty in the war zones of Afghanistan and Iraq. It was on his 10th tour of duty that he and his Special Operations unit (publicly referred to as Delta Force) was engaged in brutal fighting against al Qaeda-related groups which lasted two days.

This U.S./Afghan special operations mission was to attack an insurgency encampment made up of several caves and fortified bunkers in the Paktika province of Afghanistan. This fortification was made up of the Haqqanni network with close ties with al Qaeda.

This operation resulted in the deaths of nearly 80 insurgents, mostly Arab and Chechen fighters, as well as MSgt. Benjamin Allen Stevenson, who died of multiple wounds from small arms fire on July 21, 2011 in Paktika Afghanistan.

MSgt. Benjamin Allen Stevenson was awarded the following: Bronze Star (fifth award), Purple Heart, Meritorious Service Medal, Joint Service Commendation Medal with Valor Device, Army Commendation Medal with Valor Device, Army Commendation Medal (second award), Army Achievement Medal (second award), Army Achievement Medal (fifth award), Presidential Unit Citation, Joint Meritorious Unit Award, Army Good Conduct Medal, (sixth award), National Defense Medal (second award), Kosovo Campaign Medal with Bronze Star, Afghan Campaign Medal with three stars, Iraq Campaign Medal with six stars, Global War on Terrorism Service Medal, Noncommissioned Officer Professional Development Ribbon with number 3, Army Service Ribbon, Overseas Service Ribbon, NATO Medal, Special Forces Tab, Combat Infantryman Badge, Expert Infantry Badge, Aviation Badge, Military Free Fall Jumpmaster Badge, Parachutist Badge, Air Assault Badge, and seven Overseas Bars.

A funeral was held at Hope Mills, NC and his remains were interred in Sandhills State Veterans Cemetery. He leaves behind his wife: Heather, two children: Isaac and Naaman, his mother: Laura, father: John, Uncle: Robert, and two siblings: Daniel and Laura. He was only 36 years old.

Robert J. Stover, Sr.

Robert J. Stover, Sr. was born January 31, 1925 in Glens Falls, NY to Jay and Helena (Manning) Stover. He grew up in Greenwich, NY and attended school at Greenwich Central School.

Robert enlisted in the United States Army on April 2, 1943 in Albany, NY just as the storm in Europe and the Pacific was gathering intensity and strength. After basic training at Atlantic City, NJ, Robert received training as an airplane and engine mechanic in Kerns, UT, and subsequently cook and baker training while in Europe.

Tec/5 Sgt. Robert J. Stover, Sr. departed Biloxi, MS on April 22, 1945 and was assigned to Company I, 142 Infantry Regiment, 36th Division in the European Theater of Operation. Sadly, as he was boarding his ship, he was notified of his brother's death. Bud had been killed on a Rhine River bridge while crossing into Germany.

Having arrived on the eve of the collapse of Nazi Germany, Tec/5 Sgt. Robert Stover was assigned the task of helping to reconstruct a Europe, which had been devastated by six years of death and ruin.

Once, Robert found a young German boy scrounging for food scraps in the company garbage. He fixed a food tray for the 8-year-old and left it where he would find it.

"When the boy returned," Robert's wife recalled, *"someone had given him a gun and told him to shoot an American. He shot Robert in the chest. However, a pocket Bible given to him by his father saved his life."*

After almost a year of Foreign Service, Robert returned to the United States on April 9, 1946 and was honorably discharged on April 15, 1946 at Fort Dix, NJ.

He was awarded the following: Good Conduct Medal, World War II Victory Medal, American Campaign Medal, and the European-African-Middle Eastern Campaign Medal.

Robert resided in Germantown, since 1960 and was a communicant of Resurrection Church. He was active with the Boy Scouts and the Catholic Youth Organization.

Robert is survived by his wife, Elizabeth, and their seven children: Robert, Lois, Frederick, William, David, Edna and Elizabeth.

All four sons served in the Army, Robert in Vietnam and William in Grenada. Robert J. Stover, Sr. died January 15, 1979.

Robert J. Stover, Sr. and countless other Americans fought not only to attain the peace but to retain it as well. We are his legacy and we owe him our immeasurable and enduring gratitude for his dedication to the high cause for which he served.

Raymond W. Strang

Raymond W. Strang was born on December 26, 1931 in Poughkeepsie, NY to Walter and Mary (Pilch) Strang. He grew up in Columbia County, attended Chatham Elementary and High schools and worked on farms during the summer. His father, who drove a tractor trailer, passed away when he was in his teens.

On January 11, 1949 Raymond enlisted for three years in the United States Army at Albany, NY. After basic training at Fort Dix, NJ and additional training at Camp Pickett, he was assigned overseas and served in Germany.

Cpl. Raymond Strang was trained with the military police and served as a prison guard for the next three years. During this time one of the first major international crises of the Cold War resulted in Cpl. Raymond Strang being assigned temporary duty (TDY) in Berlin.

The Soviet Union blocked the Western Allies railway and road access to sectors of Berlin, thus giving them control over the entire city. In response, the Western Allies organized the "Berlin Airlift" to carry supplies to the people in West Berlin resulting in 200,000 flights in one year.

Cpl. Raymond Strang was discharged at Fort Jay, NY on September 2, 1952. He was awarded the Army Occupation Medal (Germany).

Raymond returned home and on January 30, 1953 married Margaret Scholl in Rhinebeck, NY. In the ensuing years they raised five children: Richard, Keith, Ronald, Donna and Lonnie.

Ray worked at the Hudson River Psychiatric Hospital and retired from W. B. McGuires. He enjoyed hunting and was a member of the VFW Post #7765, where he served on the Honor Guard.

Raymond passed away on July 17, 2010 and was buried in Linlithgo Cemetery. He leaves behind a loving wife, Margaret, three children, twelve grandchildren and thirteen great grandchildren. He was 78 years old.

Thomas J. Super

Thomas J. Super was born September 13, 1923 to Michael and Nellie Super in Hudson, NY. He grew up in Hudson and attended Hudson Central School. Prior to his enlistment, Thomas worked as a riveter helper.

Thomas entered the United States Army on February 12, 1943 at Camp Upton, NY. After his basic training Pvt. Thomas Super received additional training as a cannoneer on a 155mm howitzer and on June 10, 1943 he was assigned to the Mediterranean Theater of Operations with the 36th Field Artillery Battalion. Pvt. Thomas Super was assigned to the 155mm howitzer gun crew.

Each gun crew section consisted of a section chief, gunner, assisted gunners, and cannoneers. As No.1 gunner, Pvt. Thomas Super was responsible for elevating the gun and attaching the firing pin.

His units were in campaigns in North Africa, Sicily, Italy, France Germany and Austria; involved in the battles of Central Europe, Naples, Foggia, Rhineland, Rome, Arno, Sicily and Southern France. In the process, Pvt. Super made an amphibious landing.

After two years and four months, Pvt. Thomas Super returned to the United States as a result of demobilization and on October 13, 1945 he was honorably discharged at Ft. Dix, NJ.

For his service to his country Pvt. Thomas J. Super was awarded the European African Middle Eastern Service Medal with bronze arrowhead and six battle stars and the Good Conduct Medal.

Thomas met and married Reubina Quick at the Sacred Heart Catholic Church in Hudson, NY and raised two children: Michael and Stephen.

Thomas worked as a truck driver and auto mechanic, retiring after 20 years with Schermann Trucking.

He was a member of the VFW, American Legion, Washington Hose (50 yrs), Fish and Game and a communicant of Sacred Heart Catholic Church.

On June 17, 1994 he passed away and was buried in Cedar Park Cemetery Hudson, NY. Predeceasing his wife, he left behind two sons, two grandchildren and three great grandchildren. He was 70 years old.

Cyrus E. Sweet, Jr.

Cyrus E. Sweet, Jr. was the eldest of two sons born to Cyrus and Nellie Sweet. Cyrus was born January 31, 1924 in Hudson, NY. Upon graduation from high school, he enlisted in the Army Air Corps and entered the service on September 17, 1942 in Albany, NY.

Cyrus traveled by train to Atlantic City, NJ for basic training and was then transferred to Sioux Falls, SD for additional training as a radio operator and mechanic and finally to Fort Morris, FL. In a final letter to his family, dated July 14, 1943, he writes:

Dear Folks,
... I have a tough day tomorrow and can only get a few hours sleep, so will close. I will write from Savannah or somewhere along the route. Take care of yourselves and you'll hear from me as often as possible. Will write soon.   *Love, Son*

Without a furlough, Staff Sgt. Sweet's B-26 departed from the United States for England with scheduled stops in Greenland and Iceland. On August 4, 1943 his B-26 Martin Marauder departed an air base in southern Greenland. An urgent radio call for help some 200 miles off the coast of Iceland was the last communication from SSgt. Sweet and his crew.

On August 19, 1943 Cyrus's mother received a telegram from the War Department listing her son as missing in action and on August 5, 1945 he was declared dead.

The circumstances surrounding the sudden disappearance of SSgt. Sweet and his crew remain a mystery. He was 19 years old.

SSgt. Cyrus E. Sweet, Jr. was awarded the: Purple Heart, Good Conduct Medal, American Campaign Medal, WWII Victory Medal, Honorable Service Lapel Button WWII and Citations of Honor from General Arnold, Presidents Roosevelt and Truman.

One citation reads:

> *"In grateful memory of Staff Sergeant Cyrus E. Sweet, Jr. who died in the service of his country. He stands in the unbroken line of patriots who have dared to die that freedom might live, and grow, and increase it blessings. Freedom lives, and through it, he lives – in a way that humbles the undertakings of most men."*
>
> *– Franklin Delano Roosevelt*

Like most before him who selflessly pledge their lives, their fortunes and their sacred honor, Staff Sgt. Cyrus E. Sweet, Jr. gave his life so that others might live.

Louis G. Taylor

Louis G. Taylor was born to George and Betty Taylor on July 3, 1953 in Hudson, NY. He attended Hudson elementary and high schools.

Lou enlisted in the United States Marine Corp on August 30, 1972 and received basic training at San Diego, CA. Attaining the rank of corporal, Lou was assigned to the Supply Administration on the Pacific island of Guam. He received training for Marine NCO, Motor Vehicle Operator, Transportation and Storage of Hazardous Material and Passenger Travel Specialist.

Four years later he was promoted to staff sergeant in the Supply Administration as an operations man in Newark, NJ. In 1980 Lou became a traffic management officer, attaining the rank of chief warrant officer.

Lou was married to Stephanie (Cotte) on September 30, 1978 and together they raised two children: Louis Jr. and Robert Taylor.

CW2 Louis G. Taylor was awarded the following: (2) Good Conduct Medals, National Defense Service Medal, Rifle Sharp Shooters Badge, Pistol Sharp Shooters Badge, Meritorious Mast, Meritorious Unit Commendation, Navy Achievement Medal, Humanitarian Service Medal, Certificate of Special Recognition and Letter of Appreciation.

Louis G. Taylor passed away on May 5th 2013 and was buried in Union Cemetery, Mellenville, NY. He leaves behind a wife, two sons. He was 59 years old.

Philip Tkacy

Philip Tkacy was born in Hudson, NY on July 24th, 1917 to the proud parents of Stanley and Mary Tkacy. Prior to enlisting in the service, he worked at Weisack Mills in Hudson. He was active in the Federation of Polish Sportsmen and a communicant of Sacred Heart Roman Catholic Church of Hudson.

Philip entered the United States Army on February 3, 1941 prior to America's involvement in World War II. Upon completion of his training, Philip was assigned to the 27th Infantry Division.

As WWII went into full swing, Philip's unit was assigned to the Pacific Theater of Operation. In the course of four years of military service, PFC Tkacy would visit home only once and see grueling combat on the islands of Eniwetok, Saipan and Okinawa.

On April 23, 1945 PFC. Philip Tkacy was instantly killed by a Japanese artillery shell while engaged with the enemy on the Island of Okinawa. He was 27 years old. 1st Lt. Oscar Vigen wrote to Philip's mother upon his death,

"Philip was one of several men who had been with this company during the entire period of time it has been overseas. From the very first, he proved to be one of the most capable soldiers and infantrymen of the group and he soon earned the respect and confidence of the officers and men of the company. ... We will never be able to fill his place in the esteem in which all men of the company and myself had for him. We are realizing more and more each day what a wonderful friend and fine soldier we have lost."

Okinawa was the last American battle of WWII and its most costly. It claimed 49,000 America casualties before it was over.

Philip's two brother, Joseph and Donald – both navy veterans of the Okinawa Campaign, visited Philip's grave on Okinawa. After the war his remains were returned to the United States and placed in Cedar Park Cemetery, Hudson, NY.

PFC Philip Tkacy was awarded a Citation for Saipan and Okinawa along with the Purple Heart (posthumously).

Andrew Tomchik

Andrew Tomchik was born May 17, 1935 to George and Elizabeth (Gamrat) Tomchik in East Nassau, NY. Growing up in Nassau, he attended elementary, middle and high school. He received a GED while in the service and later attended Hudson Valley Community College.

Andrew entered the United States Air Force on November 11, 1953. After his basic training, he trained as a jet aircraft engine mechanic from February to July 1954 at Chanute Air Force Base, Ill.

Airman First Class(A1C) Andrew Tomchik was assigned to duty in Korea and Alaska where he worked on jet aircraft. He was discharged on October 20, 1957 at Lockbourne Air force Base, OH. He received the National Defense Medal and the Good Conduct Medal.

Andy returned home and in the ensuing years he worked as a jet engine and aircraft mechanic for Pan American World Airlines, a tractor trailer driver, and transportation supervisor for Staats Express Inc..

He married Susan Meyer on September 27, 1975 at the St. Lukes Lutheran Church in Valatie, NY and they raised a son, Christopher.

Andrew suffered from severe hearing loss as a result of working on military aircraft. It was finally recognized and he was granted 70 percent disability by the Veteran's Administration. Andrew retired in 1984 for Staats Express Inc.

Andy remained active in his community throughout his life. He was a member of the Hoag's Corners Ambulance Rescue Squad, Columbia County Sportsman's Federation, senior vice commander of the Korean War Veterans Association, vice commander of the Columbia County Chapter 283 of the Veterans of Foreign Wars, and Columbia Memorial Post chaplain of the Disabled American Veterans of Chatham. He was communicant and council member of St. Luke's Lutheran Church.

Andrew died on June 9, 2007 and was buried in the Kinderhook Cemetery. He was 72 years old. He leaves a son, Christopher, and lovely wife, Susan, who writes:

"I was introduced to Andy while I was camping. Andy loved the outdoors and nature. He was a great fisherman and loved to hunt. Andy was definitely a man of special qualities with his wisdom and knowledge of doing things with perfection. I have never met a man so gifted in so many ways. He loved to tell the stories of his life and places he visited while in the air force and on the road as a truck driver. He could quote and talk about the Bible, which really intrigued people. He was one of a kind and the Lord took the best. I sure miss him."

George H. Traver

George H. Traver was born to Charles Van and Nellie Virginia (Cramer) Traver on May 7, 1918 at Chatham, NY. He attended White Plains and Chatham public schools. The youngest of five siblings (Stener, Frank, Kathlene and Paulene), George worked as a fireman alongside his father, who was an engineer on the Harlem Line, a Division of the NY Central Railroad.

George enlisted in the Marine Corps on January 22, 1942 and completed basic training at San Diego, CA, trained as a rifleman and assigned to Company K, 3rd Battalion, 8th Marines, 2nd Marine Division.

In the fall of 1942 the 2nd Marine Division landed on the Japanese-held island of Guadalcanal in the Soloman Islands in support of the 1st Marine Division. It was during these combat operations that PFC George H. Traver was wounded in the hand and forearm and was sent to New Zealand for medical treatment.

After resupply and training, the 2nd Marine Division made a second amphibious landing on the small island of the Betio in the Tarawa Atoll located within the Gilbert Islands.

On November 20, 1943 the 3rd Battalion, 8th Marines made an amphibious landing on Red Beach 3. Unable to negotiate the coral reef several hundred yards from shore, the marines waded ashore while coming under intense small arms and heavy weapons fire from hidden fortified positions beyond the seawall.

The 3rd Battalion, 8th Marines incurred heavy losses; many of them never reaching shore. That afternoon on Red Beach 3, PFC George H. Traver received his second (fatal) wound to his upper body. He and a thousand of his fellow marines were buried on the Island of Betio. His remains, which were located in "The Lost Cemetery" were exhumed along with 35 fellow marines in June of 2015. His remains were identified with the use of DNA.

PFC George H. Traver received the following awards: Purple Heart with gold cluster, Asiatic Pacific Campaign Medal, WWII Victory Medal, Good Conduct Medal, Sharp Shooters Medal and a Presidential Unit Citation.

PFC George H. Traver's remains were transported to Chatham, NY where his funeral was held with full military honors. He was then interred in the Chatham Rural Cemetery. He leaves behind eleven nieces and nephews and their families. He was 25 years old.

Martin J. Tuczinski

Martin J. Tuczinski was born November 6, 1932 to Martin and Irene (Ryan) Tuczinski, Sr. in Hudson, NY. Raised in Chatham, he attended Chatham Central School and graduated high school in 1950 from Christian Brother's Academy in Albany, NY. Attending Albany Business College, he went to work for the NYS Health Department as a projectionist.

Martin entered the United States Army on December 11, 1952. After basic and advanced training (Aberdeen, MD), Cpl. Martin Tuczinski was assigned to the 48th Ordinance Company in Baumholder, Germany.

He was honorably discharged on November 30, 1954 at Camp Kilmer, NJ.; earning the German Occupational Medal and the National Defense Service

Medal.

Returning home Marty worked for the State Insurance Department as an investigator until 1965. For the next 24 years he was a counselor for the NYS Division of Veteran Services in Hudson, NY where he retired in 1989.

He met and married Carol (Charron) on June 11, 1953, raising three children: Daniel, Deborah and Dale.

Marty served as a committeeman for the Town of Ghent (1968-70), Town of Ghent supervisor (1970-81) and Columbia County Republican chairman (1990-02). In April 1998 Marty was appointed vice president of Off Track Betting for Schenectady and Albany until December 2002, when he continued as secretary to the board until his death.

He was past commander of Ghent VFW Post 5933, past president of Chatham Stanford W. Smith Hook and Ladder Fire Co., board member of the Public Employees Federation, the Chatham American Legion Post 42, the Chatham Rescue Squad, and Glencadia Rod and Gun Club.

Marty died on April 15, 2003 after a courageous battle with cancer. Recognized for his service to country and community, he was eulogized as an *"extraordinary leader and man,"* a *"great leader and friend"* known for *"fairness, strength and compassion, fostering partnerships,"* a *"diligent worker,"* *"an astute politician,"* a *"humanitarian"* and *"family man,"* and a *"devout, Roman Catholic."*

Then-Gov. George E. Pataki said, *"The Capital Region lost a true public servant and friend . . . no one more committed or who fought harder for the interests of Columbia County."*

Marty was laid to rest at St. James Cemetery, Ghent, NY. He left behind his loving wife, a sister, (Lorraine Bowes), three children, and seven grandchildren. He was 70 years old.

William Dudley Van Alystyne, Jr.

William D. Van Alystyne was born August 11, 1925 to William Dudley, Sr. and Gertrude Anna Van Alystyne in Albany, NY.

William entered the United States Army on November 22, 1943. After basic training he was assigned to the European Theater of Operations. Sgt. William Van Alystyne, Jr. served in Italy and saw action in the Rome-Arno, North Apennines and Po Valley campaigns.

He was honorably discharged on January 28, 1946 at Fort Dix, NJ. For his service he was awarded the following: E.A.M.E. Service Medal, Good Conduct Medal, WWII Victory Medal and a Presidential Unit Citation.

Joseph Warren Van Deusen

Joseph W. Van Deusen was born December 26, 1918 to Charles and Magdalena (Spath) Van Deusen in Hudson, NY. He attended Hudson Central School District where he was class president for three years and graduated in 1937.

Working as a shipping and receiving clerk, he entered the United States Army on August 30, 1943. After basic training Joseph received Basic Pilot Training (1051 Pilot T E) at Shaw Field, SC and the Advanced Pilot Training at Turner Field GA where he was qualified to fly B-25.

1st Lt. J. Warren Van Deusen was assigned to Squadron E. 112 AAF at Westover Field , MA flying a B-25. A B-25 with a crew of six was known as the Mitchell. It was a medium bomber that had a range of 1,350 miles with a cruising speed of 230 mph and was famous for the Doolittle Raid on Japanese on April 18, 1942.

During WWII Westover Field became the largest military air facility in the Northeast. Early in the war it was used for anti-submarine operations against German U-Boats and as a training base.

Lt. Van Deusen trained hundreds of servicemen who would fly B-25s and the P-47s in the European Theater of Operation.

After hostilities ended, Lt. Joseph W. Van Deusen was honorably discharged on December 1, 1945. For his service he was awarded the American Theater Ribbon and the WWII Victory Medal.

Returning home he met and married Alice E. Hennessy on April 26, 1947 in Hudson, NY. For the next 38 years he worked for Hudson City Savings Institution as a bank president and CEO, retiring in 1982.

He was active in his community serving on many boards: Columbia County Indus. Management Club, Empire State Cert. Devl. Corp., Greater Hudson Chamber of Commerce, president of Greenport and Hudson Board of Ed., Board of BOCES, Co-Chair Community Chest and Red Cross Drives, Hudson Jaycee Distinquish Service Award, Director AAA Hudson Valley, president of Greenport Historical Society and Hudson Rotary Club, deacon elder/treasurer of First Reform Church of Hudson, Columbia Golf and Country Club.

Joseph passed away on March 31, 2017 and was buried in Cedar Park Cemetery, Hudson, NY. Predeceased by his wife Alice who died in 2011; he left behind three children: Dirck, Kathleen, Christine, and four grandchildren. He was 98.

Charles Henderson Van Deusen, Jr.

Charles Henderson Van Deusen, Jr. was born November 15, 1914 to Charles and Magdalena (Spath) Van Deusen in Livingston, NY. He attended Hudson school and graduated in 1933.

Working as a machinist, he entered the United States Army on June 1, 1942 in Albany, NY. Qualifying as a marksman with the M-1 in basic training, Charles was then trained as an air operations specialist and assigned to the Army Air Force.

On October 16, 1942, Cpl. Charles Van Deusen, Jr. was assigned to the 11th Army Air Force in the Aleutian Islands (Alaska) as a machinist with air ground crew and runway maintenance at Kodiak and Dutch Harbor.

Cpl. Charles Van Deusen, Jr. returned to the States on November 6, 1944 and was assigned to the 4000th AAF Base Unit at Paterson Field, OH, where he was honorably discharged on October 27, 1945.

For his service he was awarded the Asiatic-Pacific Theater Ribbon with Bronze star and the Good Conduct Medal.

Returning home he met and married Doris Anderson in May 1948 at Christ Church in Hudson, NY.

He worked for Gifford-Wood Co. until 1960 as a machinist, personnel manager and then personal assistant to Ben Gifford. He then went to work for Van Tassel Tool Company in Hudson, NY until his retirement in 1978.

Charles remained active in his community with the Hudson International Rotary, Hudson Elks 787, Hudson Mystics Athletic Club, Hudson Columbia Golf and Country Club and as warden in Christ Episcopal Church in Hudson, NY.

Charles passed away on August 2, 1982 and was buried in Cedar Park Cemetery, Hudson, NY. He left behind a son, Neal, and a daughter, Allyn. He was 67.

Glenn C. Wallace

Glenn Clayton Wallace was born August 27, 1932 in Glens Falls, NY to George and Elizabeth Wallace. He attended St. Mary's Academy and after graduation he attended the College of Holy Cross and Albany Business College, where he receive an Associate's Degree in Business Administration and Accounting.

Glenn entered the United States Navy on October 18, 1954 at Albany, NY and after basic training he was assigned to the U. S. Amphibious Base at Little Creek, Norfolk, VA as a yeoman. Yeoman Third Class (Y3) Glenn C. Wallace was charged with the administrative and clerical duties necessary to the daily functioning of the United States Navy with tasks such as: preparing, typing and routing correspondence and reports, organizing and maintaining files, operating office equipment, receiving and sorting mail, receiving office visits and handling telephone communications, performing office personnel administration, while serving as office manager.

Y3 Glenn C. Wallace served in the navy reserves from April 16, 1956 to June 8, 1960, where he was then honorably discharged.

Glenn married Arlene Avery on December 1, 1956 and together they raised two children: Mark and Linda.

Glenn worked for Travelers Insurance Company for 30 years in management, marketing and underwriting; retiring in 1993. He also worked as special investigator for the Liquidation Bureau of NYS Ins. Dept. (1996-2002). Glen served as election commissioner on the Columbia County Board of Elections ('86-'97), asst. sergeant-at-arms for NY State Senate ('89-'92), and constituent service rep. for Sen. Stephen Saland '93-'96).

Glenn remained active in his community. He was a scout master for Kinderhook Troop 113 and chairman of the Mahikan District Advancement Committee. He was a member of the Friends of Lindenwald, Knights of Columbus, Kinderhook Elks (PER), Marion Stegmann Fund (chairman), Kinderhook Palmer Engine & Hose (pres./tres.), Kinderhook Sportmen's Club (tres.), Kinderhook Town councilman and communicant of St. John the Baptist.

Glenn passed away on October 2, 2014 and was buried at Linlithgo Reformed Cemetery in Livingston, NY. He left behind his son, Mark, his daughter, Linda, and three grandchildren: Sean, Sarah and Nicholas. He was 82 years old.

Richard Miller Walsh

Richard Miller Walsh was born April 4, 1924 in Hudson to Alfred Miller Walsh and Dora Lampman Walsh. While living in Mellenville, he attended school at Philmont Elementary and Philmont High School.

Richard entered the Army on January 4, 1945 at Albany, NY. After basic training he was assigned to Panama, with the responsibility to protect this vital passageway.

He attained the rank of corporal and was honorably discharged on November 24, 1946. Cpl. Walsh was awarded the WWII Victory Medal, the Panama Service Medal and the Good Conduct Medal.

Richard returned home where he married Eleanor McNaughton on November 6, 1948. Together they raised three children: Stephen, Coleen and Judith.

For 42 years he worked as a supervisor of the G.E. Naval Ordinance Department at Pittsfield, MA and was known for his dedicated work ethic. He was active in the Reformed Church and the Chatham American Legion.

Richard was known as a good and devoted family man with a good sense of humor. He enjoyed cooking, making home improvements or spending a day fishing with his son.

Richard died on June 6, 1985 at the age of 61 and he is buried at Mellenville (NY) Cemetery.

Francis M. Ward

Francis M. Ward was born June 26, 1918 in The Bronx, NY. He entered the United States Army on March 21, 1941 in Jamaica, NY.

Francis received basic training at Fort Bragg, NC and later, advanced training as a sound ranging observer at Fort Sill, OK. His group acted as cadre for new troops until January 1, 1944 when he embarked on a troop ship in New York Harbor bound for Europe.

The purpose of sound ranging observer is to operate ahead of the troops with three separate units spread out in a triangle fashion to pick up the sound of enemy guns. The coordination of data, when relayed back to the allied artillery, permits them to locate the enemy gun emplacements for counter-fire.

Cpl. Ward's job consisted of gathering data at one of three outposts near the front lines and relaying this information back to headquarters. It would then be used to locate and destroy enemy guns. He once remarked that he often found himself closer to the German lines than his own.

Francis was stationed in Ireland until D-Day (plus three) when he landed on Omaha Beach in Normandy and became part of the greatest amphibious landing in the history of military warfare. He was action in numerous engagements while attached to the First, Third and Seventh Army throughout Northern France, the Battle of the Bulge, Central Europe and the Rhineland in Germany. On one occasion he captured three German soldiers single handedly.

Fate placed him at the infamous Nazi concentration camp at Dachau, Germany where he aided in the liberation of thousands of starving men, women and children. In retrospect, he thought that these people were so grateful to get out of the war and go where there was some food. He told his wife, "They looked so emaciated."

He was awarded the American Theater Defense Service Medal, the European-African-Middle Eastern Service Medal and the Good Conduct Medal.

From 1946 until his death on September 29, 2000, Francis lived and worked in Columbia County.

He was a devoted husband, loving father, a kind and caring friend and neighbor. Francis played a significant part in what Tom Brokaw called "The greatest generation." He says, ". . . I had come to understand what this generation of Americans meant to history. It is, I believe, the greatest generation any society has ever produced."

Francis' legacy is his family, friends and a very grateful nation.

Samuel B. Webb

Gen. Samuel B. Webb was an aide-de-camp to Washington and wounded in three battles. He was a notable participant in the first inauguration of George Washington as our president.

He married Claverack's Catherine Hogeboom in 1790 and they lived as notable citizens with all seven children born on Webb Road.

They are buried in the Dutch Reformed Cemetry, Claverack. The Webb family has continued to be important in our national life. In the 20th century, they created the great Museum in Shelburne, VT.

Webb, Samuel Blatchley, soldier, born in Wethersfield, CT, December 15, 1753; and died in Claverack, NY, December 3, 1807.

He was descended from Richard Webb, of Gloucestershire, England, who was made a freeman of Boston in 1632, and accompanied the Rev. Thomas Hooker in the settlement of Hartford, Connecticut, in 1635. He was a step-son and private secretary to Silas Deane, and took part at an early age in the movements that preceded the Revolution.

In command of a company of light infantry, he left Wethersfield for Boston on hearing of the Battle of Lexington, participated in the Battle of Bunker Hill, where he was wounded, and was commended in general orders for gallantry. A letter that he wrote to his step-father describing that battle is now possessed by the Connecticut historical society at Hartford.

He was soon afterward appointed aide to Gen. Israel Putnam, and on June 21, 1776, was made private secretary and aide-de-camp to Washington, with the rank of lieutenant colonel. He wrote the order for promulgating the Declaration of Independence in New York City, July 9, 1776, and was associated with Col. Joseph Reed a few days later in refusing to receive a letter from Lord Howe that was addressed to "George Washington, Esq."

He was present at the battle of Long Island, was wounded at White Plains and Trenton, and was engaged also at Princeton. He raised and organized, almost entirely at, his own expense, the 3d Connecticut regiment, of which he assumed command in 1777.

He took part in Gen. Samuel H. Parsons' unfortunate expedition to Long Island, was captured with his command by the British fleet, December 10, 1777, and was not exchanged till 1780, when he took command of the light infantry, with the brevet rank of brigadier general.

He arranged the meeting between Washington and Rochambeau at Wethersfield, CT, May 19, 1781, and was a founder of the Society of the Cincinnati in 1783.

When Washington took the oath of office as first president of the United States, Gen. Webb was selected to hold the Bible on which he was sworn.

Arthur C. Whitbeck

Arthur C. Whitbeck was born August 4, 1923 to Arthur and Agnes Whitbeck in Hudson, NY. Growing up in Hudson, he graduated from Hudson High School.

While attending school, Arthur was recognized for his physically ability in basketball, softball; and football. He was voted class vice president ('41), elected to the student council ('42), and voted the most cheerful ('42). While working at Clough's Bowling Alley on 6th Street, Arthur developed into an excellent bowler.

Tech 4 Arthur Whitbeck received training at Fort Knox and Camp Harrison as a tanker. After he finished his training he was assigned to the Eastern Theater of Operation in the 784th Tank Battalion, an Afro-American tank force, with Gen. Patton's 3rd Army.

The Allied forces had landed in Normandy and fought its way across France, into Holland and was poised to strike for the first time at Germany.

In December of 1944, Hitler amassed a weakened, yet, very lethal Army in the Ardennes. He struck the American forces with a fury at Bastone which came to be known as the Battle of the Bulge. The allied forces turned back the Germans with a counterattack, secured a bridge at Remagen and then prepared to thrust into the Rhineland.

Attached to the 35th Infantry Division, the 784th Tank Battalion was heralded as "an effective, courageous, and dependable unit which earned the respect and admiration of the infantrymen who worked well with the tankers."

It was on March 4, 1945 and against tremendous odds, that T/4 Arthur Whitbeck's unit became engaged in hostilities against enemy forces at Sevelen, Germany. A news report at the time stated:

> *"On and off for 18 hours . . . the tank force was badly shot up and trapped when a bridge was blown up behind them. However, they unleashed their own offensive, attacking Nazi parachuters destroying enemy installations and engaging in savage street fighting."*

T/4 Whitbeck's armor unit was badly shot up and it was during this engagement that he died of wounds suffered as a result of this conflict. His remains were interned in the Netherlands American Cemetery in Margraten, Netherlands (Plot K, Row 14, Grave I).

T/4 Arthur Whitbeck was 21 at the time of his death and he was awarded the Purple Heart.

Raymond Clarence Whiteman

Raymond Clarence Whiteman was born in Spencertown on April 21, 1915 to Nellie Leana (Haner) and Harry Early Whiteman and four years later on October 11, 1919 his brother Donald Jones Whiteman, followed.

While Raymond attended Austerlitz Public School and Donald attended Austerlitz and Spencertown Union Free School, they both graduated from Chatham High School.

Majoring in business and Latin, Raymond graduated valedictorian of his class in 1934, was accepted at Albany Business College, however, did not attend.

Donald, also a business major, continued his education at RPI (Rensselaer Polytechnic Institute, a private university in Troy, NY) – a place where in later years he enjoyed teaching.

With the impending invasion of the Japanese mainland and in spite of a wife and two children, Raymond heeded the call to serve his country.

On May 7, 1945 he entered the United States Army and received basic training at Fort Dix, NJ where he scored marksman on the rifle range.

PFC Raymond Whiteman remained stateside in his service to his country and was honorably discharged on January 18, 1946. He was awarded the WWII Victory Medal, the Good Conduct Medal and the Marksman Badge.

Donald Jones Whiteman

Following in the footsteps of his older brother, Donald entered the United States Army on September 4, 1946.

After his basic training, he was assigned as a part of the Army of Occupation in Europe and on May 5, 1947, PFC Donald Whiteman was honorably discharged. He was awarded the WWII Victory Medal, the US Army of Occupation Medal and the Good Conduct Medal.

After their military service, both brothers returned to the United States, where they would continue with their lives in Columbia County.

Raymond returned to his wife, Noreene Mary (Aldrich) and continued to be active in veterans' affairs, especially Chatham American Legion Post 42. He retired from Anti-Corrosive Metal Works at Castleton, NY.

Donald married Rita (Reed) of Ghent, raised a family and started a business, the Craftech Industries of Hudson, NY; where he would remain president until his death.

In his youth, Raymond was a charter member of the Austerlitz "Lone Scouts," the precursor of the Boy Scouts, and held the highest score in Latin at Chatham High School. A devoted family man, Raymond built his own home and for decades played the fiddle at local square dances.

Similarly, Donald was noted for his dedication to his family and community. He, too, was an avid musician, played the saxophone at family gatherings. He was a charter member of the Spencertown Academy.

When their country called, they came; when needed, they served – two brothers whose dedication to country and community was a family tradition.

John Henry Whiteman

Henry Whiteman, who emigrated from Switzerland and participated in the Revolutionary War, first resided on a farm located in Germantown. Later, the Whitemans moved to Austerlitz where, in 1839, John Henry Whiteman was born and grew up on the family farm.

With the advent of the Civil War, on July 31, 1862, Col. David S. Cowles was authorized to raise a regiment in Columbia and Dutchess counties for the Union Army. John Whiteman enlisted at 22 years old in the infantry and became a part of Company A of the 128th New York Regiment, which was made up of recruits from Austerlitz and other area townships.

Mustered in on September 4, 1862 at Camp Kelly (Hudson fairgrounds), the 128th New York Regiment left on the steamship "Oregon" for New York City and then to Camp Millington, near Baltimore, MD by train where it would become a part of the defense of Washington.

In December of 1862 the regiment sailed south on the "Arago" where it was assigned to Gen. Nathaniel Banks Department of the Gulf. The 128th NY Regiment was assigned to confiscate Confederate wares and then to lay siege and to assault Port Hudson, La. (May 27, 1863). In the process they lost many men, including their regimental commander, Col. Cowles. This campaign directly resulted in opening the Mississippi River to the Union forces.

The regiment served as provost and guard duty at Baton Rouge, LA until March of 1864, when it then participated in the Red River Campaign (March 23-May 22).

With a new commander, Col. James Smith, the 128th NY Regiment sailed north to Virginia where they participated in the Gen. Sheridan's Shenandoah Valley Campaign (Winchester, Fisher's Hill, and Cedar Creek).

This campaign was immortalized in the poem "Sheridan's Ride" by Thomas Buchanan Read. As the "breadbasket of the South," Gen. Sheridan was charged to "lay waste" the valley and in so doing, it was said that at the time "a crow had to bring its own lunch" when it flew over the Shenandoah. The regiment ended the war with service in Georgia and then North Carolina.

Sgt. John Whiteman took ill and was hospitalized in Annapolis on August 1864. He mustered out on July 12, 1865 in Savannah, GA and returned to his

Pratt Hill Farm in Spencertown.

In later years he married Elizabeth Howard, and raised four children on his thriving farm renowned for its cherries. He was active in the community church (St. Peters) and fire company (Austerlitz and Spencertown).

In 1910, John died and was buried at St. Peter's Cemetery in Spencertown, NY. He was 72 years old.

Through Sgt. Whiteman efforts during a troubled time in our history, America returned to what President Lincoln called a "just and lasting peace."

Harriett F. Wiebel

Harriett Florence Gates was born October 19, 1919 in Millinocket, ME to Fredrick and Blanche (Turner) Gates. Harriett grew up and attended school in Millinocket, graduating from Sterns High School. She entered Maine General Hospital School of Nursing in Lewiston and earned a degree in nursing in 1940.

After graduation Harriett worked as a register nurse until she joined the United States Army on November 12, 1941 in Lincoln, ME. 1st Lt. Harriett Florence Gates was assigned to the 2nd Evacuation Hospital. Because she had red hair and the last name of Gates, she was nicknamed "Rusty Gate."

In September 1942, Lt. Gates arrived in Belfast, Northern Island. For the next twenty-one months she made many moves caring for the 8th Air Force.

On June 28, 1944, Cpt. Gates' Unit set up a 750 Med Evacuation Hospital on Omaha Beach. From June 1944 to April 1945 her unit earned five battle stars for St Lo, Hurtgen Forest, Battle of the Bulge, Cologne and the Rhineland. During her 33 months of service overseas her unit cared for more than 49,000 patients.

While in the Army Harriett met and married fellow officer, Wallace Williams. Together they raised four children: Wallace Jr., Harriett, Brenda and Judy Ann. Cpt. Harriett F. Gates was honorably discharged on January 27, 1946.

For her service she was awarded the following: European-African-Middle Eastern Theater Campaign Ribbon, Meritorious Service Unit Plaque and the American Defense Service Medal.

Upon her discharge Harriett worked as a registered nurse, and after 24 years as a supervising registered nurse, she retired from Long Beach Memorial Hospital in August 1985. Additionally, Harriett spent many hours serving as a volunteer in Northport, St. Albans and Kings Park VA hospitals. During her volunteer work, she met Clearance Wiebel and on July 27, 1976 they were married in Manorton, NY.

Harriett was a member of: the Southern Columbia Memorial VFW Post, Past Long Beach American Legion (past commander), Long Beach VFW, Long Island AMVETS, Belmore Post of Military Order of the Cooties, Grand Office of

Cooties of the New York State VFW and past patriotic instructor of the New York State VFW. She was the first woman commander of Nassau County Council of the VFW.

Harriet Wiebel passed away on May 29, 2004 at the age of 84 and was laid to rest in Millinocket, ME. She left behind a loving husband, four children, eleven grandchildren and fifteen great-grandchildren.

Kenneth H. Wilber

Kenneth Wilber was born February 5, 1946 to Charles L. Wilber and Bernice V. (Akin) Wilber in Hudson, NY. He attended Chatham Central School, graduating in 1963. He graduated from Albany Business College in 1965.

Kenneth entered the United States Navy on October 20, 1965 in Albany, NY. After basic training he attended additional training at Ellison Field, Pensacola, FL. He was then assigned to the USS Navasota (AO-106) in Long Beach, CA. His deployment in the Western Pacific with the USS Navasota from 1/5/68 to 8/1/68 and then again from 2/24/69 to 9/13/69 took him to the South China Sea and the Sea of Japan.

Attaining the rank of YN3, he was honorably discharged on October 19, 1971. For his service YN3 Kenneth Wilber received the following awards: Vietnam Service Medal, National Defense Service Medal, Armed Forces Expeditionary Medal (Korea), and the Vietnam Campaign Medal.

He returned home met and married Jeannette Lauster. He was employed at Columbia Corporation in Chatham (30 years). They raised two children: Tracy and Kyle.

He was elected as a Ghent Town councilman (1980-81), Ghent supervisor (1980-92) and Columbia County treasurer (1996-2011). He was a member of the Ghent VFW #5933 (commander, post quartermaster), Ghent Marching and Concert Band, Chatham, Am. Legion Post 42, 3rd Dist. NY Veterans of Foreign Wars (past commander), Rip Van Winkle Counties Council Veterans of Foreign Wars (past commander), Columbia County Honor-A-Vet (chairman), Congressional Military Academy Selection Committee (18 yrs), Columbia County Republican Committee (vice chairman), Ghent Volunteer Fire Company (president, board of directors, chaplain), Columbia County Volunteer Firefighters Assoc., Columbia Greene Comm. Col. Board of Trustees, Chatham Christ Our Emmanuel Lutheran Church (treasurer/councilman).

Ken passed away October 27, 2018 and is buried in the family plot in Ghent Union Cemetery. He left behind his wife, Jeannette (51 yrs), two children: Tracy Muller, Kyle Wilber, and four grandchildren: Troy, Regan, Owen, Riley. He was 74 years old.

Edward Martin Witko

Edward Martin Witko was born January 31, 1919 to Andrew and Rose Witko in Nassau, NY. His family moved to Hudson where he attended high school and graduated in 1937 with honors.

Upon graduation Edward went to work, sharing his time between his brother Pete's restaurant in Niverville and his mother's business at 5th and Columbia Street, Hudson, NY.

Despite his busy work schedule, he found time to pursue his favorite pastimes, hunting and fishing. Often in the company of a friend, he would return home with a squirrel, pheasant or a string of freshly cleaned fish for his mother to prepare for dinner.

The day after Pearl Harbor, Edward enlisted, along with his close friend George Karen, in the United States Navy. After completing basic training at Newport, RI, and then a short leave, Coxswain 3rd Class (Cox3) Edward Witko was assigned to a minelayer, the USS Miantonomiah (CM-10). Attached to Mine Division 50, the USS Miantonomiah assisted in efforts to reduce the menace from German submarines along the east coast.

On October 23, 1942 the USS Miantonomiah departed from Yorktown, VA, laden with a full complement of mines in anticipation of the invasion of North Africa.

Joining Center Attack Group (TG 34.9), the USS Miantonomiah laid a defensive minefield north and east of Fedala Harbor, in what became a three-pronged attack on French Morocco. Passing within 25 to 75 yards of her, she narrowly escaped damage from three torpedoes fired from two German submarines.

For the next several months while on board the USS Miantonomiah, Edward assisted in operations in Morocco, the Chesapeake Bay, the Caribbean, and Trinidad. On April 29, she sailed from Bayonne, NJ and arrived in Bristol, England to join the 12th Fleet.

In England, Cox3 Edward Witko prepared for and then participated in the D-Day invasion of Normandy, France.

Between June and September 1944, the USS Miantonomiah was assigned dispatch and escort duty from England and France. Early on the afternoon of September 25, 1944, while navigating the inner and outer harbor of LeHarve, France, the USS Miantonomiah struck an enemy mine. Having just cleared the entrance to the channel with the aid of a French pilot, a tremendous explosion erupted under the engine room.

The USS Miantonomiah sank in 20 minutes with the loss of 58 officers and men. Cox3 Edward Witko was seriously injured and taken to a hospital. At the age of 24, Edward succumbed to his injuries and was buried at St. Andre, France. Later at the request of his family, he was reinterred on April 13th, 1949 at Cedar

Park Cemetery Hudson, NY.

The USS Miantonomiah received two battle stars for action in WWII. Cox3 Edward Witko was posthumously awarded the Purple Heart along with the European-African-Middle Eastern Campaign Medal.

Donald C. Wood
Elizabeth Kerner Wood

Donald C. Wood was born September 27, 1918 to William and Jennie (Miller) Wood in Chatham, NY. He grew up there and attended Chatham Central School.

Donald enlisted in the United States Army and after basic training as an infantryman; he was assigned to the 198th Infantry Battalion, 19th Infantry Division in the Pacific Theater of Operation. While stationed in the Aleutian Islands of Attu and Kiska, he attained the rank of private first class.

For his service PFC Donald C. Wood was awarded the Asiatic Pacific Campaign Medal and the Bronze Star.

Elizabeth Kerner was born June 24, 1919 to Charles and Lola (Wolven) Kerner in Ghent, NY. Growing up in Ghent, she attended the Chatham Central School. In 1935 she went on to receive a nursing degree (registered nurse) at Vassar Hospital in Poughkeepsie, NY.

As a private nurse, Elizabeth enlisted in the United States Army Reserves on July 25,1941and then entered active duty on November 3, 1944.

1st Lt. Elizabeth Kerner was assigned to the Army Nurse Corps in the European Theater of Operation. Serving five months in England and France, she then returned to the United States where she continued to serve in Atlantic City, NJ with Section I 3440 Area Service Unit Station Medical.

1st Lt. Kerner was discharged on June 30, 1949 at Fort Benning, GA and until June 22, 1957, she continued to serve as a nurse in the United States Army Reserves.

1st Lt. Elizabeth Kerner was awarded the EAME Campaign Medal and the WWII Victory Medal.

Donald and Elizabeth met and married on October 1, 1949. They lived in Chatham where they raised three children: Lola, Linda and Charles.

Donald worked as a printer/typesetter for the Chatham Courier while Elizabeth practiced as a nurse with Drs. Marks and Greitzer in their pediatric family practice.

Donald was a member of the Ghent Sportsman's Association, former post commander of Chatham American Legion Post 42, as well as past president of the Ghent Volunteer Fire Company #1. Both Donald and Elizabeth were members of the Ghent, VFW Post 5933.

Donald C. Wood died on April 4, 1981and Elizabeth, who would live another 25 years, died on April 14, 2006. She was buried next to her husband in Ghent Union Cemetery. He was 62 years old; she was 86.

Fidelity in service to their country, to their community and to one another.

Henry F. Wood

Henry F. Wood was born to William J. and Jennie C. Wood on October 20, 1916 in Chatham, NY. There he attended elementary and high school.

Henry was a noted athlete with four years varsity baseball and two years varsity basketball. In honor of Henry and his brother Donald, the Donald and Henry Wood Memorial Award was established for a deserving graduating senior. Later, Henry's love of baseball compelled him to play in the county league.

Working in construction, Henry entered the United States Army on March 7, 1941 in Chatham, NY. He received basic training at Camp Upton, Long Island, NY. He later received chemical training at Edgewood Arsenal, MD, (now known as Aberdeen Proving Ground) and was then assigned to Savannah Airbase, GA. as service aviation support.

Cpl. Henry Wood was assigned to the Philippine Islands on October 20, 1941 just prior to WWII. After the bombing of Pearl Harbor and hostilities broke out, Cpl. Henry Wood, along with United States and Filipino armed forces fought the Japanese for three months on the Peninsula of Bataan.

Taken prisoner along with 75,000 starving and diseased American and Filipino soldiers, Cpl. Wood march for three days without food or water on what is infamously known as the Bataan Death March.

Stripped of weapons and valuables, they were beaten, bayoneted and mistreated; many died of heat exhaustion. Filthy water buffalo wallows along the roadway was the only drinking water available. Those unable to continue were summarily bayoneted, shot or ordered buried alive by fellow prisoners. Failure to do so resulted in one's immediate execution.

Cpl. Henry Wood was interned in the Philippine's POW camp, Cabanatuan, where sweltering heat, overcrowded conditions, meager rations, poor hygiene, lack of proper medical care, forced labor and disease (malaria, dysentery, beriberi) quickly thinned the ranks.

On July 13, 1942 Cpl. Henry Wood died from malnutrition and disease. Originally interred at the United States Military Cemetery in Manila, his remains were repatriated and buried in Ghent Union Cemetery on October 26, 1949 in the family plot. He was only 25 years old.

Cpl. Henry F. Wood was posthumously awarded the Purple Heart, the Asiatic-Pacific Campaign Medal with one star, the POW Medal and the Philippines Defense Medal.

Each day we live our lives, let us pause for a quiet moment to reflect and give thanks to all those who paid the ultimate price for the gift of freedom. God bless Henry F. Wood.

Edward J. Ziemba

Edward J. Ziemba was born September 26, 1913 to Anton and Katherine (Bania) Ziemba in Hudson, NY. He attended Hudson Elementary and High schools.

Edward entered the service on November 21, 1942 in Albany, NY. He was assigned to the 507th Engineer Company, Seventy Corps of Engineers of the 1120th Combat Group. During World War II his unit served in Central Europe in the Ardennes, Normandy, Battle of the Bulge and the Rhineland.

In February of 1945 it became apparent there were no other officers or non-commissioned officers present at the Roer River Site. Having completed his designated mission Sgt. Ziemba of his own accord, took charge of directing bridging operation and traffic. All this took place while under enemy observation and while shells were dropping in the area.

Sgt. Edward J. Ziemba was awarded the Silver Star for gallantry for disregard for his own personal safety during this action.

On November 24, 1945 Sgt. Edward Ziemba was honorably discharged from the United States Army at Fort Dix, NJ. He was awarded the following: Silver Star, Five Bronze Stars, American Service Medal, European-African-Middle Eastern Medal, World War II Victory Medal and the Good Conduct Medal.

On October 27, 1946 he married Helen T. Skiba in Hudson, NY. Together they raised two children: Edward and Mary Ann.

Ed was a steam derrick engineer and operated other heavy equipment for the New York Central Railroad. He was later employed as a foreman with Canada Dry; where he retired in 1975.

Ed was a member of Columbia County VFW Post #1314 (life), Washington Hose Company #3, and the Federation of Sportsmen. He was also a member of Teamsters Union Local 812, St. Mary's Church, Polkaing Club of Sacred Heart Church, and basketball coach. He was elected to the Columbia County Basketball Hall of Fame.

Edward J. Ziemba passed away on June 9, 2005 at the age of 91 and was laid to rest in Cedar Park Cemetery in Hudson, NY. He left behind a loving wife, two children, three grandchildren and five great-grandchildren.

SECTION 2
REVOLUTIONARY WAR
COLUMBIA COUNTY ROSTERS
7TH REGIMENT NYS

Baches, John
Baily, Stephen
Baily, Timothy
Bawney, John
Bell, John A. Lem
Bensk, Rudolph
Berry, William
Berry, William, Jr.
Blanchar, Abiathar
Blanchard, Abraham
Bresee, Jellis
Brewer, Abraham
Bullis, William
Burnham, Mashall
Burton, Josiah

Calder, Hendrick
Cannifif, William
Carn, John
Cecil, Richard
Chapman, Amos
Chapman, Asa
Chapman, David
Chapman, Ezekiel
Chapman, Ezra
Chapman, Noah
Claw, Andrew
Coenraut, Nicholas
Cole, Gerard
Cook, John
Cornelisan, John
Cornelus, John
Cramphin, Ralsan
Crippen, Reuben
Crocker, Amos
Curtis, Ebenezer
Curtiss, David
Curtiss, Joseph

Davis, Dennis
Davis, George
Delamattor, Benjamin
Delametter, Jacob
Deyor, Peter
Dingman, Casper
Dingman, Isaac

Dingman, Jacob
Dobs, Daniel
Dorn, Abraham

Ealon, Elijah
Earl, Moses
Earl, William Jr.
Eldridge, Joseph
Elkenbragh, John
Elkinbrach, John

Feeley, John
Feely, John
Ferguson, Jacob
Folmer, Zemtus
Fols, Conrat
French, John
Fuller, David

Gardaneer, Peter H.
Gardner, Godfrey
Goes, Derick
Goes, Ephraim
Goes, John, Jr.
Goes, Laurence
Goes, Michael
Goes, Tobias
Gould, Jesse
Graper, Ruben
Graves, John
Graves, Richard
Green, Augustus
Gwin, Oren

Haak, Christopher
Hall, Justice
Hamblin, Seth
Hamblin, Zaccheus
Hancy, Fradrick
Hare, Daniel
Hark, Daniel
Hawk, Christopher
Herder, John
Herrick, George
Hoffman, George
Hogan, William

Hoyer, George
Hrkiman, George
Hubbard, David
Huguenin, David
Humphry, Ezra
Huyck, Burger D.
Huyck, Burger I.
Huyck, John, Jr.
Huyck, John A.

Ittick, George L.
Itting, Conrat

Jenkins, Anthony
Johnson, Isaac
Johnson, John
Johnson, Peter
Joslin, Henry

Kane, William
Kelder, Hendrick
Kinne, Jesse
Kittle, John
Kittle, Nicholas
Knapp, Isaac

Lister, Frederick
Luny, William
Lusk, Jacob
Lusk, Michael
Lusk, William

McFail, Patrick
McMichael, James
McPhaile, Patrick
Mans, John J.
Marsail, John
Marshall, Enos
Miller, Casper
Miller, John
Miller, Jonathan
Mitchel, James
Mitchel, James, Jr.
Moet, Coenradt
Moet, Johannis
Molony, John

Montgomery, Alexander
Moore, John A.
Moot, Conrath
Moot, Johannis
Morey, Elisha
Morey, Elisha. Jr.
Morey, Samuel
Moshier, Jonathan
Mott, Henry
Mott, Jeremiah
Mudge, Michael
Muller, John J.

O'Briant, Cornelius
Olthousen, Nicholas
O'Neal, James
O'Neil, John

Paine, Daniel
Painter, Thomas
Pearsee, Isaac
Peersye, Isaac
Peterson, Benjamin
Peterson, Philip
Pew, John
Philip, Pelnis
Philip, Peter
Proper, Frederick

Quithot, Stephen
Randal, Nathaniel
Rees, Benjamin
Richmon, George
Richmond, Conrad
Richmond, Simeon
Robertson, George
Robinson, George
Robison, Jeremiah
Root, Asahel
Root, David
Rowland, Samuel
Rowse, Coenradt
Ryan, Edward
Ryan, William

Salisbury, Sylvester
Sally, John
Sally, Thomas
Salsbury, John
San, Moses
Saunders, Isaac
Scharaly, Peter
Scharp, Jacob
Scharp, John
Scharp, Laurence P.
Scott, John

Scott, William
Sebring, Lewis
Seley, John
Seller, Frederick
Sharp, John
Sharp, Lawrence
Sharsa, Daniel
Shutts, John
Sisson, Richard
Smith, Asa
Smith, Christian
Smith, John
Smith, Joseph
Smith, Samuel
Snyder, Peter
Snyder, Simon
Staats, Abraham
Staats, Abraham J.
Staats, Abraham T.
Staats, Jacob
Staats, John
Staats, John Jr.
Statts, Abraham
Stever, Jacob
Stoplebeen, Johannes
Suthard, Thomas

Thoma, Caleb
Thomas, Jacob
Trusdeil, Kiel
Trusdell, Richard
Trusduil, Iseel

Utly, Jeremiah
Van Aelstyn, Thomas
Van Alen, Abraham
Van Alen, Dirck
Van Alen, Cornelius
Van Alen, Gilbert
Van Alen, Henry
Van Alen, John E.
Van Alen, Peter
Van Alstine, Abraham
Van Alstyne, Leonard
Van Beuren, John
Van Buren, Cornelius
Van Buren, Ephraim I.
Van Buren, Ephraim T.
Van Buren, Francis
Van Buren, Tobias
Vanderpoel, Andrew
Van Derpoel, Andries
Vanderpoel, Jacobus
Van Deusen, Peter
Van Dusen, John
Van Hoesen, Jacob

Van Hoesen, Jacob J.
Van Hoesen, John '
Van Nass, Adam
Van Ness, David
Van Slyck, Dirick
Van Slyck, Peter
VanValkenburgh, Bartholomew
VanValkenburgh,Bartholemew T.
Van Valkenburgh, Claudius
Van Valkenburgh, Jacob
Van Valkenburgh, Jacobus
Van Valkenburgh, Joachim
Van Valkenburgh, Joachim J.
Van Valkenburgh, John
Van Valkenburgh, Lambert
Van Valkenburgh, Lawrance
Van Valkenburgh, Peter I.
Van Valkenburgh, Peter J.
Vosburg, Matthew
Vosburg, William
Vosburgh, Abraham
Vosburgh, David
Vosburgh, Joachim
Vosburgh, Peter A.
Vratenburgh, John
Vredenbergh, John
Wever, George
Wheeler, Samuel
White, Henry
Whitwood, Charles
Whitwood, Cornelius
Whitwood, Samuel
Wickham, Warren
Wilsey, Jacob
Wilson, Andrew
Wilson, Dirick
Wilson, Richard
Wiltse, Jacob
Wingand, James
Wingardt, Jacobus
Witbeck, Andrew
Witbeck, Andrew, Jr.
Witbeck, Andris
Wolf, George
Wolf, Peter
Wolfram, John Tice
Wolfrem, Philip
Wolfrom, Mathise
Wright, Arl
Wright, Daniel
Wyngart, Jacobus
Wynkoop, Peter

Yeralewyn, John
Young, Frederic

Revolutionary War Albany County Rosters Militia 10th Regiment

Colonel Morris Graham
Colonel Henry Livingston
Major Dirck Jansen
Major Samuel Ten Broeck
Adjutant Philip Rockefeller
Qrt. Master. Christen Van Valkenburgh
Surgeon Thomas Thompson

Captains

Joseph Elliott
Adam Hurst
Conrad Kline
Henry Pulver
Diell Rockefeller
Dirck Rockefeller
Jacob F. Shaver
John Shaver
Philip Smith

Nicholas Power
William Rockefeller
Jacob Roschman
Harmanes Ross
Casparus Schultz
Charles Shaver
John Shuts
Jonhannes Staat
Jonhannes Stall
Peter Van De Booart
Henry Will

Lieutenants

John Best
William Casper
Jacob Hagedorn
Bartle Hendricks
Henry Irvine
John McArthur

Ensigns

Leonard Dacker
Asa Holmes
Philip Knickerbacker
Marx Kun
Colin McDonald

Additional names on state treasurer's pay book

Lieutenants

Wandel Pulver
Adam Segendorph

Ensigns

John Herder
Bastain Lesher
James Robinson

ENLISTED MEN

Adams, Baily
Andon, Casper
Angle, Willia-n
Astin, Jacob
Attwood, Timothy
Bain, Casparues
Baker, John
Barganer, Peter
Barnet, John
Barnet, Simon
Bartley, Simon
Basseroom, John
Batts, Johannes
Bearsh, John
Becker, Jacob
Ben, James
Berringer, Peter
Best, Benjamin
Best, Hendrick
Best, Peter
Biest, William
Bitser, Wilhelmus
Blass, Michael
Blass, Peter M.
Blass, William
Bless, Hendrick
Bower, Nicholas, Jr.
Bownen, Hendrick
Bruiree, Johannis N.
Bruise, John F.
Phenber, Jacobus
Cain, Paul H.
Campbell, John
Campbell, Martin
Capes, Martin
Casper, Christian
Casper, Christopher
Cleeveland, Lemuel
Cline, Anthony
Clum, Adam
Clum, Adam, Jr.
Clum, Hendrick
Coale, Johannis
Coale, Peter
Coens, William
Coitrs, John, Jr.
Cole, Isaac
Cole, John
Cole, Peter
Comb, Samuel, Jr.
Concklin, Elisha
Concklin, John
Conradt, Johannes

Coombe, Samuel
Coon, Adam
Coons, Peter
Coons, Philip
Cork, John Jr.
Corol, Michael
Cotman, Conradt
Crammer, William
Cun, Samuel
Cund, Hendrick
Cunn, Adam
Cunx, William
Cunx, William H.
Currey, William
Curry, John
Dacke,r John C.
Danels, Thomis
Dannilly, William
Decker, Abraham
Decker, Benjamin
Decker, Conradt
Decker, George
Decker, Isaac
Decker, Jacob
Decker, Jacob C.
Decker, John
Decker, Lawrence I.
Delamater, Abraham
Dick, Henry
Dick, Paulus
Dicker, Charles C.
Diness, Philip
Diness, Yerry
Dings, Jacob
Dings, John
Dings, Stutfle
Dolph, John
Donnolly, William
Dougherty, Cornelius
Dounatty, William
Douy, Cornelius
Dubois, Abraham
Dunsbach, Philip
Egelston, Benjamin
Elkenbraugh, Jacob
Elkenbrugh, I'hilip
Elliott, Michael
Engell, George
Erkenbergh, Fite
Fox, Jonathan
Frasier, William
Frits, William
Funck, Christian

Funck, Jacob
Funck, Peter
Gardner, James
Gardner, John
Gobobe, John
Graves, Bort
Haber, Johannos
Hagadom, Jacob
Hagedoom, William
Hagedorn, William
Halter, John
Halter, John, Jr.
Halter, Michael
Halter, PH"-
Hatter, John
Hatter, Michael
Hatter, Peter
Haver, Christian
Haver, Johannis
Haver, Peter
Heiser, Petrus
Herder, John
Herder, Michel
Herder, Petrus
Herder, Philip
Heyser, Henry
Heyser, Jacob, Sr.
Heyser, Jacob, Jr.
Heyser, Peter
Hofs, William
Horck, John, Jr.
Houshapple, Zacbarias
Houward, Adam
Hunt, Palathia
Hus, Casper
Hyck, Abraham
Hyck, John B.
Imik, Johannis
Jacobs, Bastian
Janes, David
Jorgh, Michael
Kain, Paul H.
Keephart, Caleb
Kline, Jacob
Kline, Peter
Lape, Jurry
Lape, Thomas
Lasher, Conradt B.
Lasher, G. B.
Lasher, Garret
Lasher, Garret, Jr.
Lasher, Johannis
Lasher, Johannis, Jr.

Lasher, Jehannis J.
Lasher, Philip
Lasher, William
Laubay, Carl
Laubay, Jacob
Lawrence, John
Lawrence, Peter
Lemnery, Solomon
Lesher, Bastian
Loomis, John
Lynch, Peter
McArthur, Arthur
McArthur, John P.
McClean, Hector
McIntire, John
MacFall, Hendrick
MacFall, Neal
MacFall, Patrick
McFall, Robert
McGill, John
Mayer, Johannis
Merky, Max
Meyer, Friderick
Miller, Jonas
Miller, Matthew
Minklar, Jacob
Moor, Peter
Moor, Philip
Mower, Barent
Nash, John
Needen, John
Nott, John
Ostrander, Benjamin
Ostrander, John
Parish, John
Parve, Daniel
Petri, Cunrath
Petrie, Conrad C.
Phillips, Christian, Jr
Phillips, Christopher
Phillips, ChristopherJr.
Phillips, John
Phillips, Peter
Plass, Peter
Plass, Peter M.
Polver, Jacob
Post, William, Jr.
Pulver, Wandel
Purden, Edward
Quackenbos, Daniel
Quackenbos, Garret
Race, Benjamin
Race, Ephraim

Radclift, John
Rath, Adam
Renolds, Lusia
Ringsdorph, Phillip
Risdorf, George
Robertson, James
Robinson, James
Rockefeller, Diell, Jr.
Rockefeller, Simeon
Rose, Andrew A.
Rosman, Samuel
Rossman, Adam
Roth, Adam
Russ, Hermanus
Russ, Samuel
Ruth, Adam
Ruyans, Philip
Ryfenbergh, Adam
Salback, Jacob
Salback, Johannis
Salback, Philip
Salbagh, Thomas
Schmit, Petrus
Schmit, Zacherias
Schnnyder, Ludivig
Schut, Isaac
Schut, Solomon
Schut, William
Scutt, William
Sebo, Harry
Segendorph, Adam
Sharp, Peter
Shaver, John
Shaver, Peter
Shcfter, Johannis
Shefter, Nicholas
Shiffer, Johannis
Shipperly, Barnet
Sholtis, Philip
Sholts, Barent
Shudes, Henry
Shultis, Barent
Shultis, Davis
Shultis, Henry
Shuts, Adam
Shuts, Johannes W.
Shuts, Peter
Simon, Battis
Simons, William
Sipperly, Barnet
Sisam, John
Skuts, John A.
Slos, John

Smith, James
Smith, Johannis
Smith, Joseph
Smith, Peter
Smith, Philar
Smith, Samuel
Smith, Zachariah
Snook, Conrad
Snyder, Conrad
Snyder, Conrad, Jr.
Snyder, George
Snyder, Samuel
Snyder, William
Spickerm, Philip
Spickerman, John
Spilman, Conrad
Stahl, Johann Henrich
State, Benjamin
Stimon, Baltis
Strader, Jost
Stribel, Ulrich
Temple, James
Ten Brook, Wessel
Ten Eyck, Abraham
Ten Eyck, Jacob
Ten Eyck, John, Jr.
Ten Eyck, John B.
Thomas, Johannis
Thompson, Abisha
Thompson, George
Trater, Joseph
Trever, Peterus
Tunsback, Philip
Turner,Gilbert
Valkenburgh,Christian
VanDeBogart, Arent
VanDe Bogart, James
VanDeBogart, Michael
VanDeBogen, Peter
VandeWaters, Hynis
VanDeWaters,Michael
Van Dusen, George
Van Dusen, Robert
Vonck, Christian
Vonck, Jacob
Vonck, Peter
Vosburgh, Jacob
Vosburgh, Lawrence
Vosburgh, Peter
Washburn, John
Washburn, Martinus

REVOLUTIONARY WAR
ALBANY COUNTY NY MILITIA
8TH REGIMENT

OFFICERS

Colonel Robert Van Rensselaer
Lt. Col. Barent I. Staats
Lt. Col. Henry J. Van Rensselaer
Lt. Col. Asa Waterman
Maj. Richard Esseltyne
Maj. John McKinstry
Maj. Henry Van Rensselaer
Adjutant John Pennoyer Jr.
Qtr. Master John Fisher

Captains

Ebenezer Cady
Joseph Elliot
Jonah Graves
Abner Hawley
Nathan Henrick
Cornelius Hogeboom
Michael Horton
Casper Huyck
Gideon King
Jeremiah Johannes Muller
John Osterhout
Wilhelmus Philip
Jacob Philip
Henry Platner
John Price
Diel Rockefeller
Jacob VanAllen
Isaac Vosburg

Lieutenants

Samuel Allin
Thomas Brown
Peter A. Fonda
Gerritt Grosbeck
James Hogeboom
Richard Hogeboom

Charles McArthur
David McKinstry
Nathaniel Migkell
Nathaniel Mills
Joachim Muller
George Phillips
Edward Rexford
Jonathan Reynolds
Peter Rockefeller
Nathaniel Rowley
Casparus Schult
John Scott
Gosah VanBeurin

Ensigns

Leanard Dacker
Esa Holmes
Simon Lothrop
Samuel Olmstead
Maurice Rowley
John Shutts
Adam TenBueck
Myndert VanDerBogert
Gerritt W. VanSchaik
Peter VanValkenburgh
James Wingard

Officers of Unknown Rank

Peter Groat
Dr. John Patterson
Jacob Philip, Jr.
Johannis Shuldt or Shult
Peter Weissman or Weissmer

Revolutionary War, Albany Co., NY Militia, 8th Regiment
Enlisted Men

David Acker
Daniel Adams
Noah Adams
John Adsit
Aaron Akins
James Akins
Samuel Akins
Jonathan Allen
Timothy Allen
William Alsworth
Spira Andreas
Speery Andrew
John Anneling
Samuel Aring
John Armerly
Peter Ashley
Peter Ashton
Benjamin Atwaters
Jeames Atwaters
Timothy Atwood
Peter Austin

Charles Babeck
Andrew Baker
John Baker, Jr.
Jonathan Baker
Samuel Baker
Andries Bamhower
Samuel Bantley
Thomas Bantley
James Barker
Tyman Barnet
Peter Barringer
Jonathan Barrit
Henry Bartle
John Bartle
Peter Bartle
Peter Bartle, Jr.
Philip Bartle
Philip H. Bartle
John Bartley
John Bay
Asher Bayley
Michel Beach
Aarent Becker

Cornelius Becker
John Becker

William Beeraft
Jonathan Beeroft

Abraham Begraft
George Begraft
Jonathan Begraft
Thomas Begraft
Thomas Begraft, Jr.
Daniel Benjamin
Ebenezar Benjamins
George Benn
Cornelius Bennum
Doctor Bentin
Henry Berger
Benjamin Best
John Bibbins
Evert Boent, Jr.
Jacob Boent
Jacob Boent, Jr.
Matties Boent
Mindert Boent
Peter Boent
Jorst Boerst
Jorst Boerst, Jr.
David Bonestail
David Bonestail, Jr.
Frederick Bonestail
Peter Bonestail
Edward Bostwick
Johann Christ Braun
Cornelius Bresee
Gabriel Bresee
Nicholas Bresee
Joshua Brooks, Jr.
Edward Broon
Jurry Browen
Abraham Brower
David Brower
George Brower
Peter Brower
Amos Brown
John Brown
John Bryan
Constant Buebee
Ephraim Bunt
Peter Bunt
Hendrick Burgart

Hendrick Burgat
Peter Burger
Henry Burghart
Jeremiah Burghart
Peter Burnett
Nathan Burns

Daniel Burson
John Bush

Johann George Cable
James Cacoll
George Cadman
David Cady
Jacob Camer
John Campbell
George Caner
Carel Caring
William Carlett
Thomas Carrey
Jacob Carter
Jacob Carter, Jr.
John Carvel
Petter Casper
Jacob Caul
Hendrick Cavel
Peter Cavel
Thomas Cayry
Job Champion
Stephen Chapman
Joseph Chatsy
Stephen Churchill
Frederick Clapper
George Clapper
Henry Clapper
John Clapper
Peter Clapper
William Clapper
Abram Clark
David Clark
John Clark
Ezecheal Cleaveland
Lemuel Cleaveland
Christopher Clinchman
Andrew Coal, Jr.
Joseph Cohoon
Hesparus Cole
Isaac Cole
John Cole
Peter Cole
David Colley
Matthew Colley
Thomas Colley
John Colman
Jacob Concklin
Philip David Constaver
Casparus Conyne
John Cool

Peter Cool
Peter Cool, Jr.
William Cool
Samuel Coon
Adam Coons
Jacob Coons
John Coons
John Coons, Jr.
William Corlett
John Cotton
William Coventry
Andres Cowle
Thoda Cowle
Lawrance Cramer
Hendrick Crepes
Henry Criselar
John Criselar
Christian Crousious
Johanny Crowsioni
William Cudney
Thomas Culley
David Cully
John Cyser

Broer Dacker (or Decker)
Daniel Danvor
David Darling
Jesup Darling
Jedidiah Darrow
Amos Davis
Daniel Davis
George Davis
Jacobus Davis
William Davis
Aron Day
Laurence Deal
Abraham Decker
Broer Decker
Christopher Decker
George G. Decker
Hendrick Decker
Johannis Decker
Joris Decker
Joris Decker, Jr.
Frederic Dederick
Christian Dedrick
Johannes Dedrick
Peter Dedrick
Gloride DeLamater
Jacobus DeLamater
Jeremiah DeLameter
Jeremyes DeLameter
Dirck DeLametter
Jeremiah DeLamatter, Jr.
James DeLamatter
Daniel Deming

William Denions
Ezechael Dennis
Mathew Deneger
Elias DePew
Adam Derring
Jacobus DeYeae
Jacobus DeYeae, Jr.
Richard DeYeae
Francis Dicker
Walter Dickson
George Didemer
John Didemore
William Dinghmanse
Dolves P. Dingmansa
Adolphus Dingmanse
Adolphus Dingmanse, Jr.
Andsiel Dingmanse
Hendrick Dingmanse
Johannis Dingmanse
Johannis Dingmanse, Jr.
Peter Dingmanse
William Dirck
William Dixson
Glonde D'Lameter (DeLamater)
Jores H. Docker (Decker?)
Isaac Doty
Joseph Doty
Samuel Doty
Peter Dox
John Hendrick Droel
Jonathan Duff
Henry Dutcher
Rulef Dutcher
Sampson Dyckman

Joseph Earl
David Ekker
Abel Edwards
Samuel Edwards
Benjamin Egelston
George Egars
Aaron Egins
James Egins
Jacob Elias
Abraham Elling
John Elliot
Peter Elliot
David Ellison
William Ellison
Rufis Elswort
James Elting
John Elting
Adam Emrich (Emrigh)
Francis Emrich (Emrigh)
George Emrigh
Matties Emrigh

Jacob Enderson
John Enderson
Jacob Enderson
James Ergie
Gabriel Esselstine
Abraham Esseltyne
Andries Esseltyne
Coenradt Esseltyne
Isaac Esseltyne
Jacob Esseltyne
Jacob Esseltyne, Jr.
Richard Esseltyne
Abraham Ettinge
John Ettinge
John Everts
John Everts, Jr.
Thomas Evertson

Stephen Fairchild
Conrath Feith
Timothy Ferris
Stephen Filka
John Finger
John Finkle
Isaac Finney
Frederick Fisher
Peter Flaus
Abraham Fonda
Cornelius Fonda
Douw Fonda
Jacobus Fonda
Jeremiah Fonda
Lawrence Fonda
Peter A. Fonda
John Foot
John Fortal
Jonathan Fox
Abraham Frayer
Isaac Frayer
John Frayer

John French
John Frogran
Isaac T. Fryer
Cornelius Funday

Jacob Gaal
James Gardiner
Jeroan Gardiner
William Gardiner
John Garrison
Jacob Gaul
Joseph Good
Ephraim Goes
Matisse R. Goes
William Gordon

John Gott
Hendrick Graat
John Graat
Wilhelmus Graat
Peter Graats
Isaac Graff
Hyron Grautt
Hendrick Grautt
John Grautt
Peter Grautt
Wilhelmus Grautt
Noadjah Graves
Seldon Graves
Ebenezer Green
Thomas Green
Thomas Green, Jr.
William Green
Christian Grihdelmyer
Christopher Grindelmyer
Jabez Griswold
John N. Groat
Hendrick Groat
Henry Groat, Jr.
Huron Groat
Hyrone Groat
John Groat
Peter Groat
Wilhelmus Groat

Johannes Haber
William Haddick
Christopher Hagedorn
John Hagedorn
Jonas Hagedorn
Peter Hagedorn
Joseph Hagedorn
Daniel Hale
Andries Halenbeck
Dirck Halenbeck
Hendrick Halenbeck
Jacob Halenbeck
Jeroan Halenbeck
John J. Halenbeck
John R. Halenbeck
John W. Halenbeck
John William Halenbeck
Matthew Hall
John Hallenback
Johannis Haltsapple
Christopher Haner
Jacob Haner
Peter Hanner
Adam Harder
Jacob P. Harder
Michal Harder
Peter Harder

Eliab Harlow
Rowse Harman
Hendrick Harmanse
Garrit Hartick
Joneton Hartick
John Harvy
William Hatch
Antrin Hauver
Andries Haver
Andrew Haver
Christian Haver
Daniel Hawkins
James Hawley
William Hawley
Zadok Hawley
Peter Hayner
Hendrick Heermanse
John Hegeman
Jacob Heirmanse
Richard Heldridg, Jr.
Baltus Helicus
Christian Helicus
Frederick Helicus
Lodewick Helicus
Jonas Helm
Peter Helm
Peter Helm, Jr.
Johan Jost Helmer
John Hendricks
Benjamin Hendrye
Jacob Henry
Adam Herder
Benjamin Herder
George Herder
Jacob Herder
Jacob Herder, Jr.
Jacob H. Herder
Jacob J. Herder
Jacob P. Herder
John Herder
Jores Herder
Michael J. Herder
Michel Herder
Michel Herder, Jr.
Nicholas Herder
Peter Herder
Abraham Herdick
Francis Herdick, Jr.
Franck Herdick
Gerrit Herdick
Jacob Herdick
Jacob F. Herdick
Jeroan Herdick
John Herdick
John F. Herdick
Jonathan Herdick

Justice Herdick
Peter Herdick
Peter Herdick, Jr.
William Herdick
William Herdick, Jr.
William L. Herdick
Andres Hermance
Jacob Hermance
Michel Hess
Sybrant Heydenbergh
Christopher Heydorn
Hendrick Heyser
Hendrick Heyser, Jr.
Stephen Hight
Daniel Higley
Jacob W. Hilten
Sander Hines
Charles Hnye (Hyne?)
William Hoff, Jr.
Jacob Hoffman
Johan Nicoll Hoffman
Michel Hoffman
Bartholomew Hogeboom
Cornelius Hogeboom
James Hogeboom
Jeremiah Hogeboom
Johannis Hogeboom
Peter Hogeboom
Stephen Hogeboom
Tobyas Hogeboom
Henry Hoghtaling
Jacob Hoghtaling
Zephaniah Holcomb
Matthias Hollembick
Samuel Hollenbeck
Henry Holliday
Asa Holmes
Jedediah Holmes
William Holsappel
Johannes Holsapple
Johannes Holsapple, Jr.
John Holsapple
William Holsapple
John Holtsapple, Jr.
Thomas Hopp
William Horton
Zephaniah Hough
Dirck Houghtaling
Samuel How
Enos Howard
William Hubbard
Augustus Huffman
David Huguenin
Marten Huick
Simon Huller
Johannes Hultsapple, Jr.

William Hultsapple
Daniel Huston
Casper Huyck
Johannis Huyck

Isaac Jackson
James Jackson
Robert Jackson
John Jacobs
Hendrick Jager
David Jennes
Henry Jolley
William Jorean
Negro Jubb
William Jurden

John Jurey Keble
Peter Keble
Hendrick Kelder
Jost Kelder
William Kelder
Daniel Kelley
Hendrick Kells
John Kells
Jonathan Ketchum
Stephen Ketchum
Daniel Kettil
Daniel Killey
Phillip Killmore
George Kilmore
Hendrick Kilmore
Conrade King
Charles King
John Kittle
Anthony Kline
Henry Kline
Gerret Kool
Wilhelmus Krath
Hendrick Krisler

Andries Laap
George Laap
Thomas Laap
George Land
Jeremi Land
Jeremiah F. Land
Frederck Landt
George Landt
Jeremiah Landt
Johannis Landt
Johannis Landt, Jr.
Johannis L. Landt
John Landt, Jr.
Lawrence Landt
Jurry Lant
Elisha Larvey

William Larvy
John Lasher
Ephraim Lee
Israel Lee
James Legges
Tobyas Legges
Tobies Legit
William Lemon
Abraham Lewis
Peter Lewis
William Link
Andrew Loomis
Bastian Loop
Christian Loop
Martin Loop
Peter Loop
Josiah Lothrop
John Lott
Andrew Lovejoy
Benjamin Lovejoy
Henry Ludlow
Henry Ludlow, Jr.
William H. Ludlow
Barent Lych

Robert McCall
Alexander McCulley
McDonald
Henry McFale
Robert McFall
James McGee
Jacob McGinnis
John McGoraghey
Charles McMollen

Neal Madfall
Abraham Maier
Matthew Mandiville
Docter Mannol
Frances Mantle
Wynant Mantle
Danel Marchell
Daniel Marhill
Nicholas Marte
Nicolaes Marten
William Martin
Frederick Maul
Amos Meerit
Seth Meggs
Anthony Melius
Stephen Merrit
Thomas Merrit
Fite Mesick
Hendrick Mesick
Jacob J. Mesick
John Misick

John J. Misick
Peter Mesick
Peter J. Mesick
Thomas Mesick
Frederick Meyer
Henry Michel
Jacob Michel
Anthony Michels
William Mighel
Anthony Miles
John Milham
Andries Miller
Christopher Miller
Dirck Miller
Frederick Miller
Jacob A. Miller
Jeremiah Miller
Jeremiah C. Miller
Peter Miller
Samuel Miller
Samuel A. Miller
Stephen Miller
William Miller
William A. Millet
Eshable Mongomry
George Monnal
Ezekial Montgomery
David Moon
Paul Moon
Richard Moon
Paul Moore
John Morris
Judg Morris
Nicholas Morris
Richard Morris
Robert Morris
Elisa Mory
Fraderick Moul
John Moul, Jr.
Jacob Moull
Johannis Moull
Frederick Mowal
Johannis Mowal
Johannis Mowal, Jr.
Jacob Mowel
John Mowel, Jr.
Frederick Moyer
Hendrick Moyer
Ebenezer Mudge
Christopher Muller
Cornelius Muller
Cornelius C. Muller
Cornelius C.S. Muller
Cornelius H. Muller
Cornelius J. Muller
Cornelius Johannes Muller

Cornelius R. Muller
Cornelius S. Muller
Dirck Muller
Fretireck Muller
Henry Muller
Hessen Muller
Jacob Muller
Jacob Muller, Jr.
Jacob C. Muller
Jeremiah Muller
Jeremiah C. Muller
Jeremiah C. S. Muller
Jeremiah J. Muller
Jeremiah T. Muller
Jeremiah W. Muller, Jr.
Jeremy C. Muller
Jocham Muller
Johannis Muller
Johannis C. Muller
Killian Muller
Peter Muller
Stephen Muller
Stephen C. Muller
Stephen H. Muller
Stephen I. Muller
Stephen J. Muller
William Muller
William C. Muller
Jeremiah Johs Mullory
Paulies Mun
Daniel Munsee
Joseph Murgethroydt
Samuel Murphy
Henry Myer
John Naile
Charles Neer
Henry Neer
Jacob Neer
John Neer
Peter New
Simeon New
Nicholas Nicoll
Thompson Nooney
John Noyes
Frederick Nuan
Cornelius Oostrander
Hendrick Oostrander
Jacobus Oostrander
John Osterhout
Arent Ostrande
Hendrick Ostrande
Hendrick Ostrande, Sr.
Jacobus Ostrande
Philip Ostrande
Wilhelmus Ostrande
Aron Ostrander

Hendrick Ostrander
Henry Ostrander, Jr.
Wilhelmus Ostrander

U. Briggs Pabody
John Palmer
Stephen Palmer
Silas Pardee
Zebulon Patchen
James Patrick
Thomas Patrick
Jacob Patterson
James Patterson
John Patterson
Richard Patterson
Nehamiah Paulding
Daniel Payn
Benjamin Petterson
John Phelps
Adam Philip
Christian Philip
David Philip
George Philip
Hendrick W. Philip
John H. Philip
William Philip
William Philip, Jr.
Adam Philips
Christian Philips
Ebenezer Philips
Christeana Phillip
Hendrick Phillip
Hendrick H. Phillip
Jacob Phillip
Jacob Phillip, Jr.
Wilhelmus Phillip
Isaac Phinney
Jacob Pictell
Thomas Pictell
Thomas Pictell, Jr.
John Pierce
William Pike
Isaac Pitcher
Michael Plank
Coenradt Plass
Johannis Plass
Hendrick Platner
Jacob Platner
David Plunt
Henry Plunt
John Plunt
Bill Pratt
Robert Pratt
William Pratt
Isaac Preston
Timothy Price

Andries Raadt
Coenradt Raadt
Hendrick Raadt
Philip Raadt
Ephraim Race
Henry Race
Jonathan Raes
Johannis Ralf
William Rament
Coenradt Rath
Andries Raudt
Hendrick Raudt
Adam Raut
Andrew Raut
Conrad Raut
Philip Raut
William Raymond
Daniel Ree
Hendrick Rees
Hendrick Rees, Jr.
John Rees
Jonas Rees
Jonathan Rees
Jonathan Rees, Jr.
Jonathan H. Rees
Jonathan J. Rees
Jonathan W. Rees
Philip Rees
Thomas Rees
William Rees
Jonathan Relgen
Lewis Reynolds
Joseph Richardson
Hendrick Rifenberger
Coenradt Ring
Jacob Risedorf
Thomas Robbins
William Robbins
John D. Roberson
Peter Roberts
Henry Robins
Robart Rocbaugh
Thoms Rodman
Ebenezer Roe
Othaniel Rogers
John Rolf
William Rome
Robert Rooreback
Robert Rorapaugh
Barent Roseboom
Bastean Rosman
George Rosman, Jr.
Harman Rous
Hendrick Row
John Row
William Row

John Rowland, Jr.
John Rowley
Dirck Russell
George Russman
Jurry Russman
Sebastian Russman
Lawrence Ryne
John Rysen

Jacob Salback
Johannes Salback
Johannis Salsbury
Amos Sarring
James Saxton
Amos Scerrin
Lawrance Scharp
John Schermerhorn
John Schermerhorn, Jr.
William Schermerhorn
Hendrick Schoenmaker, Jr.
Henry Schoenmaker
Hendrick Scholtus
Coenradt Schoudt
Peter Schudt
Henrick Schult
Peter Scism
James Scott
William Scott
David Segar
Phillip Shafer
Cornelous Sharp
Jacob Sharp
Johannis Sharp
Johannis Sharp, Jr.
Nicholas Sharp
Andres Sharts
Johannes Sharts
Juriah Sharts
Nicholas Sharts
Nicholas Sharts, Jr.
Adam Shaver
Peter Shaver
Philip Shaver
Henry Sheaver
James Shephard
Jonathan Shephard
Jurry Shirts (Juriah Sharts?)
Nicholas Shirts (Sharts?)
Nicholas Shirts, Jr. (Sharts?)
Godfree Shoemaker
Hendrick Shoemaker
Hendrick Sholt
Hendrick Sholt, Jr.
Andres Showerman
Jeremiah Shufelt
Henry Shufelt

Peter Shufelt
Hendrick Shuldt
Hendrick Shuldt, Jr.
Johannes Shuldt
Johannis Shult
Abraham Shurts
David Shurts
Nicholas Shurts, Jr.
Uriah Shurts
Abraham Shuts (Schutts?)
David Shuts
Simon Shuts
James Silky
Peter Silvernagel (Silvernail?)
Jacob Simon
James Simson
Robert Simson
Henry Skinkle, Jr.
Henry I. Skinkle (Schankle?)
Jacob Skinkle
Jonas Skinkle
Josiah Skinner
John Smart
Benjamin Smith
Christopher Smith
Coenradt Smith
Coham Adam Smith
Derick Smith
Dirck Smith
Francis Smith
George Smith
George Smith, Jr.
George A. Smith
George Adam Smith
George P. Smith
Henry Smith
Henry P. Smith
Jacob P. Smith
Jered Smith
Jeremiah Smith
Jeremiah C. Smith
Jerry Smith
Johannis Smith
Johannis C. Smith
John Smith
John G. Smith
John P. Smith
Peter Smith
Peter A. Smith
Peter Adam Smith
Peter Johannis Smith
Philip Smith
Richard Smith
Timothy Smith
Tuenes Smith
Tunis Smith

Tunis P. Smith
William Smith
John Snook
Martinus Snook
Coenradt Snyder
George Snyder
Henry Snyder
Hendrick Snyder
Peter Snyder
Peter Snyder, Jr
William Snyder
William H. Snyder
Peter Sours
Uldrick Sower
Anthony Spanord
Samuel Spencer
Samuel Spencer, Jr.
Cornelious Spoor
Jesse Squire
Embrew Stalker
John Stalker
Joseph Stalker
William Stanze
James Stark
Henry Stever
Gerlough Stolp
Peter Stolp
George Adam Stoppelbean
Faltin (Valentine?) Stoppelben
Jacob Stopplebean
Jacob Stopplebean, Jr.
George A. Stopplebeen
Hendrick Stopplebeen
Hendrick Stopplebeen, Jr.
Michael Stopplebeen
Michel H. Stopplebeen
Nicholas Stopplebeen
Peter Stopplebeen
Valentine Stopplebeen
John Storm
William Strickland
Jacob Stuppelban
Nichol Stuppelban
Nichol Stuppelbean
Jacob Stupplebean
Nichol Stuppleban
Jacob Stuppleban
Hendrick Stupplebean
George Sufelt
George Sufelt, Jr.

John Tallmage
Elisha Talmage
Georgwe Teater
John Tedmore
Anthony TenBroeck

Henry L. TenBroeck
Jeremiah TenBroeck
John TenBroeck
John Jeremiah TenBroeck
Peter TenBroeck
Peter B. TenBroeck
Samuel J. TenBroeck
Samuel Jeremiah TenBroeck
Samuel John TenBroeck
Barent TenEyck
Alexander Thompson
John Thompson
Benjamin Tickner
Abraham Tileman
John Tittemood
Abraham Titteman
Seth Toby
Dyer Tolley
Johan F. Tolley
John Tran, Jr.
Teas Treat
Theas Treat
Isaac T. Trier
Anthony Tripp
John Trull
John Tunnecliff
Gilbert Turner
Gysbert Turner
William Y. Tuttle

David Utley

Zachariah Vallance
Adam VanAlen
John VanAlen
William VanAlstyne
Nicholas VanBack
George VanBeuren
Peter VanBeuren
Peter VanBregan
Jacob VanDeboe
Michael VanDeBogert
Dirrik VanDekar
Joghem (Jochem?) VanDekar
Soloman VanDekar
Dirck VanDerKar
Jacob VanDerKar
Jocham VanDerKar
Johannis VanDerKar
Nicholas VanDerKar
Abraham VanDeusen
Cornelius VenDeusen
GlondeVanDeusen
Glouds VanDeusen
Jacob VanDeusen
Johannis VanDeusen

Johannis J. VanDeusen
John I. VanDeusen
Mattawe M. VanDeusen
Matthew VanDeusen
Robert VanDeusen
Tobyas VanDeusen
Michael VanDeWater
Barent VanDusen
Henry VanDusen
Malacher VanDusen
Martin VanDusen
Evert VanEpps
Abraham VanHoesen
Albertus VanHoesen
Burry VanHoesen
Cornelius J. VanHoesen
Cornelius N. VanHoesen
Gerrit G. VanHoesen
Hendrick VanHoesen
Jacob VanHoesen
Jacob VanHoesen, Jr.
Jacob C. VanHoesen
Jacob F. VanHoesen
Jacob I. VanHoesen
Jacob J. VanHoesen
Jacob Jacob VanHoesen
Jacob Jurry VanHoesen
Jacob L. VanHoesen
Johannis VanHoesen
Johannis Janse VanHoesen
John VanHoesen
John Hoes VanHoesen
John Hoes VanHoesen, Jr.
John Jacabse VanHoesen
John Joseph VanHoesen
John Jurry VanHoesen
Justice VanHoesen
Nicholas VanHoesen
Peter VanHoesen
Cornelius VanHuesen
William VanNess
William VanNess, Jr.
Killyaen VanRensselaer
Henry VanRensselaer
John R. VanRensselaer
Peter VanRensselaer
Robert VanRensselaer
William VanRensselaer
Cornelius VanSalsburg
Lukas VanSalsburg
Abraham VanValkenberg
Bartholomew VanValkanberg
Bartly VanValkenberg
Matties VanValkenburg
William VanValkenberg
John VanValkencis

Justice VanValkeneer
Peter VanValkeneer
Gerrit VanWagenaer
Peter Vasberry
Abraham Venson
Bastian H. Vischer
Peter Vonck
Abraham Vosburgh
Dirck Vosburgh
Evart Vosburgh
Isaac Vosburgh
Isaac P Vosburgh
Jacob Vosburgh
Jacob Vosburgh, Jr.
Jacob D. Vosburgh
Jacob P. Vosburgh
Jacobus Vosburgh
Peter Vosburgh
Matthew Vosburgh
Isaac Vrendenburgh
Jacobus Vrendenburgh

John Wadsworth
Carel Wagenaer
John Wagenaer
Peter Wagner
Jacob Ward
Peter Warne
Richard Warne
Peter Warner
Richard Warner
Samuel Wattles
John Waymar
Henry Weager
Jacob Weager
Philip Weager
Peter Weissman
Walter Wemple
Garrit Wendell
Benjamin West
William West
Benjamin White
John White, Jr.
Jurry White
Peter White
Uriah White
William White
Peter Wiessmer
Peter Wiessmer, Jr.
Alexander Wiley
Willams Willams
Simeon Willcocks
Nathaniel Wilcox
Thomas Williams
Cornelius Wilsey
Cornelius Wilsey, Jr.

Henry Wilsey
Jacob Wilsey
Jeames Wilsey
Thomas Wilsey
Jacob W. Wilton
Thomas Wiltse
George Wineradt
Michel Wise
Hendrick Witbeck
Jacob Witbeck
John Witbeck

Lukas Witbeck
Thomas Witbeck
John Hartick Witlow
James Wood
John Wood
John Wood, Jr.
William Wood
Asa Woodward
Peter Wyat

Hendrick Yager

Peter W. Yates
Robert Yates
Jacob Yorker
Calvin Young
Philip Young
William Young

Robert W. Zanegall

REVOLUTIONARY WAR
ALBANY COUNTY NY MILITIA
9TH REGIMENT

Col. Peter Van Ness
Maj. Jacob Ford

Captains
Bartholomew Barrett
Jonah Graves
Josiah Graves
Abner Hawley
Joshua Whitney

Lieutenants
Benjamin Allen
Daniel Barnes

Abner Kellogg
Charles McArthur
David McKinstry
Nathaniel Mead
Amaziah Phillips
Jonathan Pitcher
Eleazer Spencer
Abel Whalen
Daniel Wilson

Ensigns
Stephen Graves
Phiniheas Rice

ADDITIONAL NAMES ON STATE TREASURER'S PAY BOOK

Lt. Col. David Pratt
Capt. Joseph Allen Tanner
Lt. Caleb Clark
Lt. Thomas Hatch

Charles McKinstry
Thomas McKinstry
Will Ove
John Reynold

ENLISTED MEN

Ackley, James
Adset, John
Adsit, Samuel
Andreas, Ebenezer
Andress, Ebenezer
Andrews. Elisha
Bagley, Asher
Barret, Ebenezer
Baret, Eleazer
Barrows, Ebenezer
Benjamin,
Blackman, Joel
Bont, Matthias

Borghordt, Lambert
Bower, Daniel
Brown, Benjamin
Bunhas, Charles
Bunt, Ephraim
Bunt, Matthias
Bogert, Hennerey
Burget, Johoicam
Cadman, John
Cadman, Joseph
Carrier, Amos
Casterrar, John
Castor, John

Chaimberlain, Benjamin
Chaimberlin, Gurden
Childendon, Benjamin
Benjamin Chittendon,
Cisel, Peleg
Cleaveland, Oliver
Cohoon, Joseph
Colver, Ebenezer
Crippen, John
Crippen, Roswell
Culver, Ebenezer
Darner, Christopher
Darrow, Ammerus

Darrow, Christopher
Davis, Andrew
Day, David
Deen, Gains
Denison, Christopher
Devonport, Jonathan
Dibble, Henerey
Dolittle, Timothy
Doolittle, Heckaliah
Dudley, Simeon
Earle, Benjamin
Elmer,
Foot, Samuel
Foster, John
Frask, James
Freamon, Jonathan
Freeman, Daniel
Gardner, John
Goff, Oliver
Gold, Jonathan
Gould, Elijah
Gould, Jonathan
Graves, Increase
Graves, Soldon
Green, Thomas
Green, William
Griswell, John
Griswold, David

Hacket, Joseph
Hall, Benijah
Hamblin, Jesse
Harris, Eliphalet
Hatch, Thomas
Hawkins, Daniel
Hawley, Daniel
Hawley, Zadok
Hewit, Arthur
Hollister, Smith
Horsford, Ithamer
House, Thomas
Howes, Thomas
Huit, Arthur
Huntly, William
Hurlbert, Jesse

Jackson, James
Joal, Ebenezer
Johnson, Thomas
Johnson, Abner

Keeney, Roger
Ketcham, Jesse
Killogh, Benjamin

Lawrane, Judah M.
Lawrence, Joseph
Leonord, John
Lee, Joel
Liment, Archibald Jr.
Limont, John
Lothrop, Ebenezer
Lovejoy, Andrew

McArthur, John
McKever, James
Malleray, Samuel
Martin, Robert
Meaker, Robert
Mirit, Amos
Mortain, Robert
Mudge, Ruben

Nicols, Eliachim
Palmer, John
Palmer, Stephen
Palmitier, Benjamin
Palmmer, Gilbert
Palmmer, James
Parks, Samuel
Penfield, Isaac
Phelps, Jonah
Pottor, Gideon
Pratt. Samuel

Rea, Hugh
Reiss, Matt
Reynolds, Jonathan
Richinson, Joseph
Robbins, Daniel
Robinson, Hector
Rodman, Joseph
Rodman, Thomas
Roldman, Joseph
Root, Joshua
Root, Moses
Root, Nicholas
Rowland, John
Rowland, John, Jr.
Rowley, Jabesh

Salsbury, __idion
Saxton, Ebenezer
Scoot, Matt
Shepherd, Jonathan
Smith, Eli
Smith, Elijah
Snyder, William
Spalding, John
Spalding, Nehemiah
Spalding, Samuel
Speer, Cornelius
Spencer, Amos
Spencer, Asa
Spencer, David
Spencer, Eleazer
Spencer, Eliphas
Spencer, John
Spencer, Matthias
Spencer, Phineas
Spencer, Samuel
Spencer, Tuneas
Stark, Amos
Stuart, John

Taylor, David
Taylor, James
Teeckner, Benjamin
Thomlinson, Lemuel
Tickner, Benjamin
Tickner, Jonathan
Tilman, Jacob
Titus, Silas
Tyler, Ebenezer

Valcomburgh,   Johocicam
Van Hoesen, Francis
Van Valcomburey, George
Vawn, Edward
Vawn, Richard
Virgin, Asa
Walch, Thomas
Welch, Jonathan
West, Samuel
White, Johoicam
White, William
Wise, Samuel
Witmore, Reuben
Woodin, Rubin
Wrolen. John

CIVIL WAR
NEW YORK 128TH REGIMENT

FIELD & STAFF OFFICERS

Col. David S. Bowles
Lt.Col. James Smith
Maj. James P. Foster
Adjutant Abraham Ashley, Jr.
Quartermaster Alexander Annan
Surgeon Palmer C. Cole
1st Asst Surgeon Charles H. Andrus
2nd Asst Surgeon Daniel P. Van Vleck
Chaplain Rev. John Parker

NON-COMMISSIONED STAFF
Sgt. Maj. S. H. Brady
Commissary Sgt.E. Augustus Brett
Quartermaster's Sgt. George S. Drake
Ordinance Sgt. John Mathers, Jr.
Color Sgt. James M. Braley
Hospital Steward John E. Schuyler
Surgeon Orderly Jacob Carl
Sutler Joseph Wild

ENLISTED MEN

Abbott, George F.
Abernetty, James
Ackley, Jr., Ezra M.
Agnew, William
Albertson, Andrew S.
Alexander, James
Allen, Ethan
Allen, James
Allen, John
Allen, John E.
Allen, Phillip
Allen, William J.
Almsted, Alonzo H.
Althause, William H.
Alverson, Oscar C.
Alverson, Uriah
Ambler, Joseph
Ames, Jacob M.
Anderson, Charles R.
Anderson, John E.
Andrus, Charles
Annan, Alexander
Anthony, James M.
Appleby, Charles F
Appleby, William H.
Argast, Christopher
Arhom, Augustus
Armstrong, Daniel
Armstrong, George
Armstrong, Jacob
Armstrong, James
Arnold, Anning W.
Asher, Jacob Howard
Ashley, Jr., Abraham
Austin, Henry A.
Austin, Henry D.

Aweng, Augustus
Bailey, William H.
Baker, Charles H.
Baker, Jesse
Baker, John C.
Baker, Lewis
Baker, Peter S.
Baker, William H.
Baker, William W.
Ball, Isaac P.
Ballard, Albert A.
Bantlin, Augustus
Barker, Albert M.
Barlow, John E.
Barrett, Benjamin
Barrett, James
Barrett, Lorenzo
Barringer, Robert R.
Bartlett, George L.
Bartley, William H.
Barton, John
Bates, Ezekial E.
Baxter, James
Beach, William H.
Becker, Charles E.
Becker, John
Becraff, William
Bell, Charles M.
Bellows, David
Benaway, Garret M.
Beneston, Frank
Beneway, C. Willis
Bennett, Barent
Bennett, John H.
Bennett, William R.
Benson, Benjamin T.

Benson, Henry L.
Benson, Manasah
Best, Benjamin
Best, John
Best, Lewis
Bieri, Christopher
Bingall, William
Birch, Richard T.
Bishop, Bartlett H.
Bishop, George
Blauvelt, Edwin J.
Blauvelt, Isaac W. C.
Blinn, Daniel
Blunt, Robert M.
Bogardus, Edwin H.
Boice, Jeremiah
Boon, John
Bostwick, Charles E.
Bowman, Jacob S.
Bowne, Theodore
Bowne, William H.
Boyce, Charles
Boyer, Joseph
Boyle, Stephen
Bradbury, Augustus U.
Bradley, Barney
Brady, Sylvester H.
Braley, James M.
Brant, James
Breman, William
Brennan, Michael
Brett, E. Augustus
Brett, Francis H.
Brewer, Sylvester
Brewer, Wallace
Briggs, John R.

Briggs, William B.
Brill, Egbert
Broadhead, Abram
Brooks, Levi L.
Brooks, Louis C.
Brower, Charles W.
Brower, George W.
Brown, Benjamin H.
Brown, Derrick
Brown, George
Brown, James H.
Brown, James K.
Brown, John
Brown, Joseph
Brown Sylvanus
Brown, William B.
Browness, George
Brownell, Isaac
Brownell, Jr., Milton
Brownell, Randolph
Brundage, Henry
Brundage, Webster
Brush, Robert A.
Brusie, Walter
Bryant, Simeon
Buckingham, Herman
Budd, Jacob S.
Buircth, Ebenezer
Bundy, North
Bunt, John
Bunt, William H.
Burch, Jacob
Burdick, Isaac
Burdick, Riley
Burhance, James E.
Burhans, James E.
Burke, William
Burnett, Alfred
Burns, Robert H.
Burritt, John
Burroughs, Henry
Burroughs, John
Burton, William
Butts, James
Byrnes, John
Cable, Edmund
Caine, Edward J.
Callaghan, James
Campbell, James
Cannon, Jr., Arnout
Card, Walter D.
Carl, Jacob
Carle, John
Carlow, Peter
Carlow, William L.
Carnes, William

Carpenter, Martin P.
Carroll, John
Carter, Alonzo
Carter, George A.
Case, Henry
Case, Smith G.
Casey, John
Cashdollar, Lewis W.
Chamberlain, Benjamin F.
Chase, Amos
Chase, Charles D.
Chase, David
Chase, William
Chase, William H.
Cheever, Jr., Henry
Cherry, John
Cherry, Joseph
Cherry, William
Chicherter, Palaeman A.
Childs, Frank J.
Chiman, Adam
Chittenden, Charles B.
Chittenden, John H.
Churchill, Benjamin
Churchill, Joseph L.
Churchill, Robert P.
Churchill, Sidney F.
Churchill, Walter E.
Clapper, Charles A.
Clark, Albert R.
Clarke, Charles
Clark, James E.
Clarke, Andrew M.
Cline, Norman
Clum, Louis H.
Cody, Martin P.
Coffin, George
Coffin, Jacob B.
Cole, Albert
Cole, Cyrus W.
Cole, Gilbert
Cole, Henry B.
Cole, J. Emry
Cole, John E.
Cole, John E.
Cole, Palmer C.
Cole, William H.
Cole, George W.
Collins, David C.
Collins, Peter G.
Colvin, Samuel B.
Comstock, Samuel N.
Conklin, Virgil L.
Conklin, William S.
Conklin, Samuel
Conlon, William

Connor, Daniel
Connors, Patrick
Conrad, John
Coon, Henry
Coons, Jr., Jonas
Coons, John F.
Coope, James
Cooper, Benjamin H.
Corning, William M.
Cottrell, Dwight
Courtney, Henry A.
Couse, Hiram
Covey, Leonard C.
Cowles, David S.
Cox, Isander F.
Cox, Samuel
Coyle, Augustus C.
Cramer, Francis E.
Crawe, J. Mortimer
Crawford, William E.
Crissey, Robert H.
Croff, William B.
Croff, William H.
Cronan, James
Cronk, George D.
Cronk, Peter D.
Cronk, Wheeler G.
Croshline, Abraham
Croskier, Samuel
Crossman, Bruce G.
Crowther, Joseph W.
Culver, George N.
Cummings, Henry
Cummings, William
Curtis, Samuel P.
Cypher, John B.
Daniel, Alfred
Darling, Smith W.
Dascum, George H.
Davidson, Charles M.
Davis, Orville L.
Davis, Thomas N.
Davison, Uriah
Day, Nathan
Day, Robert A.
Deacon, George T.
Dean, Clement R.
Dearborn, Charles L.
Decker, Allen
Decker, James
Decker, John B.
Decker, John I.
Decker, Jr., Peter
Decker, Richard
Decker, William
Dedrick, Gilbert

Defrece, Thomas
De Groff, John E.
De Groff, Samuel
De Groff, Theodore A.
Delamater, Edward H.
Delamater, John C.
Delamater, John L.
Deming, Willard F.
Denany, William
Denegar, Horace
Denn, Ralph
Dennis, Charles E.
Dennis, David R.
Depew, James E.
Devine, William
Dewint, Arthur
Dewint, Jasper
Dewint, Martin V.
Dillon, Garret F.
Dingee, John
Dingee, John
Disbrow, Francis
Dobler, John
Dodge, Charles S.
Dolfinger Martin
Donnelly, John
Doolittle, Jacob
Doolittle, Robert B.
Doran, Thomas
Doty, John E.
Doty, Spencer C.
Doty, William M.
Downing, Joseph M.
Doxey, Joseph W.
Doyle, James
Doyle, Wesley
Drake, George S.
Draper, Charles H.
Drury, Edward L.
Drury, George A.
Duncan, Dewitt
Duntz, William
Dusenbury, John J.
Dutcher, Thomas N.
Dutton, John
Dyer, Peter
Dyer, William H.
Dykeman, George
Dykeman, Jacob J.
Dykeman, Robert D.
Dykeman, Wilson
Earl, Ephriam H.
Earl, George H.
Earl, John W.
East, William
Eckert, John T.

Eddy, Hiram B.
Ellingham, Francis
Ellingham, William
Elting, George
Ennist, James
Enoch, Richard
Ensign, Charles H.
Eshleman, Uleric Peter
Evans, John J.
Eyth, Augustus
Fairbanks, Lewis B.
Fairchilds, Austin
Falconer, George F.
Falk, Major
Farrington, George W.
Faust, August
Feilds, Archibald
Felts, Albert P.
Ferguson, Alexander
Fero, David
Ferrell, John M.
Ferrington, Stephen A.
Ferris, Charles H.
Filkins, James
Filkins, Martin V.
Finch, George
Finger, Montgomery
Finkle, Jacob
Fitchett, George H.
Fitzgerald, John
Fitzgerald, Michael
Fitzgerald, John
Fleck, Frederick
Fleming, James
Flinn, John
Flint, George
Flynn, Michael
Flynn, Thomas
Fogarty, John
Foland, Leonard
Ford, Lorenzo D.
Foshay, John S.
Foster, Jesse
Foster, James P.
Foster, Matthew
Foster, Peter
Foster, Thomas
Fout, Michael
Fox, Joseph
Fradenburgh, Morris
Fraleigh, James A.
Frear, William
Friss, Phillip H.
Frost, James K. P.
Fuller, Elmore E.
Fuller, Frederick

Funk, George A.
Furguson, John R.
Furlong, Thomas
Gaddis, Alexander
Gaddis, John
Gallagher, Edward
Gardner, Abram
Gardner, William
Garner, Edward G.
Garrison, John H.
Garvey, Cornelius
Garvin, James
Gauley, Richard
Gay, John
George, Edgar
Gerard, Henry
Germaond, John
Geron, Levi
Gifford, Edward
Gifford, James E.
Gildersleeve, Stephen
Gilkinson, David H.
Gilroy, Philip
Glendhill, William
Gobel, Augustus
Gordenier, Edward
Gordon, George J.
Gorton, George H.
Gott, Nelson S.
Graf, Matthias
Graves, Oliver
Gray, George W.
Green, James
Griffin, William
Griswold, Cyrus
Griswold, Lucian S.
Guinan, Michael
Gulliver, William
Gurney, Isaac B.
Hadden, George W.
Hadden, John S.
Haeber, Karl Frederick
Hagar, John H.
Hague, John N.
Haight, George
Haight, William E.
Hainer, Robert N.
Hall, George V.B.
Hall, William
Halleck, Egbert
Halpin, Michael
Ham, Charles
Ham, Horace C.
Ham, Jacob
Ham, Robert
Ham, Virgil

Hamilton, George W.
Hamilton, William E.
Hamlin, Thadius
Hammond, Ephraim
Hammond, Nicholas P.
Hammond, William P.
Hanaburgh, David H.
Hand, Benjamin
Hand, William B.
Haner, David
Hanley, David
Harder, Michael
Hardick, John S.
Harner, William H.
Harris, Robert M.
Harrison, Jared
Harrison, John R.
Harrison, William
Harrop, Robert S.
Hart, Ambrose B.
Hart, John
Hartman, Karl
Hartson, Napoleon B.
Harvey, George H.
Harvey, James
Harvey, William
Haskins, William H.
Hauvber, Taylor
Hauver, Charles H.
Hauver, George W.
Hauver, Henry S.
Haviland, William V.
Haw, Daniel
Hawes, Granville P.
Hawkins, Martin V. B.
Hawkins, William B.
Hawks, David
Hawver, William H.
Head, James
Healy, James
Heath, Charles H.
Hedges, William
Heilig, Francis
Heilman, John B
Hermance, Harrison
Hermance, John
Hermance, Norman E.
Hermance, William H.
Heroy, James I.
Heuver, Ezra
Hewitt, James M.
Hicks, Caleb
Hicks, Henry R.
Hicks, Lansing
Hicks, Walter
Hill, Alson

Hill, James H.
Hill, James W.
Hilliker, Edgar
Hilliker, Fernando
Hines, William
Hinkle, John
Hinman, Edward R.
Hitchcock, Alfred J.
Hoag, Benjamin F.
Hoag, John B.
Hodes, Francis
Hoes, Charles
Hoes, Charles
Hoffman, Mandaville
Hogeboom, Joseph T.
Hogle, Edward
Holdridge, James M.
Holmes, Lewis
Holsapple, Ambrose
Holt, John L.
Hopkins, William H.
Horan, Timothy
Horane, Larnes
Horton, Elijah T.
Horton, Leonard
Horton, Myron
Hosier, John H.
Hotaling, Caleb M.
Houck, Charles S.
House, Henry L.
Hover, William
Howard, Murray
Hubble, Lambert J.
Huddleston, Charles
Hughes, John W.
Hulbert, Henry B.
Hulet, Peter
Hull, William H.
Humeston, Charles
Humeston, Merritt
Humphrey, John H.
Hunt, William H.
Huntzing, Peter
Husted, Hiram A.
Husted, Robert T.
Hustis, Harvey
Ingles, Henry
Ireland, Cornelius
Jackson, Andrew
Jeffers, William H.
Johnson, Augustus E.
Johnson, Edward
Johnson, Thomas A.
Jones, Alexander
Jones, Edward
Jones, Robert T.

Jones, Theron
Jones, Thomas L.
Kahoe, Henry
Keane, Michael
Keese, Francis S.
Keese, John W.
Kellerhouse, Stephen
Kellerhouse, William
Kelley, Benjamin
Kelley, John
Kelley, Patrick
Kelley, William
Kells, Charles
Kells, Job
Kells, Theodore
Kells, William
Kelly, Edward
Kelly, James
Kennicutt, Elijah
Kennicutt, Jr., Elijah
Ketterer, Charles
Keys, Columbus L.
Keys, John F.
Kieselburg, Augustus
Killerhouse, Albert
Kilmer, Norman
Killmer, Ruben
King, William
Kingsley, Charles P.
Kipp, George
Kipp, John W.
Kipp, Theodore
Kisselburgh, Stephen
Kisshower, Charles E.
Kline, Leonard
Knapp, Anson O.
Knickerbocker, Everett
Kniffin, Gilbert H.
Krafft, Ferdinand H.
Kraft, Theodore W.
Kron, Wilhelm
Krum, George
Lacey, Charles
Lachlin, Terrence
Lafferty, John
Lafferty, William
Lake, Jeremiah J.
Lake, John B.
Lake, John B.
Lake, Moses W.
Lampear, Oliver
Lane, Jeremiah
Langdon, Adrian
Langdon, John Isaac
Lanighan, Thomas
Lape, John E.

Lapham, Robert
Laray, Isaac
Lasher, George E.
Lattin, Ethan S.
Laughlin, William
Lawrence, Charles A.
Lawrence, Henry
Lawson, Leonard B.
Lawson, Solomon
Lay, Henry C.
Leary, James A.
Lee, William
Leins, John M.
Leonard, Martin
Le Roy, Harrison M.
Lester, William J.
Lewis, James M.
Lewis, William T.
Light, Robert B.
Lineberg, Edward
Lineberg, Le Roy
Linsey, Frederick H.
Lockwood, Henry D.
Lodge, Godfrey
Loucks, Leonard
Loucks, H. Walter
Lovelace, Daniel
Lovelace, Stephen
Low, John P.
Ludlam, David
Luster, Eliphalet
Lutz, Charles
Lyden, Patrick
Mac Intire, David N.
Mackey, Charles L.
Mackey, Jr., Henry
Mackey, Noah W.
Mackey, William H.
Mahon, Thomas
Mallbach, Mathias
Manning, John D.
Mansfield, Leverett O.
Marks, Seneca H.
Marquart, George
Marquet, Charles W.
Marquet, Samuel
Marsh, William Willis
Marshall, John J.
Marston, Francis
Martow, Napoleon
Mase, Abner R.
Mase, Sylvester H.
Masten, Hezekiah
Mastin, John H.
Mathers, Jr., John
Mattoon, Thaddeus H.

McAllaster, Isaac A
McArthur, Henry L.
McCambridge, William
McCamley, James
McCann, James
McCann, William
McCarty, Chandler
McCord, Charles W.
McCormick, Henry
McDonough, Thomas
McGeorge, Adam
McGreth, Patrick
McIntyre, Bennett
McIntyre, John
McIntyre, John T.
McIntyre, Peter H.
McKinney, John
McKown, Charles W.
McKown, George W.
McManany, Cornelius
McQueen, John
Medler, John W.
Meguert, Christopher
Melius, Sidney
Melius, William Crawford
Merch, Alvin G.
Merch, Charles P.
Merrit, Frank
Merrit, Thomas E.
Mexted, Thomas
Meyers, Delancey L.
Mickle, Isaac J.
Millard, John E.
Millard, William H.
Miller, Abram Edgar
Miller, Alonzo
Miller, Andrew
Miller, Benjamin F.
Miller, Charles
Miller, David
Miller, Henry
Miller, Jacob H.
Miller, John
Miller, John J.
Miller, Jonas
Miller, Josiah
Miller, Stafford
Miller, Sylvester, C.
Milroy, Robert
Milroy, William C.
Minkler, George W.
Mitchell, Francis
Mitchell, HowardE.
Mitchell, Isaac O.
Mitchell, Robert J.
Moett, Jacobus C.

Monahan, Patrick
Monfort, Theodore
Monfort, Washington
Mooney, George W.
Moore, Arthur A.
Moore, Charles R.
Moore, Harrison
Moore, Milo P.
Moore, James
Moore, John G.
Moore, Joseph
Moore, Peter
Moore, Phillip H.
Moore, Stephen H.
Moore, Wallace
Moore, William B.
Moores, Reuben
Morgan, Elijah D.
Morgan, Gilbert D.
Morgan, Samuel G.
Morgan, Willard
Morhimer, James
Morris, Edward H.
Morris, Jr., Henry W.
Morris, James
Morris, Jersey
Morrison, George
Morse, George W.
Morse, Howard H.
Mosher, Allen
Mosher, Alexander W.
Mosher, Joseph C.
Mosher, Renseller
Moshier, Theadore
Mosier, John
Mulharin, Edwin
Mullen, Aaron K.
Munger, James E.
Murch, Joshua
Murphy, James
Murphy, Traver
Murray, Horatio E.
Murrell, George
Myers, Augustus M.
Myers, Benjamin
Myers, James W.
Myers, John W.
Myers, William
Navin, William B.
Near, Andrew H.
Near, Samuel
Neenan, Daniel
Nesbitt, David A.
Nevens, Theodore
New, John T.
Newent, George F.

Nichols, Frederick
Nichols, Hiram D.
Nichols, Platt
Nichols, William H.
Niver, Levin
Noble, Alfred
Noble, Goodman T.
Norcutt, George A. G.
Norris, John
Noxon, Dewitt C.
Noxon, William A.
Noyes, George M.
O'Connor, Jefferson T.
Oddy, Samuel
Odell, Harvey
Odell, William H.
O'Donnell, James
Ogden, Horace
Olivet, Lorenzo D.
Olivett, Wesley
O'Malley, Joseph
Onderdonk, James H.
O'Rourke, Joseph
Orr, David D.
Orr, Walter L.
Osborn, John L.
Osborne, Augustus M.
Osterhaut, John W.
Ostrander, Charles A.
Ostrander, Fremond
Ostrander, William
Ostrander, William H.
Ostrom, Albert
Ostrom, Ambrose W.
Outwater, James
Palen, Rufus J.
Palmatier, Harmon
Palmatier, John H.
Palmatier, Walter W.
Palmer, Jacob B.
Park, William
Parker, Daniel
Parker, George
Parker, John
Parker, William
Parks, Benjamin
Parks, Oscar F.
Parmer, Robert A.
Partington, Silas
Partington, William
Payne, George C.
Payne, John H.
Pearce, Jeremiah
Persall, Lewis
Penny, Archibald W.
Penny, James H.

Philllips, George E
Pickles, Robert
Pierce, Fletcher
Pinder, Charles H.
Pitcher, John S.
Place Isaac
Plass, John H.
Plass, Jonas M.
Plass, Peter
Plass, Peter R.
Plass, Seth G.
Platner, James
Platto, William
Plumb, David M.
Point, Emanuel
Polhamus, Martin
Pollard, Ananson
Pollock, George H.
Porter, Curtis L.
Porter, William
Portland, James
Post, James E.
Post, William H. B.
Potter, Charles H.
Potter, Robert
Potts, George W.
Potts, Peter E.
Potts, Thomas
Poucher, Myron
Poulse, Jacob
Proper, John Peter
Proper, Walter
Propson, John
Pryor, Horace
Pultze, David H.
Pulver, Edward
Pulver, William
Pye, Isaac E.
Quick, Josiah E.
Rafferty, John
Rausch, John
Records, Charles
Rector, Robert N.
Reynolds, Charles E.
Reynolds, Reuben
Reynolds, Smith F.
Rhynders, Charles
Rice, Thomas
Richmond, John
Rider, Daniel B.
Rider, Landon P.
Rieger, August
Rifenburgh, Jonas
Rifenburgh, Peter E.
Rikert, Calvin
Rikert, Franklin W.

Rikert, Martin
Riley, Josiah
Rim, David
Risedorf, Edgar
Risely, Robert
Rivenburgh, Andrew
Roberts, Edward
Roberts, Stewart H.
Robinson, P. V.
Rockefeller, Walter
Rogers, Benjamin V.
Rogers, James E.
Roney, David
Roselle, Charles
Rossell, Lewis
Rote, Allen
Rothery, Henry
Rous, Hiram
Rowe, Egbert
Rowley, William H.
Rundell, Daniel I.
Rust, Cornelius R.
Ryan, Patrick
Sackett, William B.
Sagendorf, Franklin
Sanders, Robert
Scally, Peter
Schearman, Adam
Schermerhorn, Porter J.
Schill, Joseph
Schiller, Christian
Schiltz, Sebastian
Scholl, Adam
Schouten, John S.
Schowerman, John
Schryver, John R.
Schupp, Frederick
Schury, Otto
Schuyler, John E.
Scofield, Richard H.
Scott, James
Scott, Stephen
Scutt, Martin
Scutt, Samuel C.
Seeley, Charles
Seeley, James
Selby, John
Serrine, Isaac
Seymour, Joseph
Shafer, Frederick
Shafer, George
Shaffer, Albert
Sharp, William H.
Shaw, Alexander
Shaw, Franklin H.
Shear, Egbert

Sheen, Jeremiah
Sheldon, Allen
Shelly, Henry J.
Shelly, John W.
Shepherson, Mark
Sheridan, James
Sherow, Franklin M.
Sherringer, Barent
Shook, John H.
Shove, Seth
Showerman, William R.
Silvernail, Andrew J.
Silvernail, Charles S.
Silvernail, Ira
Silvernail, John F.
Silvernail, Warren S.
Simmons, Daniel
Simmons, George F.
Simmons, Louis
Simmons, William Henry
Simpson, Theodore
Sincerbox, Henry H.
Sipperley, Henry S.
Sitser, Abram
Sitzer, William R.
Skinkle, David A.
Skinner, Freeman
Slater, George W.
Slocum, Oliver
Slocum, Theodore
Sluyter, Henry H.
Smalley, Benjamin H.
Smith, Alexander D.
Smith, Alfred S.
Smith, Andrew Jackson
Smith, Charles
Smith, Charles
Smith, Charles A.
Smith, Hervey
Smith, Isaac P.
Smith, James
Smith, John
Smith, John
Smith, John
Smith, John H.
Smith, John H.
Smith, John Q.
Smith, Martin
Smith, Philo
Smith, Robert O.
Smith, Theodore
Smith, William
Smith, William
Snydam, W. H.
Snyder, William H.
Sparks, George

Sparks, Jacob Onsar
Speed, Burgess
Speedling, Samuel
Spence, John
Spielman, William H.
Sprague, David
Sprague, George W.
Spredbury, William
Stacy, Byran
Stall, Henry S.
Stall, Robert D.
Stanbury, Charles
Stanford, Edward
Starrs, William
Stengel, Martin
Stephens, Gilbert
Stephens, James L.
Sterling, Francis N.
Sterling, Joseph
Stevens, Frank
Stevens, William A.
Stickles, Cornelius
Stillwell, Henry C.
St. John, Morgan S.
Story, George
Story, James
Story, Philo
Stotesbury, John
Stoutenburgh, Egbert
Strait, Lorenzo
Strass, Morris
Struse, Frederick
Sullivan, Michael
Sullivan, Patrick
Sunderman, William
Swords, George W.
Taff, John
Taffe, Lawrence
Tallman, Richard M. J.
Tanner, George
Tanner, John J.
Tator, Edward Frank
Tator, Harry D.
Taylor, John
Taylor, John
Taylor, John B.
Teator, John
Teator, Martin
Teator, Philetus
Teator, William
Terry, Austin H.
Thayer, James C.
Theal, Gilbert
Thomas, George E.
Thomas, Moses
Thompson, John

Thompson, William N.
Thomson, Charles A.
Thorn, John C.
Thurston, Richard H.
Tice, Matthew B.
Tipple, George A.
Townsend, George
Townsend, William
Traganza, Amos
Trainor, John
Traver, Evert
Traver, Franklin H.
Traver, Harry S.
Traver, William H. H.
Traver, Charles S.
Travis, Dominick
Tremper, George W.
Trimper, Jacob S.
Tripp, Andrew
Tripp, John
Turner, Abram T.
Tweedy, Charles
Vail, Jesse D.
Van Allen, Stephen H.
Van Alstyne, Lawrence
Van Amburgh, David E.
Van Auken, John J.
Vanback, William
Van Curen, Robert
Vandawater, Hazzard
Van De Bogart, Ward
Van Deusen, Brasell
Van Deusen, James V.
Van Deusen, Loron
Van Dyck, Isaac
Van Etten, John
Van Etten, John H.
Van Hovenburg, John
Van Keuren, John A.
Van Nosdall, Edward
Van Nosdall, Horton
Van Nostrand, Valentine
Van Orsdoll, William
Van Slyck, Charles Lewis
Van Slyck, George Whitfield
Van Tassel, Robert
Van Tassell, John W.
Van Tine, Charles
VanValkenburgh, John W.
VanValkenburgh, Robert E.
Van Vlack, John P.
Van Vleck, Daniel P.
Van Voorhis, George
Van Vort, Charles
Van Wagner, Levi
Van Wyck, Benjamin W.

Veeley, Orville
Venzele, James H.
Vincent, Anthony
Wagoner, George
Wagoner, John H.
Waldron, Adam
Walker, William
Wallace, John
Walters, Edward
Walters, George H.
Walters, Oliver J.
Walters, William H.
Wamsley, John A.
Wands, Thomas E.
Ward, Isaac S.
Warner, Gilbert H.
Warner, Gilbert II
Warner, John F>
Warren, Daniel
Washburn, James H.
Waugh, Charles C.
Way, John P.
Weaver, William H.
Wevster, Isaac
Weddel, Isaac J.
Weeks, George A.
Weller, Charles
Weller, David W.
Welles, Edward S.
Wesley, Daniel I.
Wheeler, William
Whitbeck, John V.

Whitbeck, Samuel H.
White, Anthony
White, George T.
White, John
White, Ransom A.
White, William H.
Whiteman, George W
Whiteman, John H.
Whitman, Edmund A.
Wilber, Charles S
Wilbor, George T.
Wilbur, Henry D.
Wilcox, Cary
Wilcox, Charles Wesley
Wilcox, Justin A.
Wilcox, Martin V.
Wilcox, Simon
Wilhelm, Johannes
Wilkinson, Frederick
Wilkinson, John D.
Wilkinson, John P.
Wilkinson, Robert Frederick
Williams, Alonzo
Williams, Charles
Williams, Cornelius B.
Williams, Frederick M.
Williams, Henry
Williams, Levi F.
Williams, Moses
Williams, Peter
Williams, Sherman H.
Williamson, John J.

Wilson, Charles P.
Wilson, Charles P.
Wilson, Mortimer D.
Wilson, John V.
Wilson, John W.
Winans, Isaac T.
Winans, William H.
Wing, Elisha
Winslow, Leonard C.
Winters, James
Woldron, William
Wood, George N.
Wood, Henry I.
Wood, Henry V.
Wood, James
Wood, Jeremiah D.
Wood, William
Wooden, Benjamin P.
Wooden, Charles W.
Wooden, John James
Wooden, John R.
Wooden, William H.
Wooden, George H.
Woodin, Solomon M.
Woodward, John S.
Worden, John W.
Wright, John
Wright, Orra P.
Yelverton, Stephen A.
Youmans, Stephen D.
Young, William H.

WORLD WAR I
COLUMBIA COUNTY VETERANS

Abele, William John
Abrams, Edward C.
Abrams, Harry James
Abriel, Walter Gearing
Adriance, Jesse Edwin
Agar, Justus B.
Aikien, Jr., Arthur Louis
Aken, Barton, Taylor
Aken, JamesNelson
Akins, Henry Jacob
Alderesio, Michael
Allen, Harry
Allen, JohnAllen
Allen, Malcolm Henry
Allen, Reben Pierce
Allen, Stanley Garner
Almstead, Arthur Amasa
Almstead, Coert
Almstead, Vernon
Alvord, Harold Benedict
Ames, John Frederick
Anderson, Andrew M.
Andres, Charles S.
Arcuri, Philip
Arkinson, Mark V.
Arnold, Elbert James
Arnold, Ernest Kenneth
Avery, Harbey Kilmer
Badalementi, Joseph
Bailey, Oscar
Bainer, Clinton George
Baker, Andrew Philip
Baker, Floyd Jay
Baker, Frederick Edward
Baker, George Arthur
Baker, Baldwin
Balos, Peter Dionysius
Bame, Donald Vance
Bannister, Harry James
Barden, Elvin
Baringer, Harold Charlesworth
Barksdale, Thomas
Barnard, John Drury
Barneck, Joseph
Barnes, Thurlow Weed
Barnes, Williams Tompkins
Barringer, Jacob Richard
Barringer, Russell Harra
Barton, Charles Reuben
Barton, George Bennet
Bates, Arthur C.

Battershall, Charles LeRoy
Battershall, Harrison Miller
Battershall, Raymond J.
Bauer, Jr., Augustus William
Baxter, Gregory Phipps
Beaucage, Joseph Howard
Beaufre, Ephraim Joseph
Becker, Joel Curtis
Becker, Peter Benjamin
Begley, John Harold
Belanger, Arthur Joseph
Belcher, Robert Morgan
Belcher, Sheldon Cadman
Belknap, Harold Chester
Bell, Archibald Douglas
Belska, Joseph G.
Bennett, Edson Loran
Bennett, Harold Livingston
Benson, Walter Van Ness
Berger, Walter Henry
Berlin, Delmar L. F.
Berlin, Frederick H.
Berlin, Henry Christian
Berlin, John Frederick
Berninger, George John
Bernockie, Leo Paul
Best, Clifford Charles
Best, Edward
Best, Jr., Francis Milton
Best, LeRoy
Betz, Dean Henry
Be Vier, Clifford Lee
Biancofiore, Antonio
Bidwell, Frank Alvia
Biesel, William Trimble
Bingham, Wells Anderson
Bingle, John Alwin
Blair, Edward
Blashfield, Roscoe Westover
Blass, Ward B.
Blessing, George
Blinn, Philo Buel
Blunt, Charles Robert
Blunt, William Washington
Bogardus, Robert Henry
Boice, Eugene Thomas
Boice, Guy A.
Boice, Lee
Bollinger, Charles John
Bollinger, William George
Bondsman, Arthur

Booth, George Lyle
Boucher, Hubert Alfred
Boucher, John Edmund
Brabender, Edward
Brabender, Theodore H.
Brackett, Ben H.
Bradley, Arthur W.
Bradley, Lincoln Maurice
Bradley, Oliver Avery
Bradley, Otis Howard
Braker, Harry David
Bradley, Jr., John August
Brandon, John Henry
Brandow, Albert Otis
Brandt, Frank
Branion, Robert Vincent
Bratton, Stanley
Bratton, Thomas
Breizy, Everett
Brennan, Edgar George
Brennan, Frank J.
Brennan, William Patrick
Bresky, Hillard
Brignull, Alfred James
Brignull, Edward Ernest
Brignull, John William
Bristol, Albert Crane
Britt, Charles
Briwa, Charles
Briwa, William D.
Brizzie, Lee
Brooks, Henry
Broomfield, Charles William
Broszio, Marx, Frederick
Brower, Charles
Brown, Ernest Vivian
Brown, Floyd E.
Brown, Jr., Philip
Brown, Thomas Joseph
Brugger, Joseph William
Brush, Miltimore Witherell
Bubb, William John
Buckman, Henry Carl
Bugel, Daniel Nicholas
Buika, John
Bujnosky, Stephen
Bullinger, Frank Benjamin
Bullinger, Louis Napoleon
Bulliger, Theodore Martin
Bunk, Michael Thomas
Bunt, Everett

Burdick, Willis Nelson
Burdwin, George Harder
Burke, Harold Edmund
Burke, Thomas Robert
Burns, James Clarence
Burns, William Francis
Burns, William Thomas
Bush, Edward Charles
Bush, Harry Jobes
Byfornski, William Joseph
Cadalso, Ciro Eloy
Cade, Henry
Callan, Albert Stevens
Callan, Francis Marvin
Callan, John Lansing
Candlen, Francis Joseph
Cannon, John Henry
Canny, Michael Edward
Cappelli, Joseph Thomas
Cappelli, Paul Eugene
Cardinale, Frank Joseph
Cardinale, George Michael
Carle, Clifford Harry
Carle, Westley Scott
Carle, Elise E.
Carlson, Raymond John
Carlton, Floyd Archie
Carlucci, Augusto
Carmell, Ralph
Carpenter, John Henry
Cashman, Henry Sheridan
Cashman, John Howard
Cashman, William Russell
Caul, Cecil Charles
Ceaser, Luther
Cellela, Charles
Cesternino, Salvatore
Childs, Charles Edward
Chodecov, Benjamin
Ciancetta, Justino
Cistone, Joseph
Clapper, Clinton
Clapper, Harry
Clark, Frederick Holley
Clarkson, Frank Dederick
Clarkson, Louis Vincent
Clayton, Richard
Cleary, William Francis
Closson, Clarence Lewis
Clum, Elbert John
Clum, Philip
Cobb, Harold Vernon
Cochrane, Francis
Cochrane, John
Coffin, Clarence
Coffin, Robert George Anthony

Coffin, Tristram
Cole, Harry George
Cole, James Stanley
Collier, Charles Sager
Colwell, John Bernard
Colwell, Robert Emmet
Conine, William Russell
Conklin, James
Connors, James
Conroe, Irwin A.
Coons, Clayton Francis
Coon, Ernest Charles
Coons, Harold John
Coons, Harry Philip
Coons, Harry William
Cordato, John
Corniello, Nick
Corpi, Louis
Corsey, Alfred Lincoln
Costa, Joseph John
Coster, Harry
Coster, Robert
Countryman, Peter
Coursen, Peter William
Cox, William Gordon
Coxon, Charles John
Cozza, James
Craft, James Albert
Cramer, Alfred Kilmer
Crandell, Edwin Davis
Crank, Arthur Lee
Crank, John
Craver, Clarence Harvey
Craver Harry Burton
Crawford, George Edgar
Crawford, Julius Frederick
Crego, Arthur Van Voorhis
Crego, Ernest Roy
Crego, Ralph Nelson
Crosby, Edward
Cross, Frank
Crouse, William Patrick
Cruise, William John
Crumley, Charles W.
Cuddy, John
Cullen, Richard Eugene
Cunningham, Arthur B.
Curtis, Frederick
Curtis, George
Curtis, Kenneth B.
Curtis, Martin F.
Dacy, Cornelius
Dahm, John Martin
Daley, Eugene Reynolds
Daley, Jr., William Bell
Dallas, Abram Samuel

Daly, Frank Owen
Dalzell, William M.
Damalacago, Michael
Damm, Irving Clarence
Darrow, Parker Northrup
Darrow, William Wallace
Dauski, Anthony Joseph
Davi, Frank
Davis, Chester Russell
Davis, Guy Pratt
Davis, Lewis Anson
Dayton, Frank Blackman
Dean, Harry Ellsworth
Deane, Irving Minkler
Decker, Bernard Caleb
Decker, Clarke Harvey
Decker, Clifford
Decker, Earl George
Decker, Edward Leonard
Decker, Everett Westley
Decker, Harry Cornell
Decker, Robert Storm
Decker, Wilfred
Dederick, Edward
De Fazio, Paolo,
De Freest, George
DeLamater, John Sherman
Delaney, Leo Joseph
Delaney, Paul John
Delavan, Ralph
Della Salla, Pasquale
Delmonaco, Sabatino
De Prosse, Alexander R.
De Santis, Giovanni
De Witt, Sherman Edgar
Deyoe, Cornelius
Diamond, Harry
Diamond, Samuel
Dietter, Frederick
Dietz, Jacob A.
DiGioia, Pasquale
Dillion, Edward Joseph
Dillion, George Phillip
Dimock, Asa Redmond
Diskin, James E.
Dixon, Dysart
Dolan, Edward Leo
Doland, John Walter
Dolan, William Henry
Doland, Max Timothy
Domonic, Anthony
Donahue, Joseph Paul
Donegan, John Francis
Dougherty, Thomas Patrick
Doviskie, Frank James
Doyle, Frank Hopper

Doyle, Michael James
Doyle, William James
Drumm, Mark Hanna
Du Bois, Coert
DuBois, Jacob Lenard
Dugan, Jesse Joseph
Duggan, George Joseph
Duggan, John Charles
Dunlap, Horace Guv
Dunn, Alexander John
Dunn, Joseph Patrick
Dunphy, Francis Walter
Duntz, Raymond William
Durham, Charles Edward
Durkin, John Joseph
Dwyer, Edward Carroll
Dymond, George Herbert
Earll, George David
Eaton, Frederick A
Eaton, Harry Patrick
Eaton, Joseph Francis
Eaton, Martin C.
Eberle, Harold Frederick
Eberlein, Carl W.
Ebertein, Martin L.
Eckerson, Earl Budd
Eckerstein, Ernest M.
Edelman, William Floyd
Ederer, Charles Joseph
Edgley, Francis Raymond
Edwards, John Lounsberry
Edward, Leonard Percival
Egan, Jr., Charles Wiley
Egan, John Thomas
Ehlers, Charles Herman
Eighmy, George Lawrence
Eitleman, Frank
Eitleman, Grant Sheldon
Eitleman, Louis D.
Eliff, Dennis Timothy
Elliot, Eric James
Elliot, Jefferson Bryan
Ellsworth, Grover
Ellswoorth, Harry
Eltz, Seth Floyd
Ershler, Louis
Ershler, Max
Ershler, Philip
Evans III, Cornelius Henry
Evans, Harold Brown
Evans, Ralph
Evans, Jr., Robert W.
Everett, Henry
Faifitz, Aaron Lewis
Farrell, James Jay
Farrell, John Joseph

Faulkner, Sanford
Fearon, Joseph John
Fehl, Jr., Philip
Feller, Frederick
Fellows, Ward Lynton
Felts, Ralph Dewey
Filipello, Fellipo
Finch, Arthur
Fingar, Floyd Adam
Fingar, Warren Lloyd
Fingar, Willis Emphraim
Finkle, Matthew Walter
Finn, James Joseph
Fitzgerald, Patrick Joseph
Flanagan, Thomas A.
Flatley, Thomas William
Fletcher, Horace
Folz, Edwin
Ford, Thomas Henry
Ford, Thomas Vincent
Fortunatio, Giaganto
Foster, Leonard Jr.
Fowler, Earl
Fowler, Harold Van S.
Fox, Carl William
Fox, Paul
Fox, Walter
Fox, Ward Joseph
Francis, James Chalmers
Francis, Norman William
Franko, Jr., James J.
Frederick, William John
Freinberg, Arthur
Freinberg, Philip
Frese, Carl Dick
Frese, Jr. Christian Herman
Friss, Leon Norman
Fritts, Harold Ellsworth
Fryman, Frederick Allen
Fuchs, Joseph
Fuller, Charles Buckmaster
Funk, Fred George
Funk, Harry Benjamin
Funk, Myron
Funk, Otha Ray
Funk, Roscoe C.
Furtak, Louis
Gabriele, Pasquale
Gaddis, George P.
Galster, Henry Christian
Gannon, John Edward Gannon,
Martin Edward
Gannon, Thomas Martin
Gardenier, David
Gardenier, Wilbur Ambrose
Gardner, William

Gardner, Edward Nelson
Garner, Claude Hand
Garnsey, Nathan David
Garrison, Arthur Ernest
Garrison, Claude
Garrison, Le Roy
Garvey, Frank Amsted
Garvey, Ralph
Garvey, Wright Barnes
Gaskell, William Austin
Gates, Wilfred
Gaylord, Walter Charles
Gehbauer, Christine Edna
Gerlach, Philip George
Geron, Jeremiah
Gibbons, Thomas William
Gifford, Benedict
Gifford, Isaac Collier
Gifford, Jr., Malcolm
Gilfoy, John Joseph
Gill, John A.
Gill, John Henry
Gillet, Arthur Delavan
Gillet, Ransom Hooker
Gillette, Jr. John Westfield
Gillette, William
Girdler, Charles Norman
Glover, Guy
Glover, Horace Thumbert
Glover, William Newton
Glynn, Oscar
Gohl, William Robert
Gold, Abraham
Goldberg, William
Golden, Elmer John
Goldstein, Samuel
Gordon, Joseph Emile
Graf, William
Gravino, Marco
Gray, Donald McKinstry
Greene, Harold S.
Green, Kathryn E.
Gregory, Jr., Edward S.
Groat, Earl Schermerhorn
Grogan, John B.
Grogan, John Willliam
Gronwoldt, William
Grossman, Milton E.
Grossman, Samuel Leslie
Groves, Jr., Daniel Niles
Groves, John Almon
Gumprecht, Carl
Hack, Daniel M.
Hack, Jesse Frazer
Hageman, Herbert Carl
Hagen, Raymond Alfred

Haigh, Earl Franklin
Haigh, Paul Newton
Hall, Benjamin Leo
Hallenbeck, Thurman Derick
Hallenbeck, William Hiram
Halloran, John Joseph
Halloran, Michael James
Halloran, Thomas
Halstead, Peter
Ham, Enos Depew
Ham, Harry Leonard
Ham, Ira
Ham, Roland
Ham, Theodore
Hamm, Burgess Sylvester
Hamm, Clarence Lockwood
Hamm, Charles Adam
Hamm, Earl Iowa
Hamm, Floyd Emmett
Hamm, Harold Barclay
Hamm, Rudolph
Hamm, Thomas William
Hamm, William James
Haner, Leland Goodrich
Haner, William John
Hannett, Lewis Christopher
Hannon, Patrick William
Hapeman, Quincy Collins
Harder, Frank Mesick
Harder, George
Harder, George Albert
Harder, George Harold
Harder, Irwin Martin
Harder, Lee Kisselburgh
Harder, Lewis Frank
Harder, Stanley Hess
Harder, Willis Frederick
Hardy, Edward Pierson
Hardy, Thomas Clarence
Harlow, Maurice Frances
Harmon, Marwin David
Harmon, Raymond Uriah
Harmon, Roy William
Harris, Carleton Tilley
Harris, George William
Harrison, William Boyd
Hartigan, William Raymond
Hartmann, Charles J.
Hartmann, Harold W.
Harvey, Martin La Verne
Hasbrouck, Harry E.
Hasbrouch, Oscar
Hassett, Edward Dennis
Hatch, Jr., Charles Gerard
Hathaway, Thomas Messer
Hathaway, William

Hatheway, James Hover
Haverlick, John
Hawkes, Jr., Charles August
Hawley, William P.
Hawver, Biard Jacob
Hawver, Frederick W.
Hawver, Raymond Tilden
Hawver, Walter William
Hay, Nelson Caul
Hayes, Leo Joseph
Hayne, Harry Walter
Haynor, Freeman Nelson
Hazelton, Melburne Morse
Hazelton, Walter Philmon
Hearn, Arthur Joseph
Hearn, William John
Heeney, Frank Hoag
Helsley, William Henry
Henderson, Alden W.
Henderson, William G.
Hendler, Irving
Henderickson, Howard A.
Henn, Charles
Hennig, Otto G.
Herb, William Ellery
Hering, John Albert
Hering, Lewis Joseph
Hermance, Edward Cooper
Hermance, John Harper
Hermance, Myron E.
Hermance, Paul Edward
Herron, William Clifton
Herzog, Julius
Hickey, George Elwood
Higgins, John Francis
Hill, Charles James
Hill, Joseph B.
Hill, Walter John
Hinds, Edward Elroy
Hinds, Jr., Zack Clark
Hinsdale, Alfred J.
Hinsdale, Harry K.
Hoag, Clarence Maurinus
Hoag, Warren
Hobbie, Roy Chancellor
Hoffman, Edward
Hoffman, Henry Delan
Hoffman, Paul Edward
Hoffman, Russell
Hoffman, William Hamman
Hofsteller, Jr., Nicholas
Hogeboom, Herbert Franklin
Holmes, Jacob Frederick
Holsapple, Ernest
Holsapple, Harold
Holsapple, Lloyd Burdwin

Hood, Harold L.
Horn, Max
Horton, Charles Henry
Houghtaling, Henry Groat
Houghtaling, William
Hover, Earl Franklyn
Howard, Charles Martin
Howe, Thomas Vincent
Howe, William Daniel
Howland, Walter Brown
Hoysradt, Russell Jacob
Hubbard, Ralph Moore
Hudson, Ernest Adams
Hughes, Edward E.
Hughs, Jr., George W.
Humphrey, Lewis James
Hunt, Arthur E.
Hunt, Wilson Joseph
Hunter, George Spoor
Hunter, James
Hutchings, John T.
Hutchinson, Robert Henry
Huyck, Clarence
Huyck, John
Ihlo, William
Imhof, Frederick William
Ingham, Claude
Inman, Charles Gideon
Inman, Edward Keyser
Inman, George Cornelius
Irish, Leland Wesley
Isenhart, Jacob William
Isenhart, Worthington H.
Jacklin, Allen
Jackson, Benjamin
Jackson, Roy
Jacob, John
Jadatz, Henry Ernest
Jansen, Frederick Philip
Jarocki, Stanislaw B.
Jasinski, John
Jennings, Elmer Leroy
Jennings, Frederick Henry
Jennings, Merwin Harlan
Jennings, Roy
Jennings, William McKinley
Jewell, Pincus
Johnson, Abbott Clinton
Johnson, Anthony
Johnson, Harold
Johnson, Harold Leonard
Johnson, Ivan Anselm
Johnson, Jonas
Johnson, Junior
Johnson, Leonard Franklin
Johnson, Luke

McDonald, Charles T.
McDonald, John Gerard
McDowell, David
McDowell, Robert
McEvoy, Arthur Francis
McEvoy, James Joseph
McGrath, Patrick Dominic
McGuire, Albert
McHugh, John Francis
McIntosh, Stanley Niver
McKay, Andrew
McKay, John
McKinstry, Augustus T.
McLean, Hugh
McMillan, George Scholefield
McMillan, John Baylies
McNamara, David Joseph
McNamara, Francis, T.
McNeil, Edward N.
Melius, Floyd Sheldon
Melius, Norman Leo
Melius, William H.
Mercer, William B.
Merritt, Ray Welsey
Mesick, Albert Barton
Mesick, Henry Thomas
Metz, Samson Francis
Mieske, Otto Peter
Mieske, Richard
Miller, Arland Jacob
Miller, Barton
Miller, Charles
Miller, Chester LeRoy
Miller, Claudius George
Miller, Clifford Stall
Miller, David William
Miller, Edward Sheldon
Miller, Edward Sheldon
Miller, Frank James
Miller, Gilbert Edward
Miller, Harry Parker
Miller, John Eugene
Miller, John Henry
Miller, Joseph Leo
Miller, Levi
Miller, Lloyd Lasher
Miller, Malcolm Rockefeller
Miller, Merle
Miller, Norman Wallace
Miller, Stanton William
Miller, William
Millias, Ward Winthrop
Milne, David
Miner, Edward F.
Miner, William
Minkler, Eugene

Minkler, Guy
Molesky, Samuel
Moll, Frederick Colbert
Molyneaux, Wilbur Ludlam
Montague, William Edward
Montaldo, Victor
Monthie, Herman Lawrence
Moon, Floyd Snyder
Moon, Francis Morton
Moore, James Edward
Moore, Lucius
Moore, Percy John
Moore, Ralph J.
Moore, Van Rensselaer
Moore, William Reuben
Morgan, William E.
Morgillo, Antonio
Morgillo, Pasquale M.
Moriarty, Michael
Morris, Joseph
Morris, Thomas Earl
Morrison, Arthur Jerome
Morrison, Oscar Paul
Morrison, Sanford C.
Morsier, Clifford Morris
Mossman, Charles T.
Moul, Cornelius Ferris
Muldowney, James Francis
Muller, Jr., Konrad
Mullins, Michael
Mulson, William
Murphy, John H.
Myers, Jr., Cyrus
Myers, Harry
Nack, Paul
Nadler, Charles Carl
Nash, De Lloyd Daniel
Navarra, Joseph
Nawrockey, Frank Lawrence
Near, Robert Horton
Nelson, Cornelius Hanes
Nemeth, Frank
Nero, Domenico
Nero, Frank
New, Howard Albert
Nichols, Le Roy Charles
Nolan, Carroll Lalor
Nolozny, Frank
Nonamaker, Harold
Nonamaker, William
Nordsiek, Charles Luers
Novak, Anthony Stephen
Novine, Edward J.
Obuhski, Walter
Ochibovi, Tony
O'Connell, Thomas Joseph

O'Connor, Charles Bradford
O'Connor, James Edward
O'Connor, William Joseph
Ogden, Robert
Oldriek, Joseph Albert
Oldreik, William Joseph
Oliver, Charles Augustus
Oliver, Ellwood Hendrick
Olm, Edward Ernst
Olson, Otto Ludwig
O'Neil, Thomas Anthony
Opszonski, Joseph
O'Reilly, James Bernard
Orsted, Floyd Peter
Ossenfort, William Peter
Ostrander, Frank
Ostrander, George William
Ostrander, Wallace
Ottaviano, Settimio Luigi
Oxbrough, William Van
Padalinski, John Joseph
Paladucci, Peter
Palatsky, Charles Louis
Palatssky, David
Palatsky, Ralph
Palen, Virnest
Palmer, Clarence Bedford
Palmer, Earl Schuyler
Palmer, Frank Van Vleck
Palmer, Oscar Zimmerman
Park, Francis Ward
Parke, William Hall
Parry, Charles George
Parslow, George W.
Patten, Charles Ellsworth
Patterson, David Chapin
Patton, Andrew Louis
Paul, Esmond Franklin
Payn, Harold Ernest
Payne, Rector Lewis
Pectal, Otis C.
Pederson, Frederick
Peper, Charles Christian
Perlee, Lawrence Rockefeller
Perry, William Walter
Peters, Eli William
Peterson, Robert Morgan
Petry, Martin John
Petsel, Kenneth Homer
Petsel, Stanley Conrad
Petucha, Stephen
Philip, John Van Ness
Piester, Jr. Charles John
Pinkowski, John Thomas
Pitcher, Henry Payson
Pitcher, Hubbard McKenzie

Johnson, Robert Groat
Johnson, William Grant Reed
Jones, Herman Ephrim
Jonker, Reverend Philip
Joseph, William Nathan
Kane, Aloysius Charles
Kane, James Bernard
Kane, Raymond William
Kearney, Ambrose Alfonso
Keefer, Adam
Keeler, John Paul
Keil, Jr., George Phillip
Keller, Rudolph J.
Kellerhouse, Charles
Kellerhouse, William Lincoln
Kellogg, Raymond Austin
Kelly, Berlin Dennis
Kelly, James Edward
Kempf, Jr., Titus N. C.
Kemter, Paul Max
Kennedy, Harold Clark
Kennedy, Joseph Bernard
Kennedy, Margaret
Kennedy, Raymond Dennis
Kenny, Christopher
Kent, Frank Leslie
Kern, Ezra George
Kern, Floyd Dewitt
Kerner, Edwin
Kerr, Edmund L.
Kerr, Harold Jerome
Kestenbaum, David
Kestenbaum, Herbert H.
Kie, James Herbert
Kiel, Conrad
Kiernzel, Leon Joseph
Kilmer, Chauncey
Kilmer, Earl William
Kilmer, Elger Van Dyck
Kilmer, Frank
Kilmer, Frank Merwin
Kilmer, Harry
Kilmer, Sidney
King, Harry Francis
King, John J.
King, William Snyder
King, Winnie Samuel
Kinney, George Martin
Kirby, Jacob
Kisselburg, Wesley Charles
Kittle, Carlton Leggett
Kittle, Sanford Henry
Klein, Carl H.
Klein, George M.
Klein, Henry Louis
Klein, Harold Nicholas

Klimas, William Vincent
Kline, Arnold Manuel
Kline, Emil
Kline, Jacob
Kline, Manuel Edward
Klingelsmith, Clyde Joseph
Knapp, John Christian
Knight, Hollet A.
Knight, Howard
Knoblock, William Andrew
Knott, James
Kovatch, John
Kovats, Joseph
Kraft, Earl Abraham
Kraft, Leonard Christian
Krasnoborski, Anthony
Krasowsky, John
Kritzman, Charles Morton\
Kukon, Jr., John James
Kurtznacker, Lewis C.
La Bella, Tony
Labrie, Harold Langdon
Lafferty, Arthur
Lamasure, Albert Beyer
Lamb, William Edward
Lambadini, Guiseppi
Landeck, Harry William
Landry, Leo Bernard
Lane, Clifford Hitchcock
Langlois, Henry Russell
Lanphear, Harold Elwood
Lapointe, Charles Dayton
Lappies, Raymond Phillip
Lasher, Earl E.
Lasher, Edward Clark
Lasher, George E.
Lasher, Harry M.
Lasher, Lewis Homer
Lasher, Matthew Connor
Le Bois, Henry
Leggierri, Raffaele
Lemon, Lincoln L.
Lesoeck, Charles A.
Levy, Clyde E.
Lewandowski, George
Lewis, Harold Nelson
Link, Ezra A.
Livingston, Edmund P.
Livingston, Henry Hopkins
Livingston, Robert Reginald
Loman, Arthur James
Longley, Frederick Jessup
Loomis, Henry Milham
Loonie, Thomas Chester
Loos, Frank Sanford
Loos, Harold Stowell

Lorenz, Herman
Loveday, James
Lutsker, Simon
Macy, Harold
Macy, Harold Edward
Madison, John H.
Magarian, Malcolm Garabed
Magley, Irving Hannon
Mahon, John Thomas
Mahoney, John Clement
Main, Earl Tator
Maisenbacher, Frank Peter
Malinoski, John Paul
Malinoski, Michel William
Mallory, Roy Wesley
Malone, John Henry
Maloney, William Augustine
Mambert, John Wellington
Manchuk, Martin Frank
Marcuschewitz, Simon
Margolis, Benjamin
Margolis, Jack Simon
Markessinis, Angel L.
Markuson, John
Marshall, Edward Walter
Marshall, George Finch
Marshall, Peter John
Marshall, Richard Henry
Marshall, Roy
Marshall, Jr., William Henry
Martin, Arthur Clark
Martin, Arthur Edward
Martin, Leo Clark
Mastin, Harold Leonard
Masters, Jr., Francis Robert
Matheis, Leland V.
Matheis, Otto
Mattoon, John Elbert
Mawhinney, Arthur Stuart
Maxfield, William
Maxwell, Harry
Maxwell, Philo
Mayer, Frederick J.
McAree, Michael Francis
McArthur, Edward Gaul
McCarthy, Jr., Timothy
McClellen, Jr. George
McConnell, John Felix
McConnell, John William
McConnell, Joseph Bernard
McCoull, Samuel Frank
McCue, Edward James
McCullough, John Brewer
McDarby, Harry
McDarby, Harvey
McDermott, William Joseph

Plass, Harry Stickle
Plass, Levi Simons
Plass, William
Platner, Walter Wilkins
Plemley, Edward
Plemley, John
Plotz, David Plotz
Podlek, Peter
Popham, A. Fleming
Popham, Lewis Charles
Porter, Frank
Porter, Joel
Potts, Ernest
Potts, Everett Conrad
Potts, Floyd
Potts, Frederick Richard
Potts, Roger Elroy
Potts, Vernon Edward
Poultney, Charles Daniel
Powell, William Marshall
Prestigiacomo, Rocco
Price, Harold
Primo, Emilio
Prior, Harold James
Prior, Willard Francis
Proper, Irving Samuel
Proper, Myron Peter
Proper, Theodore
Pultz, Burton E.
Pultz, John Frank
Pulver, Arthur John
Pulver, Benjamin
Pulver, Edward James
Pulver, Frederick
Pulver, Orville
Purcell, Mary McConnell
Purcell, Jr., Philip
Quarteri, Joseph
Quigg, Murray Townsend
Quinn, Leavitt, F.
Quirk, Jr., Edward Michael
Quirk, John Melville
Race, Christopher
Race, Millard
Radler, Martin Canrad
Rainey, Eugene Howard
Randazzo, Vito
Rapp, George E.
Rappa, Guiseppe
Raught, Lee F.
Raught, Lester Henry
Raught, Winfield Chester
Raup, Harold J.
Reader, Oliver T.
Recor, Frank Hadley
Redmond, George Leroy

Regan, Eugene
Reid, Green
Reid, William Cornelius
Reiss, Charles William
Reiss, Harry Henry
Reynolds, Harold Oliver
Reynolds, Herbert Edwin
Reynolds, Jared
Richardson, John Stephen
Rider, Jonathan Benjamin
Riegel, Lloyd Charles
Rifenburgh, Foster
Rifenburgh, Raymond
Riley, Arthur William
Ring, Donald Barringer
Ring, Erik
Rivenburgh, Jr., Frederick
Rivenburgh, Lloyd Horace
Rixon, Frank Edward
Roberts, George Raymond
Roberts, Harvey
Robinson, Charles John
Rockefeller, Ralph Foster
Rockefeller, Sherman V.
Rodmond, Frank Harper
Rodman, Leander
Rodriquez, Harry M.
Roe, Walter Cavert
Rogers, John Joseph
Rogers, Timothy A.
Roney, Leo Dewey
Roosa, Carleton Egbert
Root, Frank Ett
Ross, Frank
Rossman, Leonard Jacob
Rossman, Richard Allen
Rouse, Harold Edward
Rouse, Seth Joseph
Rowe, Donald G.
Rowe, Floyd
Rowe, George G.
Rowe, Percival
Russell, John Joseph
Russell, Robert Daniel
Russell, Thomas James
Russell, Willis Waren
Sackett, Aaron Eugene
Sackett, Ransom GIllet
Sackett, Robert Emmett
Sagendorph, William Walter
Sager, William J.
Sallerola, Angelo
Sapko, George Edward
Saulpaugh, LeRoy Warren
Saupaugh, Milton Vincent
Saulpaugh, Richard Morrison

Sausbier, Frederick Henry
Scalere, Carlo
Scalley, Joseph John
Schaefer, Henry Lawrence
Schermerhorn, Charles
Schermerhorn, Edward
Schermerhorn, Ellis
Schermerhorn, John Eitleman
Schilling, Ernest Raymond
Schilling, Harold Clifford
Schmidt, Herman Frederick
Schmoyer, Paul Samuel
Shoemaker, John Joseph
Schoonmaker, Clinton James
Schoonmaker, Theodore B.
Schoonmaker, Wardell A.
Schwab, Anthony
Schwab, Charles John
Scism, Carlyle Vance
Scott, Frederick Biesel
Scott, William Arthur
Scoville, Olan Oscar
Scrodin, Leo
Scutt, Earle Charles
Seaman, Clarence Haviland
Seduto, Frank
Seery John William
Seibert, Elizabeth Anna
Seipel, Claude Kline
Seymour, Henry Miller
Seymour, Stewart Marion
Shadic, Leo
Shafer, Harry
Shamulski, John A.
Sharkey, Owen Thomas
Sharp, Albert Sharp
Sharp, Frank Clarence
Sharpe, Earle George
Shattuck, Adrian Levi
Shattuck, Earl James
Shaver, Edwin Roy
Shaw, Archibald Robert
Shaw, Donald Schofield
Shaw, William E.
Shea, Andrew George
Shea, Donald Vincent
Shea, John Edward
Shea, Walter James
Shea, William James
Sheak, William
Sheffer, Albert Morton
Sheffer, Ernest Reed
Sheffer, Jr., Frank
Sheffer, Le Roy James
Sheffer, Percy Livingston
Sheffer, Sheridan Phillip

Sheldon, Curtis Miller
Sheldon, Edward Kipp
Sheldon, Grant Elwood
Sheldon, Henry Christian
Sheldon, Ralph Charles
Sherman, Earl David
Sherman, Lyle George
Shook, Fred
Shook, George Edward
Shook, John Elbert
Shook, Roy Leonard
Shraeder, William Glen
Shufelt, Harold Austin
Shufelt, James V.
Shufelt, Wallace
Shutts, John Kenneth
Shutts, Ralph
Sigler, Jesse G.
Silverberg, Abraham
Silvernail, Louis Amasa
Simmons, Clarence Howell
Simmons, John Edward
Simon, John Benjamin
Simonson, Julius Charles
Sitcer, Clarence
Sitcer, James
Sitter, Alfred Benjamin
Skalla, Leon Francis
Skinkle, Alton Edward
Skinkle, John J.
Smith, Andrew
Smith, Asabel Blakeman W.
Smith, Charles Anthony
Smith, Charles Chauncey
Smith, Chester David
Smith, Clarence
Smith, Clarence W.
Smith, Foster Rensselaer
Smith, Frank J.
Smith, George Edward
Smith, George Newell
Smith Henry Frederick
Smith, Jared William
Smith, Jesse Benjamin
Smith, Leon Van Rensselaer
Smith, Melvin
Smith, Walter Edward
Snyder, Bernard Matthew
Snyder, Cecil Edward
Snyder, Edward Chauncey
Snyder, George Louis
Snyder, John J.
Snyder, Lewis Carskaden
Snyder, Theodore
Soloman, Alvin Henry
Solomon, Morris Harry

Southard, Herbert W.
Souther, Joseph William
Southerland, Harry Murry
Southworth, Hamilton Munn
Splittberger, Arthur
Staats, Edward
Staats, Ellis Stillwell
Staats, Frank De Witt
Staats, Garrett
Staats, Philip
Stackman, Christopher
Stahlman, Willard Edward
Stebner, Rhinehardt A.
Steele, Samuel T.
Stehle, William
Steitz, Ralph Henry
Stemple, Lewis F.
Steuerwald, Arthur Harold
Steuerwald, George Ernest
Steuerwald, William Hyde
Stevens, Edward
Stickle, Emil Frank
Stickles, George Peter Stickles, Harry
Stickles, Jr., Robert Hinsdale
Stickles, Calvin Frederick
Stickles, Edward James
Stickles, Ezra
Stickles, Harold M.
Stickles, Philip Daniel
Stickles, Royal
St. John, James Henry
Stokes, Leo Francis
Stoliker, William Jack
Stone, Emerson Law
Storm, Chester Miller
Storm, Richard Aitken
Stouter, John Henry
Strain, David
Streeter, Carl Trimper
Strehler, Aldolph Edwin
Strever, John James
Strever, Roy George
Stuart, Walter
Stupplebeen, Seymour
Sullivan, Daniel James
Sullivan, Eugene Francis
Sullivan, Harold James
Sullivan, Helen Elizabeth
Sullivan, William Henry
Sutton, Harry G.
Sweet, Cyrus
Sweet, Lisle Wells
Sweet, Percy
Sweet, Raymond E.
Swezey, Christopher

Swint, Charles Joseph
Szabo, Elmer Lewis
Tallmadge, James Goodale
Tanner, Dewey
Tanner, Floyd Gardener
Tanner, Lewis Montimer
Taylor, Charles Raymond
Taylor, Herbert Vernon
Taylor, Leslie George
Teal, Edmund Jacob
Teator, Frederick Martin
Teator, George Dewey
Terry, Anderson
Terry, David
Thomas, Ernest Reed
Thomas, John Henry
Thomas, Robert Ellsworth
Thompson, Bradley Edward
Thompson, Charles
Thompson, Edward Tremain
Thompson, Royce Clarence
Thorne, Curtis Leroy
Tiemaszkiewicz, Waclaw
Tiffany, Jay Rossman
Tile, Joseph
Tillson, John Lester
Tirk, Floyd Henry
Tobias, Charles
Tobias, James Oscar
Tomlin, Andrew
Tomlin, Jr., Frank
Tompkins, Jr., Daniel Davis
Tootell, Augustus Leutian
Tracy, Augustus Cadman
Tracy, De Loss Kellogg
Tracy, Martin
Tracy, Van Belston
Traver, Arthur
Treanor, John
Tremper, Charles Edward
Tucker, Edward Harrison
Turner, Ernest Lester
Uliano, Giuseppe
Van Allen, Edgar
Van Allen, Louis Henry
Van Alphen, Willis
Van Alstine, Walter Isaac
Van Alstyne, Albert Henry
Van Alstyne, Jacob
Van Alstyne, Lewis
Van Alstyne, Pruyn John
Van Alstyne, Robert
Van Bramer, William Alden
Van Buren, Edward W.
Van Buren, Harry Leonard
Van Buren, Raymond James

Van De Boe, Louis Bristol
Van De Bogart, Ernest Otto
Van de Carr, Cornelius V.
Vanden Burgh, Paul W.
Van Deusen, Charles Werter
Van Deusen, Donald Higgins
Van Deusen, Fay
Van Deusen, George Earl
Van Deusen, Leslie Marshall
Van Etten, Jr., Luther
Van Hoesen, Charles R.
Van Hoesen, Henry Raymond
VanKuren, William Chester
VanLoan, Howard Wm
Van Patten, Frederick
Van Vaulkenburg, Edward J.
Van Vaulkenburg, Frank J.
VanVaulkenburg, James M.
Van Vleck, Clarence
Van Vleck, Harry Jacob
Van Vleck, Lester Decker
Van Vleck, Roy Abram
Van Zandt, William H.
Vatalaro, Raffaele
Vincent, Archie Miller
Vincent, Elbert Harold
Vincent, George Chester
Vogel, Frederick
Voight, Charles Henry
Vosburgh, Frank Edward
Vosburg, Lee
Voss, Harry Lewis
Wager, Robert Bert
Wagner, John Arthur
Waldorph, Ray
Walker, John James
Walker, William Henry
Wallace, William
Walsh, John Harold
Waltermire, Albert Louis
Waltermire, Homer George

Walters, Harold D.
Wamback, Arnold
Ward, Joseph Harry
Wardle, James McClure
Warner, Earl James
Washburn, Elliott Rhodes
Washington, James M.
Weaver, Albert Oscar
Weed, Russell Arthur
Weinstein, Norman Lewis
Wells, Ethel Marion
Wenk, George W.
West, Charles Jacob
West, Edward Jacob
Westover, George Earnest
Westover, George Jerome
Westover, Jesse Edwin
Whalen, Harold Joseph
Whalen, Jr., Sebastian D.
Wheeler, Edward
Wheeler, Perry Hermance
Wheeler, Thorne Lake
Wheeler, Worthy Nathan
Whitaker, Sylvester S.
Whitbeck, William John
White, Frank Thomas
White, John Hallenbeck
White, Peter
White, Russell Deane
Whitehouse, Arthur E.
Whiteman, Jr., Jarvis Setchuel
Whitty, Edmund Alward
Whitty, Vincent Joseph
Wilber, Delbert Jared
Wilber, Lloyd Clifton
Wilcox, Jr., Oscar
Wilder, Wallace David
Willets, James Bailey
Williams, Charles Fuller
Williams, David Andrew
Williams, George Stanley

Williams, Harry V.
Williams, Lawrence
Williams, Roger
Williams, Sidney Fletcher
Wilt, Reginald
Wiltse, Stanley Bailie
Wiltsie, John Henry
Winne, Raymond A.
Winstian, Leo
Winstian, Philip
Winters, William Louis
Wise, Edward
Wisewell, Jr., Francis Henry
Wisockis, Stasis
Witkowski, Michael Edward
Wolcott, Ivan
Wolven, Vernon
Wood, Cornelius Jones
Wood, Harry Doty
Wood, Winthrop Adams
Woodward, Fred
Worth, Clarence Joseph
Wortz, Matthew
Wurstel, Frank
Wyckoff, John Sterling
Yacone, Amedeo
Yerick, Edward Joseph
Yerick, Frank George
Yerick, John Francis
Young, Earle Delbert
Young, George Henry
Young, Harold
Young, Philip Henry
Young, Roy
Yozwak, John Joseph
Zanchilli, Dominic
Zegular, Joseph Charles
Zellmer, Philip
Zenovitch, Anthony J.
Zimmerman, Herman C.

WORLD WAR II
COLUMBIA COUNTY VETERANS

Abitable, Anthony Vincent
Abrams, William Francis, Jr.
Adam, Robert Charles
Adams, John P.
Adam, John Wesley
Adams, William McMillan
Adriance, Alexander Bruce
Adriance, Edward Jesse
Aery, Thomas Paul
Agins, Samuel
Agne, Henry Francis
Ahrens, William Fred
Aichele, Frederick
Aimstead, Arthur Herbert
Aimstead, Kenneth William
Aimstead, Stewart Coert
Alamillo, Keneth
Alamillo, Malcolm V.
Alamillo, Raymond
Albright, Clifford Spencer
Albright, Earl Marion
Albright, Harold Paul
Aldrich, George Byron
Aldrich, Hubert Justus, Jr.
Alger, Donald Jesse
Alger, Earl Paul
Alger, Frank Robert Jr.
Allen, Edward Crosier
Allen, Elmer W.
Allen, Emma Barbara
Allen, Louis A.
Allen, Marvin
Allen, Weldon, Newgens
Allen, William David
Alspach, Edward J.
Althiser, Charles Edward
Althiszer, Robert
Alto, John
Alvertson, Egbert, Jr.
Ambrose, Alger L.
Ames, Donald
Anderson, Albert Edward
Anderson, James H.
Anderson, Jean Wilber
Andrews, Lawrence James
Andrews, Vern Hewitt
Andrusky, Morris
Anelle, James Dominick
Angell, Fred Decker
Armstrong, William M.
Army, Nancie Marguerite

Arnold, Allen
Arnold, George Dagley
Arnold, Gordon Lewis, Jr.
Atkins, Richard Winfield
Atkinson, Normand Smith
Avery, Kenneth H.
Avery, Ralph Peter

Babcock, Marvin Simeon
Babjeck, Michael James, Jr.
Bader, Peter Nordolf
Bailey, Charles Alvy
Bain, Barbara Rose
Bain, William Sherwood
Bair, Fredrick Haigh, Jr.
Baker, Andrew Philip
Baker, Donald Elwood
Baker, Edward Franklin
Baker, Everett W.
Baker, Louis G.
Baker, Lewis Thomason
Baker, Roy Donald
Ballway, Harold Edward
Bame, Clifford Vance
Bame, Crawford Thornton
Banks, Oakley G.
Bannister, Robert James
Barber, Arthur James, Jr.
Barca, Angelo Gerald
Barden, Charles Vernon
Barden, Donald Charles
Barden, Harrison Lee
Barden, John Wesley
Barden, Paul Wood
Barden, Robert William
Baretsky, John Jr.
Barford, Burns F. Jr.
Barner, Charles Leonard
Barnum, Anette Esther
Barratt, Martin Lindy
Barringer, Otis Nelson
Bartholomew, David William
Bartholomew, William Peter
Bartlov, Percy A.
Barto, Peter Wilber
Barton, Donald William
Basen, Jacob
Basen, Julius
Basen, Samuel S.
Bassakalis, Franklin George
Batchelder, Frank Monroe

Bates, Herbert V.
Bates, Joshua B.
Bathrick, Archie John
Bathrick, Kenneth
Battistello, Andrew
Bauhoff, Frank
Beaumont, William Gene
Beckel, George William
Becker, Clarence Jacob
Beckers, Joseph H.
Beebe, Charles
Beebe, Donald E.
Beebe, Howard Francis
Beebe, James Gordon
Beecher, John Joseph
Beers, Raymond Winfred
Beers, Willard Truscott
Beldnap, Raymond David
Belknap, Elsie Green
Belknap, Harold Chester Jr.
Belknap, Robert Jackson
Bell, Thomas James Jr.
Bemis, Bert W.
Bemiss, Charles Wolcott
Bemiss, George R.
Bender, Albert William
Benedict, Harold Bradley
Benedict, John Coleman
Bennar, Albert Stephen
Bennett, Donald B.
Bennett, Edson Loran
Bennett, Marcus Aldelbert
Benson, George Egbert
Benton, Orsmer J.
Benton, Talcott Barnett
Berg, Bernard
Berger, Sam C.
Bernhoft, Bernard Billy
Bernhoft, Fred Carl
Berninger, John II
Bernockie, Frederick Paul
Bertram, Donald George
Bertram, Stanley Frank
Bessman, Michael A.
Best Donald R.
Best, Edward Harrison
Best, Henry Bodley Jr.
Best, Martin
Betts, Robert C.
Bevens, William Edward
Bezbroda, Samuel

Biedrzicki, Lee Joseph
Bier, Joseph Otto
Bikes, William J.
Bishop, Alfred, Jr.
Bishop, Charles Edward
Bither, William Martin
Bixby, Burdell, R.
Black, Edward John
Blake, Francis Joseph
Blake, William F.
Blanchard, Charles W.
Blass, John Harmon
Blass, Wallace Theodore
Bleadow, John William, Jr.
Bliss, Floyd Russell
Bliss, Gerald Steward
Bliss, Roger Courtenaye
Block, Alan Edward
Bloomfield, John Jordon
Bluteau, Thomas J.
Bob, William John
Bobalko, John Charles
Bocholz, Arthur B. Jr.
Boffardi, Joseph Mayo
Bogarski, Frank John
Bogarski, John Francis
Bogarski, Louis John
Bogarski, William
Bohnsack, Donald Charles
Bohnsack, Warren Hardy
Boice, Belden Charles
Boice, Roy, Jr.
Boice, Vernon Allen
Bordeux, Richard David
Boris, Alex Joseph
Borrele, Frank John Jr.
Bossert, Charles William
Bost, Charles Edward
Boswell, Elwood Lyman
Boucher, Louis Edward
Bouer, Saul David
Boughton, Charles Spencer
Boughton, Harold Frederick
Bowers, Elmer M.
Bowers, Richard Duane
Bowman, Ralph J.
Bowsh, William
Boyce, Jack Nelson
Boyd, George R.
Boyko, Nicholas William
Boyles, Henry F.
Boyles, Russell E.
Bozik, Philip S.
Brady, Ashton Perry
Brady, Joseph James
Brady, Paul Dillion

Brahm, Antony Charles
Braker, John James
Brandley, Ada Marie
Brandow, Roy
Brash, Frank Jacob
Bratton, Marshall F.
Braudt, Augustus Herman
Bravender, Harold
Bray, Francis James
Brearley, Kenneth George
Brearly, Frank Edward
Bregman, Robert
Brenenstuhl, Elwin John
Brenner, Julius Peter
Brignull, Alfred W.
Brignull, James Edwin
Briscoe, Harold J.
Bristol, Norman Richard
Bristol, Robert Thompson
Briwa, Charles Jr.
Brizzie, Eugene
Broderick, Charles John
Broderick, Eugene Joseph
Brodwoski, John
Bronk, Frank Lincoln
Brooker, Kenneth Edward
Brooker, Walter Eric
Brooks, John William
Brooks, Josiah Alexander
Broomer, Irving Julius
Brorup, Erlind Madsen
Brosky, George Joseph
Broszio, Marx Robert
Brothers, Blandfort Bert
Brough, Henry Jr.
Brower, Frank Charles
Brown, Arthur Francis
Brown, Charles Jay
Brown, Charles F.
Brown, Chester L.
Brown, David Speer
Brown, Donald Robert
Brown, Frank Melville Jr.
Brown, Fred Jay
Brown, George Edward
Brown, Lyford Martin
Brown, Thomas Joseph
Brown, Warren Curtis
Brown, William Russell
Brueckmann, Gordon Frederick
Brush, Miltimore W.
Brush, Roberick McLeed
Brusie, Charles R.
Brusie, Fay William
Bryant, Charles Ernest
Bryant, Clement Arthur

Bryant, Louis
Bryfonski, Lewis Francis
Bucci, Dominic Joseph
Bucci, Peter John
Buchan, John Merwin Jr.
Bucholz, Jr. Arthur B.
Buckbee, Bertran Harry
Buckbee, Willard Howell
Bugel, Leonard Geiger
Bujnovsky, Steven Jr.
Bunk, Vernon Augustus
Bunlak, John Jr.
Bunlak, Stephen
Burch, Alvin J.
Burch, Charles
Burch, Emma Catherine
Burch, Raymond
Burch, Raymond R.
Burger, Floyd Edward
Burgess, Walter
Burke, Cornelius Garretson
Burke, Leverett C.
Burley, Harry Jay
Burnett, Arthur C.
Burnett, Warren Harding
Burns, Arthur Lewis
Burns, Hugh Rodney
Burrows, Mortimer Townsend Jr.
Bush, Charles Leverett
Bush, Henry Galster
Bussett, Claude
Butler, Mary Martha
Byron, Raymond J.

Cadby, Robert Andrews Jr.
Caggianelli, Antonio M.
Cagianelli, Michael E.
Call, Bien Fradenburg
Call, Clayton James
Callaghan, John W.
Callahan, Andrew Richard
Callahan, George Aleysius
Callahan, Timothy Joseph
Callan, Albert Stevens Jr.
Callan, Albert Stevens Sr.
Callan, John Lansing #
Calyer, Theodore H.
Campbell, Clifford Henry
Campbell, Donald Hugh
Campbell, Donald Oscar
Canape, Louis Salvatore
Canavan, Vincent Walter
Canetto, Joseph
Canetto, Libero
Canning, Lester
Cantine, Frank Martin

Cantine, Henry T.
Cantine, Walter Sheppard
Caparoso, Arthur Joseph
Caparoso, Carmine
Cappozzo, Frank Fred
Card, Donald Howard
Card, Edward Frank
Card, Francis Charles
Card, Frank Epson
Card, Gerald B.
Card, James Marcus
Card, Robert
Card, Stanford
Card, Wilmer Jr.
Cardinale, Frank J.
Carhart, Harry S.
Cariseo, Sisto J.
Carl, George Lester
Carl, Howard N.
Carl, Lyle Frederick
Carl, Ray D.
Carl, Ruth Earline
Carl, Wesley J.
Carle, David Edward
Carle, Ralph G.
Carle, Wesley Scott Jr.
Carlson, Torbjorn Vincent
Carlson, Torsten Emanuel
Carlucci, Nicola
Carpenter, Leonard Doty
Carter, Frederick J.
Carter, Melvin B.
Cascioli, Leonard P.
Case, Frederick Martin
Cash, Warren O.
Caswell, William Joseph
Cavallari, Augustus Irving
Cavallari, Domenic
Celelli, Eugene Michael
Centocanti, Americo Carlo
Cernak, John James
Cesternino, Lenord
Chace, Malcot
Chaikowski, Stephan
Chaikowski, Walter Edward
Chairella, Frank Philip
Chamberlain, Robert J.
Chamberlin, Wendell Everett
Chapman, Ellsworth W.
Chappell, Kenneth Edward
Charlton, Harold Howard
Charney, Samuel
Charron, Leonard Edmund
Charron, Nelson Joseph
Chase, Warren R.
Chisoim, James Juenes

Christiana, Albert H.
Christiana, Alvan
Church, Harold Lloyd
Ciampa, Vincent Michael
Cianetta, Angelo
Cipkowski, Joseph Anthony
Clapp, Donald John
Clapp, Edison
Clapp, Harold Clinton Jr.
Clapp, William R.
Clapper, Raymond Eber
Clark, Clayton
Clark, Harold M.
Clark, Kenneth Thomas
Clark, Robert Aaron
Clark, Thomas Leo
Clark, Westley Harry
Clarkson, George Henry
Cleary, William Patrick
Clemente, Anthony Milan
Closson, Clyde F.
Clough, Paul L.
Clum, Elbert John
Clum, Roy
Coburn, Le Roy Edgar
Cody, John T.
Colbeck, Nelson C.
Colbert, Clarence
Colby, Arthur B.
Cole, Conrad Hugh
Cole, Everett
Cole, George
Cole, Theodore
Coll, James Joseph
Collins, Robert Wilson
Colville, William Alton
Colwell, Leo Edward
Colwell, William Leo
Compton, Earl Dwight
Congdon, James L.
Conklin, Francis Andrew
Conklin, Paul Stanley
Conklin, Walter James
Conklin, Willis Bertram
Conley, Calvin B.
Conley, Sherwood Decker
Connell, Bernice Irene
Connelly, William F.
Connors, James Thomas
Conte, Anthony Peter
Conte, Armando Patrick
Conte, Ferdinand John
Conte, Joseph Paul
Conte, Louis Raymond
Conte, Thomas R.
Conway, Roland E.

Cook, Alan James
Cook, Leon Foster Jr.
Cook, William Graf
Cookingham, Robert Francis
Cookingham, Thomas Albert Jr.
Cooley, John Henry
Coons, Albert
Coons, Alfred Andrew
Coons, Archie William
Coons, Arthur William
Coons, Chauncey David
Coons, Clifford Russell
Coons, David F.
Coons, Elmore Berton
Coons, Franklin A. B.
Coons, Frederick John
Coons, Herbert Oakley
Coons, Kenneth B.
Coons, Myron E.
Coons, Robert A.
Coons, William DeForest
Cooper, Floyd George
Cooper, Ralph
Cooper, Thomas Woodrow
Copp, Joseph
Corapi, Anthony S.
Cordato, Anthony John
Cordato, Joseph P.
Cordato, Joseph R.
Cordato, Leonard G. Jr.
Cordato, Michael Anthony
Cosby, Jack
Cossolino, Anthony J.
Cossolino, Joseph
Costello, Thomas Lawrence
Coster, Joseph
Coughlan, Joseph Daly
Couse, Earl L.
Cowardin, Samuel Pendleton
Coxon, Charles Leroy
Coxon, Raymond Frank
Cozzolino, Frank M.
Cozzolino, Nicholas
Craft, Charles
Craft, George Irving
Cramer, Charles Edmund
Cramer, Malcolm
Crandell, Edwin Hawley
Crandell, Walter Bain
Crans, Elmer Henry
Crans, Preston Milton
Craver, Clayton Francis
Craver, Robert Edward
Crawford, Douglas Watson
Crawford, Raymond R.
Crego, Arthur V.

Crego, David Nelson
Crego, Ralph Nelson
Cresky, Stanley
Crispino, James Joseph
Crosby, John Howard
Crosby, Robert H.
Crosier, Oliver D.
Cross, Parker Jarvis Jr.
Crouse, John Francis
Cruise, James Joseph
Cruise, John William
Cullison, Donald Harris
Cunningham, Ivy Lee
Cunningham, William J.
Curd, Arvella Irene
Curd, Charles Joseph Jr.
Currier, Franklin James
Currier, Willis Earnest
Curtin, Tessie Marion
Curtis, Paul R. Jr.
Curtis, William Mueller
Czajka, Frank J.
Czajkowski, Joseph John
Czajkowski, Stanley E.
Czirr, William Joseph

Dagget, Leonard
Dallas, William E.
Dalzell, Edward
Damon, Keneth Roland
Darness, David Niles
Darness, John
Dauski, Alfred.
Dauski, Harold
David, Benjamin Edmund
Davis, Cecil Carl
Davis, Charles
Davis, Howell Arthur Jr.
Davis, James Dalton
Davis, Laurence F.
Dawson, Robert William
Day, Clarence Jr.
Day, Douglas Hollister
Dean, Edward Gordon
Dean, George Richard
Deans, Stephen Thomas
DeBella, Cosimo
DeCintio, Joseph
Decker William S. Jr.
Decker, Armand Roy
Decker, Charles M.
Decker, Donald Milo
Decker, Edward Leonard
Decker, Gordon, M.
Decker, John Bradley
Decker, John Evans

Decker, Lee William
Decker, Margaret Alice
Decker, Neil Bidwell
Decker, Philip Spencer
Decker, Ralph Forrest
Decker, Russell Eugene Jr.
Decker, Vernon Sherwood
Decker, Vernon Wesley
Decker, Walter Claudius
Decker, William Henry
Decker, William Lewis
DeCrosta, Anthony John
Decrosta, Emrick Louis
DeFile, John Joseph
Defile, Patrick James
Defile, Patrick Michael
DeGroodt, Jesse Jay
DeGuzman, Robert Vincent
DeJoy, Joseph Thomas
Delaney, Bartholomew Frances
Delaney, Robert Vincent
Delginski, Alexander M.
Dellea, Fred Richard
DeLuke, John
DeLuke, Peter Joseph
DeLuke, Ralph W.
DeLuke, Sisto J.
Demler, George Walter
Demos, Christopher Harry
Denegar, Reginald Arthur
Denegar, Richard J.
Denegar, William Harry Jr.
Dennis, Edward P.
Dennis, Floyd William
Dennis, Henry Harris
DePeyster, Robert Boyd
DeShaw, Albert S.
Detel, Howard
DeVane, Jack Ramon
DeVane, Robert Ellard
Devenski, John
DeWitt, Edna Ruth
Dexheimer, Harold F.
DeYoe, Frank Searing Jr.
DeYoe, Warner Stanley
Dick, James Caird Jr.
Dickeson, Essex Hunt
Dickson, Christine Elizabeth
Diehl, Harry Jacob
Diel, Carlyle Henry
Dietter, Ernest Stanley
Dinardi, Thomas P.
Dinehart, Frederick Herbs
Dinehart, William Henry Jr.
Dingee, Alfred Shedrick
Dingman, Earl Edward Jr.

Dingman, Harry
Dingman, Howard Asbury
Dings, Lester Carle
Diokas, Frank J.
Disbrow, Howard Henry
Disher, Pershing A.
Diskin, James Edward Jr.
Diskin, Thomas Patrick
Dittmar, Robert Willits
Dixon, Lloyd Randall
Dobrowski, Edward Victor
Doddridge, Donald Samuel
Dodds, Mary Jean
Dodge, William Dayton Jr.
Dolan, Everett Marvin
Dolan, Louis F.
Dole, John Markman
Doleski, Alexander Adam
Domkoski, Harold Joseph
Donegan, Michael W.
Doolittle, Edward
Doolittle, Henry James
Doolittle, Richard Henry
Doolittle, Robert Bernard
Dorland, Charles Ellwood
Doviskie, George
Downing, Frederick
Doyle, Clyde Oakleigh
Doyle, William Francis
Drabick, Nickolas J.
Drabick, Stephen J.
Dragan, Denny
Drahushuk, Andrew
Drahushuk, John
Drake, Murray Frederick
Driscoll, John Fred
Drobnicki, Benjamin Walter
Drowne, Roland Charles
Drucker, Theodore Ewald
Drumm, Orville
Drumm, Robert Willard
Dubois, Raymond B.
Duff, Joseph F.
Dugan, Jesse Joseph
Dugan, Michael William
Dunham, George Hubert
Dunn, Bernard
Dunn, John James
Dunn, Thomas James
Dunspaugh, William Edward
Dunton, Benjamin Fish
Dunton, Clifford Raymond
Dunton, Lawrence Earl
Duntz, Henry Seipel
Durkee, Forrest Jay
Durkee, William Duncan

Durniak, Daniel
Dutcher, David Howell
Dutton, Linwood Carlton
Dykeman, Clyde Maynard
Dykeman, Elmer Harry
Dykeman, William James
Dymond, Earnest Ezra
Dymond, Elbert Osborne
Dzirnksski, Frank William
Eames, David Monroe
Eaton, William M.
Eckel, Malcolm William
Edgley, Francis Raymond
Edgley, Kathleen Anne
Edgley, Ralph Healey
Edwards, Allan Vincent
Edwards, Harry Henry Jr.
Edwards, John R.
Edwards, Leonard H.
Egan, Joseph A.
Egan, Peter Francis
Egnasher, Joseph Martin
Egnasher, Lawrence S.
Eisner, Howard F.
Eisner, Lawrence Wilfred
Eitleman, Lawrence Edward
Elliot, William R.
Ellis, Robert Winthrop
Emmett, Herbert Edward
Ennis, David C.
Erers, William Clancy
Ericson, Jr., William Gustave
Ernst, Lydon Hofferd
Ershler, Arthur
Estok, Paul P.
Evans, George Root
Evans, John T. Jr.
Everett, Cecil Maxton
Everett, Hilton Harding
Everett, Merrill Thomas
Everett, Vernon Henry
Everin, James Edward
Every, Charles Jr.
Every, Roy C.
Ewasick, Steve

Fabiano, Francis
Fabiano, James
Fabiano, Joseph Anthony
Face, Ellis Leo
Face, Otto P.
Fagan, Joseph E.
Falkner, Harry LeRoy
Falkner, Ralph Jay
Falkowsky, Edward
Falter, Christine A.

Falter, Denis S.
Farling, Edward Dudley
Farrington, George Briggs
Fass, Max
Fayerweather, John
Feger, William Andrew
Feller, Delmar W.
Felter, Frederick Wallace
Felter, Frank Charles
Feltner, John Barmore
Fennhahn, William Paul
Fenoff, Theodore Ebenezer
Fero, Melvin George
Ferriss, Charles Cochrane
Field, Walter Sanford
Fiero, Franklin William
Fiero, Oscar Harry
Finch, Walter Douglas
Finck, Robert Frederick
Fingar, Claudius da Silva
Fingar, Ralph Warren
Fingar, Robert A.
Fingar, Victor J.
Fink, Melvin Jordon
Finkle, Philip H.
Finkle, Richard Samuel
Finkelstein, Edwin William
Finkelstein, Harold
Finn, Clifford James
Fino, John Albert
Fino, Louis Fred
Fiorillo, Michael Phillip
Fischer, Frederick Charles
Fischer, Marold A.
Fishbough, Edna (Wohlfarth)
Fisher, Byron Lansing
Fisher, Frank
Fisher, Raymond Hall
Fitting, John Philip
Fitzgerald, John Robert
Flaum, Benjamin
Flaum, Samuel
Fletcher, Horace Charles
Fletutor, Charles
Flick, Bernard
Flick, Clyde Duane
Floeter, John Carl
Florio, John Vincent
Foladelli, John Fr.
Foladelli, Mary D.
Folmsbe, Theron C.
Folmsbe, William C.
Folz, Edwin David
Fontaine, Louis Dean Jr.
Forando, Leo
Ford, John Edward

Ford, Joseph O'Connor
Forgham, James Duane Jr.
Fosegan, Anthony John
Foss, Carl Alstien
Fournier, Edward Joseph
Fowler, Frank Joseph
Fox, John
Fox, Paul Harold
Francis, Albert Edward
Francis, Donald Franklin
Francis, Elden Vernon
Frank, Paul Floyd
Franklin, Walter D.
Franz, John Charles
Frederick, Alexander Donald
Frederick, Henry George
Frederick, Nathanal
Freinberg, Eleanor
Freinberg, Harold Bernard
Freinberg. Herbert Davis
French, George A. Jr.
French, John Harpin
Frichette, Walter Crawford
Frick, Frederick Robert
Frick, George W.
Frick, John
Frier, Robert, William
Frisbe, Charles Van Alstyne
Frisbee, Edward
Friss,Arland
Friss, Howard Avery
Friss, Richard, Le Roy
Fritts, Crawford Ellsworth
Frost, Chester Frank
Fumasoli, Maurice
Funk, Benjamin Andrew
Funk, Cecil H.
Funk, Raymond Leroy
Funk, Rodney Wilber
Funk, Vernon Wilson
Funk, Vincent Oscar

Gabaccia, Felix
Gabaccia, Remo Palmo
Gabriel, Carman Joseph
Garbiel, Orlando Louis
Gabriel, Victor Michael
Gaffney, Joseph M.
Gaffney, John R.
Gagliardi, Joseph F.
Gage, Alfred Kittell
Gagliardy, Patrick J.
Gagliardy, Terence Michael
Gallagher, Hugh J.
Gallup, Francis Marion
Gambacorta, Lorenzo Vincent

Gambacorta, Santo Louis
Gamello, Charles Philip
Gamello, Samuel Anthony
Gangloff, Joseph Arthur
Ganley, Joseph M.
Garafalo. Philip C.
Gardina, Claude
Gardinier, Claude Donald
Gardinier, James Simeon
Gardner, Ralph
Garner, Philip Klinsing
Garrigan, Thomas William
Garry, George E.
Garry, John Bernard
Garvansites, Anthony V.
Garvey, John Lawrence
Garvey, Mary Genevieve
Garvey, Wright Barnes
Gattone, Patsy
Gauthier, Rollin Henry
Gawron, Edwin Casmer
Gaylord, Alden W.
Gelhorn, Elmer Richard
Gawron, Stanley Jr.
Gawron, Walter
Gaylord, Alden Woodruff
Gazzera, Alfred
Gelbert, Martin
Gelhorn, Harold George
Gembala, George
Gembala, Stephen John
Gendar, Bertram Elmer Jr.
Geraldi, Edmund Charles
Gerst, Robert Francis
Geyer, Carl Conrad
Giabalvo, Saverio M.
Giannattasio, John Thomas
Giannattasio, Joseph Paul
Gibbons, Charles Francis
Gibbons, James Gilbert
Giggen, Steven Stanley
Gilbert, Harold Robert
Gilbert, William
Gillette, Ezra Berry
Gillette, Florence Lyle
Gillette, Ira F.
Gilroy, Robert James
Ginsberg, Morton
Girdler, Charles Norman Jr.
Glasser, Lloyd
Glick, Philip Paul
Glickman, Harold
Glines, Leon Edgar
Glines, Sidney Jasper
Glovanovitch, Henry Hinz
Glynn, Walter A

Godbolt, William Elmer
Godfroy, Louis Emil Jr.
Godstrom, Oscar Hilmar
Goeke, Ralph Eugene
Goetz, Elmer Race
Gold, Joseph H.
Goldberg, Abie
Goldberg, Arthur Morton
Golden, Charles David
Golderman, Julius
Goldman, Irving
Goodermote, Earl J.
Goodfellow, Hubert Traver
Goodman, George C.
Goodman, Hyman
Goodrich, Lloyd Kenneth
Goodrich, Quentin E.
Goold, Gordon C.
Gorecki, Frank
Gorecki, Helen B.
Gorsline, Donald Douglas
Goux, Edward Frederick
Graboski, Arthur A.
Gramlich, Wilbur A.
Grant, Clifford Joseph
Grant, Willard E.
Grasso, James Vincent
Grater, John J.
Grau, Elmer J.
Graziano, Frank Louis
Graziano, Patrick Nick
Graziano, Peter P.
Graziano, Phillip
Graziano, Ralph
Graziano, Tony J.
Green, George Daniel
Green, William David
Greene, Alfred Thomas
Greene, Lawrence V.
Gregpru. John William
Grener, Floyd
Grener, Kenneth N.
Grener, Reginald Claude
Griffin, Bernard Joseph Jr.
Griffin, John Howard
Griffin, Thomas Joseph
Griffin, William Roland
Grimes, Guy W.
Groat, Earl I.
Gross, Gerard P.
Gross, Robert Adam
Grossman, George Francis 3rd
Grossman, Stanley H.
Grubb, John Edward
Grube, William C. Jr.
Grzyb, Charles

Gueidner, Richard George
Gumaer, Bruce R.
Gurny, Mitro
Gutch, John
Gutheil, Edith Majorie
Gutheil, Warren Heisser

Haag, Joseph
Hacker, Paul
Hadsell, Frederick Kent
Hafner, Stephen F.
Hafner, William John
Hagen, Marcellus Burr
Haggerty, Raymond Joseph
Hall, John William
Hall, Thomas James
Hallenbeck, Alexander Fyfe
Hallenbeck, Arthur Riddle
Hallenbeck, Arthur Thomas
Hallenbeck, Earl Clifford
Hallenbeck, Frank LaRue
Hallenbeck, Geoffrey Russell
Hallenbeck, Harmon
Hallenbeck, Harold F.
Hallenbeck, John W.
Hallenbeck, Marshall Lewis
Hallenbeck, Jr., Morton
Hallenbeck, Paul Spanburg
Hallenbeck, Stanley G.
Hallenbeck, Jr. Thurman
Halloran, James David
Ham, Melvin George
Ham, Ralph Charles
Hamitton, Russell Frank
Hamilton, William Murray
Hamm, Arthur Willard
Hamm, Charles Elbert
Hamm, Claude E.
Hamm, Elwood Ross
Hamm, Erwin C.
Hamm, George Henry
Hamm, Harold LaVerne
Hamm, Paul R.
Hamm, Ralph A.
Hamm, Robert Earl
Hamm, Robert Harry
Hamm, Warren Harold
Hamm, Wesley L.
Hamy, Joseph
Hand, Bruce R.
Hand, James Sanderson
Haner, Richard Leland
Hanlon, Leroy
Hannett, Louis Kane
Hansen, Gerhard William
Hanson, Donald Earnest

Hanyen, Raymond Frederick
Hapeman, William Raymond
Harangozo, Joseph
Harder, Byron T.
Harder, Clarence K.
Harder, George Albert
Harder, George Mesick
Harder, John Francis
Harder, John Witbeck
Hardner, Martin Irvin
Harder, Perry Addison
Harder, Robert Keith
Harding, James Curtis
Hardy, John Clifford
Harling, James C.
Harlow, Hubert Gregory
Harms, Charles Joseph
Harms, John Frederick
Harp, Jr. John H.
Harrington, Carl L.
Harrington, James P.
Harrington, John Francis
Harris, Charles Tobias
Harrison, William Rogers
Hart, Charles H.
Hart, Frederick Seward
Hart, Gerard Francis
Hart, Raymond J.
Hartcorn, Louis Ambroso
Hartigan, John Vincent
Hartigan, William Boyd
Harvey, Barton L.
Harvey, Earl Dolbert
Hastings, John Frazco
Hatch, George Padgett
Hatch, James Asher
Hatch, Lewis Asher
Hatch, Norman William
Hatch, Russell Stephen
Hauck, John
Haverlick, Henry Levi
Hawkins, Harvey Henry
Hawver, Biard Franklyn
Hawver, Carl H.
Hawver, Charles Vincent
Hawver, Claude William
Hawver, Clifton John
Hawver, Earl Mervin
Hawver, Easten B.
Hawver, Elmer Thomas
Hawver, Lloyd Howard
Hawver, Walter Vincent
Hayes, John Granley
Hayes, Norman Mailler
Haynes, Everett Williams
Haywood, Ellwood Orson

Haywood, Roland Ellsworth
Haywood, Morris C.
Hazelton, George B.
Hazelton, Maynard W.
Hazen, Joseph George
Heald, Raymond
Healy, Martin James
Healey, Richard Thomas
Healy, William Arthur
Hedrick, Jr., Gustav Frank
Heeney, Leo Martin
Heeney, William F.
Hegardty, Arthur L.
Heintz, Conrad
Heintz, Emanuel
Heintz, Jr., Henry
Heintz, Henry Harold
Heintz, Samuel Albert
Heintz, Walter Edwin
Heintz, William
Heinz, William
Heist, William James
Helliwell, John Thomas
Helsley, Leonard William
Leisley, Llewellyn Sherwood
Hendler, David Anthony
Herbs, Jr., Lorenzo C.
Herbs, Paul Casper
Hermance, John T.
Hermance, Richard Thomas
Hermans, Howard Grant
Hermans, Worden M.
Heron, Frederick David
Herrick, Jr., Frank Edwin
Herrick, Kenneth Daniel
Herrick, William Mairs
Herron, Robert Irving
Herron, William L.
Herzberg, Robert Waldron
Hester, Jr., Martin J.
Hettesheimer, Henry Foster
Hettisheimer, Sherwood Andrew
Hewitt, Ernest Clater
Hickey, Calvin J.
Hickey, Eben L.
Hicks, Harold Benjamin
Hiebeler, Jr., George E.
Hieber, George
Higgins, Francis W.
Hildebrant, Harry
Hill, Clifford Mabrey
Hilton, Gordon Edgar
Hinch, Evelyn P.
Hines, Roland
Hiscox, Joseph
Hitchcock, Donald Earl

Hoag, James
Hobbie, Jr., George
Hobbie, Leon Jacob
Hocking, Jr., Lenord Alvin
Hector, Joseph Louis
Hoddick, Arthur Booth
Hoder, Andrew Anthony
Hodge, Clifford Maurice
Hodge, Jean Francis
Hodina, Alfred
Hodowansky, Michael Americo
Hoefer, Charles E.
Hoes, Isaac J.
Hoes, John Spotsweed
Hoes, Peter Van Buren
Hoffman, Clifford Joseph
Hoffman, David Joseph
Hoffman, George W.
Hoffman, Joseph
Hoffman, Nelson Lawrence
Hoffman, Ralph Oliver
Hoffman, Jr., Robert S.
Hofstetter, Clarence
Hofstadter, Warren Jay
Hogue, Alfred M.
Hoke, Donald Robert
Hoke, Vernon P.
Holdridge, Edward Louis
Holley, Edmund F.
Holmer, Edwin
Holmes, Eric John
Holmes, Jacob F.
Holowaty, Samuel J.
Holsapple, Clifford Arthur
Holsapple, Edward P.
Holsapple, Henry Taylor
Holsapple, Vincent Henry
Holsten, George Frederick
Hood, Emery E.
Hook, Willis Eugene
Hoose, Harold R.
Hopfenspirger, Joseph William
Horton, Robert J.
Horton, Sheldon M.
Horton, William H.
Hosier, Lewis N.
Hotaling, Charles D.
Hotaling, Nathan David
Hotchkiss, Jessee Alfred
Houck, Milo Edward
Houghtaling, Herman Henry
House, Clifford Henry
Hover, Charles Edward
Hover, Frank Lee
Hover, John Edward
Hover, Warren Charles

Howard, Edward Bristol
Howard, Clifford E.
Howard, Edward Van Alstyne
Howard, James
Howard, Samuel Lawrence
Howard, William E.
Howarth, Robert R.
Howe, Arthur L.
Hoystrant, James O.
Hucaluk, John
Huggard, Frances Grace
Hughes, Bradford
Hughes, Donald J.
Hughes, Emmett Bernard
Hughes, James Cleve
Hughes, John W.
Hughes, Martin J.
Hughes, Wilfred G.
Hull, Paul
Hunt, Harold H.
Hunter, William Cullen
Hurta, John J.
Husak, Stephen
Huston, George Albert
Hutchings, Duward E.
Hutchings, George Guernen
Hutchings, John H.
Hutchingson, Clarence Holmbs
Huvar, John Martin
Huyck, John Benson
Hyman, Harold Leon

Ignasher, Jr., Anthony
Ignasher, Walter Lewis
Ihlenburg, Richard Charles
Ingham, Edward L.
Ingham, John
Ingham, Jr., Thomas
Ingham, Harry L.
Irish, Margaret Taylor
Isaacson, Jr., Alfred Henry
Iwetz, Theodore A.

Jabianski, Andrew Anthony
Jablanski, Joseph
Jablanski, Michael Frances
Jablanski, Michael W.
Jacklin, Edward
Jackson, Archie Louis
Jackson, Raymond Philip
Jackson, William Wynne
Jagobia, Arthur Charles
Jacobia, Kenneth Howes
Jacobs, Roswell Fred
Jahns, Donald
Jahns, Harold Henry

Janes, Elisha Paul
Jarocki, Edmund
Jaseinski, Matthew A.
Jasinski, Edwin John
Jasinski, Felix Joseph
Jastrombeck, Sigmund Theodore
Jefferies, George Marchant
Jefferies, Louis Gardner
Jennings, Arthur Fred
Jennings, Norman
Jennings, Raymond
Jennings, Warren Clyde
Jennings, William T.
Jensen, Harold Elwood
Jewett, Allyn C.
Jezwrski, Leo Joseph
Johnson, Cortland
Johnson, Grant Edward
Johnson, Herbert Rolan
Johnson, King
Johnson Lawrence R.
Johnson, Lawrence Walter
Johnson, Leonard James
Johnson, Nathan
Johnson, Stanley
Johnson, William R.
Johnston, Barson Wilson
Johnston, Donald Milton
Jones, Donald P.
Jones, Felix P.
Jones, Jr., John
Jones, Louis Sidney
Jones, Norman Edward
Jones, Paul Kingsbury
Jones, Thomas Clark
Jones, Jr., Vincent William
Jornov, Jr., Anthony Harold
Jubie, Michael Z.
Juchem, Donald LauVern
Judson, Jr., Paul
Judson, Robert B.
June, Charles Burton
June, Lionel D.

Kaghuba, Michael
Kaczanowcke, William
Kaemmerlen, Paul
Kandrach, Andrew G.
Kandrach, Peter Bernard
Kardash, Joseph
Karic, Peter
Karic, John
Kasnowsky, Julius Joseph
Kass, Kenneth C.
Kavanaugh, Arthur F.
Kavanaugh, Robert Francis

Kay, Anthony Francis
Kazukenus, Bernard Joseph
Keffer, Earl Hamilton
Keeler, Clinton Henry
Keeler, Duane Christian
Keeler, Edward Joseph
Keeler, Edward Roland
Keeler, Elwood E.
Keeler, Ralph Arthur
Keeler, William Raymond
Kehrer, Anthony V.
Kehrer, John J.
Keil, Chester George
Keil, Daniel Emanuel
Keil, Frederick
Keil, John L.
Keil, Richard Harold
Kelch, Raymond M.
Kelleher, Bernard John
Kellerhouse, George H.
Kellerhouse, Robert Henry
Kelley, Charles Stephen
Kelley, John Herman
Kells, Abram Andrew
Kells, Jacob
Kelly, Jr., Edward Joseph
Kelly, John Warner
Kelly, Robert Francis
Kelly, Truscott Martin
Kendall, Charles Paul
Kendall, Donald J.
Kendall, James Yale
Kendall, John Francis
Kendall, Jr., Robert E.
Kenneally, John Francis
Kennedy, Fr., Paul J.
Keough, Herbert Charles
Kern, Horace Andrew
Kern, Robert G.
Kerner, Edwin
Kerner, Elizabeth Della
Kerschner, Charles Franklin
Lestler, John Wesley
Keyes, Edmund Frank
Keil, Calvin Jack
Kiel, Clifford Leslie
Killeen, James Hugh
Kilmer, Alfred Dexter
Kilmer, Charles W.
Kilmer, Harold F.
Kilmer, Harry Arthur
Kilmer, Robert Curtis
Kilmer, Wallace John
King, Doris Elizabeth
King, Hinton
King, Lester Harry

Kinne, Charles Harvey
Kinnes, Wilmot J.
Kipp, Robert James
Kipp, Walter M.
Kirbey, George Myron
Kirwin, William Rossman
Kisselback, John Lloyd
Kitchie, Joseph Anthony
Kittell, Harold King
Kittell, Roy Berry
Kittle, Jr., Earl Haledon
Lklein, George Louis
Klima, Joseph Edward
Kline, Jr., Benjamin Linwood
Kline, Bernard Charles
Kline, Floyd Edward
Kline, Herbert Evander
Klitsch, Francis Emil
Knabbe, Robert
Knapp, Clement W.
Knights, Jr., Howard Edward
Knitt, Charles W.
Knott, Bernard
Knott, Raymond
Koberlein, Hans George
Koch, George
Koeppe, Walter
Kogiman, William
Koll, Thomas
Koncelik, John Joseph
Konderwich, Joseph Frank
Konig, Jr., Frederick William
Kontra, John
Koren, George Anton
Kosa, George
Koscinszczek, Alexander Stanley
Koskowski, Stanley J.
Koslow, Arnold
Kosnick, Alexander
Kosnik, Joseph S.
Kosoff, Bernard
Kostszewski, Frank John
Kostszewski, Janice A.
Kostszewski, Martha Teresa
Kostik, Paul
Kovatch, Richard John
Kowal, John R.
Kowalski, Edward
Kowalski, John William
Kowalski, Walter Bernard
Kozel, Frank Oliver
Kraft, Christopher, John
Kraft, Remington George
Krapf, George Edward
Krauss, George Frederick
Krauss, Walter Robert

Kreeber, Clarence W.
Kreig, Jr., George E.
Krein, Anthony F.
Krein, Felix J.
Krein, Frank P.
Krieg, Howard Allen
Krisniski, Edward
Kuhner, Herbert August
Kukon, John James
Kurtznacker, Arthur Guertin
Kurzyna, Joseph Sigmund
Kutski, John
Kwasnowski, Henry P.
Kwasnowski, Samuel J.

La Bella, Joseph
Lacovara, Vincent A.
La Due, Harry Charles
Lafin, Burton Samuel
Lagitch, William J.
Laing, Frederick William
Lamont, Edwin Isaac
Lamont, Henry C.
Lamont, James H.
Lamoree, Charles Pasha
Lando, Sherwin
Landry, John O.
Lankenau, Walter John
Lanphear, Cornelius Bartlett
Lanphear, Henry Thomas
Lanphear, Richard F.
Lansing, Williams
LaParre, Robert Russell
Lape, Bradford Claude
Lape, Viven F.
Lappies, Robert Rurton
Larabee, Arthur C.
Laraway, Herbert Harrison
Laraway, Richard Lansing
Laraway Willard Starks
Larkins, Raymond Abram
Larry, Mason Edward
Lasher, Edward R.
Lasher, Ernest Reginald
Lasher, Gerald Rodman
Lasher, Ralph Harry
Lasher Roland Delbert
Lasher, Willis W.
Lashway, Ernest N.
Lashway, Harold Frederick
Laska, Joseph
Laurange, Clifford Willard
Lauster, George Henry
Lauster, Gustave A.
Lauster, William Henry
Law, Jr., Franklin James

Law, Homer G.
Law, William Alfred
Leach, John Edward
Leard, Bruce E.
Leavenworth, Le Roy J.
Leavy, Harry K.
Lebrecht, Archie Clinton
Lebrecht, Charles Edward
Lebruk, Jones
Leck, John P.
Leck, Michael
Leck, Stanislaw Edwards
Lee, Donald E.
Lee, Edward Michael
Lefkowitz, Alvin Martin
Lefkowitz, Edward Herbert
Leggett, Paul
Leggett, Washburn K.
Leggieri, Charles Ralph
Leggieri, Gerald M.
Lehmer, Donald Jayne
Lemuth, Harold Irwin
Lemon, Arthur Henry
Lemon, James George
Lemon, Wallace Lee
Lenehan, Jr., John Joseph
Leonard, Marcel Frederick
Levanites, Frank John
Levanites, John S.
Lewicki, Michael T.
Lewis, Gordon
Lewis, John Francis
Lewis, Paul Lawrence
Lezette, George Ira
Libardi, Frank S.
Libruk, John
Lichtel, Richard Lewis
Lichtenhan, Sr., Charles Edward
Lichtenhan, Sanford A.
Lieberman, Harold
Liepshutz, George
Light, Jr., Edward William
Link, Maurice William
Link, Charles Willig
Lins, Thomas W.
Linsky, Wayne, K.
Linville, Byron Milo
Little, Charles N.
Lobdell, Earl Willard
Lobdell, Lawrence Orthel
Lobdell, Richard Francis
Lockwood, Albert J.
Lockwood, Ralph Bernard
Logan, Frank Michael
Lomax, James W.
Loos, John Nicholas

Lopez, Rafael Anthony
Lorch, Henry S.
Lorenz, Jr., Wesley Frederick
Lose, Chares III
Losee, Henry B.
Lubera, Joseph L.
Luckett, Albert
Ludington, Harold Vincent
Lugert, Alfred Philip
Lugert, George Arthur
Lugert, Paul Eugene
Lukas, Jerome Henry
Lumpkin, Ozzie
Lunde, Otto Helmer
Lupinos, Joseph
Lupinos, William
Lustiber, Frank Paul
Lydon, Edward
Lyman, Charles Joseph
Lyman, Irving Senn
Lyman, Robert E.
Lynch, David Anthony
Lynk, Donald Preston

Mabb, Charles W.
Mabb, Frederick Joseph
Mabb, Richard Albert
MacArthur, James L.
MacCormack, Thomas Paul
MacCormack, Warren
Mace, Lester J.
Macfarlane, Colin A.
Macfarlane, John P.
Macfarlane, Peter
Macfarlane, William Robert
MacGiffertm John Robert
Macher, Frank Joseph
MacKenzie, Frank Robert
Mackey, George Francis
Mackey, Reginald Irwin
Macy, Donald R.
Madison, Sherman
Madsen, Walter A.
Magee, William Mitchell
Mahar, Jack Woodard
Mahokin, Michael
Mahota, Charles R.
Maiewski, Paul Edward
Malley, Thomas F.
Mallon, John Francis
Maimberg, John Francis
Malone, William Emmett
Maloy, Donald Francis
Maloy, Jr., James Albert
Mancarella, Charles Paul
Manchuck, Harold F.

Mangan, Rita Mary
Mangione, Emanuel Joseph
Mansfield, Leverett F.
Mapes, John Wesley
Maquelin, Cornelius Paul
Marchionne, Mitchell Anthony
Mariak, Michael
Markay, George Joseph
Markessinis, Jr., Angel Lambros
Marmulstein, Albert Irving
Marsh, Francis George
Marsh, Irad Herbert
Marsh, Raymond F.
Marsh, Richard Northrup
Marshall, Donald I.
Marshall, Jr., Floyd Burton
Marshall, Jr. James George
Marshall, Thomas F.
Marston, Stillman W.
Martin, Albert Louis
Martin, Armando Stephen
Martin, Arthur James
Martin, Arthur Pultz
Martin, Fred Maurice
Martin, John Leonard
Martin, Joseph Francis
Martin, Richard E.
Martin, Robert William
Martino, Joseph A.
Maruniak, Michael Joseph
Masters, Francis Robert
Mastronuncio, Alfred H.
Matteson, Jr., Guy A.
Matteson, Robert Daniel
Matties, Aldolph
Mattoon, Benjamin Kline
Maturi, Frank V.
Maviglia, Frank Augustus
Maxwell, Clarence M.
Maxwell, Claude
Maxwell, Gordon
Maxwell, John F.
Maxwell, Wallace J.
Mazel, Jr., Arthur
Mazel, James
Mazur, Frank J.
Massacano, Fred R.
MacCaffrey, Samuel James
McCagg, Charles Howard
McCagg, Harvey J.
McCagg, Willard S.
McCarthy, Jr., Berton J.
McCarthy, Clifford Walter
McClellan, George
McConnell, John F.
McCoon, Donald R.

McCoon, Gerald Grant
McCormack, Everett Campbell
McCoy, Tyler Marsh
McCulloch, Jr., David Stephen
McDarby, Cecil Le Grange
McCarby, Clifford George
McDarby, Harold F.
McDarby, Jr., Ward
McDonald, Frederick Joseph
McDonald, Henry James
McDonald, James Patrick
McDonald, John Francis
McEvoy, Alexander Vosburge
McEvoy, James Joseph
McEwan, John Alexander
McEwan, William George
McFaul, Francis Edward
McGeary, Henry F.
McGee, Albert E.
McGee, William Wallace
McGinnis, Horace E.
McGinnis, Robert F.
McGuire, Lewis James
McGuire, Philip Howard
McIntyre, Edward H.
McIntyre, Stephen Cecil
McIntyre, William Pultz
McKay, Charles E.
McKay Edward T.
McKay, George E.
McKay, James Francis
McKay, Walter J.
McKeown, David M.
McKern, Edward L.
McKibbin, William Henry
McLean, Robert Andrew
McWhirt, William W.
Meacher, Paul James
Meade, Leland Rudolph
Meade, Oliver G.
Meccarello, Constantino
Meccarello, George Lindbergh
Medeiros, Armando
Medwid, John
Medwid, Michael
Meier, Kenneth Lincoln
Meiner, Jack S.
Meister, Victor Miles
Meizinger, Joseph Paul
Melino, Angelo J.
Melino, Rocco Vito
Melius, Clifford R.
Melius, Everett Charles
Melius, George Elton
Melius, Jr., George H.
Melius, Jay H.

Melius, Milton
Melius, Vernon R.
Melnick, Anthony Michael
Meredith, Edward Palmer
Merrick, Nelson Albert
Merrifield, Morehouse Nash
Meschter, Alfred Taylor
Meschter, Daniel Y.
Mesick, Frank S.
Mesick, Harry McNamara
Mesick, Herman Hageman
Mesick, John
Mesick John A.
Mesick, Jr., John Lockwood
Mesick, John Thomas
Mesick, LeRoy Russell
Mesick, Richard M.
Mesick, Sherman W.
Mesick, William G.
Mesick, William M.
Mettler, Jr., John Joseph
Metz, Floyd Elbert
Metz, Marie Babetto
Metz, Sterling Adam
Metz, Willard J.
Meyers, Robert F.
Meyn, Charles Henry
Michaluk, Joseph
Michel, Robert
Mickle, Grover Sherwood
Mickle, Philip DeLeyer
Mieske, Jr., Edward Lewis
Miles, Vincent
Miller, Jr., Addison Whitney
Miller, Andrew Bortler
Miller, Barton Gilbert
Miller, Bernard Edward
Miller, Cecil Clifford
Miller, Charles Franklyn
Miller, Jr., Clifford L.
Miller, David W.
Miller, Elbert W.
Miller Emmett Adam
Miller, Francis
Miller, Jr., George
Miller, Gerard Thomas
Miller, Guy H.
Miller, Harold John
Miller, Harrison B.
Miller, Harry
Miller, Harry Jacob
Miller, John E.
Miller, John Henry
Miller, John Irving
Miller, Margaret Barbara
Miller, Maude Carl

Miller, Newton Robert
Miller, Paul Charles
Miller, Ralph Henry
Miller, Richard Warren
Miller, Robert William
Miller, Roland Boyd
Miller, Samuel
Miller, Stanley Cecil
Miller, Verner
Miller, William Levi
Miller, William Whitney
Millman, Morris
Mills, Ralph Samuel
Mills, William Wilber
Miner, David Raymond
Miner, Donald Ross
Miner, Paul Wesley
Mink, Clayton A.
Minkler, Clyde W.
Minneci, Charles
Minshell, Marvin
Mitchell, William H.
Mitchinson, Wilfred
Mixa, Michael
Moe, Louis James
Molier, William Robert
Monfette, William O.
Montague, Howard Paul
Montague, John William
Montague, Ronald Charles
Montana, Paul Robert
Monthie, Carl Edward
Monthie, Herbert Paul
Monthie, Hugh John
Moon, Roland Floyd
Moore, Arnold H.
Moore, Charles Alexander
Moore, Donald Richard
Moore, Garfield Crawford
Moore, Fred S.
Moore, Howard Pollock
Moore, Milton George
Moore, Jr., Myron
Moore, Robert Rossman
Moore, Stephen Harrison
Moore, VanRensselaer
Moore, Wallace Edward
Morgan, Adele Eleanor
Moritz, Herman Frederick
Morrison, Frank
Morrison, Harris Gordon
Morrison, John Edward
Morrison, Nathan H.
Morrison, William Lawrence
Morrone, Louis H.
Mortefolio, Joseph

Moseley, Burnett
Mosher, Harold Calvin
Moshimer, Harvey William
Moshimer, Henry A.
Moskaluk, Joseph
Moskowitz, Albert
Moss, George Henry
Mossman, Clifford William
Mossman, Clinton James
Mossman, Louis
Mossman, Richard Phillip
Mould, Jesse Albert
Moy, Joseph Daniel
Moyer, Wilmer R.
Mueller, Robert A.
Mull, Charles Hubert
Mullins, John William
Mullins, Priscilla Jane
Mulvaney, Jr., Garrett Francis
Munch, William Fred
Murray, James L.
Murray, John Patrick
Myers, Claude Roland
Myers, James Martin
Myers, Joseph G.
Myers, Lean Raymon
Myers, Milton L.
Myers, Peter Walter
Mynter, Kenneth Harold

Nabozny, Anthony Raymond
Nabozny, Frank Joseph
Nabozny, John Paul
Nabozny, Joseph Peter
Nack, Clyde Ellsworth
Nack, Gladys D.
Naegeli, Fred A.
Nagy, Frank
Nagy, Fritz
Napolitano, Ralph John
Nartiwicz, Adam A.
Near, Alfred Jerome
Near, Robert H.
Nedosko, John
Neefus, Jr., Wendover
Neer, Ralph D.
Neer, Stanley Hollis
Nelson, Edna Lucille
Nelson, Lewis R.
Nero, Anthony F.
Nero, Anthony Frank
Nero, Garmon Emilio
Nero, Charles
Nero, Joseph Marice
Nero, Joseph Michael
Nero, Pietro

Ness, Fred Charles
New, Jr., Harry Sharp
Newbauer, Theodore Joseph
Newcomb, Willie B.
Newton, Herbert Mortimer
Nichols, Donald John
Nicolich, Carl C.
Nielsen, Albert Arnold
Nimons, Valentine V.
Nixon, Jr., David Gray
Nixon, Joseph H.
Noble, Adelanide M.
Nocker Jr., William Barney
Noerling, Jr., Henry Joseph
Nolan, Francis Vincient
Nohamaker, Sherwood W.
Nooney, Harold Franklin
Nooney, Jr., Lyle James
Nooney, Stanley Joseph
North, Arlan Charles
Northup, Russell Jacob
Norton, Vernon John
Novack, Michael J.
Novack, Peter H.
Novack, Walter Joseph
Novack, Alexander Stanley
Novack, Barney
Novack, Edmond V.
Novack, Edward Bernard
Novak, John Clarence
Novak, John H.
Novak, Joseph Paul
Novak, Marion Alice
Novak, Stanley F.
Novak, Stanley Lewis
Novine, Stanley P.
Nytransky, John J.

Oakes, Kermit W.
Ochodnicki, John
O'Connell, Ronald Francis
O'Connell, Jr., Thomas Joseph
O'Connor, Harold William
Oelkers, Kenneth
Oelkers, Jr., William Tell
Ogden, Jr., Robert
Ogren, Charles
O'Hara, Almerin C.
O'Hara, Walter J.
O'Krinsky, Paul William
O'Krinsky, Stephen
Olchowy, John
Oles, David James
Oles, Merton F.
Oles, Richard Seymour
Oles, Russell William

Oles, Washburn Charles
Oligee, Maurice Robert
Oliver, Jr., George William
Oliver, Irving Telford
Olmstead, Lawrence G.
Olson, Lawrence Boughton
Omelanchuk, Steven
O'Neil, Charles Augustus
O'Neil, Jr., Daniel James
O'Neil, Edward James
O'Neil, Eugene Willard
O'Neil, Franklin
O'Neil, Franklin T.
O'Neil, Kenneth
O'Neil, William Francis
Onufrychuk, Jacob
Onufrychuk, John
Onufrychuk, Michael
Oram, George F.
Oram, Leonard G.
Oravetz, Julius Martin
Orbon, Thomas Francis
Orsted, Clayton F.
Orsted, Stanford Joseph
Orsted, Warner Everett
Osswald, Albert A.
Osswald, Jr., Herman
Ostyich, Joseph S.
Ostrander, Franklyn
Ostrander, Gardner Benjamin
Ostrander, Harold
Ostrander, Richard E.
Osuch, Mikel P.
Overlock, Jr., Albert Gardner
Owens, Herbert John
Ozack, Joseph John

Paavola, Lennard Kalervo
Palen, James P.
Palmatier, Leonard R.
Palmer, Frank Dean
Palmer, Harold Gardner
Palmer, Mildred Caroline
Panigot, Charles Gerard
Pantozzi, Stephen Vincent
Paone, Tony S.
Papp, Jr., Joseph
Paradis, Joseph A.
Parchuck, Martin Edward
Parker, John Harold
Pariman, Calvin Franklin
Pariman, Robert Gerald
Parry, Henry Laurens
Parry, Jane Helen
Parsons, Bernard Harry
Parsons, Bradford C.

Parsons, Harold Charles
Parsons, Kenneth O.
Passino, Earl A.
Patchin, Chester W.
Patterson, David Chapin
Patterson, Remington P.
Patterson, Robert Burns
Patton, John Joseph
Patton, Luther Alfred
Patzwahl, Jr., Otto Oscar
Pauley, George Dewey
Pawlik, Joseph Francis
Pawluk, Edward
Pazera, Vincent W.
Pearsall, Irving George
Peck, Charles Buel
Peck, Rodney Dean
Pectal, Clyde Martin
Pectal, George E.
Peduzzi, Jr., Eugene Louis
Peduzzi, John N.
Peduzzi, Rose M.
Pepper, James Brooks
Perlee, Lester Herbert
Perlee, Willard Earl
Perry Donald
Peters, Walter Frank
Petersen, Carl Otto
Petersen, Roy William
Petith, Charles Frederick
Petith, James Emmitt
Petrishen, Stephen
Petry, Robert Martin
Pettinicchi, Anthony
Pettinichi, Arthur J.
Pfeiffer, Harold R.
Pfeiffer, Martin Henry
Pfeil, Karl Philip
Philip, Jr., John Van Ness
Philip, Nicholas Worthington
Phillip, David Hardie
Phillips, Ambrose Wendell
Phillips, Edward S.
Phillips, Edwin Dana
Phillips, Franklin
Phillips, George Thomas
Phillips, Harold T.
Phillips, Howard E.
Phillips, Stanley Louis
Piazza, Frank
Pickett, John Joseph
Pickett, Robert Thomas
Pierro, Louis Alfred
Pierson, William Meeks
Piester III, Charles John
Piester, John Milton

Piester, Richard Frank
Piester, William Henry
Pillionnel, Jaques Henri
Pinkowski, Eugene Thomas
Pitcher, Calvin Sherman
Pitcher, William Burling
Pixley, Robert Lee
Piazza, Anthony
Pizza, Harry Michael
Plackett, Edwin L.
Plasky, Joseph
Plass, Arnold Richard
Plass, George Frederick
Plass, Richard Arthur
Platner, Alton Brooks
Platner, Beekman Whitney
Platner, Clarence Cecil
Platner, Donald
Platner, Walter Wilkinson
Platt, Clifford Kenneth
Ploss, George Edward
Ploss, Howard Albert
Podmijersky, John William
Poleschner, Charles
Polidor, Frank Joseph
Pollack, Edward J.
Ponkos, Rudolph George
Popeckie, Frank Paul
Popp, August Peter
Poppiti, Anthony C.
Poppiti, Charles J.
Porpa, Harold
Porreca, Angela J.
Porreca, Charles Anthony
Porreca, Louis Phillip
Porreca, Nicholas Joseph
Porter, Frederick H.
Porter, Hoysradt
Porter, William Stanley
Pospisil, Jr., William
Post, Calvin B.
Post, Edwin G.
Post, Lester Elmer
Post, Peter, H.
Pott, Warren Ellwood
Potts, Albert Floyd
Potts, Clayton D.
Potts, Jr. Frederick Richard
Potts, John J.
Potts, Lewis John
Potts, Robert Elmore
Poucher, Burton George
Poucher, Clarence M.
Poucher, Harold J.
Boucher, Leonard
Poucher, William Arthur

Pough, Ralph W.
Pound, Clarence Dwyer
Powers, William H.
Pratt, Ashley James
Pratt, Phillip Francis
Predpall, Daniel Francis
Price, Irving
Price, Kenneth V.
Primsky, Jr., John Joseph
Prior, Harriet Mary
Proper, Charles B.
Proper, David S.
Proper, Lester Gifford
Proper, Otis Walter
Proper, Samuel Edward
Proper, Stanley
Proper, Timothy H.
Proper, William Albert
Propst, Paul Henry
Prusky, Jr., Victor
Pryshlak, John
Prystupa, Michael
Ptaszek, John Edward
Ptaszek, Walter R.
Puckett, Eldridge Marion
Puckett, Milton Runyon
Pula, Stanley Walter
Pulcher, John T.
Pulcher, Leo John
Pulcher, Madlyn Julia
Pulcher, Paul Joseph
Pulling, Clarence M.
Pulling, Robert Leroy
Pultz, Clarence Silas
Pultz, Harrison G.
Pultz, Jr., John Frank
Pulver, Adam Harris
Pulver, Charles Woodrow
Pulver, George Edward
Pulver, George W.
Pulver, Harry Eugene
Pulver, Herbert D.
Pulver, Mervin
Pulver, Orson C.
Purcell, John William
Putnam, Alfred Demerest
Pyndus, Michael

Quackenbush, Burt E.
Qualtierie, Michael
Quarta, Frank Leo
Quigley, William James
Quirino, Thomas G.

Raab, Howard Arthur
Raab, Walter Harrison

Race, Alfred J.
Race, Bradford John
Race, Cornelius
Race, Earl Eugene
Race, Floyd Martin
Race, Gerald D.
Race, Harry S.
Race, Herbert J.
Race, Jr., Leonard Allen
Race, Orion J.
Race, Vernon Arthur
Radley, Charles Frederick
Radley, Donald Richard
Radley, Robert F.
Raines, William Warner
Rainey, Clarke Mitchell
Randall, Sr., John Edward
Ranford, Arthur V.
Rankin, Arthur H.
Ranford, Lawrence V.
Rath, Walter Paul
Rathbun, John Howard
Rathbun, Louis Henry
Ravish, Anthony Michael
Raymond, Louis C.
Raynor, Alice Perlee
Reach, Marie Alice
Reardon, Thomas
Reed, Harold P.
Reed, Harry William
Reiner, Frank H.
Reinhardt, Theodore
Reinhart, Jr., Fred Leonard
Relie, Robert Ralph
Relyea, Carl Miller
Remmler, Olaf Donald
Repp, Henry P.
Repp, Victory E.
Ressler, Edward J.
Ressler, Jr., Paul Anthony
Reutenauer, Harold Peter
Reutenauer, Henry Adam
Reutenauer, James
Reutenauer, Marguarite C.
Reynolds, Frank Walker
Rhinehart, Jr., William H.
Rhines, Sherwood D.
Richards, William C.
Richardson, Jr. John Stephen
Richardson, John W.
Richardson, Phillip S.
Rider, Jonathan Benjamin
Rider, Robert Bruce
Ridgeway, Alden Sherwood
Ridgeway, William Evans
Riedmuller, Frank

Riegel, George
Rifenburgh, Albram
Rifenburgh, Asabel Eitleman
Rifenburgh, Harry C.
Rifenburg, Reginald
Rifenburgh, Vernon C.
Rifenburgh, William Douglas
Riggins, Charles S.
Rightmyer, Ivan Post
Ring III, John Elbert
Ringer, Jr., Harvey L.
Richie, Donald Alfred
Rivenburgh, Alfred Wilbur
Rivenburgh, Clyde Benjamin
Rivenburgh, Henry M.
Rivenburgh, Leonard Albert
Rivenburgh, Lloyd Frederick
Rivenburgh, Sterling Richmond
Rivers, Edwin Austin
Roberson, Henry Dalton
Roberts, Allen John
Roberts, Bradley Mathews
Roberts, Donald L.
Roberts, Edward Allen
Roberts, Kenneth Harvey
Roberts, Raymond
Robertson, Russell Eugene
Robertson, William Eugene
Robinson, Charles Werter
Robinson, Francis Malcolm
Roche, Edward Jay
Rockefeller, Donald H.
Rockefeller, Gordon George
Rockefeller, Vernon Ralph
Roeder, Albert Edgar
Roetina, James Francis
Rogers, Charles Howard
Rogers, Curtis William
Rogers, Donald Delos
Rogers, Franklin R.
Rogers, George Sterling
Rogers, James Louis
Rogers, John Armstead Courtnay
Rogers, Lee L
Rogers, Louis C.
Rogers, Willard Brownell
Rogers, William Edward
Rogers, Wilson
Rhode, Douglas Lewis
Rollins, Paul Kenneth
Romanchuk, John
Romanchuck, Michael
Rosani, Angelo
Roney, Raymond
Roraback, Richard E.
Ross, Charles Everett

Ross, Donald Arthur
Sossi, Edward Peter
Rossi, Michael Joseph
Rossi, Romeo M.
Rossman, Emmett Edward
Rossman, Robert C.
Rothermel, Charles William
Rothermel, Claude A.
Rothermel, Edward George
Rothermel, John Herbert
Rouse, Donald E.
Rouse, Jr., Irving
Rousseau, Frederick F.
Rowe, Edward L
Rowe, William C.
Rowen, Elliot A.
Rowen, Harold W.
Rowles, Wililam Sidney
Rubio, Richard A.
Ruggles, Jr., George Wilbur
Ruhmke, Henry William
Rundell, Horace Jermiah
Rundell, Robert Morris
Rundell, William S.
Rushkowski, Jr., John A.
Russell, Francis James
Russell, Jr., George William
Russell, John Merrill
Russell, Paul
Russell, Robert Francis
Russell, Thomas James
Russo, Joseph
Rutkowki, Joseph John
Rutschmann, Thomas Emil
Ryan, Jr., John Aloysius

Sabo, Frank T.
Sabo, John
Sacco, Jr., Joseph
Sacco, Michael James
Sacco, Sameul A.
Sackett, Warren Granger
Sagendorph, Roland Ostrander

Sagendorph, Roland Ostrander
Sagendorph, Winfield
Salerno, John Albert
Saim, Heinz
Saim, John J.
Samsel, Rose Marie
Sandagato, Joseph Ralph
Sandstrom, Jr., Hugo Richard
Sandstrom, Lloyd W.
Sanford, Charles Arthur
Sandord, Floyd
Santana, Andrew

Sapko, Frank
Sartori, Antonio
Sartori, Austin C>
Savastano, Jr., Frank Saverio
Savitsky, George Bernard
Savitsky, Solomon Charles
Sawicky, Aldolph J.
Sawicky, John A.
Sawyer, Charles D.
Sawyer, Delbert James
Sawyer, Franklin Martin
Sayles, Robert M.
Scalley, Howard T.
Scannell, Thomas J.
Schafer, Harold W.
Schaffer, Jr., John Joseph
Schaltegger, Jr., Oscar B.
Schaumann, Jr. Carl Donald
Schell, Charles Joseph
Schell, John Harry
Schell, John Henry
Schell, Thomas
William
Schemerhorn, Lyle
Schermerhorn, Allen Freeman
Schermerhorn, Earl N.
Schermerhorn, George P.
Schermerhorn, George Richard
Schermerhorn, Ivan J.
Schermerhorn, Raymond F.
Scheu, Jr., Charles Herbert
Scheu, Matthew Frederick
Schierich, Albert Frederick
Schiller, Kenneth Edward
Schilling, Charles Bristol
Schlegel, Julius Frank
Schlotterer, August Francis
Schlupp, George Robert
Schlupp, William
Schmolz, Francis W.
Schneidt, Norman William
Schneid, Sylvan Bert
Schools, Henry Knitt
Schools, William Henry
Schram, Jr., Earl
Schreiner, Edward
Schulman, Hugh Jerry
Schultz, William J.
Schunk, Abram Bernard
Schunk, Jasper H.
Schuster, Harold Ludwig
Schwarzchild, Eric S.
Scism, Byron Ray
Scott, Anna Marilyn
Scott, Florence Ethel
Scott, Harold E.

Scott, James
Scovel, Clinton Howard
Scribner, Arthur John
Scrodin, Benjamin Anthony
Scrodin, Thomas John
Scully, Arthur W.
Scully, Lillian Brorup
Scutt, Francis Elwood
Scutt, Robert Edward
Seaman, John Richard
Seaman, Richard Eric
Seaman, Robert Odell
Secor, Everett Harold
Seddon, Francis William
Sedgwick, Melvin Bernard
Sedgwick, Ruth I.
Sedlak, Karl
Senison, Anthony
Senison, Harry G.
Serafin, John Stephen
Seymour, Edward White
Seymour, Harold Hawley
Seymour, John Hawley
Seymour, Thomas Cornell
Shackett, George Joseph
Shaeffer, John Lee
Shafer, James Harry
Shallo, Augustine Lawrence
Shallio, Paul Veto
Sharp, Franklin James
Sharp, George Edward
Sharp, Harold
Sharp, Herbert Wilfred
Sharp, Horatio Frederick
Sharp, Leland J.
Sharpe, Jr., Earle George
Sharpe, Kenneth Donald
Sharppetts, Benjamin Keller
Sharretts, Marshall Godefrey
Shaver, Glendon
Shaver, Jr. William F.
Shea, Harold J.
Shea, Hubert W.
Shea, Lester W.
Shea, Patrick James
Shea, raymond
Shea, Wilson George
Sheak, Luther M.
Sheff, Willie Franklin
Sheffer, Bernard Clifford
Sheffer, Clifford
Sheffer, Samuel
Sheldon, Clyde Lorranine
Sheldon, Harold Leonard
Sheldon, John Edward
Sheldon, John Leonard

Sheldon, Robert R.
Sheldon, William Gerald
Sherbin, John
Sherman, Kenneth David
Sherman, Theodore
Sherpey, James TenBroeck
Sherpey, Theodore Robert
Shetsky, John Joseph
Shetsky, John Joseph
Shew, Philip Lee
Shields, Edward J.
Shields, Joseph F.
Shields, Robert Walter
Shirley, Anne R.
Shook, Jr., Edward
Shook, Elmer
Shook, Gerald Sylvester
Shook, Kenneth Grant
Short, Jr., Frank Albert
Shortell, John Eward
Shriver, Thomas Haines
Shriver, William Francis
Shufelt, Clarence H.
Shufelt, Donald E.
Shufelt, Earl Ashley
Shufelt, James VanValkenburgh
Shufelt, John Austin
Shufelt, Robert P.
Shufelt, William Joseph
Shult, Edgar George
Shultis, Owen Albert
Shuman, Charles Joseph
Shumsky, James J.
Shupa, Steve
Shutts, Alfred
Shutts, Cliffort Emmett
Shutts, Clyde Marshal
Shutts, Floyd Ray
Shutts, Garner, C.
Shutts, Ralph
Sibert, Edward Franklin
Sickler, Augustus
Siegel, Bernard Lewis
Siegel, Irving Philip
Sieger, Gilbert G.
Sigler, Donald L.
Sigler, Kenneth Harvey
Sigler, Richard Avery
Silcock, Joseph Albert
Silliman, Thorne Clark
Silliman, William H.
Silverman, Seymour
Silvernail, George Louis
Silvernail, Thomas Edward
Simmons, Dale F.
Simmons, Earl Joseph

Simmons, Earl Joseph
Simmons, Francis
Simmons, Jr., Harry Leo
Simmons, John Wood
Simmons, Raymond Rossman
Simmons, Robert Eli
Simmons, Samuel Scutt
Simpson, Oscar Gordon
Singer, John
Sipperly, Harold Philip
Sitser, George William
Sitzer, Albert Fred
Sitzer, Earl C.
Sitzer, Ernest L.
Sitzer, Harry L.
Sitzer, Ralph Alfred
Skiba, Joseph J.
Skibo, Joseph Peter
Skiff, Robert Bruce
Skiff, Terry D.
Skurski, Matthew
Skyberg, Victor Oliver
Slattery, Francis L.
Slattery, James Bartholomeu
Slattery, Martin F.
Slauson, Thomas Joseph
Smalley, Malcolm
Smalley, William Henry
Smart, Richard George
Smegoski, Edward W.
Smegoski, Jr., Frank Joseph
Smegoski, Jacob A.
Smith, Albert A.
Smith, Albert H.
Smith, Arthur V.
Smith, Charles Raymond
Smith, Chester Michael
Smith, Chester Pershing
Smith, Clifford A.
Smith, Clifford Lawrence
Smith, Earl P.
Smith, Edwin S.
Smith Frank DeForest
Smith, Gerald Leonard
Smith, Harold E.
Smith, Harold Earl
Smith, Harold J.
Smith, Harry E.
Smith, Herbert Foster
Smith, Hugh
Smith, Jr., James Gilson
Smith, John Lampman
Smith, Kenneth E.
Smith, Levi L.
Smith, Jr. Normand Fedor
Smith, Robert Leroy

Smith, Roland Foch
Smith, Stephen Keese
Smith, Sydney Reed
Smith, Theodore G.
Smith, Thomas Henry
Smith, William Stewart
Smyth III, Samuel
Snare, Jr., Archibald S.
Snare, Philip Frank
Snead, James B.
Snow, Franklin Russell
Snyder, Clinton Leroy
Snyder, Edson R.
Snyder, Edward Harold
Snyder, Jr., Floyd William
Snyder, Keith E.
Snyder, Neil George
Snyder, Ralph Eugene
Sobel, Frederick
Sobin, Alec Joseph
Solomon, Ben
Soney, Jr., Alexander
Soney, Steven
Sonrier, John Noel
Sopok, Joseph
Sottong, William James
Soule, Harold Vassar
Soul, Herbert N.
Spanburgh, Thomas H.
Spanier, Harry
Spatcholts, Jr., Leroy
Spath, Frederick Alfred
Spath, Wayne E.
Speanburg, Jr., Walter Charles
Speed, Harry Phelps
Spencer, Richard Broderick
Speery, Frank Ripley
Spickerman, Harold Carl
Spickerman, William H.
Springsteen, Jay Otto
Staats, Archie E.
Statts, Garrett Richard
Statts, John E.
Stachpool, Michael Joseph
Stadlander, Kent Webster
Stalker, Percy Orville
Stall, Oscar Phineas
Stanley, Emerson Richard
Stanley,, George Davis
Stanton, James F.
Stark, Jr., Frederick J.
Staron, Edward Chester
Steeneck, George Henry
Steerey, Richard Wendell
Stefanski, John Casmer
Stehr, Fredrick B.

Stehr, Phillip R.
Stein, max F.
Stenger, Lawrence Anton
Stenger, Robert George
Steuerwald, Carl Richard
Steuerwald, Clinton Fisk
Steuhl, Fredrick Jacob
Stickles, Albert
Stickles, Jr., Clinton Arthur
Stickles, Edmund Walker
Stickles, Ronald L.
Stickles, Stanley Floyd
Stiffler, Calvin M.
Stiffler, Clayton H.
Stimers, Clark Halliday
Stimers, James Hervey
St. John, Donald Warner
Stockman, Henry Cornelius
Stodolske, Clarence
Stoliker, Floyd Thomas
Stone, George Milton
Stone, Louis Schwarz
Stone, Paul Frederick
Stone, Ward Byron
Stoner, Alger Burton
Storm, Herbert Howard
Storms, Lloyd
Storrs, George C.
Stouter, Stephen H.
Strauss, Guenther H.
Strecker, Edward John
Strehler, Edward Robert
Strehler, Frederick William
Strever, Roy Delmar
Strombeck, Edward
Strombeck, Stanley W.
Stroud, Edward Charles
Straud, William J.
Strungosky, Jr., Michael
Studd, Edgert Richard
Stupplebeen
Stupplebeen, Jr., Leverett
Sullivan, Edward Daniel
Sullivan, John Cornelius
Sullivan, John Neill
Sunderland, Myron Joyce
Sunderland, Paul Sherman
Super, Teddy O.
Super, Thomas J.
Svingala, John G.
Swartwout, Merrill Frank
Swartz, John Allen
Swartzmiller, James Allen
Swayze, Donald R.
Sweener, Milford James
Sweet, Jr., Cyrus E.

Sweet, Harold R.
Sweet, Howard J.
Sweet, Leonard A.
Sweet, Melvin Francis
Sweetgall, Moses
Swiers, George W.
Swiers, Willard Thomas
Szafran, Paul John
Szlachetka, Frank

Tamarin, Milton Paul
Tanner, Charles
Tantillo, Leonard
Tanzillo, Frank Anthony
Tanzillo, John
Taormina, Anthony S.
Taormina, Savern Stephen
Tarddiff, Seymour Robert
Tauckus, Francis
Taylor, Edward Anthony
Taylor, Edward Donald
Taylor, Frederick E.
Taylor, George Greenman
Taylor, John F.
Taylor, Maurice H.
Taylor, Nelson Joseph
Taylor, Walter W.
Teator, Henry Lewis
Teator, John Elwyn
Teator, Louis John
Templeton, Hugh Blanchard
Tenerowicz, Raymond John
Terry, Edgar Raymond
Terwilliger, Clyde Romain
Thayer, Calvin C.
Therkildsen, Alfrield Ostrom
Thielman, Jr. Gover Arthur
Thomas, Jr., Allen John
Thomas, Maynard Mulley
Thomas, Reginald Winans
Thomasino, Dominic
Thompson, David Scott
Thompson, Edna May
Thompson, Jr., Edward Themaine
Thompson, Harry Charles
Thompson, Howard
Thompson, Mildred
Thompson, Ralph Eugene
Thomsen, Peter J.
Thomson, Lillian Ruth
Thorne, Clifton Cornell
Thorne, Douglas Charles
Thorne, Jr., William Stephen
Thorpe, Herbert Charles
Thorpe, James Woodrow
Tiano, Charles T.

Walton, Ernest William
Walton, William James
Warchol, Frank John
Ward, Charles H.
Warfield, Clarence J.
Warman, Harold Franklin
Warman, Joseph S.
Warman, Robert J.
Warren, John Vincent
Washburn, Douglas H.
Washburn, James Edgar
Washington, William
Wasuk, Michael
Waters, Thomas E.
Watson, Glennon Richard
Weaver, Arnold Clayton
Weaver, Jesse Sheldon
Weaver, Kenneth R.
Weber, Edward Russell
Weber, Robert William
Webster, George Earl
Webster, Ivan Charles
Webster, Walter C.
Weed, John H.
Weeks, Maurice Harold
Wehmann, Gerard D.
Weigelt, William
Weintraub, Herbert Joseph
Weintraub, I. Irving
Weir, Walter Franklin
Welch, Claude A.
Welch, John Edward
Welch, Kenneth W.
Welch, Lloyd Albert
Welch, Orville Warn
Welch, Walter Charles
Wemple, Roger Orlando
Wenk, George Whitney
Wentworth, Harold C.
Wentworth, Henry N.
Wenteel, Benjamin
Wentzel, Homer
Wentzel, William Edward
Wenz, Harry
West, Jr., Charles J.
West, Clarence Francis
West, Edward Clifford
West, Jr. John Joseph
West, John Robert
West, Lawrence J.
Westerman, Milton R.
Westover, Arthur Francis
Westover, George Ernest
Westover, Harold Edwin
Westover, Harry Williams
Westover, Wright B.

Wheeler, Arthur Floyd
Wheeler, Edmund Morton
Wheeler, Edward Leroy
Wheeler, Francis I.
Wheeler, Harold Victor
Wheeler, Harry F.
Wheeler, Howard Walter
Wheeler, Robert Philip
Wheeler, William Russell
Wheeler, Woodrow P.
Whitbeck, Carl Gifford
Whitbeck, Charles James
Whitbeck, Clifford Ellsworth
Whitbeck, Donald E.
Whitbeck, Irving Floery
Witbeck, Robert Lewis
White, Arthur Lee
White, Austin
White, Clarence Elmer
White, Earl Ernest
White, Edward F.
White, Frank H.
White, James Francis
White, John Daniel
White, Sewart Jerome
Whiteman, Donald Jones
Whiteman, Raymond C.
Whitman, Jr., Floyd Jay
Whitmore, Robert Brystoe
Wichroski, Joseph
Wilber, Charles L.
Wilber, George C.
Wilber, Grant Arnold
Wilbur, Webster Edward
Wilcox, Harold Allen
Wilcox, Henry E.
Wilcox, Lyndon Ecloff
Wilder, Clifford Walter
Wilder, Marion Alice
Wildermuth, Clarence Bradley
Wildermuth, Richard Anthony
Widermuth, Robert Claude
Wilkins, John N.
Williams, Charles A.
Williams, Earl Emerson
William, Edward H.
Williams, George E.
Williams, Jack
Williams, Jay G.
Williams, John N.
Williams, Leonard Franklin
Williams, Ralph I.
Williams, Robert
Williams, Russell Bailey
Williams, Sidney F.
Williams, Stanley C.

Williams, Walter Franklin
Williams, William Donald
Williams, William Frederick
Willingham, Benjamin
Wilsey, Betty
Wilsey, Harold M.
Wilsey, Helen Katherine
Wilsey, Walter Talcott
Wilska, Albert E.
Wilska, Henry
Wilson, David
Wilson, Henry Harrison
Wilson, John P.
Wilt, Kenneth F.
Wilt, Peter C.
Winfield, Harry Halford
Winig, Charles Anthony
Winn, Edward S.
Winn, George Mynderse
Winters, Philo J.
Wischhusen, Frederick George
Wischhusen, George John
Wishengrad, Rose
Wishon, Charles William
Wishon, Robert George
Wishowaty, Floyd Joseph
Wishowaty, Joseph West
Wit, John Frank
Witko, Adolph R.
Witko, Edward Martin
Witko, Edward Stanley
Witko, Jr., Joseph
Witko, Joseph Thomas
Witko, Michael Joseph
Witko, Peter Paul
Witko, Raymond John
Wlock, Jr. Charles
Wlock, Stephen H.
Wolcott, Robert John
Wolcott, Rodney M.
Wolfe, Charles J.
Wolfe, George Bernard
Wolfe, Gerald M.
Wolferstieg, Harold Richard
Wolferstieg, William Burr
Wolff, George F.
Wood, Donald C.
Wood, Henry F.
Wood, Richard Evans
Wood, Robert Lewis
Woodward, Herbert C.
Woodward, Ralph Frederick
Woodward, William Peter
Worthington, Eugene Bartlett
Woznieski, Jr., John Joseph
Woznieski, Michael P.

Woznieski, Stanley S.
Wright, Charles Franklin
Wright, Samuel Charles
Wurster, Harold C.
Wyant, Ralph
Wyckoff, Donald Ledyard
Wyckoff, Jr. John Sterling
Wyda, Metro P.
Wyman, Charles George

Yablansky, Frederick Edward
Yablansky, Frederick Edward
Yakman, Charles Anthony
Yakman, William J.
Yandik, Emil Stephen
Yannacone, Michael John
Yasinski, Frank M.
Yates, Charles J.
Yates, George Angles

Yates, George Melvin
Yerrick, Donald William
Yost, Carl M.
Yost, Harold Burnett
Yost, William Rudolph
Young, Joseph A.
Young, Paul E.
Young, William H.
Youzwak, Frank Martin
Youzwak, George Joseph
Youzwak, Joseph John
Youzwiak, Martin Paul
Yunker, Albert E.
Yunker, John C.
Yusko, Stanley
Yusko, Theodore

Zaayenga, Werner F.
Zaremba, Chester John

Zawyski, Theodore Stanley
Zayac, Jr., Paul
Zellinger, George Joseph
Zellinger, Paul
Zelman, Mitchell John
Ziemba, Edward J.
Ziemba, Louis Joseph
Ziemba, John J.
Zilliox, Robert Gernett
Zimmermann, John Alwin
Zink, Oswald Arthur
Ziotkowski, Maxmillian
Zito, Carlo Henry
Zito, Joseph
Zollo, Francis M.
Zukowski, John
Zyko, John J.
Zyko, Jr., William W.
Zyryi, William

KOREAN WAR
COLUMBIA COUNTY VETERANS

Albers, William G.
Althizer, Edward Myron
Baumli, Gregory Sr.
Bertram, Donald G.
Beveridge, Albert J. Jr.
Beveridge, Robert H.
Boor, John
Bowes, Lee Marshall
Bozik, Joseph Peter
Bozik, Lee Marshall
Cantele, Benjamin
Carl, Harry
Davi, Salvatore
De Caprio, Anthony Jr.
De File, Patrick J.
De Freest, Jon Edward
De Long, Bruce C.
Decker, David Lawrence
Decker, Gordon
Di Rocco, Robert W.
Dietter, Avery
Diokas, Frank J.
Dixon, George C.
Dupont, Robert H.
Esposito, Vito James
Everett, Beverley George
Friedrich, William L.
Gabe, Robert E.
Gamello, Guy J. Jr.
Geel, Robert W.
Glover, Harold B.

Hamilton, William Murray
Hamm, Frank David
Hamm, Stanley E.
Hamm, William J. Jr.
Hatch, James Asher
Hatheway, James H. Sr.
Havlik, John
Hollenbeck, Joel George
Hotaling, Leon C.
Jones, Robert R.
Kendall, Robert P.
Kern, Robert G.
Knight, Hallet R.
Koch, Paul F.
Koester, Henry
Kriloff, Herbert
La Pierre, Robert P.
Leggieri, Anthonio Rudolph
Lindmark, Richard
Lipsky, Robert J.
Lupsa, Thomas
Mann, Warren F.
Mlincsek, John N.
Monthie, Mynard G.
Morris, Alfred E.
Morris, John William
Myers, Lawrence B.
Nash, Bradley F.
Nichols, Charles R.
Nimmons, Raymond
Occhibove, Anthony Jr.

O'Neil, Eugene W. Sr
Pawlak, Richard P.
Pierro, Louis A.
Pitcher, Clayton L.
Poucher, Claude N. Jr.
Prata, Ralph
Proper, Paul John
Ranum, Rolf I.
Reetz, Daniel B.
Rivenburgh, David H.
Rotter, Stephen J.
Salerno, James L.
Scalley, John Joseph
Schaummann, Boyd G.
Schrader, Barry E.
Sheldon, Richard Elmer
Shook, Gerald S. Sr.
Stalker, Evi Leon
Stickles, John P. Sr.
Thatcher, Robert E.
Tuczinski, Martin John
Urbaitis, Joseph V.
Urban, Joseph John
Van Alystyne, James Reed
Wallace, Cornelius Edward
Weeks, Arthur
Wilt, Pete
Wischusen, Robert Walter
Wood, William Alfred

VIETNAM WAR
COLUMBIA COUNTY VETERANS

Abitabile, Paul R. Jr.
Adams, Robert S
Akin, Walter James
Alberson, Charles H.
Albright, Edward J.
Albright, Paul H.
Alecksynas, Harold C.
Alford, James David
Alford, Nelson R. Jr.
Alger, Thomas F.
Auletta, Vincent Stephen

Baker, Gail Charles
Balaban, Stuart L.
Barone, John M. Jr.
Bartholomew, Robert A.
Baseheart, George M.
Beecher, Stephen P.
Bemiss, Robert L.
Blair, George N. Sr.
Boswell, Lance C.
Brady, Mark A.
Brahm, Donald H.
Brash, Richard
Broast, Bernard P.
Brown, Charles DeWitt
Brown, Lawrence A.
Brown, Mark D.
Bryant, Gary Michael
Buchan, Bradley T.
Burch, Timothy Ward
Burger, Kenneth E.
Bush, George E.

Calvin, Lynn E.
Cannetto, William H.
Card, Edward F. Jr.
Carr, Thomas
Cavagnaro, Lawrence R.
Choon, Joe Philip
Christensen, Annamae Sue
Christianna, Chauncey H.
Christie, Kenneth O.
Cichetti, Charles J.
Cilwell, Michael J.
Clapp, Donnald J. Jr.
Collins, Jimmy D.
Conte, Louis D.
Conway, Edward J.
Cook, Albert C. Jr
Cook, William Graf Jr.

Coon, Gerald E.
Coon, Lyle P.
Coon, Philip A.
Coons, David Everett
Coons, Edward T.
Corbett, James A.
Cordato, John D.
Costanzo, Salvatore John
Couch, John C.
Couchman, Barry J.
Craft, William J. Jr.
Cranna, Donald
Craver, Harry L. Jr.
Crolius, Robert
Crowell, Luella Ann

Dacey, Ronald J.
Dallas, Robert W. Jr.
D'Angelo, Frank G.
Dauski, Mark Alfred
Davis, Erwin O.
Davis, Robert W. Jr.
Davis, Terrance P.
Davis, Thomas M.
Davis, Wesley Paul
Dawson, William Ernest
De Ruzzio, Robert A
Deane, Robert C.
Delaney, Bartholomew F. Jr.
Dell, George Arthur
Demarest, Anthony R. Jr.
Demski, Eric E.
Depew, Douglas Lee
Di Giuseppi, Marc Christopher
Diamati, David J.
Dietter, Le Roy
Dobrosieski, David T.
Drahushuk, John B.
Drowne, Gordon Brooke
Dunham, Raymond D.
Duntz, George E. Sr.
Dupier, Paul J.
Dutcher, Arthur V. Jr.
Dwyer, Michael J. Sr.
Dysard, William Philip Sr.

Engel, Walter G.
Esposita, Carman A.

Ferraro, Louis V.
Fila, Frank G.

Finkle, Richard C
Fiorillo, Domenic
Florio, Neil
Foiadelli, John Carl
Folmsbee, Todd W.
Francis, Robert C.
Fredericks, John Jacobs Jr.
French, Jeffrey W.

Gabe, Robert E. *
Gilbert, Donald P.
Gilbert, Thomas M.
Golden, Robert A.
Graham, John Richard
Grasso, Paul David
Green, Frederick A.
Grimaldi, Vincent C.
Gross, Robert D.
Gruntler, Daniel W.
Guarney, John P. Sr.

Hall, Leonard W.
Halstead, Peter
Hamar, Joanne G.
Hanson, William A.
Harter, Edward D.
Hausman, Paul
Hendrickson, Donald E.
Hopkins, Thomas C.

Jacklin, Edward David
Jacobia, Carl H.
Jenkins, Marc M.

Kavanaugh, Robert Miles
Keeler, James Michael Jr.
Keeler, Keith S.
Kelly, John W.
Kilmer, Stanley Edwin
Klawson, Steven C.
Koepp, John R.
Kohn, Jacob S.
Kopec, John Z
Kopec, Michal
Krein, Eugene A.

Lanpear, John A.
Lashway, Keith
Laurange, James E.
Laurange, Ricky Allen
Lauster, William H. Jr.

Little, Bruce E.
Loomis, David W.
Loos, John N.
Lovell, Jonathan B.
Lowery, Thomas A.
Lynch, John J.

MacFarlane, Robert J.
Madsen, Guy A.
Main, David Donald
Maleonskie, Robert Paul
March, Kenneth C.
Margan, John M.
Martin, Frank M.
Martino, Louis A. Sr
Maynard, Terry J.
McCagg, Harvey J.
McDarby, Allen
McDonald, Daniel J.
McDonald, Joseph
McWhirt, Vernon E.
Michael, Robert L.
Miller, David C.
Miller, John H.
Miller, Lance S.
Miller, Nelson R. Jr.
Miller, Walter W.
Mink, Charles E.
Mink, Jon R.
Mitchell, John A.
Moore, James G. Jr
Moore, Stephen A.
Morris, Alfred E. *
Morris, John William *
Nesbitt, Richard A.
Neven, Alfred E.
North, John Clay
North, Oliver L.
Northup, Charles E.
Novak, Walter M. Jr.

Ogden, Edward J. Jr.
O'Neil, Eugene W. Jr.

O'Neil, Kenneth
Otty, Richard D. Sr.

Papas, Joseph Michael Jr.
Pawlik, Joseph F. Jr
Penn, Jackie E.
Pfeiffer, John Clifford
Pilieri, Edward J. Jr.
Podlaski, Virginia Ann
Popow, Robert S.
Popow, Thomas G.
Poynte, Ronald W.
Proniske, David Michael
Proniske, Thomas J.
Pulver, Wayne R.

Race, Clark
Radley, Charles James
Rector, Thomas G.
Repko, Edward S.
Rich, Ronald I.
Ritchie, Calvin B.
Robert William David
Rogers, Cornelius Richard Jr.
Rogers, William Stanley
Rose, Wayne Louis
Roxbury, John J.
Ryan, Michael J.

Sanders, Glenn H.
Sartori, Donald Edward
Schermerhorn, George M.
Schneider, Frederick C. III
Schrenkeisen, Karen
Schrenkeisen, Raymond S.
Shook, George Jr.
Shook, Gerald S. Sr. *
Simmons, Brian P.
Sitzer, Richard Harold
Sleezer, David W.
Smith, Carolyn A.
Smith, Joanne
Smith, Raymond H.

Stalker, George W.
Stevens, David
Stever, Frederick R.
Stickles, Rodney J.
Strungosky, John Melvin
Strykiewicz, Michael
Super, Michael T.
Sutherland, Kenneth L.

Tuominen, Timothy N.
Turek, Mark Wayne
Tuthill, Thomas Adams Jr.

Van Alphen, Donald J.
Van Loan, John Scott
Van Wagner, Raymond Franklin
Vitetta, George Dominic Jr.
Vogel, Gary L.

Watson, William A.
Watson, William A.
Wemitt, Jerome N.
Wemitt, Patrick
Wenz, Robert
Wilber, Kenneth H.
Williams, David R.
Williams, Eugene
Wilt, Pete *
Winig, Vincent A. Jr.
Winn, David M.
Wood, Jack Richard
Wood, Lucene Hellen
Wood, Marcus Scott Jr.
Wood, William Alfred*
Woodward, Peter
Wright, Gerald J. Jr.

Yusko, Michael Jr.

Zbierski, Russell L.
Zincio, Walter

SECTION 3

BIBLIOGRAPHY

Annual Report Adjutant-General State of New York, 1903

Columbia County in the World War, Albany J. B. Company 1924, By The Home Defense Committee of Columbia County, New York

Columbia County's Veterans' Service Record for the Korean and Vietnam Conflicts, Columbia County Board of Supervisors, Benjamin Murell (4th Ward)

"World War II" Veterans, Columbia County State of New York, April 11, 1949, Columbia County Board of Supervisors, Gordon Decker (Hudson).

ACKNOWLEDGEMENTS

I would like to thank my wife, Susan, for her insight and editing; Dina Heisey for her initial preview and suggestions with the nascent manuscript; Joanne Concra for her secretarial skills; and Cindy Casey whose editing and publishing acumen was the glue that pieced the shards of parchment together and nurtured the manuscript to its conclusion.

A special thanks goes to all those men and women who selflessly and tirelessly honored the veterans of Columbia County, New York, for the past twenty years on the Honor-A-Vet Committee.

The following is a list of the committee members (many of whom are no longer with us) in alphabetical order:

Arnold Anderson
William M. Armstrong
Jerry Benvenuto
Roger Bradley
JoAnn Concra
Salvatore Costanzo
Joseph Dybas
Gary Flaherty
Jeff French
John Funk
Vince Grimaldi
James Haggerty
Jack Hallenbeck
Robert LaPorta

Shirley Lewis
Benny Murell
John Neary
Wilson Shea
Gerald R. Simons
David Sleezer
Chester Smith
Fred Stark
Holly Tanner
William Van Alstyne
Elizabeth Young
Patrick Wemitt
Ken Wilber

Made in the USA
Columbia, SC
27 June 2021